T0270543

CLIMATE OF CONTEMPT

CENTER ON GLOBAL ENERGY POLICY SERIES

CENTER ON GLOBAL ENERGY POLICY SERIES
Jason Bordoff, series editor

Sustainably meeting the world's energy needs is the defining challenge of the twenty-first century. The Center on Global Energy Policy (CGEP) at Columbia University's School of International and Public Affairs advances actionable solutions to this challenge through research, dialogue, and education. We operate at the intersection of geopolitics, climate, and the economy on the understanding that energy is at the heart of each. The Center on Global Energy Policy Series furthers this mission by offering readers accessible and policy-relevant books, grounded in the highest standards of research and analysis.

Jeffrey Rissman, *Zero-Carbon Industry: Transformative Technologies and Policies to Achieve Sustainable Prosperity*

Michael D. Tusiani with Anne-Marie Johnson, *From Black Gold to Frozen Gas: How Qatar Became an Energy Superpower*

Mark L. Clifford, *Let There Be Light: How Electricity Made Modern Hong Kong*

Johannes Urpelainen, *Energy and Environment in India: The Politics of a Chronic Crisis*

Agathe Demarais, *Backfire: How Sanctions Reshape the World Against U.S. Interests*

David R. Mares, *Resource Nationalism and Energy Policy: Venezuela in Context*

Ibrahim AlMuhanna, *Oil Leaders: An Insider's Account of Four Decades of Saudi Arabia and OPEC's Global Energy Policy*

Amy Myers Jaffe, *Energy's Digital Future: Harnessing Innovation for American Resilience and National Security*

Jim Krane, *Energy Kingdoms: Oil and Political Survival in the Persian Gulf*

Richard Nephew, *The Art of Sanctions: A View from the Field*

For a complete list of books in the series,
please see the Columbia University Press website.

DAVID B. SPENCE

CLIMATE OF CONTEMPT

How to Rescue the U.S. Energy Transition
from Voter Partisanship

COLUMBIA UNIVERSITY PRESS

NEW YORK

Columbia University Press
Publishers Since 1893
New York   Chichester, West Sussex
cup.columbia.edu
Copyright © 2024 Columbia University Press
All rights reserved

Library of Congress Cataloging-in-Publication Data
Names: Spence, David B., author.
Title: Climate of contempt : how to rescue the U.S. energy
transition from voter partisanship / David B. Spence.
Description: New York : Columbia University Press, [2024] |
Series: Center on Global Energy Policy series / Jason Bordoff,
series editor | Includes bibliographical references and index.
Identifiers: LCCN 2023059232 (print) | LCCN 2023059233 (ebook) |
ISBN 9780231217095 (hardback) | ISBN 9780231217088 (trade paperback) |
ISBN 9780231561556 (ebook)
Subjects: LCSH: Climate change mitigation—Political aspects—
United States. | Energy transition—Political aspects—United States. |
Energy policy—United States. | Communication in politics. | Truthful-
ness and falsehood in mass media. | Partisanship—Political aspects.
Classification: LCC TD171.75 .S68 2024 (print) | LCC TD171.75 (ebook) |
DDC 333.79/40973—dc23/eng/20240129
LC record available at https://lccn.loc.gov/2023059232
LC ebook record available at https://lccn.loc.gov/2023059233

Printed in the United States of America
Cover design: Milenda Nan Ok Lee
Cover photo: R. J. Hinkle / Alamy

For Maria, Jack, and Michael

CONTENTS

FIGURES AND TABLES

ABBREVIATIONS

BBB	Build Back Better bill
BP	British Petroleum; now just BP
BTI	Breakthrough Institute
CAISO	California Independent System Operator
CCS	carbon capture and storage
CO_2	carbon dioxide
CPP	Clean Power Plan
DAC	direct air capture
DER	distributed-energy resource
DSA	Democratic Socialists of America
EPA	U.S. Environmental Protection Agency
ERCOT	Electric Reliability Council of Texas
EV	electric vehicle
FERC	Federal Energy Regulatory Commission
FPA	Federal Power Act of 1935
FPC	Federal Power Commission
GDP	gross domestic product
GHG	greenhouse gas
GND	Green New Deal
GOP	Republican Party
GW	gigawatt

IIJA	Infrastructure Investment and Jobs Act
IOU	investor-owned utility
IPCC	Intergovernmental Panel on Climate Change
IRA	Inflation Reduction Act of 2022
ISO	independent system operator
kV	kilovolt
kwh	kilowatt-hour
LCOE	levelized cost of energy
MISO	Midcontinent Independent System Operator
munies	municipal utilities
MW	megawatt
mwh	megawatt-hour
NAAQS	National Ambient Air Quality Standards
NGA	Natural Gas Act of 1938
NGO	nongovernmental organization
NGPA	Natural Gas Policy Act of 1978
NIMBY	not in my backyard
NOAA	National Oceanic and Atmospheric Administration
NPR	National Public Radio
OPEC	Organization of Petroleum Exporting Countries
PG&E	Pacific Gas & Electric Co.
PJM	formerly Pennsylvania–New Jersey–Maryland, now just "PJM"
PM	particulate matter
ppm	parts per million
PUC	public utility commission
PURPA	Public Utility Regulatory Policies Act of 1978
PVI	Partisan Voting Index
RPS	renewable portfolio standard
RTO	Regional Transmission Organization
SO_2	sulfur dioxide
TOP	take or pay
TOU	time of use
twh	terawatt-hour

PREFACE AND ACKNOWLEDGMENTS

THIS BOOK grew out of a series of talks I gave between 2019 and 2021 on the politics of the green-energy transition. (The 2020 version of that talk can be found at https://www.energytradeoffs.com/why-all-this-is-important/.) Those talks, in turn, reflected my sense that modern media were making it more difficult for students to develop a deeper understanding of energy law and policy. Each year, more and more of the information they see comes to them from sources whose first objective is to persuade them rather than to educate them. Most are aware of this fact, and that awareness feeds cynicism in some. At the same time, many people who are not on social media seem not to appreciate how fundamentally online political discussion is affecting regulatory politics. So I decided to dive more deeply into the academic research on these questions. The upshot of that research is this book.

HOW TO USE THIS BOOK

The intended audience for this book is the set of people who want a deep understanding of the green-energy transition—past, present, and future. It is meant to be useful not only to students and faculty in courses on energy or environmental policy but also to anyone who aspires to be an energy- or climate-policy wonk.

Because the book draws on research from a variety of academic disciplines (and tries to speak to a similarly broad audience), I have supplemented the text in three ways. First, energy policy is a jargon-laden subject, so there is a glossary of acronyms provided at the front of the book. Second, many of the endnotes are explanatory and elaborate on points made in the text. Referring to them may help some readers understand the book's analysis and argument better. Last, there are seven appendices that can be found on the book website, at http://www.ClimateOfContempt.com/. The appendices provide support for parts of the analysis in longer form than could be included in the book. All of these supplemental features are intended to serve as a resource for readers of varying backgrounds who want to get into the weeds of energy-transition law, politics, and policy—in all their beautiful, messy complexity.

The book cites real-world examples of divisive online rhetoric to illustrate some of the propositions advanced in the academic literature. Of course, speech posted on social media platforms is public speech. However, I have chosen to cite by name only those social media posters who are energy-thought leaders or public figures. I assume that most of the people cited are smart, well-meaning people who make positive contributions to policy debate. Therefore, the use of their statements as illustrative examples of "what not to do" does not signify any broader critique of those people. To the contrary, some of the examples come from podcasters and writers I follow. Nevertheless, their words illustrate how norms of online discussion contribute to negative partisanship and misunderstanding of a complex problem.

Finally, one of the premises of the analysis is that a clear-eyed understanding of energy-transition politics requires distinguishing what *is* from what *ought to be* or "what is true" from "what I think ought to be so." In our pluralistic democracy, where *voters* disagree over what ought to be, separating the normative from the analytical is fundamentally important. But the modern information environment pushes us all to conflate the two. Indeed, some people reject this distinction altogether. But this book proceeds on the premise that critical thinkers need to be able to make that distinction. For additional discussion of this issue, see the introduction.

ACKNOWLEDGMENTS

Many people have made valuable contributions to this book and to my own thinking about the issues it covers. (Of course, the responsibility for any errors in the book lies solely with me.)

I owe a debt of gratitude to my colleagues at the University of Texas. I have bounced many of these ideas off them over the years. There are too many to list here, but that group includes David Adelman, Owen Anderson, Ross Baldick, John Butler, Monty Humble, Carey King, Tom McGarity, Robert Prentice, Varun Rai, Joshua Rhodes, Dave Tuttle, Wendy Wagner, and Tim Werner. This project was also informed by the perspectives of the scholars and professionals who participated in two initiatives in which I have been involved, both aimed at creating the kind of cross-disciplinary, cross-ideological dialogues this book recommends: the annual Austin Electricity Conference and the EnergyTradeoffs.com web site.

The research that went into this book has been aided by an army of capable University of Texas grad students who served as my research assistants. They include Ayo Adaranijo, Chinelo Agbim, Reem Ali, Jesse Bennett, Anne Crea, Ricardo Correa, Claire Crofford, Kimberly Dabrowski, Jay Do, Sarah Dodamead, Daniel Dyring, Adam Enochs, Christian Green, Shelley Grostefon, Kathy Guan, Aaron Jones, Daniel Kim, Fon Kunanusorn, Christopher Matos, Phillip McCarthy, Richard McNulty, Michael Patton, Jessica Patrick, Jonathan Ramirez, Caleb Ray, Hannah Schiffman, Carl Stenberg, and Bethanie Wallace. The book also benefited greatly from the contributions made by editors at Columbia University Press, including Michael Haskell, Annie Barva, and Caelyn Cobb.

I want to acknowledge the particularly valuable feedback I received on earlier drafts of the manuscript from David Adelman, Owen Anderson, William Boyd, Joshua Busby, John Butler, Ken Caldeira, James Coleman, Monika Ehrman, Alison Gocke, John Howard, Sharon Jacobs, Alex Klass, Joshua Macey, Tom McGarity, Felix Mormann, Sheila Olmstead,

Dave Owen, Tade Oyewunmi, Gabe Pacyniak, Heather Payne, Rebecca Spence, Amy Stein, Wendy Wagner, Shelley Welton, Tim Werner, and the anonymous reviewers solicited by Columbia University Press. The book was also influenced by helpful feedback from participants at various academic symposia and colloquia where some of the analysis was presented in 2019–2022, including at Columbia University School of Law, the Wharton School at the University of Pennsylvania, Florida State University School of Law, Vanderbilt University School of Law, the Nicholas School of the Environment at Duke University, and the Penn/Berkeley Energy and Environmental Scholars Program.

Parts of the analysis in the book evolved from earlier scholarship, some of which was coauthored. I owe a particular debt to David Adelman, Jody Freeman, Robert Prentice, and law student editors at the University of North Carolina, the University of Pennsylvania, Boston College, the University of Notre Dame, and Yale University for their contributions to earlier versions of this analysis.

Finally, I thank my wife, Maria Winchell, whose support and patience made this project possible.

CLIMATE OF CONTEMPT

INTRODUCTION

Never let yourself be diverted, either by what you wish
to believe, or by what you think could have beneficial
social effects if it were believed.

—Bertrand Russell, "Message to Future Generations"

IT CAN be difficult to grasp the full significance of the change happening around us when that change happens gradually. So it has been with climate change and, more recently, with the impacts of changing information technology. This is the metaphor of the frog in the pot, slowly coming to a boil. Scholars have only recently begun to understand how modern media are transforming U.S. politics. The epigraph from Bertrand Russell captures part of what they are finding: namely, how emotion triggers biases that distort our perceptions and beliefs, particularly when we want something very badly. These biases are not new; they form part of the hubris that lies at the heart of ancient Greek tragedies and are a common element of business and political scandals.[1] What *is* new is how modern information technology supercharges those biases, making them a much more pervasive feature of our politics.

This book is about energy policy—specifically, the law and politics of charting a reasonably timely path toward net-zero carbon emissions in the United States. This is the so-called energy transition. The book's intended audience is the set of people across the political spectrum who are open to the belief that getting to net zero is a worthy and important policy goal—a group I refer to here as "the climate coalition"—and are interested in a deeper understanding of energy law and its historical-political context. These two objectives go together. One cannot get that deeper understanding of the status quo without understanding how it came to be. Accordingly, part 1 of this book explores the legal, political, and economic evolution of U.S. energy markets over time. That history challenges some of today's popular but misleading narratives about regulatory politics, narratives that are too cynical by half. Part 2 looks at the regulatory task ahead, exploring some of the underappreciated political obstacles to the transition and how they might be overcome.

This analysis invokes a large body of academic research in support of the following propositions:

1. Hastening the energy transition is a worthy policy goal because the world's geophysical scientists agree that climate change poses an increasingly serious threat to our current and future prosperity and well-being.

2. As a political problem, getting to net zero is more of a bottom-up than a top-down challenge. Underappreciated scholarship—from law, political science, economics, psychology, sociology, and communications research—suggests that voters in the thrall of misinformation and frustration present a bigger obstacle to the energy transition than the political influence of economic elites.

3. Today, political propaganda is sophisticated, subtle, and ubiquitous. It routinely misinforms us and invites us every day to feel and express contempt for political adversaries and their ideas. This influence slows national policy progress and distorts our understanding of energy-transition politics.

4. The process of cultivating the moral case against our adversaries, each of us from our ideological bubble, distracts us from the important task of building majorities in support of the transition. The latter task, in turn, requires engagement across ideological and political boundaries, most effectively by way of offline, iterated, bilateral conversation.

This is an understanding of regulatory politics as a messy, complex process that puts voters and omnipresent propaganda at the center of the story. In today's hypercynical American polity, this understanding is also anathema to many of the podcasters, bloggers, and writers who help frame today's energy and climate-policy debate.

So the central conceit of this book is that members of the climate coalition will be willing to move beyond simple "whose side are you on?" narrative frames to critically engage the evidence and logic offered in support of the numbered propositions given earlier. It is a conceit because those simpler narratives are entrenched. We observe bad behavior by some opponents of the energy transition and infer that the set of "opponents of the energy transition" deserve our contempt. But that is a category error that we are constantly invited to make in today's political information environment.

Understanding this error and its political implications can help the climate coalition grow their numbers. The U.S. economy cannot get to net-zero carbon emissions without national *regulatory* legislation—"regulatory" in the sense of *mandating* fundamental changes in the behavior of energy-market participants in order to reduce carbon emissions. That sort of legislation has mostly eluded Congress for several decades now, a victim of conservatives' increasing opposition to regulatory mandates and of growing partisan tribalism.[2] In lieu of regulation, Congress has been somewhat more willing to use carrots rather than sticks. In 2022, it enacted sweeping subsidies for various energy-transition technologies in the Inflation Reduction Act (IRA), described in chapter 3. Those subsidies should make the technoeconomic aspects of the transition easier, but they will not get the United States to net zero.

Nor is the IRA likely to transform electoral politics the way New Deal programs did in the 1930s. For both structural and psychological reasons explained in later chapters, most elected officials now try to please their most ideologically extreme and negatively partisan voters. Those voters' continuous exposure to propaganda means that their votes are driven less by their economic self-interest than by their sense of their own political identity. That identity, in turn, is tied to opposing the "other" party and what it wants. For this reason, the economic benefits that flow from the IRA seem unlikely to change many votes—that is, they are unlikely to overcome the effects of twenty-four/seven appeals to a partisan tribalism that reward ad hominem argument, discourage critical thinking, breed moral certainty, and amplify feelings of contempt for "the other side." Given what each side tends to hear about the other, that contempt feels more than justified.

This is the flip side of activism. Social progress often begins with activists drawing society's attention to problems that require a policy response. The spark of interest that led to my own forty-year career in energy law began that way. When I was twenty years old, the Three Mile Island nuclear power plant melted down about thirty miles from where I was living. That experience triggered my subsequent support for anti-nuclear-power activism. At the time, I was persuaded by messaging that the nuclear industry was dangerous and deeply corrupt, even evil. There was a social and cultural element to the way I formed those beliefs, one that involved not only my friends and fellow inhabitants of the political left of center (where I still reside on most issues) but also pop-cultural influences.[3] But as I studied and worked on power-sector issues, I began to see that I had been tarring the industry with too broad a brush.[4] The moral clarity I felt about nuclear power and electric utilities became muddied by a more complicated reality, and my views of these industries and their people moderated significantly.

Today's information environment pushes people away from that kind of deeper understanding *much* more powerfully and persistently than in the past. It makes group "naming and shaming" seem like a moral imperative in part because voters' partisan differences now implicate basic human values and foundational principles of American liberal democracy. Once a movement *feels* like a war, in particular a righteous one, critical questioning of group orthodoxy seems disloyal; it can diminish the enthusiasm of those for whom moral certainty motivates them to sacrifice their time, energy, or money to the cause.[5] But if in the name of rallying support we ignore the inconvenient truths unearthed by critical thinking—the thorny technoeconomic and political trade-offs that lie at the heart of the energy transition—we deny ourselves and others a full understanding of the problem. That understanding can help us avoid the pain of unnecessary missteps as the transition unfolds. A fuller understanding is always worthwhile, anyway.

It also has political tactical value. When both sides frame political conflict as a moral crusade, building congressional majorities gets tougher, all else being equal. Value pluralism is baked into American democracy. We must accept it not because all values have an equal claim to moral legitimacy but because every citizen has a vote. In the heat of battle, we overestimate the righteousness of our own cause and the evil of the adversary. It is important to see the politics of the energy transition and its trade-offs for what they are: less a heroic battle of good (us) versus evil (them) than a complex collective-choice problem involving people with both selfish and selfless motives on all sides. This book aims to fill out that picture in part by drawing readers' attention to underappreciated scholarship that illuminates these important issues in new ways.

THE CLIMATE CONSENSUS

Fortunately for the climate coalition, the energy transition is popular with most Americans, including younger Republicans and virtually all Democrats.[6] Most voters now accept the well-established scientific consensus that human behavior is driving and hastening global warming. And despite the amplification of climate-science dissenters on conservative media platforms,[7] most voters also accept the corollary expert consensus that steps taken now to reduce emissions of greenhouse gases (GHGs)—carbon dioxide (CO_2), methane, and other heat-trapping carbon compounds[8]—can help us avert the most harmful effects of climate change.[9] Atmospheric concentrations of GHGs have increased from 280 parts per million (ppm) before the Industrial Age to about 420 ppm in 2023. Technological advances in clean energy have reduced the carbon-emission intensity of the U.S. economy in recent decades, but we are still adding long-lived GHGs to the atmosphere. Many countries—and a growing minority of U.S. states—thus now mandate carbon-emissions reductions. Congress has enacted subsidies to nudge the energy transition along but has opted not to limit GHG emissions nationally.

To those familiar with the basics of climate science and the disturbing accuracy of its predictions to date,[10] this dithering evokes dread—doubly so within social media communities that constantly focus on these risks. Popular frustration with the slow pace of policy change takes its bluntest form in the verbal excoriations of governments and corporations by the young activist Greta Thunberg. In the United States, Thunberg's frustration is echoed by new climate-focused lobbying organizations dominated by young people and focused on climate action, such as the Sunrise Movement, Evergreen Action, and Justice Democrats. Such organizations have helped to put climate policy on the political front burner. Climate activists recognize that climate effects will continue to worsen over time unless and until atmospheric concentrations of carbon are stabilized, and then reduced, and they worry that the climate is experiencing serious, irreversible harm.[11] The Intergovernmental Panel on Climate Change (IPCC) has endorsed the goal of transitioning the world economy to net-zero carbon emissions by 2050,[12] so scholarship and policy discussion addressing the energy transition have coalesced around that aspiration. (The goal is *net* zero rather than zero because the IPCC anticipates that negative emissions—removal of carbon from the atmosphere—will be necessary to compensate for lingering emissions in parts of the economy that are too difficult or expensive to decarbonize.) In this context, the U.S. failure to chart a path to net zero looks to many like a failure of governance.

Hyperbolic rhetoric employed by some in the climate coalition triggers charges of "alarmism" or "catastrophism" from opponents of the energy transition. But the continuing cascade of climate-related costs cannot have escaped anyone's notice. Warming oceans are expanding, and the rising sea levels mean more frequent coastal flooding requiring massive infrastructure investments to hold back the sea. Some coastal communities in Louisiana and Alaska have already begun to relocate inland, and the California government has recommended that its pricey coastal communities plan now for "managed retreat" from the sea.[13] The land mass of the culturally unique, 170-year-old community on the Chesapeake Bay island of Tangier, Virginia, has been reduced by two-thirds already and will be completely under water in a few decades. Salt-water intrusion into nearby farmland on Maryland's eastern shore is destroying the land's productive capacity.[14] Sea levels in the Gulf of Mexico and along the southern Atlantic coast will rise more than the world average. Florida has been experiencing regular street flooding in Miami and more severe "King

Tides" for a decade or more.[15] Municipalities on North Carolina's Outer Banks face a succession of existential choices, and the region will need to invest huge sums to preserve its main transportation artery, Highway 12.[16] Warmer oceans make hurricanes stronger, all else being equal, and the northern movement of warmer water extends the range of Atlantic hurricanes.[17]

Inland, climate change is bringing different miseries. Dangerous heat waves and drought have become much more common, stressing water resources for irrigation and hydroelectric power and worsening the wildfire season.[18] Instrumental temperature records date to 1850, and according to the National Oceanic and Atmospheric Administration's (NOAA) *Global Climate Report* for 2020, nine of the ten warmest years on record occurred between 2010 and 2020 (inclusive); subsequently, 2021 and 2022 entered the top ten as well.[19] Before 2018, California's wildfire season averaged less than one fire per year that burned more than 100,000 acres: in 2018, 2020, and 2021, the number increased to three, four, and seven fires, respectively.[20] In 2023, Canadian wildfires produced dangerously poor air quality across the northeastern and mid-Atlantic states, causing school closures and cancellation of flights and sporting events. Higher temperatures increase evaporation and the capacity of the atmosphere to hold water vapor, which exposes more Americans to dangerously high "wet-bulb" temperatures, making it more difficult for the body to cool itself and rendering some currently habitable places uninhabitable.[21] More water vapor also means more moisture available for massive rain events, such as those that produced floods in the U.S. Midwest in 2019 and in Europe in 2021.[22]

All this severe weather brings not only death and dislocation but also massive economic costs in the form of record numbers of individual billion-dollar droughts, heat waves, floods, severe storms, tropical cyclones, wildfires, and cold-weather events.[23] Investments in property, infrastructure, and insurance based on historical weather norms have become much riskier. As climate models portend a future in which volatile weather accelerates, owners of land affected by these changes will find property insurance and mortgages more difficult and expensive to come by.[24] In 2021, the U.S. government announced that premiums for its national flood insurance program would increase as much as 18 percent per year to cover increased payouts.[25]

And under federal crop insurance programs, owners of newly drought- or flood-prone farmland are sharing with taxpayers the multi-billion-dollar increases in crop losses caused by climate change, according to a Stanford University study in 2021.[26]

U.S. citizens also bear some of the costs of global-warming effects that occur beyond our borders. Two military-planning scenarios commissioned by the George W. Bush administration's Department of Defense predicted that climate-related resource shortages around the world increase the probability of warfare and other forms of conflict. They concluded that "projected climate change poses a serious threat to America's national security" and has the "potential to create sustained natural and humanitarian disasters on a scale far beyond those we see today."[27] Almost two decades later, some suggest that climate change is one of several drivers of mass migration from Mexico and Central/South America to the U.S. southern border.[28]

Given that these costs will continue to grow along with atmospheric carbon levels, many ask why voters do not insist that their leaders pursue GHG-emissions regulation.[29] The answer lies in the nature of the modern political dissensus.

THE POLITICAL DISSENSUS

DEFINITIONS AND PREMISES

Polarization, Populism, and Tribalism

Ideological polarization and populism are related but distinct phenomena. *Ideology* refers to one's political philosophy: liberal, conservative, progressive, libertarian, and so on. The two major U.S. political parties have been diverging ideologically for the better part of four decades. The resurgence of populism, by contrast, is a more recent phenomenon. *Populism* implies no particular ideology. Rather, populists challenge the legitimacy of the policymaking system as a tool of dominance by distrusted or despised elites. Together, polarization and populism are driving a return to partisan tribalism in American politics after an extended hiatus.[30] Political scientists can measure these effects. They have documented among voters an increase in "*affective* partisanship," a kind of identity-based, virtually unshakable loyalty to one's political party. Affective partisanship among American voters is increasingly *negative*, more about their opposition to the other party than about any affinity for their own. Negative partisans see only the immediate battle in front of them and the imperative of defeating the enemy. This fear of governance by the other party feeds ends-justify-the-means reasoning. More Americans begin to question the liberal-democratic norms on which the health of American democracy depends—values such as respect for the truth, for peaceful resolution of pluralistic conflict, for the rule of law, and for fair political competition.

To most people, these trends are evident in the behavior of the *other* party. Research supports the conclusion that tribalism is gaining strength in both parties (see chapter 3), but that does not mean that it manifests similarly in both. Populist anger has grown more quickly in the Republican Party (GOP) than in the Democratic Party. Elected Republicans have turned against democratic norms and demonstrated contempt for political adversaries in numbers and in ways that their Democrat counterparts have not, following the lead of insistent partisans in the electorate who seem to exert more influence over the GOP than ideological conservatives or moderates do. This trend is reflected in the twenty-first-century struggles of successive Republican Speakers of the House (John Boehner, Paul Ryan, and Kevin McCarthy) to manage congressional and party business and the party's (unanimous) elevation to that position one of the leaders of the effort to overturn the presidential election of 2020 (Mike Johnson). Populism is growing within the Democratic Party as well but so far is manifesting mostly in the form of *intra*party disagreements over issues such as the meaning and value of liberal democracy, the drivers of political division and voter behavior, and how best to hasten the energy transition.[31] These disagreements are in part generational and feed distrust between Democratic Party moderates and progressives. Some young progressives see a status quo they find unacceptable and infer that older Democrats must have lacked the inclination to fight for strong climate policy in the past. Chapter 3 puts some additional historical context around that idea.[32]

The tension between liberalism and populism can be traced backward in time through the turbulent 1960s to the Gilded Age and the Era of the Robber Barons, various nineteenth-century agrarian populist rebellions, the Antebellum Era, and even the founding period. Consequently, today's combatants invoke thinkers from the past, such as the economist Friedrich Hayek; the socialist Michael Harrington; the revisionist historians of the mid-twentieth century; the political philosophers Hannah Arendt, William Riker, Robert Dahl, C. Wright Mills, Louis Brandeis, L. T. Hobhouse, Karl Marx; and the various Enlightenment thinkers whose ideas shaped the American constitutional design.[33] When American democracy is especially dysfunctional, as it is today, we tend to argue about these first principles.

The U.S. Constitution was not designed to produce policy by opinion poll, but nor was it designed to preserve sustained minority rule. Rather, it aimed to produce the policy choices majorities *would* choose if they had the time and expertise to understand and deliberate over policy problems.[34] On climate and energy issues, national politicians are failing to translate informed majority preferences into policy in part because affective, negative partisanship has weakened the connection between voters' policy preferences and their voting choices. A former president of the American Political Science Association, the late Robert Dahl, assumed that the pluralism of American society would prevent an intense minority from frustrating majority will for too long, but he also recognized that the Constitution does not guarantee that result. Dahl inferred that "Americans seem to like" liberal democracy because it has survived periods of intense populist uprisings "except for one important interlude."[35] It is necessary to ask, Are we nearing another such "interlude"? Or, as the *New York Times* put it in 2022, "Is liberal democracy dying?"[36] Leading academic experts on authoritarianism keep warning us that they see parallels between today's U.S. politics and historical transitions from democracy to dictatorship.[37] Although our liberal democracy has survived intense partisan tribalism before now, it has never done so in the presence of the most powerful propaganda tool in human history: namely, the set of modern information and social media technologies that my generation still refers to as "the internet."

Markets and Regulation: Well-Regulated Capitalism

The structure and incentives of today's political conflict produce centrifugal forces that weaken the ideological center. More and more conservatives now characterize government as little more than a tool of oppression, seemingly oblivious to its benefits.[38] When a Republican voter warns politicians to "keep your government hands off my Medicare," or western antigovernment activists occupy federal lands, are they unaware that taxpayer money funds Medicare and the infrastructure for logging and grazing on federal land?[39] Or that it funds federal crop insurance, rural electrification, public roads, and so much more? Their rhetoric is presumably a proxy for some other complaint about government. On the left, more and more voters take a similarly dim view of markets and capitalism, seeing capitalism as irredeemable; they seem to admit no meaningful connection between a firm's market success and the benefits it provides to people. When they complain that the largest shareholders of Zoom and Amazon "profited off the pandemic,"[40] are they unaware of how those firms' products helped people in an hour of need? Their rhetoric is presumably a proxy for some other complaint about the market.

Too many voters seem to be losing sight of the symbiotic relationship between government and markets. On the one hand, *markets depend on government to function and thrive.* Fewer laws do not mean more economic freedom. To the contrary, the creation of economic value *requires* law and regulation. Aspiring entrepreneurs in dangerous, lawless regions do not enjoy meaningful economic freedom, nor do small businesses that are smothered in the cradle by underregulated monopolies or oligopolies. People would not invest in property if they could not rely on property law and criminal law—and the enforcement of such laws by courts and police—to prevent others from simply taking the fruits of their investment. They would realize many fewer gains from trade if they could not rely on the enforcement of contracts. Fewer people would engage in investment and exchange without laws ensuring disclosure of the investment risks (securities law), fair competition (antitrust law), a sufficiently healthy environment (environmental and consumer-protection laws), and government provision of public-goods infrastructure that tends to be undersupplied by the market. The absence of law and government is not economic freedom but rather Hobbesian chaos.[41]

On the other hand, the *law creates only the conditions for value creation; it does not create that value*. Countless decisions made by economic actors—to invest, to create and innovate, to persist in the face of challenges, to engage in exchanges—are the source of that value. This connection, too, ought to be self-evident. The rise of a broader anticapitalism on the ideological left is perhaps an understandable response to the extreme form of anticollectivism spreading on the ideological right, but it is fomenting an understanding of political economy that seems sometimes to miss this point. Governments need markets to function well in order for society to thrive and in order to fund regulatory regimes and public goods such as roads, police, and public education. Governments access those resources by taxing private property, income, wealth, and specific economic transactions or by borrowing from those who have accumulated wealth in the market. We know from repeated historical experience that when regulation disincentivizes too many of the choices that lead to wealth creation, the result is also ruinous in its own way.

Liberal democracy seeks a balance between these two unpalatable extremes. It seeks *well-regulated capitalism*. Each of the 536 politicians who sit in Congress and the presidency have a say in how to strike that balance. So do regulatory agencies and courts. Congress delegates important policy decisions to agencies, and courts ensure that agency decisions remain within statutory and constitutional boundaries. Each of these actors faces their own distinct set of internal and external incentives and pressures. The way they respond to them defies general characterization as either virtuous or corrupt because the collective response is ideologically and ethically complex. It comprises 536 responses that are specific to each politician and each decision.

WHY CAN'T CONGRESS REGULATE ANYMORE?

The framers of the Constitution wanted government to produce policy that reflected "the permanent and aggregate interests of the community."[42] So why is today's policymaking machine so unresponsive to the community's interest in mitigating the costs of climate change?

Top-Down Explanations: Corruption and Business Dominance

In these times of rising economic inequality, more Americans see government dysfunction through the lens of corruption or elite dominance, and it is easy to see how that view seems to fit the facts. The energy transition, for example, threatens the bottom line of the fossil-fuel industry. That industry's trade groups have promoted climate-science disinformation and funded research that promotes antiregulatory agendas. The absence of national regulatory legislation requiring an energy transition invites the inference that the industry's efforts have had their intended effect. Best-selling books tell this story, and this view is widely held on the political left.[43]

But as shown in chapters 1 through 3, this elite-dominance narrative assigns much too much agency to a few bad actors. It imputes corrupt motives to policymakers far too casually. Most importantly, it fails to acknowledge a discouraging truth: namely, ambitious politicians' desire to win *simply for winning's sake* rather than out of an allegiance to any philosophy, economic interest, or campaign donor. We cannot logically infer that elected politicians who attract the votes of oligarchs or bigots therefore view those oligarchs and bigots as their most important constituents or that they seek to enshrine oligarchy and bigotry into law.[44] If their decisions benefit oligarchs and bigots, then one might ask, "What does it matter which case it is?" But for understanding regulatory politics and formulating political strategy, this distinction between effect and intent is important.

None of which is to dispute the assertion that today's political dysfunction *does* serve the interests of the wealthy and others advantaged by the status quo. Economic inequality *does* make economic and political competition less fair. As shown in figure 0.1, income and wealth inequality in the United States have increased steadily since the Reagan administration to levels not seen since before World War II.[45] The causes of this increase are disputed, but the figure's upward-sloping curve for the late twentieth century coincides with cuts in the marginal income tax rates of the wealthiest Americans; a deregulation

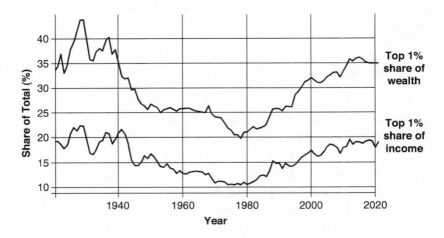

FIGURE 0.1. Wealth and income inequality over time.

Source: Wealth Inequality Database, licensed under CC-BY- 4.0.

movement across many American industries, including the energy sector; and the exposure of more of the U.S. economy to global trade. As explained in chapter 2, both Republicans and moderate Democrats supported deregulation, influenced in part by economic scholarship suggesting that it was a good idea.

One might argue (and some do) that economic inequality is not an important problem because freer markets have stimulated growth, and growth leaves even those at the bottom of the socioeconomic ladder materially better off than they would have been otherwise. But as game theory and centuries of political philosophy have demonstrated, people care as much about their *relative* socioeconomic position as they do about their absolute wealth.[46] Moreover, inequality has some demonstrably problematic consequences. The financial crises of 2001 and 2008 can be credited in part to the effects of large wealth imbalances. In each crisis, competition for shares of a massive accumulation of investment capital—what National Public Radio (NPR) once called "the giant pool of money"—proved a powerful inducement to motivated reasoning, first by a few whose corner cutting brought enormous returns and later by competitors trying to keep up.[47] In 2001, the greed and accounting deceptions of an energy company, Enron, featured prominently in the accounting scandals and the spectacular failure of the newly deregulated California wholesale electricity market. The mortgage-backed securities bubble and crash of 2008 featured massive energy-price spikes and volatility as well as turmoil in the energy-derivatives market. In both crises, established Wall Street institutions—auditing firms such as Arthur Andersen in 2001 as well as securities-rating agencies, mortgage banks, and investment banks such as Goldman Sachs, Lehman Brothers, and Bear Stearns in 2008—succumbed to the temptation to engage in illegal, ethically dubious, and reckless behavior that harmed others. These crises ended in bankruptcy for Andersen, Bear Stearns, and Lehman, triggered recessions, and imposed financial trauma for dismissed employees, small investors, and the population in general.

Economic inequality also impedes the ability of working-class people and the poor to avoid climate risk.[48] Avoiding climate risk costs money, and those with more money can more easily afford it. As property insurance and mortgage rates increase in newly vulnerable locations, each dollar increase imposes a greater burden on those with fewer dollars. Demand for housing among the wealthy pushes middle-class buyers out of safer locations and into less well-built and well-insulated abodes, exacerbating energy poverty.[49] Those who cannot afford home ownership may be locked out of cost-cutting clean-energy investments such as rooftop solar panels. Their landlords may lack the financial incentives to invest on their behalf. Many people cannot afford (or lack access to capital for) the upfront cost of investing in electric vehicles (EVs). Higher urban rents price them out of locations where mass transit offers a good transportation option. For people who simply don't want to live in urban metropolitan areas or whose jobs require them to drive long distances each day, EVs and mass transit may seem like a bad fit for their more demanding individual transportation needs. They wonder what their lives will look like in a net-zero future. In these and other ways, economic inequality disadvantages working-class and middle-class people *before, during, and after* the energy transition.

Inequality naturally breeds populist cynicism, distrust, and resentment toward elites—on the right, resentment of urban, intellectual elites; on the left, resentment of billionaires and corporations. Confronted with policy outcomes they don't like, each group infers procedural injustice.[50] Each side sees American liberal democracy as a rigged system. They disagree only over who has rigged it. But we humans infer elite dominance too often and too easily, especially when invited to do so by others.

Did Democratic Party senators from West Virginia—Jay Rockefeller in 2010 and Joe Manchin in 2021—oppose GHG-emissions regulation because of campaign or personal financial connections to fossil-fuel companies or because they feared electoral reprisals from West Virginia voters if they supported it? Did Governor Phil Murphy of New Jersey, a Democrat with strong climate-policy credentials, oppose the imposition of congestion charges on vehicles entering New York City because he was catering to Wall Street donors or to New Jersey commuters? When congressional Democrats from Oregon express opposition to siting wind turbines off the Oregon coast, are they doing the bidding of the tourism industry or responding to voter concerns?[51] As explained in chapter 1, people regularly underestimate how often politicians' behavior is driven by voters' preferences.[52] Cynicism makes us quick to ascribe different, more ethically dubious motives to politicians and to anyone who opposes our policy goals. This is the *fundamental attribution error*, the idea that because we understand our own actions in terms of our private thoughts about their context but lack access to others' internal narratives when interpreting their behavior, we fill in those blanks uncharitably. The old saying has it exactly backward: it is not familiarity but *un*familiarity that breeds contempt, at least in politics.

None of which is to urge quiescence in the presence of actual science denial, callous indifference to harm, political corruption or violence, flirtations with bigoted or repressive authoritarianism, or other threats to democratic governance. To the contrary, as discussed in chapter 6, scholars see these threats as frighteningly real and imminent, and they compel our attention. But when our emotions provoke attribution errors about adversaries or other mistaken beliefs, they exacerbate the political problem and undermine popular understanding of the transition as a complex social challenge. And when influential opinion leaders make those errors, they multiply that harm.

Bottom-Up Explanations: Voters, Propaganda, and Bias

The mathematics of majority rule in Congress are straightforward. Legislation must command the support of 50 percent + 1 of the members of the House and 50 percent + 1 (or 60 percent) of the Senate to become law with the president's signature.[53] Political scientists have long wrestled with the question of when and why Congress only sometimes overcomes these thresholds to produce popular regulatory legislation. That work confirms that businesses and the wealthy enjoy systematic advantages when lobbying Congress, but also that wealthier interests often oppose one another in policy fights. As an empirical matter, members of Congress have proven reluctant to vote against popular regulatory legislation, even (or especially) when business interests oppose it.[54] Accordingly, most of the energy-regulatory regimes we know today were enacted over the objections of some powerful business opposition. These events were *"republican moments,"*[55]in which the broader public-issue concerns overcame the systematic or institutional advantages that economic elites enjoy in battles over legislation. Unfortunately, in today's political environment the most powerful impulse driving voters' votes is not their views about climate change but rather their *contempt* for members of the other political party.

For reasons explained more fully in chapters 3 and 4, it is this climate of contempt that is making a republican moment for the energy transition harder to come by. Republican moments depend on raising the salience of commonly understood facts, but common understanding is elusive in today's "post-truth era."[56] Factual propositions that seem obviously true in one social media information bubble seem ridiculous or naive in another. Narrative frames and rhetorical norms learned online bleed into offline policy debate. When we see others persist in denying our truths, we look for the biases in *their* thinking or in *them*, not the biases in *our* thinking. Part of the problem is that we discuss policy matters online in the presence of an audience, which alters those conversations for the same reasons that "reality TV" doesn't reflect reality. When the first priority of a conversation is to persuade an audience rather than for the participants to understand one another, we are tempted to shade the truth, omit context, and mislead. And once we commit to a position before an online audience, conceding rhetorical ground when challenged poses the risk of embarrassment, and the ego comes into play. When opinion leaders and experts succumb to this kind of spin in public dialogue, it does even more harm to public understanding.

So when members of conservative online communities repeat false tropes alleging particular errors in climate science, many *do so sincerely.*[57] Mirror-image hyperbole by members of the climate coalition is sincere as well. For example, few if any climate scientists believe that our current emissions trajectory will make the earth uninhabitable by 2100 or habitable only by ten thousand humans (claims seen on Twitter/X)[58] or that the climate challenge is about "saving the planet" in any literal sense.[59] These kinds of claims may be borne of understandable frustration, but they play into characterizations of the "hysterical Left" found in right-wing information bubbles that are inhabited not only by cynics and zealots but also by thoughtful friends, neighbors, and colleagues. This kind of fracturing of political information and belief makes today's partisan divide less like the divide of the 1930s and 1960s than like the divide of the 1850s.

Now, as then, more and more partisans of each party believe that their party's victory is *necessary* to protect basic American values and a cherished way of life. This sense is provoking an upturn in political violence.[60] The shooting of Rep. Steve Scalise and others at a congressional softball game in 2017, the plan to kidnap Governor Gretchen Widmer of Michigan in 2020, the aborted assassination attempt on Justice Brett Kavanaugh of the Supreme Court in 2022, and the hammer attack that fractured the skull of former House Speaker Nancy Pelosi's husband (Paul Pelosi) that same year—all are recent examples of this trend.[61] A particularly alarming sign of this trend is Republican politicians' and voters' response to the violent insurrection at the U.S. Capitol on January 6, 2021, which sought to overturn the results of the 2020 presidential election. When the House of Representatives reconvened that day after the rioters departed, most Republican members voted *against* certifying the election results, despite the absence of evidence of electoral fraud. In the ensuing midterm elections in 2022, a *majority* of the Republican nominees to statewide and federal offices professed support for the baseless proposition that the 2020 election was illegitimate; just less than half of those candidates were elected.[62]

Thus, we are underattending to the health of our democratic institutions, and more people are losing faith in them.[63] Some see violence as a necessary and unavoidable response to evil. After all, weren't the horrors of the Civil War necessary to rid the country of the evil of slavery? At the same time, most voters presumably favor the pursuit of peaceful ways of achieving a desired result before resorting to violence—not only because of the pain violence causes but also because we cannot know in advance of a violent conflict who will prevail or what will emerge from the wreckage of liberal democracy. Nevertheless, some in the climate coalition have come to regard as naive the advice of former first lady Michelle Obama that Democrats ought to "go high" when Republicans "go low."[64]

COSMOPOLITANISM AND CONVERSATION

The admonition to "go high" is about adhering to and thereby preserving liberal-democratic norms of respect for truth, rule of law, pluralism, and fair procedure. It is a popular idea among the broader electorate but is now openly mocked on social media.[65] And to be fair, moral outrage and public expressions of contempt have driven policy change in the past.[66] But as explained in chapters 3 and 4, they aren't transforming legislative politics that same way today. Even if you believe the objects of your contempt deserve it, affirming that belief online is as likely to alienate as it is to persuade those whose support is necessary to produce a republican moment. The late Ted Halstead, founder of the Climate Leadership Council, said that the "road to success [on climate policy] runs through the Republican Party."[67] That may or may not be true, but the mathematics of majority rule mean that the road runs through the ideological median member of each house of Congress. Barring a sudden pivot in American party politics, that means securing the agreement either of Republicans or of moderate Democrats.

For the climate coalition, that implies the need to *listen and respond* to voters in swing districts and states. Listening and responding require a mindset of *fallibilism*—the idea that each of us ought to be willing to subject our beliefs to critical examination by those who disagree and to respect the possibility that *we* may be getting something wrong, either politically or practically. The political historian Hannah Arendt extolled the democratic virtues of fallibilism, urging that voters form political opinions by *charitably* considering the missing points of view: "The more people's standpoints I have present in my mind while I am pondering an issue, and the better I can imagine how I would feel and think if I were in their place, the stronger will be my capacity for representative thinking and the more valid my final conclusions."[68] Voters who are skeptical about a rapid energy transition have questions, concerns, and worries about its impact on their energy bills and service. If the United States is to make these policy choices wisely, more members of the climate coalition will need to find the will to engage open-mindedly with their ideological or partisan adversaries.

This open-minded engagement is also known as *cosmopolitanism*. Like Arendt, the philosopher Karl Popper was an articulate advocate of the importance of a cosmopolitan mindset to democratic governance. He worried openly about how the search for certainty might displace the search for truth because the former is much easier to achieve than the latter. Popper argued that "we need other people to discover and correct our mistakes (as they need us); especially those people who have grown up with different ideas in a different environment. This too leads to toleration."[69]

Today many want an easier, quicker path. They look at the accelerating instability of domestic and international politics and hope that the next crisis will catalyze the kind of political change they seek. Perhaps it will facilitate an expansion of the Supreme Court or the Senate and change the mathematics of climate policymaking.[70] This book went to press before the 2024 presidential election, an event that could trigger that sort of profound social upheaval. Or maybe climate politics will be overtaken by even more profound developments that suddenly transform the electorate, such as war or sociopolitical collapse that splits the United States in two or otherwise creates a new system of government that is more responsive to majority opinion on climate policy.[71] Or less dramatically, maybe a critical mass of Republican

voters will simply tire of their congressional representatives' tolerance of antidemocratic ideas. But none of these things seems likely
given what we know about how American politics is functioning in
the twenty-first century.

If we accept that many of the voters we demonize online are not
actually demons, the better bet is on respectful engagement with
them. Secretary of Transportation Pete Buttigieg captured the gist of
this idea in an interview in 2022:

> It's a conversation. You come at it the way you would approach a con-
> versation with a family member who you care about, who you see
> doing incredible things for their own loved ones . . ., who would give
> you the shirt off their back . . . and would be there for you in the
> toughest of circumstances. And then they open their mouths about
> politics and what they say horrifies you. But you know [that] what
> they're like is not defined by that. (Which by the way is the opposite of
> what it's like to encounter somebody on Twitter, where all you know
> about them is what you see. . . .) Then it becomes possible to see each
> other as human beings first. *That is unbelievably important.*[72]

"Seeing each other as human beings" is important because it accepts
that the strategy of directing moral outrage at political adversaries
tends to mobilize opponents and allies alike in roughly equal
measure.

Note several things about Buttigieg's advice. First, his prescription
does not guarantee success in every case. Respectful engagement may
persuade the other person, or it may not. But climate-policy progress
requires success only in a small percentage of cases. Second, his
approach respects the agency of voters; it does not infantilize them
by presuming that they must be either morally bankrupt or the
deluded pawns of the powerful. Third, it does not deny the validity of
feeling horrified by others' political views; to the contrary, Buttigieg
seems to share those feelings. Fourth, nothing in Buttigieg's prescription requires accepting or remaining quiet in the face of cruelty or
injustice or bad policy. Rather, he is addressing *how* to persuade others, not whether to do so or how to feel.

FOR SKEPTICS

Readers who find this analysis unobjectionable can skip ahead to chapter 1. But some readers will doubt the claim that American liberal democracy is endangered at all, reasoning that bitter partisanship is a feature of democracy, not a bug. Some will feel certain that the more radical members of *our* side are a less numerous, influential, or fearsome bunch than the other side seems to think; *their* radicals, on the other hand, seem truly frightening. Some may be so convinced of the irredeemability of "the other side" that they have concluded that trying to persuade voters is tilting at windmills.[73] I hope that skeptics are willing to test their predispositions by reading beyond this introduction, but this section tries to respond to some of this skepticism.

CONTEMPT IS NOTHING NEW IN POLITICS

It is true that politics has always included efforts by politicians and their partisans to take advantage of the fundamental attribution error. Lobbyists and persuaders have long understood that if a legislator casts a vote that defeats a goal I care about, I can avoid cognitive dissonance by ascribing his action to corrupt or evil motives. Political persuaders use our emotions to influence what we see in our mind's eye when we think about a party, a candidate, or an issue. Henry Adams captured this same idea when he famously observed that "politics . . . has always been the systemic organization of hatreds."[74]

Lobbyists and persuaders know that the human brain is wired to seek out patterns and that one story may be all it takes to induce belief in a generalization, especially if that belief is echoed by members of the in-group, if it *feels* good, or if we *want* it to be true. This is the danger to which James Madison famously referred in *Federalist No. 10* when he asserted that our reason and "self love" have "reciprocal effects" on one another. Modern behavioral research confirms that "what we want" does indeed dominate what we believe and decide. Thus, when Madison said that people are "not angels," he was *not* saying that they are devils, only that they fool themselves in selfish and systematic ways that endanger good governance.[75]

What *is* new is how powerfully modern media amplify this dynamic. It is not the *kind* of propaganda that is new but rather its *speed and scale.* For most of the twentieth century, the national mass media acted as a centralizing force by providing a heterogeneous citizenry with a common set of politically relevant facts. Now they exert powerful centrifugal forces, creating a political climate of contempt that is destructive to public welfare. The politician Stacey Abrams put it this way in 2019:

> When our media was [*sic*] common, there was more common cause. Right now the architecture of our political space has voices telling you what you want because they're also a filter of what you know. *When you filter your news, it creates an artificial environment that suggests that there is some war of values that is often belied the minute you talk to people.* Very few people actually experience the relationship of sitting in a committee hearing and having the conversation and realizing, especially on the state level, we agree 90 percent of the time. It's the 10 percent where we are diametrically opposed—sometimes for good reason—that gets played up.[76]

Today our phones and other devices are an omnipresent devil on our shoulder helping us decide who we should distrust or hate or ignore. This devil alters our beliefs and enlists us all in the lobbying effort. Contempt in politics may not be new, but never have we seen a technology for cultivating and sustaining contempt like the ideological and social media we have today.

ARE LIBERAL VALUES A MIRAGE?

Some skeptics may believe that liberal values were never more than a useful fiction for the naive, mere window dressing for economic-power struggles. This group includes some devotees of public-choice theory or others who do not believe in the existence of a "public interest"; right populists for whom autocracy offers a way to defeat the cultural pluralism they see as a moral threat; Marxists and left populists who see liberal-democratic norms as tools of economic dominance created and used by the powerful to protect their privileges; and scholars who are challenging the way we use ideas such as objectivity and rule neutrality by noting that procedural choices always have distributive implications.[77] But there is a distinction between acknowledging that legal rules are "political" because they produce winners and losers, on the one hand, and denying the value of liberal-democratic aspiration to truth seeking, objectivity, and fair process, on the other. The former does not negate the latter.[78]

As disciples of Enlightenment philosophy, the framers of the Constitution saw liberal democracy as a tool of social progress, a way to build a better, *fairer* society than the theocratic, semifeudal monarchies in which they lived. They sought to elevate reason over superstition and merit over heredity and privilege—at least, privilege based on familial proximity to the ruler. Enlightenment liberals hoped to use constitutional government to "establish justice" and "promote the general welfare." That politicians sometimes defeat those aspirations or pursue them in flawed ways hardly undermines their value.[79]

The first draft of this book was written in Edinburgh, Scotland, within a half mile of the graves of David Hume and (the often misunderstood) Adam Smith, two Enlightenment thinkers who influenced the framers of the U.S. Constitution directly and indirectly.[80] Neither Hume nor Smith would share modern conservatives' belief that ever-less government means ever-more freedom. Smith's notion of the "invisible hand" has made him an icon of free marketism in the public mind, but most historians, economists, and legal scholars know that he recognized that government has "the duty of protecting . . . every member of the society from the injustice or oppression of every other member . . . [and] of erecting and maintaining certain public works and certain public institutions" that the market will not provide.[81] Nor would Hume or Smith share the Democratic Socialists of America's (DSA) stated goal of abolishing capitalism.[82] Smith's views on this issue are well known, and Hume believed that commerce "encourages industriousness, helps to augment knowledge of all kinds, and renders people more sociable and humane."[83] Indeed, Hume's view foreshadowed those of the twentieth-century promoters of international-trade regimes as a response to two world wars: people who sought to promote peaceful international relations through commerce and economic cooperation.

It is not clear how much of Democrats' intraparty divide on these questions is merely semantic or reflects basic philosophical differences about American political economy. Labels such as *capitalism*, *socialism*, and *fascism* now mean very different things to different people.[84] To older Americans who grew up during the Cold War or to those familiar with Marxism and Leninism, *socialism* refers to a stage of development on the path to replacement of liberal democracy and a market economy with a dictatorship of the proletariat. To some younger voters who have grown up in an era of economic inequality and deregulation, the word may signify a simple desire for more redistribution, more public goods, and more regulation. Indeed, Bernie Sanders and the late Michael Harrington (founder of the DSA) have embraced a version of "socialism" that looks more like European "social democracy," despite the DSA's commitment to abolishing capitalism. And some of today's younger democratic socialists may see a wider gulf than actually exists between mainstream Democratic Party policy goals and DSA policy goals.[85]

Thus, when Republicans label Democratic Party initiatives as "socialist," they trigger different understandings (and reactions) in the minds of different voters; there may be a similar ambiguity effect at work when Democrats label Republicans' actions as "fascist." These semantic misunderstandings mask the fact that most voters, like Hume and Smith, seem to want well-regulated capitalism, *and* they want regulation to create a fairer, better society than the one we have now.[86]

Nevertheless, antiliberalism (or illiberalism) is on the rise in political discourse, particularly online and most alarmingly among political communities that openly support authoritarian ideas.[87] Republican megadonor and Donald Trump adviser Peter Thiel has said that he "no longer believe[s] that freedom and democracy are compatible."[88] Some American conservatives now openly express their affinity for a more authoritarian form of government, and for autocrats like President Viktor Orban of Hungary; indeed, the influential Conservative Political Action Conference invited Orban to address its annual gathering in 2022. The state legislatures of Wisconsin and North Carolina have been particularly transparent in their attempts to enshrine minority GOP rule in their respective state governments through gerrymandering and various other legal maneuvers. These developments, in turn, provoke on the ideological left anguish and fears of transitions to "fascism," which are then dismissed as hysteria by some on the right.[89] This self-feeding cycle of growing centrifugal forces whirls ever faster.

Some hope that the rise of illiberalism will provoke a defensive reaction among the greater mass of less partisan voters, as it did during World War II, when the United States was engaged in a war against European fascism and wary of Soviet communism. In 1944, a then famous jurist with the improbable name "Learned Hand" broadcast a Constitution Day speech that celebrated the importance of liberal-democratic values: "What then is the spirit of liberty? I cannot define it; I can only tell you my own faith. The spirit of liberty is *the spirit which is not too sure that it is right*; the spirit of liberty is the spirit which seeks to understand the mind of other men and women; the spirit of liberty is the spirit which weighs their interests alongside its own without bias."[90]

Human biases being what they are, this aspiration often eludes us. Perhaps because Judge Hand knew this, he avoided the language of certainty: "not *too* sure," "*seeks* to understand," and so on. The task is difficult but not impossible. Hand knew well that the framers never rejected the importance of "civic virtue."[91] Rather, they rejected reliance on *individual virtue alone* to create the kind of beneficial governance that yields decisions reflecting the permanent and aggregate interests of the community. Today, after two decades of sophisticated propaganda efficiently disseminated, that critical mass of civic virtue is rapidly depleting.[92]

CAN FLAWED PEOPLE HAVE GOOD IDEAS?

Another source of skepticism about the value of liberal-democratic norms might be stated this way: "Why should I care about the governance philosophies of dead white men whose sense of right and wrong allowed them to enslave other human beings?" The short answer is that even morally flawed people can have good ideas. This book operates on the premise that in policy debate ideas deserve to be evaluated on their own merits irrespective of who proposes them.[93] This basic idea is behind identity-blind grading of exams or double-blind scientific experiments. It is foundational to our sense of the rule of law, fair deliberation, and truth seeking.

Unfortunately, ad hominem, identity-based attacks are increasingly common, effective, and accepted in policy debate. In 2012, a conservative interest group affiliated with the oil industry, the Heartland Institute, erected billboards in several cities displaying the statement, "I still believe in global warming. Do you?" Each billboard was accompanied by a headshot of an unpopular person—such as Ted Kaczynski (the so-called Unabomber), Charles Manson, or Fidel Castro—in a crude attempt to undermine climate science by associating it with violent or unpopular people.[94] Similarly, when progressive scholars attack economic ideas by detailing the moral failings of the ideas' proponents, they are employing the same faulty logic.[95] In the same way, the racism of the founders of major environmental nongovernmental organizations (NGOs) and the continuing overrepresentation of wealthy, white people in these NGOs' ranks do not negate the value of the environmental-protection work those organizations do.[96]

The drafting of the U.S. Constitution omitted the perspectives of huge swaths of the population in ways we find tragic and morally condemnable today. Those omissions justify critical inquiries aimed at determining whether the ideas produced by such a narrow and homogenous slice of society have continuing value today and whether the legacy of exclusion affects the way we answer that question.[97] But that omission does not answer those inquiries. Some constitutional historians celebrate the flexibility and evolution of the Constitution from its exclusionary, racist origins to a more inclusive document today.[98] Nominating Joe Biden for president in 2020, Barack Obama put it this way: "I'm in Philadelphia, where our Constitution was drafted and signed. It wasn't a perfect document. It allowed for the inhumanity of slavery and failed to guarantee women—and even men who didn't own property—the right to participate in the political process. But embedded in this document was a North Star that would guide future generations; a system of representative government—a democracy—through which we could better realize our highest ideals."[99] Obama's use of the phrase "North Star" may have been no accident. It was the name of a widely read pre–Civil War newspaper

published by the brilliant abolitionist Frederick Douglass in Roches-
ter, New York (my hometown). Despite having lived a life profoundly
influenced by the Constitution's acceptance of slavery, Douglass
called the Constitution "a glorious liberty document" because it contained the seeds of reform in its aspirational language.[100]

Authors often cite others who articulated ideas before (or better
than) they did to show that the ideas resonate with others or to give
credit where credit is due. But the personal qualities of the people
cited do not determine the power or utility of the idea. Rather, we
evaluate an argument by grappling with *its* logical force or lack thereof
and with the evidence on which *it* is based. Political and legal institutions are social constructs that reflect the distribution of power when
they were created, but that fact should not paralyze our thought or
stop us from evaluating their utility today. In a recent essay on this
subject, the political theorist Wendy Brown notes that when fundamental social norms are hotly contested, as they are today, "we need
sober thinkers who refuse to submit to the lures of fatalism or
apocalypticism, pipe dreams of total revolution or redemption by the
progress of reason—yet aim to be more than . . . foot soldiers amid
current orders of knowledge or politics."[101] This book aspires to
reflect that sort of sober critical analysis. It defends liberal-democratic
norms of civil engagement, respect for pluralism, and aspiration to
truth and objectivity as the keys to making the energy transition a
political reality, and it explores the social forces undermining those
norms. Each reader can determine whether it succeeds in that task,
but only by engaging the analysis on its merits.

A FINAL CAVEAT

This book mostly sidesteps two big issues implicated by the energy
transition: whether economic growth is consistent with the transition
and the wisdom of hastening the transition in the United States given
the claim that emissions growth in China and India will "cancel out"
emissions reductions in the United States.

Some readers will be familiar with the history of the "growth/no
growth" debate within environmental policy, including the famous
wager between the economist Julian Simon and the neo-Malthusian

biologist Paul Ehrlich in 1980.[102] Those who see the energy transition as inconsistent with economic growth include both supporters and opponents of the transition, and both groups include some so-called doomers who spread the hashtag #ThanosWasRight on social media.[103] Certainly, differences of opinion on this issue are part of the subtext of online energy-transition debate. This book does not fully engage the growth question except insofar as it examines the empirical literature on the trade-offs between emissions reductions and affordable, reliable energy supplies in chapter 5.[104] That literature suggests that the United States can pursue a path to net zero that is consistent with continuing economic growth.

Nor does this book engage claims that pursuing an energy transition in the United States is pointless because fossil-fuel-led growth in India and China will overwhelm emissions reductions in the United States. *All* averted carbon emissions help mitigate the harmful effects of climate change, so the analysis in this book does not depend on action by China and India. Furthermore, it seems almost certain that pursuing a U.S. energy transition will trigger technological change that will facilitate emissions reductions elsewhere. The development of cheaper, better clean-energy alternatives in Organization for Economic Cooperation and Development nations will shift the future emissions path of China and India downward. Last, there is a strong argument that the United States has an ethical duty to act alone on this issue because a large share of the pollution that drives climate change was and is emitted from within the United States or was and is otherwise facilitated by American companies. The United States grew to wealth on the back of GHG emissions, and until it enacts policy creating a path to net zero, future developing nations such as China and India have an argument that they cannot reasonably be expected to do so.

THE PLAN OF THE BOOK

The remainder of this book explains energy regulation as the product of a complex mix of political forces, the most important of which is the electorate. Part 1 (chapters 1–3) offers a comprehensive political and intellectual history of the U.S. energy-regulatory state from its nineteenth-century beginnings to now. Chapter 1 provides a straightforward chronology of the creation of the regulatory regimes we know today, explaining them as the product of a series of republican moments. Most were congressional responses to public dissatisfaction with technoeconomic changes in the energy sector. Chapter 2 explains the deregulatory impulse that dominated late twentieth-century American politics, how it has shaped the evolution of energy markets, and its contribution to partisan polarization in Congress. That chapter includes a look at public-choice theory, which animates one strain of modern conservativism and provided some of the intellectual support for deregulation generally. Chapter 3 chronicles Congress's twenty-first-century failures to regulate GHG emissions and explains those failures as the product of growing partisan tribalism.

Part 2 (chapters 4–6) looks at the political challenge facing the climate coalition. Chapter 4 examines how the modern information environment supercharges affective, negative polarization, miring more and more voters in a miasma of frustration, misunderstanding, and alienation from politics and their political adversaries. Chapter 5 examines how that tribal partisan mindset impedes efforts to resolve the complicated, high-stakes trade-offs that are a necessary part of the transition. Chapter 6 concludes with thoughts on how to fashion the more productive political dialogue needed to produce a legislative path to net zero. Such a dialogue requires recognizing that reasonable people disagree over the best path forward and that reaching the net-zero goal is more important than punishing or excluding those whom we regard (rightly or wrongly) with contempt.

PART I

The Evolution of the Energy-Regulatory State

1

REPUBLICAN MOMENTS AND THE CREATION OF THE ENERGY-REGULATORY STATE

Of all the chores that befell them, ironing was the most oner-
ous. "Washing was hard work, but ironing was the worst," one
woman said. "Nothing could ever be as hard as ironing."
Properly so, they referred to their tools as the "sad irons."

—Robert Caro, *The Path to Power*

THE EXISTING energy-regulatory state is testament to Congress's periodic ability to produce national responses to national problems. Beginning in the mid–nineteenth century, as new forms of energy were developed and commercialized, they transformed people's lives so fundamentally that their use and availability became a matter of public concern. Figure 1.1, updated regularly by the U.S. Energy Information Administration, depicts how Americans' use of different primary energy resources has changed over time. These energy transitions were triggered by entrepreneurs trying to make money by finding better ways to power economic activity and individuals' daily lives. The transitions prompted sharp conflict over the distribution of the benefits and costs of using these new energy sources, eventually giving birth to new bodies of regulatory law. The regulatory regimes that emerged from these conflicts are best understood as political responses to perceived market failures and/or efforts to protect people from the economic predations of the newly powerful.

This chapter's epigraph from Robert Caro comments on the way rural communities were left behind by early electricity markets. It was part of his story of how the Rural Electrification Act of 1936 improved the lives of farm women by bringing electricity to the Texas hill

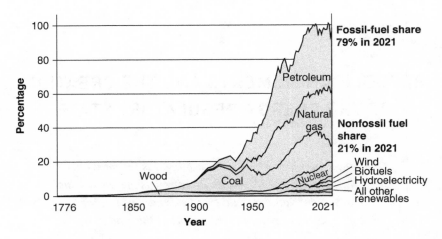

FIGURE 1.1. Energy consumption in the United States, 1776–2021.

Source: U.S. Energy Information Administration.

country. Like this act, most of the building blocks of the energy-regulatory state were responses to public demand: either for wider public access to new forms of energy or for protection from the adverse social and economic consequences of their unregulated production and delivery.[1] This chapter describes how the modern energy-regulatory state came to be. It is a story that deserves (re)telling because some of its political complexity has been lost in the cynical accounts of regulatory politics that dominate public discussion today.

THE POLITICS OF REGULATION

Today it is widely believed that corporations win most policy fights at the expense of the public interest. This view is expressed by some economists, historians, and legal scholars as well.[2] But it fails as an empirical generalization and obscures the more interesting and complicated reality revealed by a sizable body of political science scholarship. In the words of one legal scholar reviewing the empirical literature, "If you look really hard at the political science and related literatures, it is difficult to find any good, solid empirical evidence that [corporate] capture [of the policy process] exists at all. Diffuse interests often do quite well. Concentrated interests often lose, sometimes spectacularly."[3]

However, it is also true that the history of regulatory legislation is one of long periods of policymaking inertia, interrupted only every so often by short bursts of reformist legislation.[4] It is axiomatic that inertia favors the status quo and those who are benefiting from it. We expect those on whom the market is bestowing the biggest favors to oppose change and those on whom the market is imposing costs to seek change. Can we therefore infer from policy inertia that corporate power is subverting the public interest? No, not if we look at the empirical research.

WHAT BUSINESS DOMINANCE IS AND ISN'T

Scholars who study Congress start from the premise that legislators are concerned primarily with protecting their reelection prospects because they must remain in office to achieve other policy or intra-institutional goals they may have.[5] Beyond this common starting point, different scholars have framed the legislative task in different, sometimes overlapping ways: as an information problem in which members' task is to make good policy decisions and avoid bad ones; a distributive problem in which members of Congress try to bring jobs, grants, and subsidies to their constituents and to allocate their costs to others; a tug of war between interest groups in which members of Congress are little more than strands of the rope; and a representation problem in which members protect their reelection prospects by working to influence constituents' impressions of them.[6]

Policymakers are more likely to hear from business interests. Public-choice models and other interest-group theories emphasize the advantages that smaller, wealthier, more tightly organized groups—such as business interests—have in the contest to influence legislative decisions.[7] They are more likely than large, diffuse groups to band together to lobby in the first place and to invest resources in that effort. The electoral incentive means that members of Congress are more likely to listen to people who can influence their reelection prospects. This group includes wealthy individuals and businesses who can arrange significant contributions to the member's campaign coffers, firms that employ significant numbers of their constituents, and firms whose business interests fall within the subject-matter domain of the member's committee assignments.

Although social scientists recognize these lobbying advantages enjoyed by businesses and the wealthy, the empirical literature does not suggest that firms can *control* the policymaking process or its outcomes, anecdotes to the contrary notwithstanding. Studies that look for evidence that industry drives members' votes on the floor of the Senate or House, for example, have come up empty.[8] Some research even suggests that policy is instead broadly responsive to public preferences, at least within certain policy domains.[9] Other research suggests that policy outcomes tend to align with the interests of the very wealthy, but even this is disputed.[10] But this more qualified understanding of business's role in the policy process is currently getting lost in a sea of populist cynicism. As the political scientist Susan Yackee has demonstrated, when "my" side loses, I am more likely to *infer* nefarious causes for the unwanted outcome.[11] But that kind of inference is the cui bono fallacy at work: the inference that those who benefit from an action must have caused that action. *The other side won. It must have been because of the money or the lobbying coalition they had on their side.*

Today many people liken economic elites to the courtiers of old European monarchies whose proximity to power allowed them to control policy outcomes in self-interested ways. Anecdotal evidence of corrupt politicians doing the bidding of those who enrich them feeds that narrative.[12] For example, in her book on clean-energy politics in the states, the political scientist and podcaster Leah Stokes presents a view of energy policymaking that characterizes utilities and the fossil-fuel industry as almost reflexively opposed to clean energy and as the principal reason why climate and clean-energy policies are not more widespread and ambitious than they currently are. Much of her analysis is compelling, but by overcrediting industry influence Stokes predicted that it was "unlikely" that Texas would experience significant solar-power growth after 2020 and concluded that "if *all* U.S.

states acted like Texas there would be little renewable energy built."[13] These predictions were way off the mark.

In practice, firms' political strategies are varied, even within the fossil-fuel and electric-utility industries. Some firms may support strong climate policy in response to social or political pressures or for reputation enhancement.[14] Sometimes firms see new regulation as inevitable, and so they lobby less to oppose policy than to shape it. Global firms may lobby to try to harmonize regulatory requirements across jurisdictions.[15] Firms subject to foreign competition may be driven by concern that regulation will hamper their competitiveness. And so on. Nevertheless, the idea that business firms control policymaking resonates powerfully. This chapter's account of the creation of the energy-regulatory state shows that the energy-policymaking process is not nearly so simple; and chapters 3 and 4 offer some reasons why voters are increasingly prone to believe that it is.

The Role of Money in Politics

It seems logical to infer corruption or the influence of money when we can't square policy outcomes with our sense of right and wrong or with majority policy preferences. But political scientists have long warned against inferring causation from correlations between campaign spending and electoral success, noting that it is just as likely that being the preelection favorite attracts more campaign contributions.[16] Yet American political campaigns are singularly expensive, and many members of Congress must fundraise constantly. A growing literature within the social sciences details the ways in which businesses and wealthy individuals seek to exploit members' need for money and to use campaign contributions and dark money to pursue their policy goals.[17] That literature suggests that money can buy *access* to politicians that other people lack, giving rise to the inference that access equals determinative influence over policy outcomes.[18] But that inference is often wrong. In the words of a leading political science textbook on the subject, "The relationship between money and political outcomes is far from simple, largely because *where large amounts of money come into play on one side, others often mobilize as well. . . .* [S]cholars have found no smoking gun, no systematic relationship between campaign contributions and policy success, a fact that might be surprising to readers of the press, where it seems that campaign contributions are equated with lobbying power across the board. . . . One reason why it may not be so is that the policy process is so hard to control."[19]

This observation fits energy policymaking. The wealthiest Americans as a class do not oppose climate policy and the energy transition. Some do; some don't. The Koch network works assiduously to obstruct regulatory climate legislation; Bill Gates, Michael Bloomberg, and Tom Steyer seem to be working just as assiduously to support it.[20] Nor is it particularly uncommon for big-donor conservatives such as the casino magnate Sheldon Adelson and the Koch network to fail spectacularly in their giving strategies when they spend lavishly on losing campaigns.[21] Likewise, the American Legislative Exchange Council's well-funded effort to roll back state clean-energy laws in 2011–2014 was an unequivocal failure.[22]

However, the Supreme Court's long-standing endorsement of political spending as protected speech certainly confers more *potential* influence on those with more money.[23] This offends most people's sense of fair democratic process. The appearance of corruption and unfairness is important, particularly in an era of declining support for government institutions, including the Supreme Court.[24] In legislative battles pitting mixed coalitions of businesses, NGOs, and others against each other, the better-resourced side probably does have an advantage, all else being equal. In that way, the system *is* unfair. But it is a leap from that inference to the conclusion that money is the key obstacle to strong climate policy or that it was determinative in a specific policy fight.

The Role of Lobbying

When people think of industry lobbyists, they think of influence peddlers such as Jack Abramoff, who dispensed gifts and favors expertly to create a sense of emotional debt among legislators on behalf of his clients.[25] But most lobbying is less about gifts and applying pressure than about providing politically relevant information to policymakers. Legislators and regulators know that they lack information about important dimensions of a regulatory issue and that they need to acquire accurate information from those who have it, including business firms. Some research implies that this need dampens pro-industry bias because industry lobbyists, as repeat players in the policymaking game, need to maintain a reputation for providing policymakers with reliable and accurate information.[26] In the words of the political scientist Rogan Kersh,

> If you ask a Washington lobbyist about the main determinants of professional success, financial matters—campaign contributions, legislative earmarks or other monetary benefits sought by lobbyists, even client payments—will be well down the list. Ask most members of Congress and their staff, administration officials, or other Beltway insiders, and their answers will likely be similar: not money but *information* is the coin of the realm in interest group lobbying. The most sought-after lobbyists are hired not because of their ability to control, raise, or disperse funds, but primarily on the basis of their strategic capacity to deploy information in the service of their clients and policy makers as well as advance their own desired ends.[27]

Legislators' need for information provides industry with the leverage that comes from the ability to frame the issue for legislators—to make some facts more salient than others.[28] But, again, that leverage does necessarily imply damage to the public interest. For example, when Congress makes changes to bills after hearing from industry lobbyists, it may be because the lobbyist informed the legislator of a flaw in the bill that would hurt both the lobbyist's client and the legislator's constituents.

Similarly, we cannot logically infer injury to the public interest when regulatory agencies change proposed rules after receiving industry input, though scholars sometimes do make that inference.[29] Sometimes regulators decide that their initial proposal was based on a misunderstanding of the costs or difficulties of the regulatory task, or sometimes proposed rules are strategically bold as the opening position in a negotiation game.[30] Firms can wield information in influential ways,[31] but that influence does not imply significant damage to the public interest. The legal scholar Daniel Walters explains:

"Showing influence at these later stages most often means showing that business interests are successful in encouraging agencies to tinker with the technical minutiae of rulemaking. . . . Evidence that business interests (producers of electricity) succeed in influencing [the Environmental Protection Agency] to relax the permissible concentration levels of an air pollutant between a proposed rule and final rule might show up in a carefully designed empirical study as evidence of influence, but that fact alone would tend to obscure the fact that [the rule] overwhelmingly benefits the general public."[32] Sometimes regulators change proposed rules in order to take advantage of commenters expertise; this idea is supported by a recent paper finding that the U.S. Environmental Protection Agency (EPA) is particularly persuaded by comments that address the scientific details of its proposals and by comments filed by partnerships between industry firms and environmental groups.[33]

This understanding of regulatory agencies is a far cry from portrayals of regulators as either the puppets of industry or a "deep state" bent on controlling government. Regulatory agencies instead consist of a mix of career bureaucrats and political appointees, each trying to do (what they see as) their jobs. The latter are dependent on the former for subject-matter expertise, and both groups are continuously pulled and tugged by those who are affected by and interested in their decisions. Most agency careerists are attracted to work in the agency in the first place because they care about the agency's mission. Most of the political appointees are installed to try to steer the agency in directions that are consistent with the priorities of the president who appointed them. Agencies sometimes make bad decisions, and they hear from the industries they regulate much more often than they hear from others.[34] But their ability to resist politicians' or industry's efforts to divert them from their missions is routinely underestimated, and so is the ability of agency experts, deliberating in a way that is insulated from direct political control, to produce wise and democratically representative policy choices.[35]

Given the lack of empirical support for the idea that business dominance regularly subverts the public interest, the better question is: Why do policy battles produce major regulatory legislation at some times but not at others?

OVERCOMING REGULATORY INERTIA: REPUBLICAN MOMENTS

Republican moments begin with a truism that we sometimes overlook when we are unhappy with policy outcomes: that politicians worry about public opinion. Even the most powerful, autocratic rulers recognize the importance of public opinion to their legitimacy. The Roman poet Juvenal famously noted that Roman emperors used "bread and circuses" to keep the public content and to forestall unrest. The theocratic monarchs of pre-Enlightenment Europe commissioned public art and acquired holy relics to burnish their legitimacy in the public eye. Machiavelli advised princes that it was more important to cultivate the support of the mass public than that of "allies or partisans."[36] The importance that today's autocrats, such as Xi Jinping, Vladimir Putin, and Viktor Orban, place on public opinion is reflected in their efforts to shut down independent print and broadcast media and to block their citizens' access to social media.

The designers of American liberal democracy wanted to make policymakers responsive to the decisions that an informed, deliberate majority would favor. Although some scholars dispute that proposition,[37] this book proceeds on the less cynical premise that American liberal democracy was designed to *seek* noble substantive aspirations—respect for pluralism, fairness, equality of opportunity—even if it too often falls short of achieving them.[38] Among social scientists, organization theorists seem to best capture the political dynamics by which that historic aspiration is sometimes realized through congressional legislation. They model the policy process as complex and anarchic, so that durable policy change is possible only during times when particular political conditions happen to align fortuitously—that is, during republican moments.[39]

Republican moments are characterized in part by groundswells of public concern. It is that sort of bottom-up pressure that has driven Congress to enact labor laws, public-health laws, consumer-protection laws, environmental laws, and laws regulating competition and monopoly. Importantly, these groundswells are *only a necessary condition* for republican moments, *not a sufficient one*. More is required. John Kingdon's oft-cited model of legislative politics identifies three necessary conditions for regulatory legislation: a common understanding of the policy problem to be addressed, an apparent policy solution, *and* sufficient support among politicians and the public to match the solution to the problem.[40] Each of these conditions is a continuous rather than a binary variable. When the distribution of partisan control over the levers of power is especially conducive to regulatory change, less public pressure is required; when the partisan environment is particularly resistant, it takes much more public pressure to produce change. Creating that public pressure means more than cultivating widespread or intense public concern about a policy issue. It also requires *electoral* pressure—that is, creating among legislators the sense that their action or inaction on the issue might affect their reelection.

The republican moments that created the energy-regulatory state happened at times when all of the conditions emphasized by Kingdon aligned. The following chronology divides that history into two phases, each consisting of remarkably short productive bursts of regulatory energy in Congress: a *development phase* comprising roughly three decades of the Populist and Progressive Eras in U.S. history as well as the six years of the New Deal; and *an environmental health and safety phase* stretching from the late 1960s to 1990 but centered on the so-called environmental decade of the 1970s.[41] The overriding policy objective of the development phase was to spread the benefits of *reliable, affordable* energy as widely as possible by incentivizing investment in energy production. The environmental health and safety phase aimed mostly to foster *cleaner, safer* sources of energy, reflecting changing public values about how to balance development against risk, in particular environmental and health risks.

THE ENERGY-REGULATORY STATE: THE DEVELOPMENT PHASE

The modern energy markets we know today first emerged in the mid–nineteenth century following the creation of the first commercial natural gas utility in Fredonia, New York, in the 1840s, the first productive crude-oil well in western Pennsylvania in the 1850s, and the first commercial power station in New York City in the 1880s. The entrepreneurs who developed these industries became the titans and robber barons of the Gilded Age. They accumulated and used their economic clout in ways that provoked popular outrage: they misused patents, committed all manner of stock fraud, bribed politicians, and used physical violence to gain market advantages.[42] In the laissez-faire and social Darwinist ethic of this pre-regulatory era, these methods were common, and those who employed them rationalized them as legitimate competitive techniques.

The late nineteenth-century Populist Movement was a reaction to the robber barons, driven by a rural–urban social divide not unlike today's partisan divide. Similarly, in today's climate activism we can also see echoes of early twentieth-century progressivism, which was an urban-centered, morality-based social justice movement. The Populist and Progressive Eras together produced a spate of major national regulatory regimes addressing competition, labor and consumer protection, beginning with the Interstate Commerce Act of 1887, which aimed at abuses of market power by railroad companies.[43] Energy regulation was a central part of both reform movements because of the rapid growth of the oil, natural gas, and electricity markets in the late 1800s.

The regulatory response to emerging energy markets followed two parallel tracks, both focused on ensuring an adequate supply of energy to people at reasonable prices. In oil markets, Congress left the task of incentivizing and managing production to the states and employed antitrust law to punish abuses of market power after they occurred. In electricity markets, by contrast, state and federal regulators sought to control market power using the public-utility model, which accepted the premise that investor-owned utilities (IOUs) were natural monopolies that must be closely regulated for the benefit of consumers. Natural gas markets were a hybrid of these two systems: regulation of production was left to the states, while public-utility regulation governed the transmission, distribution, and sale of natural gas.

MANAGING COMPETITION IN OIL MARKETS: STATES AND ANTITRUST LAW

After Edwin Drake discovered oil in western Pennsylvania in the 1850s, the Pennsylvania and Appalachian oil patch dominated oil supply in the United States for the rest of the century.[44] This is the context in which John D. Rockefeller established the Standard Oil Company and quickly positioned it to become a dominant refiner and retailer of refined oil products. Much of Standard Oil's growth and success was attributable to Rockefeller's business acumen: his strategic sense, attention to detail, efficiency, technical innovations, and willingness to integrate vertically in order to control costs and supplies. But the company's success was also built on Rockefeller's sharp-elbowed (read: ruthless) approach to competition, which included price-fixing arrangements and the forcing of pipelines and railroads to discriminate in favor of Standard Oil.[45] Like many of the industrialists of the Gilded Age, Rockefeller believed that by absorbing or destroying weaker companies, he was providing a social benefit: not the "creative destruction" later hailed by Austrian economics as the key to competitive prices for consumers but rather a kind of market stability that only a benevolent monopolist could provide. To Rockefeller, the volatility of unbridled competition was "destructive" and "a sin" because it wreaked havoc on small firms, families, and resource-dependent communities.[46]

Most of the public saw things differently, and voters' reaction to Rockefeller's ruthlessness produced a series of republican moments in Congress. Public opposition to Standard Oil and other large holding companies, or "trusts," gave rise to the antitrust movement.[47] The movement's first major legislative accomplishment was the Sherman Antitrust Act of 1890 prohibiting "combination[s] . . . in restraint of trade" and "attempt[s] to monopolize."[48] When several exposés of Standard Oil's anticompetitive practices appeared in *McClure's* magazine between 1902 and 1904, they provoked a public outcry that built public support for passing the Hepburn Act (1906) which granted the Interstate Commerce Commission rate-setting jurisdiction over oil pipelines; passing the Mann-Elkins Act (1910), which expanded the commission's jurisdiction to several other industries; and prosecuting Standard Oil for violating federal antitrust law. In 1911, the Supreme Court decided that Standard Oil constituted an illegal monopoly and a combination in restraint of trade and ordered the company's dissolution into thirty-four separate companies.[49] Later congressional hearings featured a further dissection of Standard Oil's anticompetitive practices, many of which were subsequently defined as violations of the law within two statutes passed in 1914: the Clayton Act and the Federal Trade Commission Act.[50]

In the meantime, oil production had begun to expand to new regions, in particular California, Texas, Oklahoma, and Louisiana, where other large oil fields were discovered near the turn of the twentieth century. Each new discovery subjected the national oil market to a boom-and-bust cycle, alternating gluts and shortages accompanied by wild swings in prices—the very sort of "destructive" competition Rockefeller had lamented. Part of the problem was centered in state property law and the common-law "rule of capture," which permitted any single property owner in a multiowner oil field to draw oil across property lines to their own well.[51] The rule created a tragedy of the commons in which each owner faced the incentive to produce from their own wells as quickly as possible before other producers drew the oil away toward their wells. The resulting free-for-all destabilized pressure in underground formations, creating massive physical and economic waste.

This quirk of state common law triggered demand for state governments to regulate oil and gas production. Their incremental and successive regulatory interventions in the production market coalesced into state "conservation" statutes authorizing state regulators to establish rules to promote more efficient production.[52] These laws not only helped reduce waste but also had the happy consequence for producers of stabilizing prices, possibly at levels that exceeded long-term competitive rates. Some pipelines and producers challenged these new laws in court, arguing that the laws took away their rights to produce oil without compensation in violation of the Fourteenth Amendment and/or imposed burdens on interstate commerce in violation of the Constitution's Commerce Clause. But courts rejected both sets of challenges, reasoning that the primary purpose of state regulation was to prevent waste and manage the states' mineral resources and therefore was constitutionally legitimate.[53]

The onset of World War I paused the national regulatory impulse in Congress, but that impulse was later reawakened by the economic pain imposed by the Great Depression, which eventually produced the New Deal.[54] In six short years (1933–1939) of the Franklin Roosevelt presidency, Congress legislated with breathtaking speed to try to stimulate the Depression economy and impose sweeping new regulatory regimes on the financial, telecommunications, airlines, and the agricultural sectors, significantly increasing the size of the national regulatory state.[55] For their part, oil- and gas-supply markets remained turbulent during the Great Depression as independent oil producers evaded the production restrictions imposed by state commissions.[56] In 1933, Congress passed the National Industrial Recovery Act, a national, planning regime for oil production. This law briefly stabilized prices but was struck down by the Supreme Court as an unconstitutional delegation of legislative authority.[57] Meanwhile, the government continued to use antitrust law to punish anticompetitive behavior, most prominently in the successful prosecution of several oil companies for colluding to fix prices on spot markets in East Texas and the Midwest.[58]

After World War II, as crude-oil markets became global markets, state regulators lost the ability to use production restrictions to affect prices. By 1970, the center of price-setting power had shifted to the Organization of Petroleum Exporting Countries (OPEC), a cartel that established production quotas to prop up prices. An OPEC boycott of the United States in the early 1970s produced gasoline-price increases and shortages and provoked the Nixon administration to impose oil-price controls.[59] It also led many industrial consumers of oil—including the electric-generation sector—to shift away from oil to coal or other fuel sources.[60] These developments coincided with the growing power of government-owned national oil companies in the global market, some of which were created from the remnants of nationalized private firms. Thus, whereas the ancestors of ExxonMobil, Royal Dutch Shell, British Petroleum (BP), and Chevron once controlled the lion's share of world oil reserves, oil majors today collectively own less than 15 percent of the world's proven reserves, and each one's individual share of daily or annual production is in the low single digits.[61] The price for crude oil is now set by world supply and demand, except during periods in which OPEC chooses to exert its influence over prices.[62]

GAS AND ELECTRICITY MARKETS AND PUBLIC-UTILITY LAW

In the early history of electricity markets, some advocated government provision of electricity as a public service, an impulse that materialized as the "public power" movement of the early twentieth century. That movement gave birth to the hundreds of municipal utilities that dot today's electric-power landscape and to federal power agencies such as the Bonneville Power Administration and the Tennessee Valley Authority.[63] But the model of public control that emerged as dominant in both the natural gas and electricity markets was that of a private IOU. Instead of controlling abuses of market power after the fact through enforcement of antitrust law, policymakers opted to certify monopoly providers of natural gas and electricity within geographically defined service areas and to set the prices for those services beforehand by regulatory fiat. By the onset of the Great Depression, most states had established utilities commissions charged with regulating electric and gas IOUs in this way, setting their rates and basic terms of service.[64]

In 1927, the Supreme Court's decision in *Public Utilities Commission of Rhode Island v. Attleboro Steam and Electric Co.* circumscribed the power of state utility commissions to set rates for energy sold in interstate commerce. In response, Congress passed the Federal Power Act (FPA) of 1935, the Public Utility Holding Company Act of 1935, and the Natural Gas Act (NGA) of 1938.[65] The FPA and NGA authorized the Federal Power Commission (FPC) to regulate wholesale sales and transmission of electricity and natural gas, respectively, in interstate commerce, leaving the regulation of retail sales and local distribution to the states.[66] These laws were a reaction to continuing public concern about the market power exercised by natural gas and electricity utility trusts and to Depression Era anger at Wall Street titans, including the nation's most prominent electric-utility executive, Samuel Insull, who acceded to public-utility regulation as the lesser of two evils so as to avoid replacement of IOUs by government-owned utilities.[67]

IOUs thrived in part because the corporate form helped raise the massive amounts of capital necessary to create reliable electric grids over large service areas.[68] Over the next six decades, IOUs came to serve 75 percent of U.S. electricity customers. Municipal utilities (munies) served about half of the remaining customers and were exempted from most regulation under these statutes. They were, of course, subject to control at the ballot box. The New Deal statute that relieved farm women of their "sad irons," the Rural Electrification Act of 1936, created yet another service regime consisting of rural electric cooperatives (co-ops), which eventually came to serve the sparsely populated areas not served by IOUs or munies. Over time, the systems managed by IOUs, munies, and co-ops came to be interconnected with one another over three massive electric grids covering the continental United States.[69]

From their inception through the mid-1990s, IOUs provided energy service to customers as a single bundled product, and in many places they still do. That is, customers purchase energy and the service of delivering it in one volumetric (per kilowatt-hour, or kwh) electric bill. The FPC (now the Federal Energy Regulatory Commission, or FERC) and state public-utility commissions (PUCs) set wholesale and retail rates, respectively, under statutes requiring that the rates be "just and reasonable" and "nondiscriminatory."[70] The laws allow electric and gas IOUs to recover their reasonably incurred operating costs and a fair return on all prudent capital investments (their "rate base").[71] The utility's tariff specifies how it will recover its approved revenues through the rates it charges each of three classes of customers: residential, commercial, and industrial. As interpreted by the Supreme Court, particularly in the decision *Fed. Power Comm'n v. Hope Natural Gas* in 1944, the "just and reasonable" rate requirement implies rates that (in theory) are high enough to permit utilities to attract sufficient capital to provide reliable service to customers but not so high as to exploit ratepayers.[72] Thus, by making provision of the service profitable but not *too* profitable, public-utility regulation seeks to attract private capital into the provision of energy service to the public and thereby to ensure an adequate supply of energy at an affordable price.

While natural gas and electric utilities share this common regulatory treatment, they differ in at least three ways that are important to the energy transition. The first is in the structure of upstream energy production. In the electricity sector, IOUs were traditionally vertically integrated. That is, they generated most of the energy they sold to their customers at their own power plants. Natural gas utilities, by contrast, traditionally bought most of the gas they sold to their customers from third-party pipelines, which in turn purchased the gas from wellhead producers.

Second, power plants could be built near customers, but gas could be produced only where it was found. For that reason, the New Deal Congress saw the need for interstate shipments of gas and included a federal permitting and siting regime for interstate natural gas pipelines in the NGA.[73] In the 1930s, no one foresaw the twenty-first-century need to build power plants far from cities, in places where the sun shines or the wind blows the strongest and longest. So there was no analogous federal siting regime for transmission lines in the FPA, leaving the authority to permit new transmission lines with the states.

Third and finally, electricity cannot (yet) be stored at commercial quantities, whereas the natural gas network has long included commercially significant amounts of storage capacity. Therefore, electric-grid operators must balance the amount of electricity being added or "dispatched" to the grid by generators with the amount being removed by consumers in real time. Furthermore, the statutory requirement that rates be just and reasonable requires that grid operators dispatch the available generators with the lowest marginal costs, subject to the need to maintain reliable service. This practice is known in the industry as *security-constrained economic dispatch*.[74] As customers use more electricity, grid operators dispatch higher marginal-cost resources to serve that additional demand; when demand falls, grid operators drop the more expensive plants first. Because individual utility systems are interconnected, this balancing takes place continuously across areas that are much larger than individual utility service areas. These balancing actions are aimed at keeping the grid near its target *frequency*, which can sometimes be a delicate task.[75] Failure to keep the system in balance can result in system failure, which produces massive and deadly blackouts like those that hit the northeastern United States in 1965, the upper Midwest in 2003, and Texas in 2021.

The dispatch-order priority created by the security-constrained economic dispatch rule has profound implications for the energy transition. For most generating units, the primary component of marginal costs is fuel. Traditionally, the dispatch order of generators on the system has changed over time with fluctuations in the relative prices of the different electric-generation fuels. But fuel costs for wind and solar generators are essentially zero, placing them first in the dispatch order. This makes it easier for investors to predict their future use and therefore to estimate future revenues. At the same time, because the spot price of electricity is also tied to the marginal cost of the last-dispatched generator, the presence of wind and solar generation depresses the spot price when renewable energy is plentiful. In addition, the intermittency of renewables can make spot prices more volatile as other plants are dispatched for short periods to back up short-term, weather-based fluctuations in renewable generation. All these characteristics disadvantage higher marginal-cost generation such as coal- and natural-gas-fired plants and complicate energy-transition policymaking in ways described in chapter 5.

THE ENERGY-REGULATORY STATE: THE ENVIRONMENTAL HEALTH AND SAFETY PHASE

ENVIRONMENTALISM AND THE ENVIRONMENTAL DECADE

After World War II, the rise of a mass middle class with leisure time to spend in the great outdoors triggered popular demand for laws controlling pollution and requiring better stewardship of the environment. Postwar environmentalism was one of a family of social movements that included the consumer- and worker-protection, civil rights, and anti–Vietnam War movements. It spawned new environmental NGOs, such as the World Wildlife Fund, the Environmental Defense Fund, and Greenpeace, and swelled the coffers and membership rolls of existing groups, such as the Sierra Club and the Wilderness Society.[76] In the fields of ecology, economics, and other disciplines, it also stimulated new scholarship justifying stronger environmental regulation. Some of these works offered logical arguments in favor of government regulation; others appealed to people's moral sense. Morality-based appeals included arguments based on religious doctrine, the so-called Gaia

Hypothesis, and moral philosophy arguments that pollution is wrong.[77] Aldo Leopold's *Sand County Almanac* (1949) laid out an argument for conservation based on a notion of environmental stewardship that Leopold called a "land ethic." These ideas stimulated late twentieth-century legal scholarship exploring ideas such as the public-trust doctrine, the precautionary principle, and other ideas that would justify extending legal protection to natural resources because of their previously underrecognized social or other values.[78]

By contrast, Garrett Hardin's essay "The Tragedy of the Commons" (1968) became an influential example of a logic-based case for regulation, one that economists had long recognized: the market's tendency to undervalue and undersupply public goods. In Hardin's words, individually rational behavior leads to collective "ruin." The solution to this problem, said Hardin, is "mutual coercion, mutually agreed upon."[79] These ideas stimulated an extensive body of late twentieth-century scholarship within economics and game theory modeling the tragedy of the commons as a broader cooperation game.[80] This work intersected with economists' earlier treatment of pollution as an *externality* problem, a cost not born by the producer but instead shifted to society. That literature, in turn, established economists' preference for market- or incentives-based solutions to this externality problem, such as pollution taxes or marketable permits, rather than for regulatory mandates.[81]

By the 1960s, the case for some kind of regulation had become politically popular. These broader social demands for stronger environmental regulation went unmet for a while in part because conservatives, many of them southern Democrats, bottled up all sorts of reformist legislation in Congress, including environmental bills. Eventually, however, the political logjam broke, and Congress enacted a long list of new consumer-protection, health and safety, and environment-protection statutes, many of which profoundly affected the energy industry. Most of the energy-relevant laws were enacted in a twelve-year span extending from 1969 to 1980 (inclusive), a stretch of time that subsumes the environmental decade. Figure 1.2 puts the most energy-relevant statutes on a timeline.

The first of these statutes was the National Environmental Policy Act of 1969, which created the now-familiar obligation to prepare an

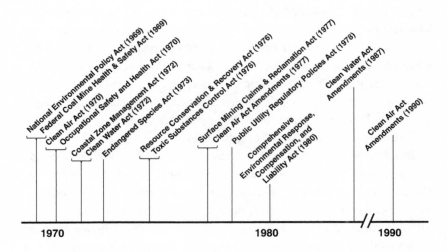

FIGURE 1.2. Major U.S. environmental statutes, 1968–1990.

environmental impact statement before undertaking any "major federal action significantly affecting the quality of the human environment."[82] Many of the other statutes are also familiar pillars of modern pollution-control law: the Clean Air Act of 1970, Clean Water Act of 1972, Resource Conservation and Recovery Act of 1976, and Comprehensive Environmental Response, Compensation, and Liability Act of 1980 (also known as the "Superfund" law).[83] These laws were the product of prototypical republican moments—responses to catalyzing events that raised the salience of environmental health and safety in the public mind. For example, many credit the Cuyahoga River fire and Santa Barbara oil spill, both in 1969, with building support for passage of the Clean Water Act in 1972, and the latter disaster certainly contributed to passage of the Coastal Zone Management Act that same year.[84] Similarly, the discovery of buried toxic waste at Love Canal, New York, built public support for the passage of hazardous-waste cleanup laws such as the Superfund law.

Several of the regulatory regimes created during this phase addressed the presence of toxic or especially hazardous substances in the environment or workplace. The Clean Air Act, Clean Water Act, and Resource Conservation and Recovery Act singled out toxics as a special category of pollution deserving of special regulation.[85] The Mine Safety and Health Act of 1977 and the Occupational Safety and Health Act of 1970 established safety-hazard regimes and indoor air-pollution regimes for mines and other workplaces, respectively. The Toxic Substances Control Act of 1976 imposed new limits on the petrochemical industry by regulating the introduction of new chemical compounds into the market. The Surface Mining Claims and Reclamation Act of 1977 required coal-mining companies to reclaim mined lands after cessation of mining operations and was aimed largely at preventing toxic water pollution in mining.[86] The aforementioned Superfund law imposed strict, retroactive, and joint and several liability on companies that had arranged for disposal of toxics and other hazardous substances in the past, imposing billions of dollars of new liability on oil companies, electric utilities, and mining companies.

Another statute from this era that exerted a profound effect on energy markets was the Public Utility Regulatory Policies Act (PURPA) of 1978. PURPA mixed financial incentives with mandates to promote "alternative" (read: "renewable" or "more efficient") energy production.[87] It introduced a new class of market participant into wholesale electricity markets: namely, non-utility-owned merchant generators. It required IOUs to purchase electricity from these merchant generators,[88] and in so doing it incentivized the first generation of U.S. wind farms, hundreds of new small hydroelectric projects, and other new utility-scale clean-energy projects. These developments, in turn, prompted many state legislatures to enact "renewable-portfolio standards" (RPSs), requiring electric utilities to buy specified percentages of electricity from renewable sources.[89]

Each of these laws altered the status quo in favor of protecting health, safety, and the environment in energy production and use. Many enjoyed bipartisan support. President Richard Nixon, a Republican, created the EPA and signed the National Environmental Policy Act, the Clean Air Act, and several other regulatory bills into law.[90] Indeed, more than half of the laws listed in figure 1.2 were signed into law by Republican presidents and enacted by Democratic Congresses. That bipartisan support for environmental regulation extended into the early 1990s, when George H. W. Bush signed the Clean Air Amendments of 1990, having run for election as "the environmental president."[91] However, that bipartisanship did not include the senior Bush's predecessor in the White House, Ronald Reagan, whose veto of the Clean Water Act Amendments in 1987 was overridden in Congress by votes of 401–26 in the House and 86–14 in the Senate.[92]

IMPORTANT CHARACTERISTICS OF THESE REGULATORY REGIMES

Many of the environmental regimes of this era created systems of shared regulatory responsibility between the federal government and the states. That is, Congress allocated responsibility for establishing regulatory standards to federal agencies but authorized those agencies to delegate to states the permitting, enforcement, and other activities required to implement those standards. Legal scholars call this division of authority *cooperative federalism*.[93] The Clean Air Act, the Clean Water Act, and the Resource Conservation and Recovery Act followed this template, as did the Occupational Safety and Health Act, the Mine Safety and Health Act, and (in some respects) the Coastal Zone Management Act of 1972.[94] Naturally, in today's era of partisan polarization, these relationships are now often more contentious than cooperative, so much so that some scholars speak of *uncooperative federalism*.[95]

Many of these statutes also include so-called *citizen-suit* provisions that empower environmental NGOs to bring suit to enforce the law when government enforcers do not, subject to prior notice and judicial-standing requirements. Of the statutes listed in figure 1.2, at least six have citizen-suit provisions: the Clean Air Act, Clean Water Act, Endangered Species Act of 1973, Resource Conservation and Recovery Act, Surface Mining Claims and Reclamation Act, and the Superfund law.[96] Tens of thousands of citizen suits have been brought under these statutes. Conservative jurists have long expressed discomfort with citizen suits as an enforcement tool, and as the Supreme Court has become more conservative over time, it has used standing doctrine to impose restrictions on their use.[97]

Finally, most of the regulatory regimes created during this regulatory phase are what economists would call *command-and-control* regimes. That is, they impose prescriptive and proscriptive mandates, often by way of permitting requirements backed up by administrative and judicial enforcement powers. One of the more unqualified "commands" in Congress's command-and-control oeuvre is the Endangered Species Act prohibition against any action that would harm a listed endangered species, irrespective of the social or economic benefits that action may have.[98] One of the few exceptions to Congress's general preference for command-and-control regulation is found in the Clean Air Act Amendments of 1990, which created one of the first market-based regulatory instruments in U.S. environmental law: a cap-and-trade program that reduced sulfur dioxide (SO_2) emissions from old coal-fired power plants.[99]

A CLOSER LOOK AT THE CLEAN AIR ACT

When people think about regulating the environmental impacts of energy production, many think of the Clean Air Act. Long before experts developed a full understanding of the contribution of GHGs to climate change, they understood that fossil-fuel combustion emits other harmful pollutants and that coal combustion produces particularly deadly emissions. Particulate matter (PM), or fine dust, causes respiratory problems, heart and lung disease, and regional haze.[100] Mercury is a toxic metal that can enter the food chain through deposition of combustion particulates into waterways. SO_2 and nitrogen oxides are precursors of acid rain, and the latter is also a precursor of ground-level ozone (smog), which triggers respiratory problems in some humans. The emissions rates of different types of fossil-fuel pollution are shown in table 1.1. A well-established epidemiological and toxicological literature demonstrates that PM emissions from coal combustion kill thousands of Americans prematurely each year and millions of people annually worldwide.[101] Consequently, when the EPA estimates the net benefits of proposed rules that would reduce coal combustion, the largest benefits are the lives saved from reduced PM emissions. That is why the EPA has consistently prioritized controlling emissions from coal combustion in implementing the Clean Air Act.

Figure 1.3 shows the shares of U.S. electricity generation from different fuels and technologies since 1949. It reflects a long period of

TABLE 1.1 Pollution from Fossil Fuels, in Pounds per British Thermal Unit

Fuel Pollutant	Natural Gas	Oil	Coal
Carbon dioxide	117,000	164,000	208,000
Carbon monoxide	40	33	208
Nitrogen oxides	92	448	457
Sulfur dioxide	1	1,122	2,591
Particulates	7	84	2,744
Mercury	0	0.007	0.016

Source: "Natural Gas Issues and Trends," U.S. Energy Information Administration, 1998, https://docplayer.net/20283086-Source-eia-natural-gas-issues-and-trends-1998.html.

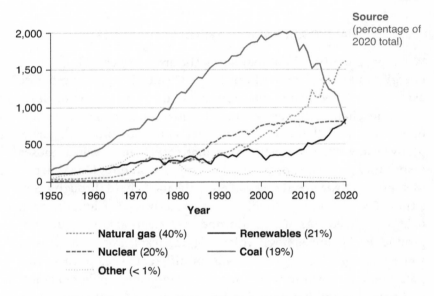

FIGURE 1.3 Fuels as a percentage of U.S. electric generation, 1950–2020.

Source: U.S. Energy Information Administration.

dominance by coal that began following the energy crises of the 1970s, when the U.S. electric-generation sector almost completely weaned itself from oil.[102] Coal's recent decline can be ascribed mostly to a combination of technoeconomic developments and regulatory pressures. The first was the development of more efficient forms of hydraulic fracturing, or "fracking," to produce natural gas in the middle of the first decade of the twenty-first century.[103] This fracking revolution reduced and stabilized natural gas prices, moved gas-fired power plants ahead of coal-fired plants in the electric-generation dispatch order in many parts of the country, and thus hastened the closure of aging coal-fired power plants. Second, a series of EPA regulatory initiatives described later put additional cost pressure on coal-fired power in the second decade of the twenty-first century. Third, the average cost of generating power from utility-scale wind and solar power fell rapidly to levels below those of all other generation technologies, pushing coal-fired power plants farther down in the dispatch order.

The Clean Air Act creates different regulatory regimes for different classes of fossil fuel pollutants—*criteria (or conventional) pollutants* versus *toxic (or hazardous) pollutants*. Among the pollutants listed in figure 1.3, PM, SO_2, and nitrogen oxides are criteria pollutants (the latter as a precursor to ozone), while mercury is regulated as a toxic pollutant. The EPA establishes National Ambient Air Quality Standards (NAAQS) for each criteria pollutant—maximum concentrations of the pollutant in the outdoor air that "protect public health" with "an adequate margin of safety" (for primary NAAQS) or that protect public welfare (for secondary NAAQS).[104] States are required to develop plans for complying with the NAAQS.[105] Periodic reviews of the NAAQS tend to result in more stringent standards over time as epidemiological and toxicological research improves our understanding of pollution's impact on public health and welfare. And the statute contains provisions allowing for regulation of new pollutant risks that do not fit neatly into this criteria pollutant versus toxic pollutant taxonomy.[106]

Chapter 3 takes up the legal question of how and whether this regulatory regime can be used to limit GHG emissions. Regardless, the statute has been a success story. Each year the EPA publishes an updated version of figure 1.4. It is a simple and clear depiction of the sharply declining pollution intensity of American life even in the face of consistent economic growth. The EPA doesn't publish a graphic representation of its progress regulating toxic pollution, but its regulation of mercury emissions from coal-fired power plants has helped reduce both mercury and criteria-pollutant emissions.[107] Emissions of CO_2, methane, and other GHGs have not fallen as much per capita, per unit

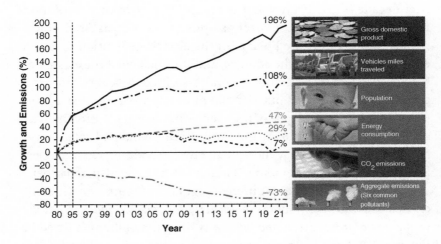

FIGURE 1.4. Comparison of growth areas and emissions in
the United States, 1980–2022.

Source: U.S. EPA.

of gross domestic product (GDP), per vehicle miles traveled, and so on
as they might have had they been given a similar regulatory push.[108]

Similar success stories can be told about most of these other environmental statutes. The Clean Water Act has produced drastic
improvements in the quality of the country's lakes and rivers. In the
1960s, the Great Lakes were often unsafe for swimming, and Lake Erie
was referred to as ecologically dead.[109] Across the United States, rivers and lakes that were once dumping grounds of untreated industrial
and municipal waste are now "fishable and swimmable," as the statute puts it. Similarly, the Endangered Species Act has helped restore
populations of endangered species such as the Bald Eagle.[110] These
and other laws created during the environmental health and safety
era were openly aspirational, and their reach sometimes exceeded
their grasp. The Clean Water Act's stated goal of *eliminating* industrial
discharges has not been (and may never be) achieved, for example.[111]
But the fact that these laws aimed high may be part of the reason why
they produced as many environmental health and safety benefits as
they did.

THE POLITICS OF REGULATION REVISITED

As described earlier, the statutory foundation of the energy-regulatory state was laid one brick at a time in those historical moments when Congress was able to overcome its inertia to enact major regulatory legislation. The statutes enacted during the development phase made investment in the provision of new energy resources attractive to holders of private capital and thereby made energy more available to and affordable for more U.S. citizens. The success of congressional regulation gave rise to a "New Deal Consensus" in American party politics after World War II, a period of relative cross-party agreement on the principle that regulation can improve lives and the operation of markets. That cross-party ideological comity helped produce the environmental health and safety regulation that forced firms to internalize some of the external costs of energy production and made the working and living environment better and more sustainable for both producers and consumers.[112]

Of course, none of these regulatory regimes perfectly maximizes social welfare.[113] Regulation has been applied poorly at certain times and places. For example, scholars have long understood that public-utility law offers IOUs an incentive to overinvest in capital, a phenomenon known as the "Averch-Johnson effect."[114] That understanding is part of what motivated the restructuring of the industry in the late twentieth and early twenty-first centuries (see chapter 2). Similarly, environmental law has sometimes erred by imposing draconian civil or criminal liability on nonblameworthy defendants.[115] But for the most part, the regulatory legislation that created the modern energy-regulatory state has greatly improved people's lives, even if it also benefited self-interested investors seeking profit or was enacted by self-interested politicians seeking reelection.

FRAGMENTED REGULATORY AUTHORITY

Today's energy-regulatory state is the product of many individual republican moments, an aggregation of individual statutes rather than an organic whole. It has created a system of diffused regulatory responsibility with many veto gates—a "regulatory anticommons" in which the power to approve or disapprove of an energy project is spread across multiple regulatory bodies at the federal, state, and local levels.[116] This "anticommons" represents a problem for the energy transition because it gives local opponents of new energy infrastructure legal and political leverage to block new project development.

We can distinguish two types of permitting requirements for new energy projects: the primary license required for any particular energy project, or the *lead-agency approval*, and the important but *ancillary approvals* that the project will need to secure from other agencies. Table 1.2 summarizes the regulatory environment of energy-project

TABLE 1.2 Energy-Project Siting Authority—Lead Agency

	Federal	State	Local	Common Ancillary Reviews (Federal)
Nuclear-power plants	Nuclear Regulatory Commission*			National Environmental Policy Act (NEPA), Clean Water Act (CWA)
Fossil-fueled power plants		PUC or other siting agency*	Municipalities (in some states)	Clean Air Act (CAA), CWA
Wind farms—onshore		PUC or other siting agency*	Municipalities (in some states)	
Wind farms—offshore	Dept. of Interior (beyond state waters)	Various state agencies (within state waters)		NEPA, Coastal Zone Management Act (CZMA), Endangered Species Act (ESA)
Solar farms		PUC or other siting agency*	Municipalities (in some states)	ESA
Transmission lines		PUC*	Municipalities (in some states)	CWA
Oil- and gas- production facilities— onshore		Oil and Gas Commission*	Municipalities (in some states)	CAA
Oil pipelines		PUC, state oil and gas commission, or legislature*		CAA, CWA
Natural gas pipelines	Federal Energy Regulatory Commission*			NEPA, CAA, CWA
Liquefied natural gas terminals— onshore	Federal Energy Regulatory Commission*			NEPA, CWA, CZMA

*Lead agency.

siting today. To many observers, it looks complicated, and it is. It can also be unpredictable. The number and height of the regulatory hurdles facing prospective energy projects will vary by type of project, project location, and the current priorities of the regulators involved. Sometimes lead agencies help developers run the gauntlet by coordinating the management of all the necessary approvals. Sometimes well-established interagency coordination procedures or systems of cooperative federalism define the jurisdictional boundaries more or less clearly.[117] Sometimes there are lingering, unresolved disputes between regulators over subject-matter jurisdiction. Sometimes federal permitting preempts state jurisdiction, or state requirements preempt local jurisdiction.[118] Other times, they don't.

The process of passing through this complex, fluid system of veto gates can seem daunting to project developers. The politics of siting are inherently difficult because the benefits of new energy infrastructure—greater energy security and affordability or environmental benefits—tend to flow to a geographically broad set of people, whereas the costs—pollution, land use, aesthetic, traffic, and other impacts—tend to be localized. Therefore, there is a self-interested logic to local opposition to energy projects, and the more power a licensing regime devolves to state and local governments, the more difficult it is for the project to navigate regulatory hurdles successfully, all else being equal.

But even under centralized siting regimes, passing through veto gates can be a challenge. For example, FERC is the lead agency for licensing hydroelectric-power projects, and the Nuclear Regulatory Commission is lead agency for nuclear-power licensing.[119] Both agencies' permitting regimes preempt broad swaths of state regulatory authority, seemingly easing the path to project completion, at least on paper. But federal regulators are often reluctant to overrule states irrespective of their power to do so.[120] And even when they are inclined to overrule state objections, powerful local veto gates remain. For example, the FPA (originally enacted as the Federal Water Power Act in 1920) does not preempt state water-rights law, and the Atomic Energy Act of 1954 does not preempt state power to regulate certain nonsafety aspects of nuclear power.[121] States can sometimes use those windows of leverage to stop projects. Even more significantly, some federal statutes authorize *state agencies* to exercise *federal power*. For example, section 401 of the Clean Water Act requires host states to certify that federally licensed energy projects will not endanger water quality.[122] The state of New York has used that provision to veto new natural gas pipelines that would deliver gas to New England, where the electricity sector must sometimes rely on diesel generators and more expensive, imported liquified natural gas during winter cold snaps.[123]

Congress designed these various provisions for shared authority as brakes on project development whose forward momentum is economic. But they provide leverage to opponents of clean- and dirty-energy infrastructure alike and slow down the development of new energy infrastructure.

THE OVERWHELMING POPULARITY OF DURABLE REGULATORY REGIMES

The political history of the regulatory state reveals an even more important truth: that durable regulatory regimes tend to have been *very* popular at their creation with both voters and members of Congress. This is true of almost all the regulatory legislation enacted during the Populist Era, the Progressive Era, the New Deal, and the years surrounding the "environmental decade." Table 1.3 lists the major regulatory statutes enacted during these eras. Together, these laws created most of today's administrative state, and they enjoyed very strong support in Congress. The Clean Air Act, for example, passed by a margin of 171 votes in the House of Representatives (273–102) and unanimously in the Senate (73–0). The FPA and NGA passed by voice acclimation in one or both chambers; and the Sherman Act and the Clean Water Act (like the Clean Air Act) passed at least one house of Congress unanimously. Indeed, among the regulatory bills listed in appendix A for which roll-call votes were held, *all commanded at least 75 percent support* in each chamber.[124]

Consistent with Kingdon's model, these kinds of republican moments happen *either* when one party controls the policymaking branches of government with large congressional majorities *or* there is a critical mass of bipartisan agreement on the issue in question. For example, the regulatory legislation of the Progressive Era and the New

TABLE 1.3 Major U.S. Regulatory Legislation

Populist Era	New Deal	Environmental Health and Safety Era
Interstate Commerce Act (1887)	Emergency Banking Relief Act (1933)	National Environmental Policy Act (1969)
Sherman Antitrust Act (1890)	Emergency Conservation Work Act (1933)	Clean Air Act (1970)
Erdman Act (1898)	Emergency Relief Act (1933)	Occupational Safety and Health Act (1970)
	Agricultural Adjustment Act (1933)	Clean Water Act (1972)
Progressive Era	Tennessee Valley Authority Act (1933)	Consumer Product Safety Act (1972)
Elkins Act (1903)	Securities Act (1933)	Endangered Species Act (1973)
Hepburn Act (1906)	Banking Act (1933)	Resource Conservation and Recovery Act (1976)
Pure Food and Drug Act (1906)	National Industrial Recovery Act (1933)	Clean Water Act Amendments (1977)
Mann-Elkins Act (1910)	Securities Act (1934)	Public Utility Regulatory Policy Act (1978)
Federal Reserve Act (1913)	Communications Act (1934)	Comprehensive Environmental Response, Compensation, and Liability Act (1980)
Clayton Act (1914)	National Housing Act (1934)	Superfund Reauthorization and Amendments Act (1986)
Federal Trade Commission Act (1914)	Soil Conservation Act (1935)	Clean Water Act Amendments (1987)
Keating-Owen Child Labor Act (1916)	Federal Power Act (1935)	Clean Air Act Amendments (1990)
Adamson Act (1916)	Public Utility Holding Company Act (1935)	
	National Labor Relations Act (1935)	
	Social Security Act (1935)	
	Rural Electrification Act (1936)	
	Robinson-Patman Act (1936)	
	Bankhead-Jones Act (1937)	
	Bonneville Project Act (1937)	
	U.S. Housing Act (1937)	
	Civil Aeronautics Act (1938)	
	Fair Labor Standards Act (1938)	
	Natural Gas Act (1938)	

Deal was enacted during periods of unified party control of government in which the one party enjoyed large majorities in both congressional chambers. The New Deal legislation listed in table 1.3 was enacted by Congresses in which the Democrats' *smallest* margins were 196 seats in the House and 23 seats in the Senate.[125]

The regulatory legislation enacted during the environmental health and safety era, by contrast, was enacted with bipartisan support from a Democrat-controlled Congress and Republican presidents who were eager to claim the mantle of environmental leadership for their party. The same is true of much of the early regulation enacted during the Populist Era. These bipartisan republican moments can happen when there is partisan competition for leadership on a newly emerging set of issues. Just as Republicans and Democrats competed for the mantle of environmental leadership in the 1970s, the regulatory legislation enacted during the Populist Era and early Progressive Era was enacted by Republicans and Democrats competing in the early twentieth century for the mantle of progressive leadership—a competition led on the Republican side by Theodore Roosevelt.

* * *

These are the political conditions to which Kingdon referred when he observed that a receptive partisan political environment is one of the necessary conditions for regulatory legislation. Troublingly for the climate coalition, neither form of partisan receptivity is present in Congress today. The few major regulatory statutes enacted by Congress in the twenty-first century, such as the Affordable Care Act and the Dodd-Frank Wall Street Reform and Consumer Protection Act of 2010, have passed by smaller majorities along partisan lines.[126] Not coincidentally, these laws have faced almost continuous postenactment attacks that have weakened their effects and/or narrowed their original scope.[127] Chapter 2 explains part of the reason why regulatory politics has become more difficult. The growing popularity of free-market conservatism has transformed both politics and energy markets in the late twentieth century. Chapter 3 completes that history, examining how populism and partisan tribalism are transforming energy politics today.

2

IDEOLOGICAL CONSERVATISM
AND DEREGULATION

A society or an economy can be Pareto-optimal and still be
perfectly disgusting.

—Amartya Sen, *Collective Choice and Social Welfare*

EVEN BEFORE Congress added the last major regulatory regimes
to the energy-regulatory state, partisan polarization in the
United States had begun to grow. That growth coincided with
the policy community's increasing skepticism toward many forms of
regulation and growing faith in the ability of markets to produce
socially beneficial outcomes. That sea change in thinking was not
driven by corruption or ignorance but rather by the rise of economics
to a hegemonic position among the social sciences in the late twentieth century. Accordingly, energy policy over the past four decades has
been a mostly *de*regulatory affair.[1] Federal regulators have opened
wholesale gas and electricity markets to competition, and some states
(a minority) have opened retail energy markets to competition. Thus,
the institutional structure of today's U.S. energy markets varies significantly by geographic location, creating a sort of natural experiment in
which the energy transition will progress within very different regulatory environments.

Some of the economic critique of regulation has lost its luster
recently, and there is certainly no current consensus on the relative
benefits of energy-market restructuring. Some energy-transition advocates see competitive markets as mostly a good thing; others disagree. On the one hand, competition seems to have facilitated the

replacement of dirtier forms of energy with cheaper, cleaner ones in many places: first natural gas for coal and then renewables for fossil-fueled power. On the other hand, competition has seemed to work better in gas markets than in electricity markets. The promise that competition would lower retail prices for residential consumers of electricity has not been borne out in practice, and competitive power markets have struggled to provide consumers with a simultaneously reliable and affordable supply of energy, occasionally failing spectacularly at that task. Regulators continue to try to make markets work by experimenting with different institutional structures. Meanwhile, just about every path to net zero envisioned by experts calls for massive growth in the electricity supply and rapid contraction of oil and gas consumption.

How (and how fast) we can steer these restructured markets toward affordable, reliable net-zero energy remains an open question, one explored more deeply in chapter 5. The current chapter sketches the history of energy-market restructuring. This chronology includes a deeper explanation of how and why policymakers chose to introduce more competition and market pricing into energy markets, how competitive markets have evolved since restructuring, and how those markets have adjusted to accommodate renewable energy and other green-energy technologies. Understanding that story requires a critical examination of public-choice economics as a driver of both deregulation and political polarization. That is where we will start.

PUBLIC-CHOICE ECONOMICS: BIASED BUT NOT EVIL

Figure 2.1 comes from a data set called DW-NOMINATE, created by political scientists to measure the ideology of individual members of Congress on a left–right scale based on their votes.[2] The data set scores every member of every Congress on two ideological dimensions: a regulatory-policy dimension and a social/cultural issues dimension.[3] Figure 2.1 uses data from the regulatory-policy dimension. It depicts the *ideological distance* between the parties—between the mean Democrat score and the mean Republican score—in both houses of Congress during the past century and a half. It illustrates that the

FIGURE 2.1. Ideological distance between U.S. congressional party means, 1879–2022.

Source: Voteview.com.

congressional parties are more ideologically polarized today than at any time in the existence of the energy-regulatory state. As part of this divergence, each party has grown much more ideologically homogenous: by this measure, there is *no* ideological overlap today between the parties in either chamber (in other words, there is no Democrat to the ideological right of any Republican and no Republican to the ideological left of any Democrat in either chamber of Congress). This is a relatively recent development.[4] The disappearance of liberal Republicans and conservative Democrats makes it more difficult for members of one party to find ideological kindred spirits in the other and so to build bipartisan support for legislation.[5] According to the underlying data, polarization in Congress on this dimension began with Republican movement to the right during the Reagan presidency; Democratic movement to the left lags Republican movement to the right by about two decades. This divergence has made the legislative process more prone to gridlock.[6]

The GOP's movement to the ideological right coincided with the spreading influence of public-choice theory in American policy circles. Public-choice scholars applied economic methods to the study of political and policy problems in ways that challenged the New Deal Consensus.[7] Public-choice economics first emerged in the United States in the 1950s, coincidentally around the same time as the publication of Ayn Rand's libertarian novel *Atlas Shrugged* (1957). But it took hold more broadly in the 1970s and 1980s. Intellectually, it descended from mid-twentieth-century Austrian economists who had written in reaction to the rise of centralized, authoritarian economies on the ideological left (Soviet Union) and ideological right (Nazi Germany). These writers criticized central planning, fleshing out Adam Smith's earlier claim that the invisible hand of the market would steer self-interested behavior toward social benefits.[8] Some members of the Austrian school went further, arguing that most regulatory constraints on free choice are morally illegitimate threats to freedom, even those imposed by democratically elected policymakers.[9]

More than any other Austrian economist, Friedrich Hayek is credited with inspiring modern public-choice scholarship. Writing in the 1940s, he questioned regulators' ability to have the foresight to regulate wisely. He depicted markets as complex adaptive systems likely to do a better job of allocating the benefits and costs of economic activity than regulators ever could.[10] Hayek and his disciples argued that knowledge in these systems is not centralized and is therefore inaccessible to regulators; rather, it is diffused and unevenly distributed among economic agents. The price signal transmits knowledge from agent to agent over time, unleashing a process of constant adaptation to constant change. From this process there arises a kind of "spontaneous" or "emergent" order that will produce more socially beneficial outcomes, said Hayek, than would any attempt to regulate the market. He did not explicitly apply his framework to energy markets, but others have, challenging the notion that regulators can "get prices right" or otherwise achieve the goal of mimicking textbook competition.[11]

The appeal of these ideas to political conservatives ought to be obvious, suggesting as they do the virtues of small-government conservatism and faith in markets. Mainstream economists, for their part, remained firm in their support for taxing externalities such as pollution, but they too had begun to rethink the logic of public-utility regulation. For all of these reasons, the deregulatory impulse spread quickly within Republican policy circles in the late twentieth century—but not only among Republicans. Some Democrats saw certain forms of deregulation as good policy and a winning electoral strategy. Along with the massive defeat suffered by the liberal Democrat George McGovern in the 1972 presidential election, these economic ideas may explain the more moderate, partly deregulatory approach to regulation taken by the Carter administration.[12] And in 1992 as Democrats contemplated the possibility of a fourth successive Republican presidential term, Bill Clinton ran for president as a "New Democrat," touting a more moderate economic-policy message. The popularity of deregulatory sentiments was seemingly underscored two years later when Republicans gained 54 seats in the House and 8 seats in the Senate in the 1994 midterms, securing the party's control over both houses of Congress. Rep. Newt Gingrich was credited with engineering this victory based in part on the claim that Clinton had reneged on his pledge to govern as a New Democrat by pursuing (unsuccessfully) a national program of universal health insurance. Against this backdrop of electoral defeats associated with going "too far to the left," it is hardly surprising that late twentieth-century Democrats became cautious about regulatory overreach.[13]

Today, popular accounts of the spread of public-choice ideas among American conservatives ascribe their popularity to far more nefarious causes: the efforts of a racist economist, wealthy donors, and corporate lobbyists seeking to preserve their social and economic privileges. The historian Nancy MacLean's book *Democracy in Chains* (2017) places an apparently segregationist public-choice scholar (James Buchanan) and a corporate villain (the Koch network) at the center of that narrative. Jane Mayer's work *Dark Money* (2016) offers an account of the policy process that credits difficult-to-trace corporate money with determining policy outcomes. Neither author gets her central facts wrong, and those facts are a *part* of the history of public-choice ideas. Some very wealthy people have worked assiduously to spread public-choice ideas, James Buchanan apparently was a segregationist, and corporations do use dark money to seek private benefits from government. Conservative donors such as the Koch network have been particularly furtive about pushing academic scholarship and public-policy debate in conservative directions.[14] However, these popular accounts ascribe *far* too much agency to a few people, neglecting other, more important forces responsible for the spread of public-choice ideas in the late twentieth century. The historian Jack Rakove's review of *Democracy in Chains*, for example, puts it this way: "Buchanan and his students are hardly alone in applying economic modes of analysis to political phenomena. Had MacLean prepared a better intellectual history, she would have done more, even by way of a survey, to convey the diversity and complexity of these approaches."[15] By focusing on a few bad actors, these narratives do a disservice to the thousands of social scientists, legal scholars, judges, and policymakers across the political spectrum who have found public-choice scholarship to be either persuasive or analytically useful.

More importantly, these sorts of ad hominem attacks distract attention from more important problems with public-choice analysis. Seminal works of public-choice literature include theories that dismiss the very notion of the public interest as a fiction and government regulation as nothing more than rent seeking by private interests.[16] Public-choice thinking justifies monopoly and oligopoly by arguing, first, that barriers to market entry are frequently lower than we think, such that we can rely on the threat of new entrants into the market to discipline the avarice of monopolies, and, second, that economies of scale are often more common than we think, justifying bigger firms in the name of efficiency.[17] For many good reasons, these ideas have been losing scholarly support in recent years, but their penetration into the antitrust community has resulted in more concentrated, less competitive markets.[18] Today the federal bench includes public-choice scholars and their disciples, many of whom continue to inject public-choice ideas into their judicial decisions.[19]

The biggest problem with public-choice scholarship, however, is that it doesn't actually *show* what many believe it shows; it instead employs assumptions that systematically bias its conclusions against regulation and redistribution.[20] That is, it borrows from neoclassical welfare economics the assumption that we can know what people want only through their "revealed preferences" and we must infer those preferences from what people are *willing to pay* (or accept) for a good or service. This assumption is at the core of economists' measures of efficiency and social welfare.[21] The obvious flaw in using aggregated willingness to pay as proxy for social value is that willingness to pay is a function of one's *ability* to pay. Dollars are far more precious—that is, they provide more value or utility—to people who have fewer of them. This flaw in public-choice theory is intuitive to most, including most economists. Regardless, many economists and others continue to use willingness to pay as the most scientifically defensible (or mathematically straightforward) measure of social value. Moreover, it is an idea that resonates with some conservative students. In 2010, an MIT business student put it this way: "A man receives from the free market what he gives to it, [and] his material worth is a running tally of the net benefit that he has provided to his fellow man. A high income is not only justified, but there is nobility to it."[22] In a world plagued by accelerating economic inequality, however, willingness to pay looks like a particularly poor measure of social value.

Public-choice scholars compound their error by pairing willingness to pay as a measure of welfare with a reverence for the "Pareto criterion," which prefers only those changes to the status quo that make some better off while making *no one* worse off.[23] In a world full of distributional conflict and trade-offs, it is easy to see how this preference skews public-choice analyses against both redistributive policy and government regulation, which produce both losers and winners.[24] This is why the Nobel Laureate Amartya Sen criticized the Pareto criterion in such strong terms, as in this chapter's epigraph. As with willingness to pay, use of the Pareto criterion makes some theoretical problems more mathematically tractable for academics, but at the price of biasing analyses of regulatory and policy questions in obvious and predictable ways.[25]

With this theoretical backdrop in mind, it is no surprise that public-choice scholars helped popularize "capture theory."[26] Capture theory proposes that regulators become "captured" by the industries they regulate—innocuously by gravitating toward the industry perspective over time or insidiously via control by members of Congress who are beholden to the industry.[27] This idea seems especially attractive after the evident corruption and pro-industry orientation of the Trump administration and the exposure of Supreme Court justices' receipt of valuable, unreported gifts from GOP donors.[28] Capture theory is popular not only among mostly right-leaning public-choice scholars but also among mostly left-leaning revisionist historians who have incorporated it into their critiques of liberal democracy, legal scholars focused on the energy transition, and a cynical voting public.[29] But despite anecdotal examples of firms exerting undue and corrupt influence over policymakers, capture theory is misapplied as a general descriptor of regulatory behavior.[30]

Regulators have their own policy and professional goals, and, as for all people, their behavior is guided by situationally specific mixtures of those motives and external pressures.[31] Inferring capture to explain disfavored policy decisions assumes away that complexity, along with the practical difficulty of capturing the agency decision process.[32] We cannot assume in any given instance the sublimation of regulators' other goals to those of industry or political overseers. For most of the history of the energy-regulatory state, agencies' missions have put reliability and affordability of supply before environmental or climate concerns because voters and politicians prize a reliable, affordable supply of energy above other concerns. Most energy regulators know that they risk their jobs when they deviate from that priority ranking, and so this bias is built into the mission of state PUCs and FERC.[33] It is therefore a mistake to infer (without further evidence) that agency decision makers would have made different, more pro-climate decisions but for their capture by business lobbyists. Nevertheless, that inference is commonly made in scholarly and public discussions of regulation.

As noted in passing in chapter 1, the capture hypothesis has not fared well under more rigorous empirical scrutiny. A political science text on the subject concludes that scholars have had difficulty "demonstrating the existence and degree of capture" even when their "evidentiary standards . . . are rather low."[34] For example, one might expect capture to be most prevalent at the state level given the relatively low pay and reduced public attention to state agencies' work. That is what Leah Stokes found in her case studies of clean-energy policymaking in four states. But Paul Teske's broader quantitative study of capture in the states concluded that capture is not the norm even there.[35] The public-policy scholar Christopher Carrigan and the legal scholar Cary Coglianese note that the canonical pieces in the capture literature consist mostly of "theory-plus-anecdote" accounts, and they conclude that the theory "exaggerate[s] the power of business over regulators[,] . . . [suggesting] the existence of nearly an iron law of business control that clearly does not exist."[36] The political scientists Daniel Moss and Daniel Carpenter describe this gap between the public perception and reality this way: "The old rendition of capture—in which powerful incumbent firms inevitably buy (or otherwise influence) regulators to build barriers to entry in their industries, and always eviscerate the public interest in the bargain—continues to enchant many onlookers in both academic and policy circles, but is increasingly difficult to reconcile with the world as it is."[37]

Carpenter sees some support for the innocuous version of capture based on industry's persistence in attempting to influence regulation aimed at standard setting.[38] And my colleagues Thomas McGarity and Wendy Wagner have shown how firms and their political agents sometimes try to "shackle" agencies by impeding their ability to pursue the agency mission, particularly in today's polarized political environment.[39] But for federal government agencies, the transparency requirements of the Administrative Procedures Act of 1946 may make capture too costly to become a norm.[40] Redirecting reluctant agency careerists consumes scarce political capital and risks being overturned in court, even if it occasionally happens. Careerists often prevail in these struggles, as when the Trump administration's attempts to force FERC to favor "generators with 90 days of fuel stored on site" (read: coal-fired power plants) ultimately failed.[41] Perhaps capture theory remains popular because anecdotes resonate more than rigorous empirical studies, or perhaps inferring capture is a psychologically tempting explanation for policy choices we dislike.[42]

Nevertheless, public-choice scholarship, including theorizing about regulatory capture, drove part of the economic critique of energy regulation. That critique argued that ex ante price regulation harms consumers and that competition and market pricing ought to correct those failures.[43] But the rationale for the deregulation movement of the late twentieth century also had broader support within economic theory beyond public-choice scholars. Indeed, deregulation had (and has) many sincere, well-intentioned supporters. If some proponents of deregulation harbored selfish or nefarious motives in advocating for it, many others believe that deregulation has improved social welfare. In energy markets, we tend to eschew the term *deregulation* and instead use the term *restructuring* to describe the late twentieth-century loosening of public-utility regulation because those markets are still characterized by substantial regulation. The remainder of this chapter chronicles that restructuring and explains some of the reasons why reasonable people can disagree over its merits.

RESTRUCTURING ENERGY MARKETS: A CHRONOLOGY

In the 1970s and 1980s, gas and electricity markets faced supply and price crises that suggested to some observers that existing market institutions were failing. In hindsight, regulation did contribute to those failures, but the fault did not lie with agency regulators. Rather, in gas markets the crisis was precipitated by the Supreme Court and Congress; in electricity markets, it was the product of sharp shifts in market conditions that few if any experts foresaw. Nevertheless, these shocks added force to the arguments of economists and other scholars who had begun to question whether the production and sale of energy (as opposed to its delivery) are really the kind of natural monopolies that require price regulation.[44]

NATURAL GAS MARKETS

Figure 2.2 depicts the structure of U.S. natural gas markets before the late twentieth century. Then, as now, the natural gas supply chain began with the thousands of individual wellhead producers of gas, mostly small independent companies alongside the major vertically integrated companies. Wellhead producers sold their product to a few big companies that owned interstate pipelines, making this part of the market a monopsony at the upstream end of the pipe and a monopoly at the downstream end,[45] where pipelines sold the gas mostly to natural gas utilities, which in turn sold it to their retail customers.

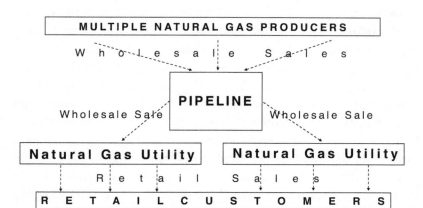

FIGURE 2.2. Structure of U.S. natural gas markets
before restructuring (before Order 636).

Recall from chapter 1 that the NGA regulates wholesale sales in interstate commerce. For the first two decades after the act's passage in 1938, the FPC set rates for gas sold *by* interstate pipelines to natural gas utilities but not for sales *to* pipelines by wellhead producers. The agency reasoned that sales at the upstream of the pipeline were competitive and that market forces kept wellhead prices low. None of the thousands of wellhead sellers could exert market power over the price to the detriment of buyers. However, in 1954 the Supreme Court held in *Phillips Petroleum Co. v. Wisconsin* that the NGA required the FPC to regulate the price charged by wellhead producers to pipelines because the statute covers all wholesale sales.[46] However, because there were thousands of wellhead producers, the Court had presented the FPC with an impossible task,[47] and the agency struggled to implement the Court's mandate. The process ultimately yielded wellhead rates that reduced the incentive to find new supplies of gas, and by the 1970s the United States faced an alarming natural gas shortage.[48] This shortage in turn prompted Congress and the Carter administration to enact the Natural Gas Policy Act (NGPA) of 1978, which established a complex schedule of gradually increasing price ceilings for different location- and age-based categories of natural gas.[49]

In the immediate aftermath of the NGPA's passage, pipeline companies rushed to secure future supplies of still-scarce natural gas by signing long-term "take-or-pay" (TOP) contracts with producers: that is, contracts in which pipelines promised to pay for all of the producer's gas at prices corresponding to the NGPA price ceilings. Meanwhile, the prospect of rising prices incentivized producers to look for new supplies and consumers to use less natural gas. More supply and less demand meant that spot-market prices for natural gas were soon lower than the NGPA ceilings and therefore lower than the prices to which pipelines had committed in their TOP contracts. Reduced end-user demand meant that natural gas utilities didn't need all of the gas to which the big pipeline companies had committed themselves, which left interstate pipelines obligated to pay for more natural gas than they could sell and at higher prices than the market price. Several "too big to fail" pipelines faced the prospect of bankruptcy.

This existential crisis for the pipeline industry was solved by a series of FERC-supervised, negotiated settlements that split the losses associated with pipelines' TOP liabilities among the pipelines' shareholders and customers.[50] As part of this process, FERC pushed pipelines to convert their TOP obligations to gas-transmission (delivery) contracts and to let wellhead producers sell gas directly to natural gas utilities. FERC then let the market set the price of these direct sales, a decision that was ratified when Congress fully deregulated wellhead prices in the Natural Gas Wellhead Decontrol Act of 1989.[51] FERC eventually required interstate pipelines to get out of the business of buying and selling gas altogether in Order 636 , which required pipeline companies to fully *unbundle* (separate) gas-transmission services from gas sales and to operate the pipeline as a common-carrier service for delivery of gas bought and sold by others.[52]

In relatively short order, the interstate pipeline system became an open-access platform for wholesale market transactions. Local natural gas distribution utilities and other wholesale customers were free to buy their gas from producers or marketers at the best available price, hiring the pipeline only to transmit the gas at posted, regulated rates. Thus, as the twentieth century drew to a close, gas *transmission* remained subject to rate regulation under the NGA, but most

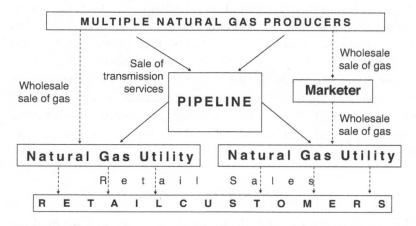

FIGURE 2.3. Restructured U.S. natural gas markets after Order 636.

wholesale sales of natural gas were made at market rates.[53] Figure 2.3 is a simplified depiction of restructured gas markets.

Most observers regard restructured wholesale natural gas markets as a success. The resulting enhancement of the incentive to profit in natural markets may have catalyzed advancements in hydraulic fracturing (fracking) and horizontal drilling in the early 2000s, which eventually stabilized natural gas prices at relatively low levels after the 2008 financial crisis.[54] Low gas prices, in turn, stimulated the licensing and construction of multiple liquified natural gas export terminals in the second decade of the twenty-first century. In 2022 and early 2023, those terminals were exporting liquified natural gas to European consumers facing severe energy-price shocks caused by the war in Ukraine. Stable, low natural gas prices also changed the economics of the power sector. Natural-gas-fired power plants became cheaper to operate and began to displace coal-fired power in the dispatch queue. This substitution of gas for coal is credited with driving reductions in GHG emissions from the electric-power sector between 2006 and 2019.[55]

Today, natural gas is traded as a fungible commodity at more than twenty U.S. trading hubs, such as the Henry Hub in Louisiana.[56] Prices vary with location, and regional price differences reflect the cost of transporting gas from producers to consumers. Unlike oil markets, natural gas markets are still regional, not (yet) global. That situation is changing with the growth of liquified natural gas markets, but the United States still produces most of its own natural gas and gets most of its imports by pipeline from Canada. The pandemic, export growth, and the war in Ukraine have increased prices, but most analysts continue to regard the restructuring of natural gas markets as a policy success.

ELECTRICITY MARKETS

The restructuring journey within the electric industry followed the same conceptual path as that of natural gas restructuring, but the bumpiest parts of that path have come after restructuring, not before it. The seeds of change were sown with the passage of PURPA in 1978 (see chapter 1), which (like the NGPA) was part of the Carter administration energy package. The statute opened the electricity-generation market to new, nonutility generators. Their presence, in turn, created pressure to relax IOUs' exclusive control over the electric grid so that these nonutility generators could sell their electricity directly to other retailers or industrial customers. Congress responded to that pressure in the Energy Policy Act of 1992 by expanding FERC's authority to order IOUs to transmit power for third parties over their transmission lines.[57] As with gas industry restructuring, FERC used that expanded authority experimentally for a few years before promulgating Order 888 in 1996, mandating that electricity transmission be unbundled from wholesale power sales and that owners of transmission lines act as common carriers providing transmission service on a nondiscriminatory basis to affiliated and nonaffiliated companies alike.[58] FERC thereafter allowed most wholesale sellers of electricity to charge market rates for power, conditioning those grants of authority on sellers' lack of market power.[59] Transmission rates remained regulated.

At around the same time as Order 888, a sizable minority of states— including California, Texas, and New York—began to unbundle their *retail* markets and to introduce competition and market pricing in place of monopoly service and regulated rates.[60] The incumbent IOUs in these states were required to sell most of their generation assets or spin them off into independent affiliates, thus increasing the profile of independent merchant generators, power marketers, and brokers within the industry. New nonutility sellers entered the retail market in these states, giving consumers choice over their power supplier.[61] All of these new buyers and sellers on the wholesale market meant that more power was being shipped beyond the boundaries of the old IOU service areas and thus straining the capacity of a transmission grid that was built for that old, Balkanized system. Anticipating this problem, FERC encouraged owners of transmission lines to form geographically broader, nonprofit membership organizations through which they could manage the grid regionally: so-called independent system operators (ISOs) and regional transmission organizations (RTOs).[62]

Where they exist, ISOs and RTOs play multiple roles. They work to ensure system reliability, to guard against discrimination and the exercise of market power in the provision of transmission services, to balance the grid, and to manage electricity spot markets. By the turn of the twenty-first century, robust wholesale markets existed within most of these ISOs and RTOs,[63] and today a majority of American households are served by retailers (competitive retailers or IOUs) that no longer generate most of the power the retailers need but instead acquire it on these competitive wholesale markets. Figure 2.4 shows the ISO/RTO boundaries as of late 2023.

Because some states have competitive retail markets, while others don't, and because some regions have organized, competitive wholesale markets, while others don't, U.S. electricity markets take one of three forms based on their institutional structure. *Fully competitive* markets are those found in places such as the Electric Reliability Council of Texas (ERCOT), the New York ISO, and (most of) ISO New England, where both wholesale and retail sales are fully unbundled from power-delivery services and subject to market pricing. Retail buyers in these locations can choose their power provider and shop for preferred terms of service, including price. The transmission and distribution services that deliver the power from generator to consumer are provided by different companies, the owners of the wires, whose rates remain regulated. In *traditional* markets, places such as the Southeast, monopoly IOUs continue to generate most of the power

FIGURE 2.4. Map of U.S. RTOs and ISOs.

Source: Sustainable FERC Project, https://sustainableferc.org/.

they sell to their customers. Their generation assets are part of their rate base, and they sell a bundled service to their retail customers. In places with *hybrid* markets, such as Minnesota, states retain traditional public-utility regulation, and so the retail customer continues to buy power supply-and-delivery service, bundled together, from a monopoly IOU at regulated rates. However, that IOU acquires most or all of its power on a robust, competitive wholesale market: for Minnesota, that market is the Midcontinent ISO, or MISO.

These differences in institutional structure matter in ways that are sometimes overlooked by experts and laypeople alike in contemporary discussion of the energy transition. Owning energy infrastructure entails very different risks in these different institutional settings, and buyers of energy face very different risks across these different environments. The next section explores how those risks complicate the reconciliation of competitive electricity markets with the public interest.

COMPETITIVE MARKETS AND THE PUBLIC INTEREST

MAINTAINING RELIABILITY *AND* AFFORDABILITY

Economic theory suggested that restructuring would yield efficiency gains in electricity markets. But "efficiency" is a tricky concept for a product that consumers view as an essential good or service and that cannot be stored in commercially significant quantities. The *ancillary services* that IOUs provided to the grid before restructuring—keeping reserves and grid resources ready to supply power when needed—became "products" that ISOs/RTOs procured from third parties by contract after restructuring. Accordingly, competitive markets have been plagued by an ongoing worry that is a kind of mirror image to the Averch-Johnson effect: namely, that market pricing and competition may not incentivize enough investment in reserve generation to maintain a reliable electricity supply. This worry continues to hang over competitive markets, fed by periodic price shocks and other growing pains that restructured markets have experienced during the twenty-first century. These problems bring to mind Nobel laureate Ronald Coase's theory of the firm, which concerned the issue of whether firms should "make or buy" products or services they need. Coase's analysis never stood for the proposition that market acquisition from third parties was always or usually the better, more efficient choice; sometimes network efficiencies make intrafirm provision of the good or service—that is, vertical (or horizontal) integration—the more efficient option.[64]

California Electricity Crisis of 2000–2001

California decided to move to a competitive electricity market in 1996, and its wholesale market worked well for its first few years. But in the winter of 2000–2001, the market experienced unusually severe and sustained price spikes. Monthly average prices rose to more than five times historical norms and daily averages to sometimes two hundred times historical norms.[65] The grid operator, the California Independent System Operator (CAISO), imposed rolling blackouts that winter to avoid grid failures. Because retail-price caps prohibited California's IOUs from passing along these exorbitant wholesale costs to their retail customers, Pacific Gas & Electric (PG&E) fell into (its first) bankruptcy, and Southern California Edison was nearing the same fate when the governor of California shut down the competitive market.

A variety of forces contributed to the crisis, including insufficient generating capacity to meet peak demand, short-term fuel-supply interruptions, a rapid rise in generator costs, transmission bottlenecks, retail-price caps that kept demand high, and extensive manipulation of the market by sellers of power.[66] In hindsight, the California market design facilitated manipulation by channeling most sales through the spot market, a set of daily power auctions in which all sales were made at the auction's market-clearing prices.[67] Because buyers on the market had customers to serve, they could not refuse to pay the auction prices, and sellers knew this. Because demand frequently exceeded available supply during the periods of peak use, individual sellers could demand exorbitant prices during these peak periods, resulting in windfall profits for all sellers.

Postcrisis investigations of California's dysfunctional electricity market revealed that many sellers took advantage of these conditions not only to capture scarcity rents but also to engage in a variety of forms of fraud and manipulation.[68] Some withheld generation to increase scarcity and drive up prices.[69] Some scheduled transactions designed to create congestion on the electric grid so that they could claim congestion-relief payments by canceling the transactions.[70] Some sellers scheduled multiple, high-volume "wash trades," whereby each party to the transaction agreed to sell the other an identical amount of electricity at unusually high (or low) prices. These trades had no economic value to the trading parties other than to influence published indices of daily power prices, thereby increasing the value of other assets they held (such as futures contracts).[71] Many of these techniques were devised by Enron, but their use during the crisis was widespread.[72] FERC, the Commodity Futures Trading Commission, and the U.S. Department of Justice brought civil and criminal enforcement actions against the manipulators of the California market, resulting in jail time for a few individual defendants and more than $4 *billion* in fines, penalties, and disgorgement of profits for about twenty-five corporate and individual defendants.[73] For its part, Congress reacted by amending both the FPA and the NGA in 2005 to clarify FERC's authority to fight market manipulation.[74]

The failure of the California market shocked the proponents of competitive electricity markets, stalled the transition to retail competition and market pricing in several states, and led to re-regulation in others. California's angry voters recalled Governor Gray Davis by referendum before the completion of his term, kickstarting the political career of Arnold Schwarzenegger, Davis's successor. Competitive retail markets have remained in place in most states in the Northeast, a few mid-Atlantic states (such as Pennsylvania and Maryland) and midwestern states (such as Illinois), and in the ERCOT region, but thereafter most of the rest of the country decided to retain traditional retail-rate regulation.

Other Supply Shocks and Worries

Without the revenue guarantees provided by traditional rate regulation, investors considering large capital investments in long-lived power plants might doubt their ability to recover their investment from energy sales alone. Wholesale-price caps imposed by ISOs/RTOs feed those doubts and, some argue, interfere with the ability of prices to signal scarcity and the need for more generation.[75] Academics and others refer to this issue as "the missing-money problem" in power markets, and it may be part of why competitive markets sometimes struggle to ensure adequate reserves.[76] Some ISOs and RTOs address this problem by operating separate markets for the procurement of future reserve capacity, holding periodic auctions for this purpose. The provision of capacity through these auctions offers generators an additional source of revenue besides power sales. However, some criticize capacity markets for their inefficiency and charge them with bias against cleaner-energy resources.[77]

The PJM region (see figure 2.4) has long operated a capacity market, but during a polar vortex that brought a record-breaking cold snap to the region in 2014, PJM chose to allow prices to rise above its $1,000/ megawatt-hour (mwh) price cap for short periods in order to avoid blackouts.[78] The ERCOT region has no capacity market, and for most of its existence used a much higher $9,000/mwh cap in an effort to make price signals a more powerful incentive to invest in reserves. But in February 2021, Winter Storm Uri created severe power-supply shortages that forced about half of ERCOT's otherwise available generating capacity offline, driving wholesale prices to the $9,000/mwh cap for seventy-two consecutive hours. This steep increase meant that retailers buying electricity on the spot market owed more for power during those three days than they owed for the combined total of their power needs during the remaining 362 days of the year.[79] This imposed crippling debts on wholesale-market buyers, and Texas politicians opted to bail out wholesale buyers by financing these costs through bonds that ERCOT ratepayers will repay over thirty years; regulators also lowered the price cap to $5,000/mwh and changed market rules to limit the maximum amount of time prices could remain at the cap.[80]

Both the PJM and ERCOT crises involved coordination problems between gas and electricity markets. More than two hundred people lost their lives in Winter Storm Uri, many because of the extended power outage.[81] The primary cause of the outage was the failure to winterize Texas's lightly regulated natural gas production and pipeline system, an issue identified during previous cold snaps but unremedied by regulators thereafter.[82] Like Governor Gray Davis of California years earlier, the commissioners of the Texas Public Utility Commission and the ERCOT Board of Directors lost their jobs after Uri, though Texas politicians went mostly unpunished by voters. The next winter, another cold snap, Winter Storm Elliott, caused widespread blackouts in the northern United States as gas supplies once again failed, and ISOs/RTOs badly underestimated demand for electricity.[83] Some climate scientists believe that climate change will bring more frequent polar vortices—geographically broad, extended cold snaps—and thus test the ability and willingness of regulators to compel preventative action and better coordination between gas and electricity markets.

Meanwhile, California and Texas have also experienced summer grid-stress events in recent years, with associated temporary price spikes. In the late summer of 2022, the California grid experienced almost a week of extreme heat that taxed grid resources. CAISO was able to avoid outages through a combination of steps, including electricity imports from other regions and the use of conservation measures. The ERCOT system had to request voluntary conservation measures from its customers to avoid blackouts in the summers of 2022 and 2023.[84] By depressing economic activity, these events impose costs beyond the immediate pain of higher electric rates. The Federal Reserve Bank of Dallas estimates that for each one degree increase in average summer temperatures, Texas's GDP declines by 0.4 percent; it estimated the cost of Texas's heat wave in 2023 at $24 billion, a one percent decline in GDP.[85]

These periodic crises reflect the ongoing struggles of regulators to incentivize investment in supply in an increasingly unpredictable electricity market. ISOs/RTOs use various forms of guaranteed payments to generators to induce them to be available in the future when needed, beyond the capacity auctions used by the northeastern ISOs/RTOs. All ISOs/RTOs also use ad hoc bilateral contracts with individual generators for the same purpose. California has employed a resource-adequacy requirement that is a variant on capacity markets. Even ERCOT, which long disavowed capacity-assurance mechanisms in favor of free-floating wholesale prices, pivoted after the trauma of Winter Storm Uri to adopt a requirement that power retailers procure reserve capacity.[86]

Structural Defects or Growing Pains?

These energy-market struggles crystallize today's regulation-versus-markets ideological divide. On the one hand, few would dispute that there is a strong public interest in maintaining a reliable, affordable energy supply. State and federal statutes require that energy prices be "just and reasonable" regardless of whether those prices are established by regulators or by market competition. On the other hand, where regulators have chosen to try to ensure just and reasonable prices by way of competition and market pricing, achieving the benefits of market efficiency implies allowing prices to float freely—to signal producers and consumers that energy is either plentiful and cheap or scarce and expensive. When regulators adopt policies that deny producers the scarcity rents that come with high prices, they mute the price signal. At the same time, politicians have shown little appetite for uncapped market prices, as demonstrated by their reactions to the California and Texas electricity crises.

Some scholars predicted this problem and worried that this partial embrace of market competition might create supply shortages.[87] And the evidence suggests that competition has not produced lower prices, for residential customers at least.[88] The missing-money problem remains a challenge, and extreme weather events continue to stress the grid.[89] As we add more variable renewable generation to the electricity supply, the question of how we reconcile competition with the public interest in reliable, affordable, *and greener* energy supplies grows more urgent. Those with faith in markets blame regulatory decisions when competitive energy markets break down; others see more fundamental problems with reliance on market forces to achieve public-policy goals. The legal scholar William Boyd argues that electricity ought to be "de-commodified" and market pricing replaced with "social rate making" by government.[90] The American Public Power Association and an NGO headed by former governor Parris Glendening of Maryland, Power for Tomorrow, are among the other persistent critics of competitive power markets.[91] Others, such as the economist Lynne Kiesling and the legal scholar Joshua Macey, argue that better-managed competitive markets offer a more promising alternative. They advocate various tweaks to market structures that they say will enable low-carbon markets to reconcile reliability with affordable prices, consistent with Hayek's observation that "an intelligently designed and continuously adjusted legal framework" is necessary for markets to function well.[92]

The line between top-down planning and Hayekian adjustments may be clearer in theory than it is in real life. For now, those who oversee the competitive parts of the U.S. electricity market continue to struggle to make those markets work for the benefit of consumers. Green-energy policies have changed the nature of that task as well by altering the electric-generation mix.

RELIABLE, AFFORDABLE, *AND GREEN*

These efforts to reconcile competition and market pricing with the provision of reliable, affordable energy coincided with the spread of national and state policies designed to make the electricity sector greener.

RPSs and Subsidies

By the turn of the twenty-first century, many states had established *renewable-portfolio standards*, or RPSs, mandating that a specified percentage of the electricity sold by retailers come from renewable sources. In practice, electricity retailers comply with these mandates by purchasing renewable-energy credits, which represent electricity dispatched to the grid by wind, solar, and other qualified generators. State RPSs have proliferated over time, and some have been broadened into "clean-energy standards" that specify carbon-emissions targets. As of late 2023, there are thirty states with RPSs or clean-energy standards, several of which have established goals of zero or net-zero carbon emissions in the future. Hawaii has established a 100 percent renewable-electricity target.[93] Just as PURPA's financial incentives helped to jump-start renewable-energy development in the 1980s, RPSs gave an additional boost to wind and solar industries by creating a market for their product that would not otherwise have existed.

Government subsidies have been a consistent presence in electricity markets for most of the past fifty years. Since the 1970s, Congress has put in place short-lived (usually one- or two-year) tax credits for wind and solar projects.[94] During most of the twenty-first century so far, those credits have taken the form of an up-front investment tax credit for solar projects and a production tax credit (per kilowatt-hour [kwh] of delivered electricity) for wind projects.[95] The Energy Policy Act of 2005 added grants and loan guarantees for investments in energy efficiency, nuclear power, biofuels, and hydrogen-powered vehicles. It also attempted to lower regulatory barriers to entry for hydroelectric and geothermal projects and added a variety of subsidies for fossil-fuel development as well. The bipartisan Energy Independence and Security Act of 2007 added still more subsidies for energy efficiency and biofuels, as did the American Reinvestment and Recovery Act of 2009.[96] And in 2022, Congress created its most powerful set of energy subsidies yet in the Inflation Reduction Act, which is described more fully in the next chapter.

FERC, for its part, has worked to reconcile market competition and green-energy development, regardless of its own partisan makeup.

Republican commissioners have supported energy-market competition for philosophical reasons, and Democrats have done so as a way to overcome IOU resistance to renewable-energy development. Jon Wellinghoff, a former FERC chair and Obama appointee, repeatedly extolled the virtues of markets while overseeing a series of rulemakings designed to force grid operators to open competitive wholesale markets to renewable generation, demand-response resources, and energy-storage resources. And FERC commissioners actively resisted the Trump administration's efforts to slow or reverse that process and to revoke policies that promote a greener grid.[97]

Collectively, these green-energy policies have contributed to the steady downward cost of renewable energy. According to the Lawrence Berkely National Laboratory, the levelized cost of energy (LCOE) for wind energy was about $600/mwh in 1980;[98] today most estimates put it at less than one-twentieth of that number. Solar power has experienced an equally sharp decline in the LCOE . These price trajectories are chiefly responsible for the sharply upward-sloping "renewables" curve in figure 1.4 (in chapter 1). Table 2.1 reports LCOE estimates for 2021 from two widely cited sources, a consultancy called Lazard and the U.S. Energy Information Administration. They reflect the fact that in many places wind and solar are now the least expensive sources of electricity available.

TABLE 2.1 LCOE Estimates for Electric-Generation Technologies ($/mwh)

Technology	Lazard	U.S. Energy Information Administration
Coal	65–152	82
Natural gas—combined cycle	45–74	39
Natural gas—combustion turbine	151–96	
Nuclear—conventional	131–204	
Nuclear—advanced		88
Hydroelectric		64
Geothermal		39
Wind—onshore	26–50	40
Wind—offshore	83	136
Solar—utility scale	30–41	36
Solar—residential rooftop	147–221	

Sources: Ray 2021, 3–5; "Levelized Costs of New Generation Resources in the Annual Energy Outlook 2022," U.S. Energy Information Administration 2022, table 1b.

Renewables and the Transmission Bottleneck

There is tremendous unmet demand for grid-based renewable energy because of a shortage of transmission capacity to get that power to market.[99] Transmission lines are very long-lived assets, and investment has failed to keep pace with the changing needs of geographically broader electricity markets and demand growth.[100] Depending on how one defines *transmission*, there are between 120,000 and 200,000 miles of transmission lines on the continental U.S. electric grid. Most models of a net-zero electricity system (see chapter 5) foresee at least a doubling in size of the transmission grid. Yet in 2022 only 674.6 miles of new transmission were built in the United States; of that total, only 198 miles were the highest-voltage lines (345 kilovolt [kV] and 500 kV) that are in shortest supply.[101]

The primary barriers to transmission investment are regulatory and political. Because the FPA reserves permitting authority for interstate transmission lines to the states, barriers to entry are especially high for long-distance lines that cross multiple states.[102] State siting laws favor local interests, empowering NIMBY (not in my backyard) opposition, and incumbent utilities over nonutility investors.[103] Congress's attempts to address the problem have been halting and timid. The Energy Policy Act of 2005 tried to encourage states to form compacts to manage the process of transmission planning. It also provided FERC with limited "backstop authority" to site transmission lines within designated "national interest transmission corridors."[104] After two circuit courts narrowed that authority, Congress strengthened it in the Infrastructure Investment and Jobs Act (IIJA) of 2021.[105] As of late 2023, FERC has not used that power, and the U.S. Department of Energy has taken only a few baby steps toward the designation of transmission corridors in which FERC could exercise that power.[106]

Transmission projects face another front-end hurdle, a positive-externality problem.[107] The set of people (and utilities) that benefit from new transmission investment is broader than the set whose retailers will enter into contracts to use the line. New transmission improves the reliability of the entire regional system and allows cheaper, cleaner power to displace more expensive, dirtier power in the dispatch queue. It provides congestion relief, reduced power and transmission costs, and other benefits, many of which flow to non-customers of the line.[108] For an asset that will last many decades, quantifying these benefits is speculative and difficult, but the federal courts require FERC to do so anyway, following a "cost-causation" or "beneficiary pays" principle that they read into the FPA's "nondiscrimination" requirement. This requirement sometimes restricts ISOs/RTOs from allocating the costs of new lines across their footprint. The late Judge Richard Cudahy was an eloquent critic of this approach: "However theoretically attractive may be the principle of 'beneficiary pays,' an unbending devotion to this rule in every instance can only . . . discourage construction while the nation suffers from inadequate and unreliable transmission. Unsurprisingly, it is not possible . . . to calculate the precise value of not having to cover the costs of power failures and of not paying costs associated with congestion, and all of this *over the next forty to fifty years*."[109] Despite this obstacle, FERC has tried to encourage transmission tariffs that would internalize these positive externalities, approved attractive rates of return on transmission investment, and nudged transmission owners to engage in more regional and interregional transmission planning.[110]

The power of these FPA cost-allocation constraints is illustrated by what has happened within the ERCOT region, where those rules do not apply. ERCOT avoids some federal regulation by walling itself off from most of the interstate electricity market—that is, by maintaining no alternating-current connections across state lines. Within ERCOT, the state of Texas procured a series of high-voltage power lines connecting windy West Texas to demand centers in East Texas and spread the costs across the entire ERCOT footprint.[111] The presence of those lines incentivized the construction of massive amounts of wind generation in a short period. Investment in high-voltage transmission outside ERCOT would presumably yield similar results.

The National Renewable Energy Laboratory has estimated that increased investment in high-voltage, long-distance transmission lines would yield large reductions in power prices, improved reliability, and a variety of other sizable benefits.[112] In 2022, the MISO region approved cost-allocation rules for a group of interstate transmission lines that would facilitate development of 53 gigawatts (GW) of renewable energy in the north MISO region. That renewable energy would more than double renewable capacity in the MISO region and would almost certainly displace expensive, fossil-fueled power on which the region relies for more than half of its electricity. But the lines will cross multiple states and will be built only if the transmission projects can secure approval from each of the states through which they pass or if the Department of Energy and FERC decide to use their backstop siting authority to overrule state vetoes.

Decentralizing Electricity Markets

Some see the expansion of distributed-energy resources (DERs) as a way around the problems of building transmission or grid-based generation reserves as electricity markets rely more on greener energy. DERs are forms of generation, storage, and demand responsiveness that sit "behind the meter"—that is, on the customer's property. They include rooftop solar units, batteries such as the Tesla Powerwall, EVs, hydrogen fuel cells, as well as dirtier sources such as diesel generators.

In most states, "net-metering" policies compensate DER owners for the excess energy they send to the grid at retail rates, usually at multiples of the wholesale rate.[113] Critics of net metering charge that in locations where customers pay a bundled retail rate, net metering is a regressive cross-subsidy because it enables wealthier DER owners to drastically reduce their electric bill without reducing their peak reliance on the grid. Net metering shifts some grid maintenance costs to other, less wealthy customers because their electric bills pay not only for the power they consume but also for the costs of maintaining the grid. Traditional IOUs argue that net metering could trigger a utility "death spiral," eroding the IOUs' revenue as more DERs come on line.[114] Defenders of net metering respond that these cross subsidies are tiny, at least at current DER penetration rates. Some note that utility rates include other cross subsidies and so ask why critics single out this one in particular to criticize. More directly to the point are defenders' claims that DERs bring benefits to the grid in the forms of deferred fossil-fuel generation, reduced spot-market prices, avoided pollution, and (perhaps) deferred future grid investment.[115]

Proposals to alter net-metering regimes in Nevada, Florida, and California have provoked intense, bitter conflict.[116] Some proponents of net metering dismiss claims of economic regressivity, characterizing them as disingenuously made by self-interested IOUs. In any case, the people whose rates might increase due to net metering seem not to be concerned (or organized) about the issue. In bundled markets other than California,[117] DER penetration has not yet hit levels that would make the cross-subsidy effect salient to other ratepayers. Consequently, net metering remains a relatively popular norm across most states for now. The regressive cross-subsidy problem is not a concern in competitive retail markets because retail customers in those markets pay separately for transmission and distribution services at a regulated rate. Thus, because ratepayers in competitive retail markets pay a separate bill to cover grid costs, using net metering for their power consumption does not shift any grid costs to others.

Some experts envision a more ambitious decentralized energy future, one in which smart-grid technology and widely adopted DERs will enable retail customers to buy and sell energy services—power from our rooftop solar panels, storage services from our EVs or Tesla Powerwalls, and so on—across the distribution grid. Lynne Kiesling uses the term *transactive energy markets* to describe this kind of decentralized electricity market in which information technology enables market agents (read: customer owners of DERs) to use price signals to automate exchanges of energy services and thereby obviate the need for more expensive top-down planning solutions.[118] This vision of a decentralized net-zero future would accommodate a bigger role for microgrids and other grid-connected institutions that supply their own power needs during grid outages.[119]

At first blush, the case for decentralization seems to be strengthened by the increasing liability risk faced by IOUs in California and Hawaii for wildfire damage caused by transmission lines. Burying long-distance transmission lines is expensive, yet climate change is increasing this wildfire risk.[120] Perhaps local, decentralized energy systems can offer cheaper, better service. However, transactive markets will require massive computing power and time-varying retail rates to send the price signals that will make those markets work and make investments in DERs attractive. But the price shocks that hit

California and Texas may have dampened enthusiasm for the sort of dynamic retail pricing that sends that kind of powerful signal.[121]

It also remains to be seen whether a decentralized grid can offer a better mix of environmental performance, affordability, and reliability than the centralized grid has provided. Shortly after Superstorm Sandy in 2012, New York State embarked on a program it called "Reforming the Energy Vision" to encourage the formation of transactive energy markets on the state's distribution grid.[122] However, that initiative has not yet produced a successful low-carbon transactive energy market on the distribution grid. Since 2016, the Consolidated Edison Co. and the State of New York have run the Brooklyn microgrid, an attempt to create a low- or net-zero-carbon, local transactive energy market. But the Brooklyn microgrid continues to rely on gas-fired power from ConEd, and its planned investments in locally sited net-zero technologies have met with neighborhood opposition.[123]

Nevertheless, proponents of decentralization remain hopeful. The technologies that enable DERs to participate in energy markets are new, and more utilities are beginning to offer time-of-use (TOU) retail rates.[124] A FERC rule written in 2022 requires RTOs/ISOs and other grid operators to open their wholesale markets to aggregators of DER resources, enabling DER owners to sell power, storage services, or demand response (through aggregators) in competitive wholesale markets.[125] Thus, when grid operators look at their dispatch queue in order to serve the next unit of demand, that queue will contain not only bids from grid-based power plants but also bids from aggregators of DERs. Time will tell how and how much DERs will contribute to the provision of clean, reliable, and affordable energy service.

RESTRUCTURED MARKETS AND
THE ENERGY TRANSITION

Liberals who support restructuring see it as a way to break IOUs' stranglehold on the power-generation sector. In many of the places where IOUs resist investment in renewable energy, restructuring has promoted renewables development by exposing incumbents to competition. In that way, the restructuring of energy markets has opened the door to nonutility investors, many of whom have invested in renewable generation. By contrast, conservative support for restructuring is ideological. Conservatives can credit restructuring for improving natural gas markets and for the way renewable generation drives down wholesale power prices. Zero-marginal-cost wind and solar power not only directly influence spot prices but also indirectly influence price in power purchase agreements between generators and retailers.[126]

The history of restructuring recounted in this chapter shows that both market competition and regulation can push renewable development. Consider the states listed in table 2.2. California's renewable growth is policy driven and regulated, with wind and solar projects driven by state mandates. Those projects must overcome multiple permitting hurdles before receiving permission to build and interconnect with the grid, yet they are being built. In Texas, there are no such mandates or permit requirements. Within the ERCOT region (most of Texas) the only state-imposed requirement for new generators, other than grid-interconnection approval, is to register with the state. Both Texas and California have long queues of wind and solar projects waiting for permission to interconnect. Both states continue to see massive renewable-energy growth.

But the environment for renewables in states such as Texas may be changing.[127] The same late twentieth-century forces that fed deregulation have fed a steadily increasing ideological polarization between the political parties that is now mixed with an increasingly bitter form of partisan tribalism, a mixture that is animating active opposition to the energy transition in conservative states, suggesting that the

TABLE 2.2 Installed Wind and Solar Generating Capacity (in GW), Top-Three States, 2022

Solar		Wind	
California	43.2	Texas	37.4
Texas	20.0	Iowa	12.5
Florida	12.8	Oklahoma	11.9

Sources: The solar data are from the Solar Energy Industries Association website at https://www.seia.org. The wind data are from the SaveOnEnergy.com website. Both sets of data are from 2023.

energy paths of California and Texas could diverge in the future. California seems likely to continue to push the energy transition along, whereas Texas policymakers seem to want to erect barriers to the transition (even if their efforts to date have been mostly unsuccessful). Republicans' turn against the transition is not mainly the product of corruption or industry influence; as explained in chapter 3, it is best explained as a response to the conservative ideology and negative partisanship that characterizes Republican voters.[128] In addition to the thoughtful conservatives who embrace an antiregulatory philosophy on its own merits,[129] negative partisans oppose Democrats' climate agenda *simply because* it is the Democrats' agenda. This opposition also explains Congress's failures to enact national climate-regulatory legislation in the twenty-first century. Chapter 3 explores that political dynamic in detail and completes the story of the evolution of the energy-regulatory state we know today.

3

PARTISAN TRIBALISM AND CLIMATE POLICY

---

*The surest way to work up a crusade in favor of some good
cause is to promise people they will have a chance of maltreat-
ing someone. To be able to . . . behave badly and call your bad
behavior "righteous indignation"—this is the height of psychological luxury, the most delicious of moral treats.*

—Aldous Huxley, introduction to Samuel Butler, *Erewhon*

AT THE turn of the twenty-first century, as the restructuring of
energy markets was gaining steam, climate change moved to
the front burner of American political discourse. Its emer-
gence coincided with growing partisan tribalism—negative, affective
partisanship—in U.S. politics. As the two major political parties continued to grow farther apart ideologically, they reorganized around
sociocultural rural/urban and education-level divides that have grown
more bitter over time. Today Democrats and Republicans encounter one another less frequently and embrace increasingly different
worldviews.[1] Each group is much more alarmed by the other's policy
goals and values than it used to be. For the strongest partisans,
winning elections and policy fights has become a *moral* imperative,
which has led to more party unity and discipline as well as more frequent use of countermajoritarian institutions such as the filibuster
to stop the other party from getting what it wants. Legislative gridlock is more common.[2] When one side uses hardball techniques
successfully to thwart the other's ambitions, it can provoke a "turn-
about is fair play" reaction. Norms of fair political competition erode,
and it becomes easier to view one another with contempt.

Despite all this, Congress came very close to enacting legislation
regulating GHG emissions in 2009–2010 and again in 2021 but fell

short on each occasion. Industry lobbying was part of the reason why the legislation didn't pass, but only part. A closer look at those defeats reveals that intensifying voter contempt for the other party and its members played at least as important a role in both outcomes. The climate bills that passed the House of Representatives in 2009 and 2021 failed in the Senate because Republicans and a few Democrats stood in their way.[3] Senators' opposition was traceable in part to their (and their constituents') continuing embrace of a sharply antiregulatory view of what "freedom" means. Both sets of opponents saw cooperation with the Democrat-led majority on climate policy as electorally risky and therefore made a show of not cooperating on the issue.

TWENTY-FIRST-CENTURY CLIMATE-REGULATION EFFORTS: A CHRONOLOGY

THE HISTORICAL BACKDROP

Because our understanding of climate science has a long lineage, many people ask why climate change did not become a salient national political issue earlier than it did. Climate science dates to the nineteenth century, when the work of the scientists Joseph Fourier, Eunice Newton Foote, and John Tyndall first developed its theoretical building blocks.[4] The first modern climate models were developed in the 1950s and 1960s, and by the 1980s there existed a community of geophysicists and policymakers who were actively focused on climate change. The founding of the IPCC in 1988 organized this climatology community within the broader field of geophysics.[5] Two years earlier, Senator John Chafee (R) of Rhode Island held congressional hearings titled *Ozone Depletion, the Greenhouse Effect, and Climate Change*. Indeed, Congress had the foresight to include language in the Clean Air Act identifying climate effects as among the factors the EPA should consider when regulating to protect public welfare. And in 1990 Congress directed the EPA to gather information on the greenhouse effect.[6]

So why, then, didn't climate science enter the national political conversation sooner? Some point to the disinformation efforts by the fossil-fuel industry and its congressional enablers.[7] Research by major oil companies had identified the role of fossil-fuel combustion in climate change as early as the 1960s, yet oil and gas trade associations continued to sow public doubt about climate science well into the twenty-first century.[8] At the same time, late twentieth-century climate science was embryonic by today's standards, as reflected by the cautious way in which the IPCC discussed it.[9] The IPCC began summarizing the findings of climate research in the 1990s, publishing periodic "assessment reports" denoted AR1, AR2, and so on. The first two reports, both published before the turn of the twenty-first century, stopped short of concluding that human activity was a primary driver of warming.[10] In 1999, the National Academy of Science echoed the tentative language of AR2, *suspecting* that humans cause climate change but acknowledging significant uncertainty around the magnitude and specifics of that relationship.[11] It was not until AR3 in 2001 that the IPCC began to attach probabilities to its summaries of the scientific literature, concluding that it was "likely" (more than 66 percent chance) that human activity was driving climate change.[12]

Those probabilities subsequently grew to "very likely" (more than 90 percent) in AR4 in 2007 and "extremely likely" in AR5 (more than 95 percent) in 2014. In AR4, the IPCC began to sound the kind of stronger alarms that have since become the norm, calling warming "unequivocal" and "unprecedented," warning of "severe, pervasive and irreversible" harms, and urging swift policy action to mitigate those harms. Those alarms grew stronger in AR5 and in the special report written in 2018 on meeting the 1.5°C warming goal (discussed in the introduction).[13] In AR6 (2023), the IPCC confirmed that "human activities . . . have unequivocally caused" warming, and it focused more attention than in previous reports on the specific projected impacts in different parts of the world.[14]

Thus, despite earlier theoretical and other breakthroughs, the IPCC didn't express firm scientific confidence in human-induced climate change until the twenty-first century. Nevertheless, other countries and regions took regulatory action, while the United States has not. In 2003, the European Union enacted a cap-and-trade regime for carbon emissions called the "carbon-trading scheme." Although the scheme was not very effective in its early years, leaders in the union repaired some of its flaws, and it now imposes a meaningful constraint on European carbon emissions. Several other nations have created national carbon-emissions regulations of varying stringency, including China, Colombia, Japan, Canada, and New Zealand.[15] In 2009, a group of northeastern U.S. states established a regional cap-and-trade regulatory regime for GHGs known as the Regional Greenhouse Gas Initiative. Membership in the initiative has fluctuated between seven and twelve states as partisan control of member states changes over time.[16] Contemporaneous efforts to create a similar cap-and-trade regime in the western United States faltered, leaving a rump GHG trading market whose members are the state of California and the Canadian Province of Quebec.[17] In 2023, the state of Washington initiated its own "cap-and-invest" carbon-trading regime, which is separate from the other regimes.[18]

So why hasn't Congress acted to restrict GHG emissions? The public debate over climate science in the early 2000s was remarkably similar to the public debate over the science of acid rain in the 1980s.[19] In both instances, industry tried to stave off regulation by lobbying aggressively and by trying to sow public doubts about the underlying science. Yet in 1990 Congress enacted acid-rain regulation in a statute signed into law by a Republican president, George H. W. Bush.[20] As with acid rain, the public understanding of climate science has moved closer to the expert view over time, but that convergence has not (so far) produced legislation regulating emissions. What accounts for the difference in outcomes?

The most likely reason is that by the time the IPCC expressed a high degree of confidence about the human causes of climate change, partisan polarization had gridlocked Congress by reducing cross-party ideological overlap to a few remaining RINOs and DINOs.[21] Gridlock began to erode Americans' confidence in their democracy, a phenomenon strengthened by the changes in political media described in the next chapter. These forces together planted the seeds of the negative partisanship that we see in full flower today. Table 3.1 puts these trends side by side and hints at why it has been more difficult to produce a republican moment for GHG regulation than for acid-rain regulation. The partisan conditions were much more conducive to a republican moment in 1990 than the early 2000s; by the latter date,

TABLE 3.1 IPCC Assessment Reports, Partisan Overlap, and Attitudes Toward U.S. Democracy

IPCC Assessment Report (stated confidence level)	Year	% Americans Satisfied with "the Way Democracy Works in the United States"[a]	Partisan Overlap (Number of Members) in the House of Representatives[b]
AR1	1990		6/14
	1995		4/1
AR2	1996	27.5	3/5
	2000	31.7	2/3
AR3 (> 66%)	2001		2/2
AR4 (> 90%)	2002	39.4	0 [0.19]
	2004	23.4	0 [0.19]
	2007		0 [0.14]
AR5 (> 95%)	2008	23.2	0 [0.14]
	2012	11.1	0 [0.18]
	2014		0 [0.18]
AR6 ("unequivocal")	2016	9.7	0 [0.18]
	2020	8.7	0 [0.23]
	2023		0 [0.39]

[a] Tracking-poll data from American National Election Studies, Cumulative Time Series Data File, https://electionstudies.org/data-center/anes-time-series-cumulative-data-file/.

[b] Measured as the number of members who sit inside the boundary of the other party's ideological distribution on the DW-NOMINATE first dimension (D/R). For the years in which partisan overlap = 0, the number in brackets is the ideological distance between the most conservative Republican and the most liberal Democrat. There was no partisan overlap in the Senate during the period covered by this table.

the GOP's movement to the ideological right made Congress less receptive to the kind of public pressure that produces republican moments. The subsequent acceleration of partisan tribalism has hardened that opposition.

LEGISLATIVE NEAR MISSES

Part 1: Legislative Failure and Regulatory Quagmire

In the years between the release of AR3 in 2001 and AR4 in 2007, members of Congress introduced legislation aimed at regulating GHG emissions. Many of these bills were bipartisan. The Climate Stewardship Act, for example, would have created a cap-and-trade regime for GHGs. Senators John McCain (R–AZ) and Joe Lieberman (D–CT) introduced this bill into the 108th, 109th, and 110th Congresses from 2003 to 2007.[22] In 2009, the House of Representatives passed a different cap-and-trade bill, the American Clean Energy and Security Act, also known as the Waxman-Markey bill, by a mere seven votes along partisan lines. Its Senate counterpart, the Clean Energy Jobs and American Power Act, or Kerry-Boxer bill, was the subject of fierce negotiations during the 2010 session, and some iterations of the Senate bill would have included a carbon tax and a national RPS.[23] Like most major regulatory initiatives, it split the business community. Many fossil-fuel producers lobbied against both Waxman-Markey and Kerry-Boxer, but these bills also attracted the support of an ad hoc association of large companies, including several major utilities, as well as BP.[24] However, the Kerry-Boxer bill was never brought to a Senate vote, despite Democrats' majority in that chamber. It was doomed by the opposition of Republicans, coal-state Democrats, and even some green groups who opposed these bills as too weak.[25] As it had with the Affordable Care Act, the Obama administration misjudged how quickly growing partisan contempt was undermining the possibility of bipartisanship, even for policies that Republicans had previously supported. Not long after the failure of the Kerry-Boxer bill, rural conservatives started posting YouTube videos of themselves "rolling coal"—spewing black exhaust from modified pickup trucks—as a form of (in their words) "Prius repellent."[26] Identity-based negative partisanship had already become a strong political force.

Into this policy breach stepped the EPA. The Bush administration's earlier refusal to regulate GHGs had led to the Supreme Court's decision in *Massachusetts v. EPA* in 2007, holding that GHGs fall within the Clean Air Act definition of a pollutant and that, given the state of climate science in 2007, the EPA would be hard-pressed to avoid concluding that GHG emissions ought to be regulated as a threat to public health and welfare.[27] After the failure of the Kerry-Boxer bill, the Obama EPA promulgated a series of rules regulating GHG emissions from vehicles as well as from factories, refineries, and other stationary sources.[28] In 2014, the Supreme Court struck down portions of some of these rules in *Utility Air Regulatory Group v. EPA* in a 6–2 decision that included an ominous warning that the Court would be less deferential to agency decisions on questions of "vast economic and political significance"—a then-emerging standard of judicial review known as "the Major Questions Doctrine."[29]

Just before the *Utility Air* decision, the Obama EPA promulgated a rule specifically targeting GHG emissions from fossil-fueled power plants, known as the Clean Power Plan (CPP).[30] The CPP treated GHGs as neither a toxic pollutant nor a criteria pollutant under the Clean Air Act; rather, it relied upon a relatively rarely used part of that act, section 111(d), which authorized the EPA to establish *guidelines* according to which states were to define emission *standards* for *sources* of the pollution covered by the EPA guidelines. Those standards, in turn, should represent the *best system of emissions reduction* that has been *adequately demonstrated*, considering costs.[31] The CPP depended on the courts accepting the agency's interpretations of each of the statutory terms italicized here, but that made the rule vulnerable to judicial challenge.[32] In particular, the CPP embraced an uncommon definition of *source* that offered states the option of "generation shifting"—reducing the use of coal-fired power plants in favor of cleaner generation rather than simply requiring that coal-fired plants install pollution controls such as carbon capture and storage (CCS).[33]

The CPP provoked fierce opposition from Republicans and coal-state Democrats, who argued that this application of 111(d) exceeded the EPA's authority under the statute. One Democrat, Joe Manchin (D–WV), featured his opposition in his reelection campaign ads.[34] Republican governors and attorneys general sued to overturn the rule, but that litigation had not run its course by the time the Trump administration rescinded the CPP.[35] Nevertheless, the Supreme Court took up the question of whether the Clean Air Act *would* have authorized the CPP, answering in the negative in *West Virginia v. EPA* in 2022. In *West Virginia*, the Court applied the Major Questions Doctrine to conclude that the EPA cannot "claim . . . to discover in a long-extant statute [the Clean Air Act] an unheralded power . . . representing a 'transformative expansion in [its] regulatory authority.' "[36]

Part 2: Reenergizing Climate Action

While the Obama administration was pursuing GHG regulation, Democrats in Congress successfully fought off Republicans' attempts to amend the Clean Air Act to prevent the EPA from regulating GHGs and simultaneously pursued climate legislation of their own. Their efforts were hampered by Republicans' control of one or more houses of Congress and/or the presidency during this period.[37] Many of the Democrat-sponsored bills aimed at complementing the Obama administration's GHG rules by addressing emissions from segments of the economy not targeted by those rules. Democrats later introduced multiple bills aimed at establishing emission caps, imposing carbon taxes and import/export carbon fees, offering financial support for the clean-energy export industry, and investing locally in green energy in economically distressed communities.[38]

Congressional Democrats' continuous pursuit of legislative action on climate during these years of divided government may seem futile in hindsight, but only with hindsight is it evident that securing *any* bipartisan cooperation was by then a futile objective. Indeed, those congresses included Republicans who supported, at least rhetorically, certain forms of GHG-emissions regulation, in particular carbon taxes. This may account for the regular appearance of multiple Democrat-sponsored carbon "fee" bills introduced into the 113th, 114th, and 115th Congresses. Some of the bipartisan energy for carbon taxes came from interest groups such as the Climate Leadership Council and the Congressional Climate Solutions Caucus. The organizers of the Climate Solutions Caucus aspired to have equal numbers of Democrats and Republicans, but that aspiration lasted only one congress, a casualty of Republicans' waning enthusiasm for GHG regulation and the rising influence of conservative populists within the party.[39]

The "blue-wave" congressional election of 2018 swept Democrats to a thirty-six-seat majority in the House of Representatives and raised the profile of the Progressive Caucus in Congress, in particular four new House members nicknamed "the Squad": Alexandria Ocasio-Cortez (D–NY), Ilhan Omar (D–MN), Ayanna Pressley (D–MA), and Rashida Tlaib (D–MA). Like veteran senator Bernie Sanders (I–VT), Ocasio-Cortez claimed the endorsement of the DSA, whose membership swelled after her election.[40] Their election was due in part to the efforts of a progressive NGO, the Justice Democrats, which pursued a strategy of trying to replace moderate incumbent Democrats with progressives, but this strategy brought to the fore intraparty tensions between the Progressive Caucus and the moderates in the New Democrats Caucus.[41] The conflict was in part ideological and in part generational. Many young progressives saw moderate Democrats as insufficiently bold or aggressive in their prior pursuit of climate legislation; some even saw fellow Democrats as obstacles to policy progress or felt condescended to by Democratic Party leaders in the House and Senate.[42] For their part, the New Democrats could point to the forty seats that flipped from Republican to Democrat in the 2018 House elections, most of them by ideological moderates. This internecine warfare set the stage for intraparty conflict over climate-policy strategy going forward.

By the time of the 2018 election, congressional climate strategists had begun to turn away from carbon taxes and toward other regulatory instruments, reflecting a growing sense on the left that stronger government action would be required to meet emissions-reduction goals. Also in 2018, the IPCC's special report on holding global warming to 1.5°C concluded that sharp, immediate reductions in GHG emissions and "rapid, far-reaching . . . changes in all aspects of society" would be required to achieve that goal.[43] That same year, the Swedish teenager Greta Thunberg began to skip school to protest the lack of policy action to mitigate global warming.[44] As noted in the introduction, her protests drew international attention, raised the salience of climate issues in the electorate, and mobilized young people in support of her goal. At the same time, new climate-focused NGOs brought renewed momentum to the efforts of existing climate-focused environmental organizations such as 350.org, Greenpeace, and the Sierra Club.[45]

These developments centered the attention of the climate coalition on a set of policy principles previously championed by Sen. Bernie Sanders called the "Green New Deal" (GND). In the 116th Congress, the GND took the form of a House resolution that seemed to track the IPCC's call for strong near-term policy action. It proposed the imposition of a "duty" on "the Federal Government [to] . . . achieve net-zero greenhouse gas emissions through a fair and just transition for all communities and workers [via a] 10-year mobilization [to meet] 100 percent of the power demand in the United States through clean, renewable, and zero-emission energy sources." It added that "the public [should] receive appropriate ownership stakes and returns on [energy] investment" and included other redistributive social safety-net and labor programs modeled after the public-works programs of the New Deal.[46] Most of the House Progressive Caucus joined Rep. Ocasio-Cortez to sponsor the GND resolution; most of the New Democrat Caucus did not. The resolution never reached the House floor, and with Republicans controlling the Senate and the presidency, no legislative version of the plan was introduced into the 116th Congress.

Democrats hoped that the 2018 election would begin a succession of elections like those that had created the durable Democratic Party majorities during the New Deal. In 2020, Sen. Sanders ran for the party's presidential nomination by articulating a New Deal–like theory of change. In an interview with the *New York Times* editorial board, Sanders suggested that his candidacy could generate a republican moment for the energy transition and renewal of New Deal values. He explicitly rejected the need for bipartisanship or significant compromise with Republicans because the GND would be so popular that it would force Republicans' hands. Sanders put it this way:

> The way you bring about real change in this country, what the history of America is about is when millions of people stand up for justice. So again, when I say to you—in due respect, and I mean that—we look at the world differently. You're saying, how do I negotiate with Mitch McConnell? And I'll tell you how I negotiate. Because when the people of Kentucky are demanding to raise the minimum wage to $15 an hour or health care for all or making their schools, public colleges and universities tuition-free, that's the basis of negotiation. O.K.?[47]

Many of the GND's policy planks did indeed command broad support within the Democratic Party and among a significant minority of Republican voters. But the elections of 2020 and 2022 did not produce the sort of voter pressure on Republicans that Sanders predicted. Democrats gained control of the Senate and presidency after the 2020 election, but fourteen of the House seats Democrats had flipped in 2018 flipped back to the GOP, shrinking the Democrats' margin of control in the House from thirty-six to eight. House moderates complained that progressive messaging—mostly over issues such as "defund the police" but also the unpopularity of the GND in oil and gas-friendly states where Democrats can win elections, such as New Mexico and Pennsylvania—undermined their chances to hold those seats.[48]

The moderates' complaints reflected the different ideological makeup of the combatants' districts. According to the *Cook Political Report*, the "partisan lean" of the average New Democrat seat in the 117th Congress was D + 3.5; the lean of the average Progressive seat was D + 15.9.[49] Post mortem analyses of the 2020 election suggested that progressive messaging energized turnout of new, left-leaning voters *but also energized opposition voters*.[50] That dynamic is consistent with the observation that when an issue attracts energy and money from one party, it also attracts energy and money from the other. In this way, activating the base poses more electoral risk for representatives in contestable seats, more of whose constituents reside in the ideological middle.

Part 3: Another Attempt at Regulatory Legislation

In the 117th Congress, the Senate was split evenly, such that Democratic Party control required party unanimity and the vice president's tie-breaking vote. Meanwhile, the Trump presidency had fanned the flames of partisan tribalism within the GOP. The party had already begun to nominate and accept into its congressional ranks supporters of QAnon, a vague, fantasist conspiracy built around the idea that within the federal government lies a shadowy "deep state" bent on taking over the United States and with a secret pedophile ring run by prominent Democrats, even Hillary Clinton.[51] In addition to the election of Marjorie Taylor Greene (R–GA) and Lauren Boebert (R–CO) to the House, nine other QAnon supporters won Republican primaries for Congress in 2022.[52] Despite reports that many congressional Republicans were privately disgusted with President Trump and with their party's most combative and nihilistic members, most refused to stand publicly against these populists' or their attacks on democratic norms because it entailed too much electoral risk.[53] Their fear of electoral punishment for standing up proved well founded. Of the ten Republicans who joined Democrats in voting to impeach President Trump, eight retired or lost their bids for reelection in 2020.[54] And, as already noted, when the House reconvened on the evening of January 6, 2021, after the violent insurrection earlier that day, most House Republicans voted *not* to certify the results of the 2020 election. Their votes reflected their constituents' belief that Joe Biden had "stolen" the election.[55]

Given the tone and solidity of Republican opposition, climate legislation in the 117th Congress needed to be acceptable to every Democratic senator and almost all of the Democrats in the House. In 2021, negotiations among the White House, Speaker Nancy Pelosi, and House progressives produced a smaller ($3.5 trillion) version of the GND called the "Build Back Better" (BBB) bill, which became a focal point for climate negotiations.[56] The BBB abandoned the idea of making the federal government responsible for building and owning new green-energy infrastructure and instead included a Clean Energy Performance Program. The program was a kind of national clean-energy standard that used carrots (subsidies) and sticks (financial penalties) to reduce the carbon content of electricity sold by electricity retailers over time.[57]

Over the summer and fall of 2021, negotiations between the House and Senate—particularly with the Senate's two most conservative Democrats, Joe Manchin (D–WV) and Kyrsten Sinema (D–AZ)—grew cagey and delicate.[58] Knowing that Manchin was a champion of the IIJA (infrastructure bill), progressive Democrats in the House withheld their approval of that bill pending resolution of BBB negotiations with the Senate. But Manchin refused to support the inclusion of the Clean Energy Performance Program within the BBB, and the program was removed; even then, Manchin continued to oppose the BBB on other grounds, and it died in the Senate.[59] Despite feeling betrayed by Manchin, House Democrats ultimately approved the IIJA in part because it included new financial supports for EV-charging infrastructure and provisions strengthening FERC's backstop siting authority for transmission lines that could serve new wind and solar farms.[60]

Progressive commenters ascribed Manchin's opposition to his connections to the coal industry through family businesses. Yet

Manchin's positions throughout the negotiations mirrored those of conservative Democrats who had opposed Waxman-Markey a decade earlier: worrying openly about the effect of the bill on energy prices and opposing a rule change to circumvent the GOP filibuster.[61] Supporting the Clean Energy Performance Program would have proven politically risky for any Democrat in West Virginia, a state the *Cook Political Report* assigned a partisan lean of R + 23.[62] For his part, Manchin explained his opposition to the BBB by noting that he has "never been a liberal in any way, shape, or form" and that if people want progressive policies, "all they need to do is . . . elect more liberals."[63]

Despite this intraparty feud, Senator Manchin surprised his fellow Democrats less than a year later by announcing that he had reached an agreement with Senate majority leader Charles Schumer (D–NY) to support a new bill, the Inflation Reduction Act (IRA). The IRA contained a long list of tax credits and other subsidies for a variety of upstream and downstream investments in energy production, including renewable energy, mining, nuclear power, hydrogen production, carbon sequestration, transmission, and domestic manufacturing of clean energy. It also included provisions addressing health-care costs, labor and wage issues, and other goals that had been part of the GND and the BBB. The tax credits in the IRA were structured so as to be more lucrative for developers who use domestic content, to meet certain "prevailing wage" criteria, and to benefit so-called energy communities and low-income communities.[64] The bill also included subsidies and other policy supports for fossil fuels.[65] The IRA was signed into law in August 2022.

Both moderate and progressive Democrats claimed credit for the IRA's passage.[66] Some progressives saw it as a definitive rejection of carbon taxes and other market-based regulatory instruments favored by economists and as a vindication of GND-style industrial policy.[67] For his part, Manchin explained his support for the bill this way:

> This legislation ensures that the market will take the lead, rather than aspirational political agendas or unrealistic goals, in the energy transition that has been ongoing in our country. The [bill] invests in the technologies needed for all fuel types—from hydrogen,

nuclear, renewables, fossil fuels and energy storage—to be produced and used in the cleanest way possible. . . . [T]his bill does not
arbitrarily shut off our abundant fossil fuels. It invests heavily in
technologies to help us reduce our domestic methane and carbon
emissions and also helps decarbonize around the world as we displace dirtier products.[68]

These contrasting narratives offered by progressives and Manchin to
explain the IRA reflected enduring ideological divisions within the climate coalition.[69] Nevertheless, for the climate coalition, the passage
of the IRA seemed to steal a victory, if not precisely the one it wanted,
from the jaws of defeat.[70]

That victory took the form of a familiar policy instrument: subsidies. Federal tax credits for wind and solar projects have been a regular feature of U.S. energy law for almost fifty years. Along with PURPA
subsidies of the late twentieth century and state RPSs, tax credits have
given renewable energy a leg up in the market when it needed such
support.[71] To be sure, Congress has also periodically offered financial
support to other forms of energy: nuclear power, energy efficiency,
and other energy technologies.[72] What makes the IRA different from
earlier subsidies is its power and reach. It addresses a broad suite of
energy-transition technologies in one bill. It extends its tax-credit provisions for ten years rather than just one or two years; it provides the
claimants with direct payments from the Treasury for qualified expenditures rather than credits against liability that must be taken only
at tax time; and it allows munies and other public entities to qualify
for some of those direct payments, even though they have no tax
liability.[73]

The IRA's incentives are sufficiently powerful that they should lower
the trajectory of future GHG emissions by reducing clean-energy development costs, all else being equal. The precise magnitude of that
effect is difficult to predict given friction in labor and raw-materials
markets and the political barriers to entry for new energy infrastructure, but it seems likely to be a sizable one.[74] Optimists within the
climate coalition also expect the IRA to provide the legislative foundation for EPA regulation of GHGs under the *West Virginia* standard
and/or to transform U.S. electoral politics in ways that will build a

durable legislative majority for new legislation charting a path to net zero. However, as explained in the remainder of this chapter, a fuller understanding of the dynamics of partisan tribalism suggests that those expectations are probably too optimistic.

ENERGY-TRANSITION POLITICS AFTER THE 117TH CONGRESS

The IRA adds to an existing swirl of economic and policy forces that will influence how the energy transition unfolds. Some of those forces put tailwinds at the back of the transition; others represent headwinds likely to slow its progress.

TAILWINDS AT THE BACK OF THE TRANSITION

As figure 3.1 illustrates, the carbon intensity of the U.S. economy has declined in recent years, even before passage of the IRA. Indeed, since the failure of Waxman-Markey/ Kerry-Boxer in 2010, carbon emissions have fallen more than would have been required under that statute.[75] In the electricity sector, these declines have been due in part to the way natural gas crowded coal out of electricity markets in the early 2000s and to the displacement of gas- and coal-fired power by renewables more recently. Today the list of new wind and solar projects waiting for permission to connect to the grid would double the grid's generating capacity.[76]

Looking forward under current political conditions, we can expect that when Democrats hold the White House, they will continue to push to limit GHG emissions from fossil-fueled power plants.[77] But the GOP's emerging anti-climate-policy orthodoxy means that the most important executive-branch climate initiatives are likely to last only as long as Democrats control the White House. We can expect state politics to be a little more stable because most states are dominated by one party or the other, and the enthusiasm of blue states for strong climate policy represents a significant tailwind for the energy transition. Some examples:

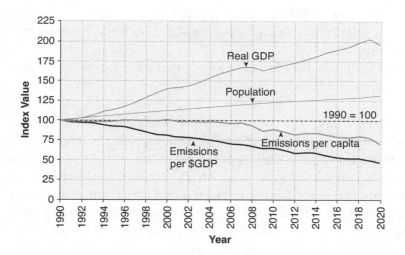

FIGURE 3.1. U.S. CO$_2$ emission trends, 1990–2020.

Source: "Climate Change Indicators: U.S. Greenhouse Gas Emissions,"
U.S. EPA, 2022, https://www.epa.gov/climate-indicators/climate-change-
indicators-us-greenhouse-gas-emissions.

- In California in 2019, Governor Jerry Brown signed a bill mandating 50 percent of California's electricity to be powered by renewable resources by 2025 and 60 percent by 2030, while calling for a "bold path" toward 100 percent zero-carbon electricity by 2045.[78]
- Hawaii has established a goal of 100 percent renewable-electricity sources by 2045.[79]
- New York State's Climate Leadership and Community Protection Act calls for all the state's electricity to come from carbon-free sources by 2030 and for 70 percent of those sources to be renewable.[80]
- A Michigan law establishes a goal of 100 percent clean energy by 2040 and 60 percent renewable energy by 2035.[81]
- Washington State's Clean Energy Transformation Act of 2019 requires all electric utilities in Washington to transition to carbon-neutral electricity by 2030.[82]

- New Mexico has mandated that the state's publicly regulated utilities receive all their electricity from carbon-free sources by 2045.[83]
- A Minnesota law establishes a goal of reducing GHG emissions by 80 percent by 2050.[84]

Similarly, more than one hundred U.S. cities have pledged to meet their electricity needs using "100 percent renewable" energy.[85]

Perhaps the most important tailwinds behind the transition are economic. Wind and solar power are inexpensive, and electricity buyers want more of it. Some electric utilities have begun to take action to reduce their carbon footprints, even in red states, with some pledging sharp reductions over time.[86] A growing number of commercial and industrial energy consumers have made similar pledges. Many of these pledges reflect customer pressure. According to Yale University polling, the percentage of Americans who are either "concerned" or "alarmed" about climate change grew from 50 percent in 2017 to 58 percent in 2021, with only 19 percent describing themselves as "doubtful" or "dismissive."[87] Companies want to highlight their procurement of zero-emission power to their customers; retailers want to offer customers more zero-emission power.

In much of the country, adding more inexpensive utility-scale wind and solar power to the electricity-generation mix would reduce electricity rates for consumers. Farmers and ranchers initially liked hosting wind turbines on their land because the turbines bring an additional source revenue (through lease payments) but include minimal interference with farming and ranching operations, but some of that enthusiasm has cooled recently.[88] Wind and solar farms also bring economic benefits to rural communities in the form of property-tax revenues. In Texas, for example, existing renewable-energy installations will bring an estimated $7.2 to $8.8 billion in tax revenue to local communities over their lifetimes, most of it in rural areas.[89] The substantial economic benefits that flow from green-energy infrastructure development, amplified by IRA subsidies, will benefit new businesses and workers, many within Republican political jurisdictions.[90] Some analysts predict that these benefits will create new voting constituencies for green energy and other transition technologies, tipping the political balance in Congress toward broad support for a net-zero future. Whether that prediction turns out to be correct remains to be seen, but it depends on an economic self-interest model of voting behavior that does *not* seem to explain the behavior of voters today.[91]

HEADWINDS IN THE FACE OF THE TRANSITION

Partisan Opposition in the States

Whatever political momentum the IRA creates will confront a growing Republican hostility to green energy and the energy transition in red states.[92] No Republican in either chamber of Congress voted for the IRA.[93] That opposition reflects elected Republicans' growing support for the argument that plentiful fossil fuels are an indispensable part of a reliable energy supply. This trend manifests in many ways. For example, after Winter Storm Uri in February 2021, Governor Greg Abbott of Texas inaccurately blamed wind and solar generators for the power failure, and Texas's subsequent pivot toward policies favoring "dispatchable" (read: fossil-fueled and nuclear) power plants reflects that same philosophy. In 2023, Republicans in the Texas Legislature introduced a suite of bills aimed at disadvantaging renewables in the electric-generation mix, though many failed to pass.[94]

Nor is this trend limited to fossil-fuel-producing states. According to the Guarani Center on Environmental, Energy, and Land Use Law at New York University, more than twenty Republican-led states have enacted laws prohibiting local governments from banning natural gas hookups in new buildings, presumably as a reaction to local bans enacted in recent years in Berkeley, California; Brookline, Massachusetts; and elsewhere.[95] And Republican opponents of the 2023 Minnesota decarbonization legislation referred to it as the "Blackout Bill," suggesting that reducing reliance on fossil fuels would jeopardize the security of the energy supply.[96] In the first six months of 2023, 156 bills were introduced into state legislatures proposing to penalize Black-Rock and other funds that address climate-related risks; as of late 2023, fourteen states, including some with no fossil-fuel industry, have enacted laws to remove state investment money from those funds.[97]

Some states take symbolic anti-green-energy action even further. In early 2023, Wyoming indicated that it would refuse billions of dollars of federal grants under the IIJA for installation of EV charging stations,[98] echoing some states' earlier refusal of federal money for Medicaid expansion under the Affordable Care Act. Around the same time, Governor Ron DeSantis of Florida proposed a tax exemption for gas stoves, explaining that "they [Democrats] want to control every aspect of your life. . . . They want your gas stove, and we're not going to let that happen." Increasingly, Republican politicians couch this political strategy as part of broader ideological battles over cultural issues, calling Blackrock's environmental, social, and governance initiatives "woke capitalism."[99] In today's hyperconnected political environment, the use of culture-war frames has turned the old axiom that "all politics is local" on its head; today it is more accurate to say that all politics is national.[100]

All of which raises questions about the continued viability of the cooperative federalism on which so many national regulatory regimes rely. For ambitious Republican politicians, climate, energy, and environmental policies present attractive opportunities to please a party base that is tuned into national, negative, partisan messaging. If Republican politicians can win votes by thwarting Democrats' climate-policy goals, the process of implementing executive-branch climate policy will be slow and litigious when Democrats control the White House and likely to stop (or move into reverse) under Republican presidents.

Judicial Hostility to Regulation

Executive action to hasten the energy transition faces another threat: from the courts. It is not clear whether or how much the executive branch can advance the transition after the Supreme Court's decision in *West Virginia v. EPA*. The Biden EPA, like the Obama EPA before it, has chosen to rely on Clean Air Act section 111(d) to regulate GHG emissions. That choice seems legally risky. The dissenting justices in *West Virginia* seemed to rule out use of section 111(d) in this way when they characterized the majority's holding: "Today the Court strips the

Environmental Protection Agency . . . of the power Congress gave it to respond to 'the most pressing environmental challenge of our time.' "[101] But some argue that the IRA patches the legal holes identified by the *West Virginia* Court, insulating the Biden EPA's reliance on section 111(d) of the Clean Air Act against legal challenge. That claim is based on two arguments. The first is that the IRA supplies the kind of explicit congressional delegation of authority to regulate GHGs that the Court said was missing from the Clean Air Act. The second is that the IRA will stimulate development that will "demonstrate" technologies such as CCS that weren't previously "adequately demonstrated" under the Court's reading of section 111(d).[102]

These readings of the IRA seem too hopeful, however. The IRA contains no explicit authority for the EPA to regulate GHG emissions.[103] And even if the relevant pollution-control technologies do become inexpensive and viable under the IRA, the Court as currently composed seems likely to view any EPA rule mandating a path to net zero as a "major question" requiring a far more explicit delegation of regulatory authority than can be found in the IRA. And if decarbonizing the power sector is a major question for the EPA, it is probably a major question for FERC and other agencies as well, constraining the power of the executive branch to mandate a path to net zero.[104]

These are frustrating realities for the climate coalition. The Supreme Court's conservative majority was approved by senators representing a minority of American citizens.[105] One member of that group, Justice Neil Gorsuch, was approved after the Senate's historically unprecedented denial of a vote to Obama administration nominee Merrick Garland. Another, Amy Coney Barrett, was confirmed by the Senate in direct contradiction of the logic by which that body denied a vote to Garland. Thus, to the climate coalition the *West Virginia* decision looks like the successful use of the courts to achieve antiregulatory *policy* objectives that conservatives could not achieve in Congress.[106] Regardless, the Court defines the constitutional boundaries of regulation. After *West Virginia*, it appears likely that the only politically secure path to a net-zero future lies in national legislation requiring (or more clearly and specifically authorizing) that future.

THE NEW PARTISAN ENVIRONMENT

Any such legislation will have to overcome a toxic mix of ideological polarization and partisan tribalism—negative, affective partisanship—that today affects every policymaking institution in the United States, including Congress. As noted in chapter 1, republican moments happen when groundswells of voter concern pose electoral risk or opportunity for members of Congress. Today, partisan polarization and partisan tribalism combine in powerful ways that mute the connection between voters' issue preferences and electoral risk. It is important to understand why.

Partisan Polarization and Safe Seats

The overwhelming majority of House and Senate seats are now "safe seats," those representing jurisdictions whose voters are solidly in favor of one party or the other. Political scientists have studied the decades long, bidirectional relationship between partisan ideological polarization, on the one hand, and the rise of congressional "safe seats," on the other.[107] Representatives of safe seats protect their electoral futures differently than representatives of competitive seats do. In safe seats, the principal threat to members' reelection comes at the nomination stage, not in the general election. This means they must cater *not* to their average constituent but rather to their more ideologically extreme and negatively partisan ones.

Scholarly explanations for the spread of safe seats credit some combination of gerrymandering and voluntary voter geographic sorting of liberals into cities and conservatives into rural areas.[108] Redistricting after the 2020 U.S. Census exacerbated this problem as state parties focused on consolidating power in the seats they already held rather than trying to expand the size of their party's congressional caucus.[109] Therefore, even though climate has become more salient to voters nationally, that concern exerts less electoral pressure on members of Congress because fewer of them represent competitive jurisdictions.[110] Republicans in safe seats now protect their reelection prospects by attending to the preferences of their *party's* median voter on climate issues, even if that means defying a majority of their own constituents in the process. In this environment, the kind of shocks to the political system that produced republican moments in the past—the abuses committed by robber barons, the Great Depression, pandemics, and environmental tragedies—are less likely to produce a republican moment today. Reflecting this change in voter behavior, table 3.2 illustrates how the wave elections that preceded the New Deal differ from recent congressional elections. In this respect, today's American political dysfunction seems more like the antebellum period than the New Deal. Before the Civil War, voters and politicians subordinated policy preferences to the moral imperative of attaining political power.[111] And that seems to be their priority today.

TABLE 3.2 The Changing Composition of Congress

		Before and During the New Deal			
President	Year	Senate		House	
		Dem (N)	GOP (N)	Dem (N)	GOP (N)
Hoover (R)	1929–1931	39	56*	163	267*
Hoover (R)	1931–1933	47	48*	217*	217
FDR (D)	1933–1935	59*	36	313*	117
FDR (D)	1935–1937	69*	25	322*	103
FDR (D)	1937–1939	76*	16	333*	89

*Denotes majority party in each chamber.

		Compared to Recent Elections			
President	Year	Senate		House	
		Dem (N)	GOP (N)	Dem (N)	GOP (N)
Trump (R)	2017–2019	48	52*	194	241*
Trump (R)	2019–2021	47	53*	235*	200
Biden (D)	2021–2023	50*	50	222*	213
Biden (D)	2023–2025	51*	49	213	222*

*Denotes majority party in each chamber.

Partisan Tribalism

Twenty-first century partisanship in the United States has become much more *affective*—more of an expression of group identity than an expression of policy preferences or a governance philosophy.[112] For more and more voters, their partisan identity is also *negative*—focused on preventing the other party from realizing its goals. Affective, negative partisanship offers incentives for GOP politicians to oppose Democrats' policy objectives even if they are popular. Opposing the other party's initiatives is a way of pleasing negative partisans, *regardless of the content of those initiatives*. Thus, negative partisanship makes it risky for Republicans who previously supported carbon taxes or cap-and-trade regimes to partner with Democrats in support of those initiatives. Less than a decade after the first "Prius repellant" videos appeared on YouTube, more and more elected Republicans now embrace a bitter, rhetorical equivalent of "rolling coal."

The Pew Research Center records a doubling since 1994 of the shares of voters in each party who hold "very unfavorable opinions of the other party."[113] In fact, that is putting their feelings mildly. Over recent decades, more and more voters have come to see the opposing party as "immoral, dishonest and close-minded," segments growing to more than 70 percent of Republicans and 60 percent of Democrats in 2022.[114] Since 1978, the National Election Study has tracked the feelings Americans have toward the opposite political party on a scale of 0 (most unfavorable) to 100 (most favorable). In 1978, the median respondent felt only mildly negatively toward the other party, reporting scores among Democrats and Republicans in the high 40s. In 2020, the average Democrat reported a score of 20 for the GOP, and the average Republican reported a score of 16 for Democrats. Fewer than 10 percent of respondents gave the opposing party a score of 0 in 1978. In 2020, *48 percent of Republicans and 39 percent of Democrats gave the opposite party a score of 0.*[115]

Partisan animosity may spring in part from the different life goals of liberals and conservatives. In the words of Pew researchers,

Liberals and conservatives are divided over more than just politics. Those on the opposite ends of the ideological spectrum disagree about everything from the type of community in which they prefer to live to the type of people they would welcome into their families.

. . . Given the choice, three-quarters (75%) of consistent conservatives say they would opt to live in a community where "the houses are larger and farther apart, but schools, stores and restaurants are several miles away." . . . The preferences of consistent liberals are almost the exact inverse. . . . [W]hile 73% of consistent liberals say it's important to them to live near art museums and theaters, just 23% of consistent conservatives agree—one of their lowest priorities of eight community characteristics. [116]

As Democrats and Republicans encounter one another less frequently, there is more space for the fundamental attribution error to do its damage, for unfamiliarity to breed contempt.

For reasons explained more fully in the next chapter, partisans see negative partisanship in the other party much more easily than in their own. It is not only that Democrats and the climate coalition hear more often about Republicans' most extreme rhetoric; the incendiary rhetoric of Democrats is also highly salient to Republican partisans. After the Supreme Court's reversal of the *Roe v. Wade* decision in 2022, some members of Congress made threatening statements directed at Supreme Court justices, statements that conservatives claimed crossed the line between frank disagreement and incitement to violence.[117] Similarly, rhetoric from congressional Democrats in the wake of the police murder of George Floyd in 2020 included the recommendation that protestors "armor up."[118] And many voters on the populist right report that they *feel* attacked. For example, after the January 6 insurrection, more Republicans (75 percent) than Democrats (46 percent) reported a belief that American democracy is "under attack."[119]

The most popular diagnoses of modern populism on the right describe it in reactive terms as a response to feelings of economic insecurity and cultural alienation. Author turned senator J. D. Vance's best-selling explanation of rural white alienation ties it to cultural decline and the loss of manufacturing jobs in the Rust Belt. The sociologist Arlie Russell Hochschild points to working-class white males' resentment of women, minorities, and immigrants, whose improving economic opportunities they see as replacing their own in a zero-sum game.[120] Some of those who trace voter alienation to economic forces point to the *illusion* of fairness in the market, the ostensibly meritocratic competition for jobs that ignores the obstacles some people face before they get to the starting gate. But both the Vance and Hochschild point more directly to social and cultural issues, and that thesis finds support in survey data.[121] A strong majority of Republicans (70 percent) believe American culture has changed for the worse since the 1950s, whereas a strong majority of Democrats (63 percent) believe it has changed for the better. And Democrats are much more likely than Republicans to endorse the ideas that the United States should be "made up of people from all over the world" (64 percent versus 30 percent) and "made up of people from a wide variety of religions" (55 percent versus 17 percent).[122]

Cultural divides are a major driver of partisan tribalism, and ambitious politicians try to exploit these feelings of cultural alienation to win votes. In Florida, Governor Ron DeSantis has targeted Disney for its open policies on sexuality and gender, and he joined Governor Greg Abbott of Texas in sending refugees seeking asylum at the southern U.S. border to "liberal" cities such as New York, Washington, DC, and Boston. Some congressional Republicans have suggested that the United States bomb or invade Mexico, reflecting media messages portraying undocumented immigrants as part of a hostile invasion of the United States. In April 2023, Abbott announced his desire to pardon a constituent convicted of murdering a Black Lives Matter protestor. The North Carolina and Texas Legislatures have followed DeSantis in seeking to weaken or restructure their states' flagship state universities for ideological reasons.[123] And so on. These are ways Republican politicians can demonstrate their contempt for Democrats' social and cultural priorities, burnish their negative partisanship credentials, and please a significant portion of the GOP voting base.

Negative Partisanship Is Bipartisan but Asymmetrical

Although survey data indicate that negative partisanship is spreading within both parties, violent rhetoric is now a fixture of political discourse among a much larger percentage of Republican elected officials than among Democrat officials. Republican candidates now compete for the support of their negative partisans by emulating Donald Trump. Trump rallies were (and are as of late 2023) orchestrated expressions of contempt that feature incidents of actual violence as well as rhetorical approval of the idea that contemptible adversaries ought to be dealt with violently.[124] The GOP's response to the various criminal prosecutions of former president Trump has featured calls to violence. As the former president pursues the GOP nomination in 2024 and the criminal prosecutions against him proceed simultaneously, the potential for political violence will grow.[125] Former governor Mike Huckabee of Arkansas warned that the presidential election of 2024 might be the "last American election that will be decided by ballots rather than bullets," echoing similar predictions of armed violence by former governors Kari Lake and Sarah Palin and by prominent right-wing commentators.[126] This is not the rhetoric of traditional, business-friendly, small-government conservatives; rather, it reflects the logic of politicians representing safe seats and an increasingly negatively partisan electorate.

FROM THE PAST TO THE FUTURE

Certainly, American liberal democracy has experienced bitter partisan rhetoric and negative partisanship before. The pundits of the Populist Era, the Progressive Era, and New Deal included writers such as Mark Twain (1835–1910) and H. L. Mencken (1889–1956) as well as political cartoonists such as Thomas Nast (1840–1902) and John Miller Baer (1886–1970), whose tools included ridicule and mockery directed at economic and political elites.[127] Some activists at the helm of social movements of the 1960s followed Saul Alinsky's influential primer *Rules for Radicals* (1971), which included among its "thirteen rules" the following:

> [No. 5] Ridicule is man's most potent weapon. There is no defense. It is almost impossible to counterattack ridicule. Also it infuriates the opposition, who then react to your advantage. . . .

[No. 11] If you push a negative hard and deep enough it will break through into its counterside; this is based on the principle that every positive has its negative. . . .

[No. 13] Pick the target, freeze it, personalize it, and polarize it.[128]

Alinsky argued that these strategies were necessary because elites rig democratic processes in ways that shut out the powerless. His book devotes an entire chapter to defending the notion that for activists the ends justify the means.[129] Alinsky's book was influential on the American political Left in the twentieth century, but it has also influenced twenty-first-century conservatives who have occasionally seen themselves as the relatively powerless battling left-leaning political elites.[130]

If major regulatory legislation emerged from Congress in earlier eras marked by bitter partisanship, might it happen again? The future is of course uncertain, but GHG-emissions regulation will have to overcome the GOP's turn against strong climate policy, the spread of safe seats, the decline in issue-based voting, and continuing amplification of negative partisanship. In the New Deal era, Democrats won votes by responding to voter unhappiness about the economic issues of the day. In the 1960s and 1970s, voters demanding environmental protection, consumer protection, and civil rights legislation triggered a partisan realignment that made Congress responsive to those concerns. The social science research of the twentieth century reflected that reality by crediting issues and ideology with exerting a strong influence over voting behavior.[131] Today, by contrast, issue-based explanations of politicians' behavior have lost favor among scholars because they no longer describe reality. Affective, negative partisanship drives more voting decisions today.[132]

Furthermore, party affiliation may now be driving issue preferences, not the other way around. Recent polling suggests that Republican support for renewable energy and climate policy may be starting to wane. That reversal may be driven in turn by negative partisanship. The rush of red-state policies favoring fossil fuels in 2022 and 2023, the declining GOP membership in the Bipartisan Climate Caucus in Congress, and the growing profile of pro-fossil-fuel narratives such as those espoused by the writer Alex Epstein are part of an ongoing integration of opposition to climate policy into GOP partisan identity.[133]

Unfortunately, bitter partisanship begets reciprocal bitter partisanship, creating a downward spiral. The authors of an analysis in 2015 concluded that in Congress "non-cooperation *multiplicatively* breeds non-cooperation. . . . Therefore, while it is incorrect to say that recent divisive political figures are responsible for increasing partisanship, they have actively contributed to it because *these are the types of non-cooperative figures and factions that the multiplicative system selects.* The exponential increase in non-cooperation shows no indication of slowing, or reversing."[134] Worryingly, each side's partisans believe that they are taking the more rational and principled stand, but the other side is not.[135]

All of which feeds a climate of contempt in which it is difficult for members of the climate coalition to acknowledge that *some* opposition to strong climate policy is not based on ignorance or ill will but rather on conservative arguments with which they nevertheless disagree. One strain of conservative thought accepts the reality of human-driven climate change but challenges experts' projections that it will cause sufficiently serious harm to justify costly action now. A second strain believes it likely that future technological innovation will solve the climate problem in ways that obviate the need to incur costs today. A third strain accepts most of the expert climate consensus but sees mitigation as a lost cause—an unsolvable collective-action problem because voters will never consent to bearing mitigation costs now in order to benefit future generations or people beyond our shores. Yet another strain of conservative opposition holds that mitigation represents an unacceptable infringement on economic freedom, whatever its social benefits.[136]

For the GOP's remaining traditional conservatives, the transformation of today's Republican Party from a conservative party to a negatively partisan one is upsetting, but it has its own electoral logic. In the words of the historian Timothy Snyder, when a party's policy proposals are relatively unpopular, it "must either fear democracy or weaken it."[137] Fomenting bitter tribalism may have been a smart electoral strategy for the GOP, but it is nevertheless a dangerous one. In the lead-up to the 2016 presidential election, many conservatives warned against "normalizing" Donald Trump's serial lies and attempts to undermine democratic institutions. Troubled by Donald Trump's embrace of bigotry and falsehoods, they worried openly about their party's future and warned against the GOP becoming "the stupid party." Some (but not all) of these people became "never Trumpers." But as more and more Republican voters urged their elected representatives to line up behind Trump, few *elected* Republicans were willing to condemn even the worst features of Trumpism.[138]

Why haven't traditional conservative Republicans withheld their votes from the new GOP? Conservative voters may base their tolerance of their party's transformation on the belief that they will achieve more of their preferred policy outcomes by voting GOP even if the party is dominated by Trump populists. They may see the party's embrace of Trumpism as a phase that will pass and Democrats' hand-wringing about American democracy as sour grapes. Or they may be persuaded by the culture-war narratives that present Democrats as a threat to their values and see the new GOP as the lesser of two evils. They may note that most Republicans don't believe that they are trying to destroy American democracy and point to the fact that increasing support for political violence is not an exclusively Republican phenomenon. Indeed, in a poll in 2023, 38 percent of Trump supporters and 41 percent of Biden supporters agreed that "it is acceptable to use violence to stop [the other party] from achieving their goals" because the other party's "ideologies have become so extreme."[139]

Accordingly, some conservatives may view the GOP's use of its power in Congress and the Supreme Court to block regulation as nothing more than the stuff of sharp-elbowed policy battle. The procedure the Senate used to reject the nomination of Merrick Garland to the Supreme Court may have been unprecedented, but so was the Senate's rejection of a highly qualified and then esteemed conservative justice (Robert Bork) in the 1980s. Bork was rejected for views deemed to be too conservative then, but those views were not unlike those of today's Supreme Court majority.[140] The New Deal Consensus is dead, say conservatives, and the Supreme Court's recent decisions weakening the regulatory state are a predictable result of Republicans' electoral successes.[141] If conservatives have enjoyed success in preserving an unpopular status quo, they are doing nothing more than using American institutions in well-worn ways to win more policy fights than they used to.

Presumably, the politicians who oppose GHG regulation are supported by elements of all these beliefs and motives, distributed unevenly among voters in every congressional jurisdiction. Many in the climate coalition are naturally frustrated by Republicans' use of countermajoritarian institutions to block majority preferences for strong climate regulation.[142] But it is a mistake to let that frustration breed narratives that misunderstand congressional politics, the heterogeneity of Republican voters, or the drivers of partisan tribalism. For those whose partisan enmity overrides their policy preferences in the voting booth, the question is how to break the spell of that enmity.

* * *

Part 2 of this book zeroes in on underappreciated forces feeding the partisan tribalism that plagues American democracy and dives into the ways those forces complicate the politics of the energy transition. That examination begins with chapter 4, which explores modern information technology as a hyperefficient propaganda machine—a conduit for misinformation, a trigger of negative emotion, and a driver of political dysfunction. Chapter 5 looks at how that propaganda machine muddies our understanding of energy-transition trade-offs and makes energy-transition policymaking more difficult. And chapter 6 explores ways to get back to the kind of productive engagement across political boundaries that might restore Congress's ability to respond to national challenges such as climate change.

PART II

Complexity, Centrifugal Forces, and the Energy Transition

4

THE PROPAGANDA MACHINE

*Anyone who has the power to make you believe absurdities has
the power to make you commit atrocities.*

—Voltaire

THE SERIES of republican moments that created the energy-
regulatory state established the value of regulation as a tool to
correct the failures and socioeconomic inequities that arise
within energy markets. Regulation has made energy more widely
available, more affordable, and less environmentally harmful than
it otherwise would be. The history recounted in part 1 also illustrates
that regulatory agency experts tend to understand complex energy-
policy problems better than judges or elected politicians do. Congress has wisely chosen to delegate to agency experts many of the
important decisions about how to accomplish regulatory goals. It is
therefore all the more unfortunate that the Supreme Court chose to
embrace a theoretically and historically dubious approach to judicial
review of agency action in its *West Virginia* decision.[1] The result has
been to circumscribe agencies' regulatory authority and to drop
important energy-transition policy decisions into the lap of a Congress that is increasingly paralyzed by partisan tribalism.

Research confirms that partisan tribalism is driven in large part
by the online spread of propaganda.[2] As suggested by the chapter's
epigraph, modern information technology cultivates partisan contempt by spreading misinformation and triggering negative emotion. Negative partisans prize nothing more than to see the enemy

defeated. Modern propaganda feeds them a constant stream of anecdotal reasons to feel that way, in part by triggering *fear*. To quote Bertrand Russell (again): "Collective fear stimulates herd instinct, and tends to produce ferocity towards those who are not regarded as members of the herd. . . . Fear generates impulses of cruelty, and therefore promotes such superstitious beliefs as seem to justify cruelty. Neither a man nor a crowd nor a nation can be trusted to act humanely or to think sanely under the influence of a great fear."[3] Today's partisan tribalism is triggered partly by fear of change. Some voters fear continuing changes in the earth's climate and what it means for their security and that of their children; other voters fear changing socioeconomic and cultural norms and what those changes mean for their security and that of their children. Some, no doubt, fear both.

One of the ways propaganda stokes fear is by undermining the set of norms that make up the civic-virtue mindset: fallibilism, respect for pluralism, truth seeking, and the like. The psychologist Jonathan Baron, author of a seminal text on belief formation, has his own term for that mindset: *actively open-minded thinking*. Baron sees the norms of actively open-minded thinking as necessary "for a democracy to function well (both for its citizens and outsiders)." Crucially, laws by themselves will not sustain these norms. Rather, they must be sustained by the way we behave in social groups as well.[4] A growing body of scholarship tells us that partisanship is becoming more tribal because the most powerful propaganda machine in human history is undermining those norms. It is encouraging presumptuous, close-minded certainty over actively open-minded thinking.

INFORMATION GATHERING, BELIEF FORMATION, AND COGNITIVE BIASES

For those people and groups whose messages were locked out of twentieth-century mass media—newspapers, radio, and eventually television—the invention of the internet and social media transformed their prospects. Modern information technology has opened markets for musicians and artists, put entire libraries of information at our fingertips, "democratized" the dissemination of information, and connected people who might never have found one another. But in politics it is wreaking havoc, contributing to what leading scholars of partisanship call a "poisonous cocktail of othering, aversion and moralization [that] poses a threat to democracy."[5] Modern media undermine the role of parties as peaceful mediators of intraparty conflict, distort our beliefs about politics, policy, and each other, and create unsustainable levels of partisan hatred.

SOCIAL MEDIA VERSUS REAL LIFE

Forty years ago, cultural and political radicals had no choice but to spread their messages slowly. White nationalists, for example, proselytized by passing around hard copies of *The Turner Diaries* and *The Protocols of the Elders of Zion* by hand.[6] They met to discuss their bigoted, anarchic, or violent ideas face-to-face. Violent groups on the left, such as the Weather Underground and the Symbionese Liberation Army, faced the same organizational hurdles. The information technology of the day kept fringe groups small by increasing the transaction costs of proselytizing and by maintaining social norms that kept them in the shadows. Today, by contrast, every politically active group across the ideological spectrum can mobilize and "educate" one another continuously online. They can grow much more quickly than ever before, maintain their insularity, and normalize their views among a much larger cohort of people.

The axiom "Twitter is not real life" is giving way to the axiom "All culture is internet culture."[7] Research tells us that *social media shapes national political life*. How? First, we know that news media frame "major issues of policy and politics as part of an ongoing [national] conversation," and *social media shape the news*. Most American adults use social media. Almost half participate in some form of issue-based political activism online, and about 25 percent of Americans regularly discuss politics on social media.[8] That 25 percent compose a strongly partisan and relatively ideologically extreme subset of the electorate. The Pew Research Center documents the "U-shaped" histogram of political engagement, with higher engagement levels among those at both ideological poles: "Consistent conservatives and liberals do share one habit that distinguishes them from other Americans: They spend a lot of time talking about politics and government."[9] These people are the "salesmen" and "connectors" of ideas (to borrow Malcolm Gladwell's terminology) who disseminate information, frames, and points of view from online to offline social networks.[10] According to a team of Princeton scientists who study the issue, this process is in part how "a polarized information ecosystem [online] can indirectly polarize the broader society by causing its individuals to self-sort into emergent homogenous social networks."[11] In other words, the poisonous environment of social media discourse is spreading to the broader society.

Second, *traditional news sources now emulate the newer forms of media* in the competition for readers and listeners (for "clicks"). They use grabbier, less informative headlines such as "Everything You Thought You Knew About [Issue X or Politician Y] Is Wrong" or "The Frightening New Study [About Issue X]" or "Did [Politician Y] Really Say That?"[12] They do so because they now serve a market that one academic describes as "ever-hungry for big stories at whatever cost." Writers know that the quest for viral stories is driven by "human emotion [and] human psychology," and so they cater to that emotion by "sanding the inconvenient edges off of facts in order to suit the narrative."[13] Journalists are aware of these perverse incentives but are subject to them anyway. And like most people, they see this problem more easily in others than they do in themselves. For example, the former Buzzfeed reporter Ben Smith wrote an entire book decrying this destructive media trend, but when asked in an NPR interview if he regretted his own decision to be the first to publish the salacious contents of the now discredited Steele Dossier, he demurred (twice).[14]

Third, traditional *mainstream news is reported by people who frequent social media.* Journalists get sources and story ideas online, which influences their sense of what is important, of who is an expert, and of who is to blame for a problem.[15] In a Pew Research Center survey in July 2022, 94 percent of journalists reported that they use social media for their jobs and that their social media site of choice is Twitter/X.[16] But in my field of energy law and policy, many of the most knowledgeable and experienced academic experts are not active on social media. For example, of the ten authors of the two leading energy-law texts used in law schools, only two or three discuss energy policy on social media.

In all these ways, social media's toxic norms and power to distort perception routinely escape those media's borders. The social psychologist Jonathan Haidt puts this assessment more colorfully: "You can tell me that 70 percent of Americans don't participate in the culture war, but it doesn't really matter. Events today are driven by small numbers that can shame and intimidate large numbers. Social media has changed the dynamic. Even if most Americans practice excellent fire safety habits, if a small minority is rewarded for throwing lit matches, we're going to live in an age of arson."[17] The remainder of this chapter explains how and why modern information technology impedes our ability to develop a clear-eyed and complete understanding of complex, contentious political issues.

COGNITIVE BIASES AND ATTRIBUTION ERRORS

The Enlightenment philosophy that undergirds the U.S. constitutional design conceived of humans as both rational *and* emotional, singular *and* social. It focused on how these forces within us are often in tension with one another. Scholars and philosophers of political economy embraced science and this broad conception of human nature. But early in the twentieth century, the discipline of political economy was divided into distinct social science disciplines. Economics, for its part, turned away from this fuller conception of human nature and toward a stylized, hyperrational model of the human decision maker, *homo economicus*. As economics grew in influence for a time after World War II, so did this circumscribed conception of human nature, one that chose not to engage most of the social-emotional parts of human behavior. Today we credit the psychologists Daniel Kahneman and Amos Tversky with pioneering research that is restoring the fuller picture, and we credit Richard Thaler and Cass Sunstein with popularizing it within economics and legal scholarship, respectively.[18] But the basic ideas Kahneman and Tversky developed and refined have an older lineage.[19]

For example, Leon Festinger's seminal research in the 1950s provides the everyday language we use to describe the emotional tension (dissonance) that arises when we hold beliefs or ideas (cognitions) that conflict with one another.[20] Cognitive dissonance is *powerful*—so powerful that it *must* be resolved or rationalized to restore inner harmony. We do this at some cost to truth seeking by rejecting one of the conflicting beliefs or by avoiding information or experiences that cause dissonance in the first place. Rationalization sometimes involves so-called (logical) *fallacies of presumption*—that is, making assumptions about uncertain or unknown dimensions of an issue in order to relieve dissonance. For example, if I believe in protecting economically vulnerable consumers from hardship, but I also believe that competitive, restructured energy markets benefit society, the price volatility characteristic of competitive electricity markets may cause me dissonance. One way to relieve that dissonance is to assume that state policymakers will enact policies that will protect vulnerable consumers from price shocks. Another way we rationalize is through *confirmation bias*, which describes how we protect cherished beliefs by holding contrary evidence to higher standards of proof or by instinctively dismissing or ignoring it.[21] For example, if I work for an organization that is publicly committed to promoting a particular technological approach to the energy transition, I will instinctively devote more effort and energy to thinking critically about studies or analyses that challenge that approach than about studies that do not.

The power of these biasing effects was so well established by the 1970s that when Kahneman and Tversky first launched their scholarly attack on *homo economicus*, they were very, very confident that it would succeed. In the words of their intellectual biographer, Michael Lewis, they "knew of course that people made decisions that [economic] theory would not have predicted."[22] The ensuing research demonstrated a series of specific cognitive biases that stray from rationality in predictable ways.[23]

As noted in the introduction, politicians, lobbyists, and others who would persuade us often try to exploit the bias known as the *fundamental attribution error*: the idea that because we understand our own motives and thinking but not those of others, we explain our own actions more charitably than we explain the actions of others. Consequently, when an adversary stands in the way of a policy we want, we are quick to ascribe blameworthy motives to that adversary. For example, when the very first U.S. political parties began to form around Alexander Hamilton (Federalists) and Thomas Jefferson (Republicans), each side believed strongly and sincerely in a particular economic and foreign-policy agenda: one tilted toward merchants, cities, and England, the other toward farms, rural communities, and France. As Hamilton and Jefferson pursued their respective visions within George Washington's first cabinet, it didn't take much of a push for each to regard the other as disingenuous, selfish, and misguided.[24] In politics, someone is always willing to give voters that push, lobbying us to make those uncharitable inferences about others. A recent study by a group of social scientists confirms that people ascribe more ethical motives—"less egoistic interests and more national interests"—to the leaders of their own party than to leaders of the other party.[25]

Attribution Errors and Voting

One reason why it is so easy to misread others' motives in politics is that most political choices are binary, but our decision criteria are multidimensional. The voter's choice is between two candidates,[26] but it is a choice driven by each person's uniquely weighted combination of considerations: the candidate's party or personal characteristics, the candidate's policy preferences, and more. Legislative choices are binary as well. Legislators vote for or against legislation or legislative amendments, but they do so for a multiplicity of reasons. Most of the major regulatory legislation described in part 1 of this book aimed at one big goal—such as incentivizing natural gas production (the NGPA) or reducing water pollution (the Clean Water Act)—but did so via dozens of specific provisions specifying how, when, and where to pursue the larger goal. Most members of Congress presumably liked parts of those bills and disliked others, but each member was forced to make the binary choice, to vote yea or nay.

Votes are observable, but voters' reasoning is not. Given that voting decisions are multidimensional, it is a leap of logic to impute to a voter some specific belief based on their vote, but we make that leap nevertheless. As the Harvard psychologists Susan Fiske and Shelley Taylor note, when making inferences about others' choices, we tend to focus on the personal attributes of those others that are most salient to us.[27] In the 2020 presidential election, progressive voters and moderate Democrats held differing views about parts of the Biden policy platform, but most progressives and moderate Democrats voted for Biden. Some conservative "never Trumpers" voted for Biden despite disagreeing with most of his policy platform. Likewise, many of the 74 million people who voted for Donald Trump in 2020 did not intend their vote as an endorsement of his venality or irresponsibility in office or of every policy decision he made.

Yet another study concludes that people tend to infer (mistakenly) that the opposing candidate's most extreme attributes "play[] an especially important role" in voters' decision to support that candidate. These mistaken inferences create cycles of contempt. According to the authors, "When [we] infer that an entire voter base was singularly motivated by an especially extreme—and divisive—policy issue, perceptions of political polarization are likely to grow."[28] Unsurprisingly, lobbyists exploit these mistaken inferences, feeding popular perceptions of opposing party extremism.[29] Online provocateurs know that provoking intemperate reactions from adversaries can accelerate that process. Recall from chapter 3 Saul Alinsky's Rule (for Radicals) No. 5: ridicule "infuriates the opposition, who then react to your advantage." The notorious attorney Roy Cohn endorsed a similar idea: "I bring out the worst in my enemies and that's how I get them to defeat themselves."[30] It bears repeating that it is *un*familiarity that breeds contempt in politics.

Attribution Errors and Groups

The *fallacy of division* occurs when people attribute the general characteristics of a group to an individual within the group. The *fallacy of composition*, sometimes also called "the ecological fallacy," occurs when people ascribe a characteristic of individuals within the group to the group as a whole. These fallacies work together to animate bigotry and other generalizations people make about out-groups, especially in the presence of negative emotion.

In the early American republic, pamphleteers told New Yorkers and Virginians disparaging stories about one another, animating what leaders of that era called "the party spirit." Then, as now, they did so simply because it could help their preferred faction win elections.[31] Today, depending on your news feed, you may read a steady diet of stories about ridiculous or blameworthy behavior by individual Floridians or Texans, New Yorkers or Californians, Muslims or Christians, Chicagoans or Los Angelinos, immigrants, corporate CEOs, welfare recipients, racial minorities, white men or women, "the Left," "the Right," Generation Z, millennials, Baby Boomers, Democrats, Republicans, fossil-fuel companies, environmental activists, gas or electric utilities, and so on. You may begin to impute the objectionable attributes of those individuals to the groups to which they belong. Lobbyists know that we are wired to seek out patterns and that we are receptive to suggestions that patterns exist even where they do not. One story may be all it takes to create a broader belief regardless of its empirical truth or falsity—especially if that belief is echoed by members of *my* social group, if it *feels* good, or if we *want* it to be true.[32]

However, public denigration of a group also alienates individual members of the group to which the statements do not apply.[33] For example, during the legislative battle over the Biden administration's energy bill in the fall of 2021, I opened my Twitter feed to an anguished tweet by a woman whose brother worked in the oil industry, pleading with her followers not to treat him as "the enemy." This is a natural human reaction to expressions of contempt for a group that she interpreted to include her brother. Statements such as "Republicans are climate-science deniers with an irrational hatred of government" and "Democrats are catastrophists who exaggerate climate risk so they can impose socialism" alienate potential allies. Escalating, reciprocal expressions of group contempt feed hatred among the in-group toward the out-group and pose the risk identified by Voltaire in the chapter's epigraph.[34]

BIASED ASSIMILATION OF NEW INFORMATION

Confirmation bias closes off critical thinking by creating instinctive doubt about information that contradicts established beliefs. Psychologists describe it as a kind of "unwitting selectivity in the acquisition and use of evidence," by which people apply much tougher evidentiary standards to dissonant claims than to agreeable ones.[35] Consequently, experimental subjects recall evidence supporting their preexisting beliefs better than they recall contradictory evidence. They require less supportive evidence to confirm a hypothesis than contradictory evidence to reject it. In one experiment, subjects who supported the death penalty concluded from an article that the article also supported it, while readers who opposed the death penalty drew the opposite conclusion about the very same article.[36] Once a person has formed a belief about the other political party—or about nuclear energy or wind farms or fracking—confirmation bias insulates that belief from contrary evidence. It protects both unfounded skepticism toward the climate consensus and the unfounded belief that the earth will be uninhabitable by century's end if GHG emissions aren't reduced to net zero by 2050.[37]

A related idea, *cultural cognition bias*, describes how people's sense of their own identity biases their beliefs. Humans' emotional commitments to their social identities are tied to group memberships. These commitments "operate as a kind of heuristic" that distorts how we process information about public-policy matters.[38] This bias is a relative of the idea of *groupthink*.[39] The retired congressman Bob Inglis (R–SC), who once tried to rally support for climate policy among congressional Republicans in the early 2000s, understood this connection between climate-policy beliefs and social identity: "[A] lot of what's going on with denial of climate science is 'I want to protect who I am' [and] 'I want to protect what I've built.' "[40]

When one's political party becomes central to one's identity, as it has for many today, this suite of social and cultural biases comes with it. Thus, people tend to believe that others who share their political values are more reliable sources of information and expertise, even on subjects that have nothing to do with politics.[41] They distrust the experts who don't share their values and even discount those experts' actual levels of expertise accordingly. Researchers at Yale's Cultural Cognition Project have demonstrated this effect across a number of issue contexts, including gun control, the death penalty, the safety of nuclear power, and, in particular, environmental risks.[42] In one study, researchers presented subjects with evidence of a national scientific consensus supporting the following two propositions: that climate change is real and driven by human activity and that nuclear waste can be safely disposed of in a geological repository. Political conservatives rated the credibility of the climate-change experts much less highly than the nuclear-waste-disposal experts; political liberals reversed those rankings.[43]

Thus, voters tend to regard in-group factual beliefs as "objective" and out-group beliefs as "biased," which is one way that our instincts mislead us.[44] "Individuals tend to assimilate information by fitting it to pre-existing narrative templates or schemes that invest the information with meaning. The elements of these narrative templates—the identity of the stock heroes and villains, the nature of their dramatic struggles, and the moral stakes of their engagement with one another—vary in identifiable and recurring ways across cultural groups."[45]

This is why ad hominem attacks work so well. If engaging contradictory information or arguments is uncomfortable, lobbyists can turn our attention away from what the speaker is saying by focusing on the speaker's attributes. *"Why would you ever listen to a [Democrat or Republican or liberal/conservative or Florida man or California hippy or millennial or Boomer, etc.]?"* The ad hominem attack is one way that lobbyists divide us into camps in which the "stock heroes" of one side become the "stock villains" of the other.

For example, imagine how people who live in a farming or ranching community might react to news that urban climate activists are urging Americans to give up their pickup trucks in favor of walking, cycling, and mass transit or to forgo the eating of beef. It is not difficult to see how ranchers and farmers might perceive those messages as an attack on their cultural identity. They might then be more receptive to and feel validated by messages that ridicule those outsiders as elites who are out of touch with "real Americans like me." How will urbanites who are worried about climate change react when they see the phrase "real Americans" used in a way that excludes them? It may sound like an attack on *their* identity, making them feel more receptive to (and validated by) messages that make fun of those farmers' and ranchers' attitudes. And so the cycle continues.

THE PROPAGANDA MACHINE IS A BIAS AMPLIFIER

Readers familiar with online political discussion will see where this analysis is headed. A large and growing body of research supports the intuition that ideological and social media amplify these biases in *extremely* powerful ways and cultivate firm and false beliefs as well as negative emotions more quickly, widely, and durably than ever before. Where mass media once were a centripetal social force—a creator of common understanding—they now are a centrifugal force, fomenting political division.

INFORMATION GATHERING AND THE NEW MEDIA ENVIRONMENT

Today most political and policy-relevant information is disseminated, consumed, and debated online.[46] Those who have come of age in this environment may regard it as "normal" and feel confident that they can guard against its belief-distorting effects.[47] But if we compare the current environment with how voters gathered information and formed beliefs during the environmental health and safety era (see chapter 1), we can begin to understand how and why truth seeking and critical thinking about complex problems are more difficult today than they used to be.

The (Re)Emergence of Ideological Media

Fifty years ago, there were of course no social media and no cable news. Television news came to Americans each evening for thirty minutes from three national broadcast television channels: NBC, ABC, and CBS. Local TV stations presented news for fifteen to thirty minutes two or three times daily. Print news came from one or more local newspapers, also delivered daily. Politically active voters may also have subscribed to a national daily paper, such as the *New York Times* or the *Washington Post*, and/or to a weekly or monthly news magazine. Radio stations might provide five minutes of news each hour. Much of the information provided by newspapers and radio came from the same three national wire services: AP, UPI, and Reuters.

Because news came less frequently and in much smaller volumes, voters could devote as much attention to its consumption as they pleased. News organizations were sufficiently profitable that they could fund long-form investigative pieces. In the case of radio and television stations, their broadcast licenses imposed a public-service obligation that benefited their news divisions.[48] Voters had time to read to the twentieth paragraph of a story, where one finds the caveats and exceptions to the more general propositions found in the headline and lede, so they learned to look for those caveats and exceptions. They developed *the habit of thinking critically* about what they were reading as they absorbed new information about politics and policy.

Furthermore, the news was curated differently than it is today. Almost all of it came from journalists who served ideologically heterogeneous audiences and whose training required them to aspire to norms of objectivity and completeness. Advocacy journalism, which was a more prominent part of the news landscape in the late nineteenth and early twentieth centuries, became less prominent after World War II. Reporters' professional norms required that sources be double- and triple-checked before a story could be published. Reporters were expected to educate readers on *all* of the important dimensions of a problem within the four corners of each story, to avoid opinion, and to err on the side of caution. Journalists had more time to prepare stories and did so knowing that readers would have the time to read them. Movies such as *All the President's Men* (1976), *Good Night, and Good Luck* (2005), and *The Post* (2017) depict this world of slower, carefully curated, longer-form news.[49]

Today's news landscape is much faster and, on cable television, sloppier. One historian summarized modern TV news this way: "Everything happens fast, but nothing actually happens. Each story on televised news is 'breaking' until it is displaced by the next one. So we are hit by wave upon wave but never see the ocean. . . . Watching televised news is sometimes little more than looking at someone who is also looking at a picture. We take this collective trance to be normal. We have slowly fallen into it."[50]

In addition, more journalists today serve ideologically narrower audiences. They deliver information tailored to a point of view. In the words of communications scholars, many of today's journalists "find relevant content, restructure it, and present[] it with added evaluation and orientation to particular audiences."[51] To be sure, many reporters are still bound by the old ways, reliant on careful curation and aspirations to completeness and objectivity. Many write for outlets that serve a broader audience. But voters will encounter these reporters' work amid a sea of advocacy pieces, interest-group lobbying, press releases, and even intentional misinformation dressed up as "news." Meanwhile, the shrinking budgets and rapidly declining fortunes of traditional news organizations are starving that older business and journalistic model. Subscriptions to daily newspapers, which peaked at about 60 million households in 1990, fell to 25 million households in 2020, even though the U.S. population grew by almost 100 million in those three decades. The market share of network evening news shows began declining even earlier, falling to about one-third of 1980 levels by 2020.[52]

Affective, Negative Broadcasting

Many mark the transition from old to new media with the founding of the Fox News Channel in 1996, the first and most successful explicitly ideological television news channel. Fox News's first chairman and CEO, the conservative political consultant Roger Ailes, adapted to television the brash, infotainment style of talk radio/TV commentator Rush Limbaugh. Ailes followed Limbaugh's lead in blurring the lines between opinion and fact, something the historian Nicole Hemmer calls "sharp-elbowed, fact-lite punditry." That style dominates cable "news" today.[53]

The Limbaugh/Fox News model was designed to build affective attachments to conservatism—and, by implication, the Republican Party—by helping viewers construct negative pictures of the ideological Left and the Democratic Party in their mind's eye.[54] Limbaugh's formula was to tell stories about the political Left and to characterize their actions in alarming ways. He told his listeners that regardless of how these political adversaries explained their actions, *what they really intended* was something far more nefarious—to endanger you, to disrespect you, or to take away something you value. His radio show ran for only a few hours a day, but Fox News hosts could plant seeds of doubt and fear in their viewership all day, every day. Fox News shows raised the salience of the issues on which Fox wanted its viewers to focus, so-called culture-war issues such as race, religion, sexuality, and reproductive rights. Meanwhile, its chyron, the text and captions at the bottom of the screen, posed questions designed to sow fear and doubt about Democrats and the Left.[55]

Within a few years after its creation, Fox News commanded the largest viewership in cable television news, a position it has held for almost all of the intervening period to now. It has been the engine—along with myriad talk radio shows and copycat TV outlets—of right populism and the fears that coalesced under the notion of "replacement theory," the idea that the American Left wants to destroy white Christian culture.[56] These same narratives are echoed on talk radio and social media. In 2022, Fox News viewership was double that of its leading competitor (MSNBC) and almost three times that of CNN.[57] Table 4.1 lists the top-rated cable news shows of 2022 based on Nielsen data.

Fox News's success spawned other consciously right-leaning news channels, including One America News, Newsmax, Townhall, and more.[58] At the same time, explicitly left-leaning news outlets arose in response to Fox News's success. Now cable television representatives from all ideological positions feed viewers a steady diet of stories

TABLE 4.1 Top-Rated Cable News Shows, 2022

Rank	Network	Program	Daily Viewership
1	Fox News	*The Five*	3,419,000
2	Fox News	*Tucker Carlson Tonight*	3,031,000
3	Fox News	*Jesse Waters Primetime*	2,857,000
4	Fox News	*Hannity*	2,811,000
5	Fox News	*Special Report with Brett Baier*	2,511,000
6	Fox News	*The Ingraham Angle*	2,269,000
7	Fox News	*Gutfeld!*	2,040,000
8	Fox News	*Outnumbered*	1,858,000
9	Fox News	*America's Newsroom*	1,761,000
10	MSNBC	*Alex Wagner/Maddow*	1,756,000

Source: Katz 2023 (citing Nielsen data).

about the worst of the other side.[59] Ideological news outlets rarely lie outright because when they do, they risk liability for defamation, so they lobby instead. They invite viewers—some in more subtle ways than others—to attribute to the other party or ideology the worst attributes of some of its members. They emphasize stories that advance their ideological agendas and reflect poorly on their ideological adversaries.

Figure 4.1 depicts the transition from the old information environment to the new one on a timeline. As the twentieth century gave way to the twenty-first, ideological news went online, triggering the competition for virality—stories and moments in which each side "owned" the other. Partisans now share these cathartic moments with the like-minded on Facebook, Twitter/X, Parler, Reddit, TikTok, Tumblr, Mastadon, Threads, Instagram, TruthSocial, YouTube, Rumble, email lists, message boards, podcasts, and the like.

This mixture of thoroughly sourced stories that aim to educate with those that aim to persuade (or even misinform) comes at voters in a never-ending deluge. There is far more political and policy-relevant information than we can possibly consume, and discerning the reliable from the unreliable sources takes more effort than even the most discerning people can muster. Many of those who would lobby us no longer have to worry about getting their stories past editorial filters,

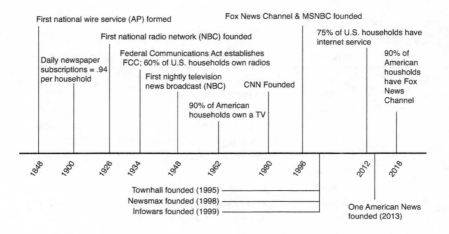

FIGURE 4.1. Old and new media.

or in some cases their editorial filters include an explicitly ideological component. We don't have time to read to the last paragraph, and so we eventually lose the habit of looking for nuance and caveats—of thinking critically about news *as* we consume it. Busy news consumers substitute podcasts for reading because podcasts allow them to multitask, but most podcasts frame information within a persuasive narrative favored by the podcaster. Back in 2008, the technology writer Nicholas Carr asked a question that seemed paradoxical at the time: "Is Google making us stupid?"

> I'm not thinking the way I used to think. I can feel it most strongly when I'm reading. Immersing myself in a book or a lengthy article used to be easy. My mind would get caught up in the narrative or the turns of the argument, and I'd spend hours strolling through long stretches of prose. That's rarely the case anymore. Now my concentration often starts to drift after two or three pages. I get fidgety, lose the thread, begin looking for something else to do. I feel as if I'm always dragging my wayward brain back to the text. The deep reading that used to come naturally has become a struggle.[60]

And as we skim our news feeds, social media algorithms exacerbate biasing effects by selecting the stories we see, placing us in informational "filter bubbles." That is, we tend to click on the stories we want to see, something researchers call "homophily." The algorithm learns what we like and gives us more of what we want and less of what we don't, hiding from us the information that challenges our views. Thus, our instinct to click on stories that confirm our preferred beliefs has the effect of censoring our news. Even if we value balance, we often cannot get it online.[61]

BELIEF FORMATION ONLINE

The propaganda machine does more than censor our information flows; it also transforms the *social* process by which we form political beliefs. The eminent anthropologist Mary Douglas once wrote that "culture puts pressure on individuals. They don't make major decisions without consulting friends."[62] Fifty years ago, after absorbing the daily news, voters would discuss it with family, neighbors, coworkers, and friends in the ensuing days and weeks. The social process of forming beliefs included subjecting those beliefs to interrogation by others *face-to-face*, with all the context that face-to-face communication provides: including nonverbal cues, the ability to discount or credit the other's opinion based on past experience, and so on. The need to maintain familial, work, or other social relationships discouraged expressions of dismissive contempt for a point of view. Norms of friendship or courtesy made the exchange of ideas mostly iterative, cautious, and slow and tended to produce conversations that were relatively conducive to learning, exploration, and deliberation.

Today one need not talk about politics or policy with friends, family, neighbors, and coworkers at all.[63] Indeed, as partisan polarization makes discussion across party or ideological boundaries more contentious and bitter, voters can preserve real-life relationships only *by avoiding* those face-to-face discussions. Voters instead find communities of interest among remote, often anonymous "friends" online and discuss issues there. Online "conversations" are almost always in writing. They are constrained by space limitations, making deep or iterated exchanges of views difficult. Some platforms impose space constraints, but even in the absence of such restrictions the transaction costs of discussion by typing impose de facto limits. So does the demand for brevity caused by the glut of information and scarcity of attention, giving rise to shorthand such as "TL;DR" (too long; didn't read). And in online groups, discussants may be anonymous. It may not be evident which members are bots or have economic incentives to advance a specific point of view. Under these constraints, it becomes easier to persuade by triggering emotion than by exchanging information.

From its inception, Fox News programming has shown a particularly sophisticated understanding of how social-emotional forces shape political belief. The network understands rural viewers' sense that urban, liberal, professional elites look down upon them. *They're laughing at you, but don't worry. We have your back—you, the real Americans.* Friendly, attractive hosts help viewers digest the news and usher them gently toward the conclusions that editors want viewers to reach.[64] The format invites viewers to equate party and ideology with identity. *These nice people are my people.* Even for viewers sitting alone in front of a screen, the presentation evokes a social response. The conservative columnist David Brooks explains the relationship between Fox and its viewers this way: "If you're in red America or in rural America, Fox is not just a news organization. It's your community center. It's . . . that news organization that pays intense attention, that [has] lots of good news stories about cops and soldiers. A lot of things that happen in red America that don't get much coverage in the coastal media get a lot of attention in Fox. And so they—it's—the loyalty there is not only about politics, and it's not only about news coverage. It's just about where people see themselves reflected."[65] Jon Stewart's version of the Comedy Central Network's *The Daily Show* was an early response to Fox News's success, one that offered its viewers a mirror-image kind of social affirmation not (then) available on traditional news channels—reassurance that there were other people who recognized the absurdity of some of the messages coming from right-wing media. Today, left-leaning podcasts (*Young Turks*, *Pod Save America*, *Majority Report*) offer that same kind of catharsis associated with making fun of those who spread misinformation on or from the ideological right.[66]

Processing these flows of political information in ideologically homogenous social media communities hardens political beliefs and loyalties quickly and tends to produce more extreme opinions. Voters now learn about a new policy-relevant development as soon as it becomes public, then share and discuss it—or monitor discussions of it—*immediately* inside their respective filter bubbles. Research confirms that this process is also how filter bubbles become more ideologically homogeneous over time: "Retweet cascades on Twitter lead to bursts of unfollowing and following activity that indicate sudden shifts in social connections as a direct result of information spreading through the social network. . . . [T]ie breaking rather than tie addition is the main driver of sorting."[67] According to one group of researchers at New York University and Princeton, these reactive "following/unfollowing" decisions are the mechanism by which "large portions of the most liberal and most conservative [Twitter/X] users *never see what the other side is saying.*"[68]

Importantly, high levels of education and political sophistication do not insulate people against these distortions. The more important factor is the lack of exposure to people who hold opposing views; ideological isolation biases belief among all sorts of people. Indeed, according to the polling firm PredictWise, "In general, the most politically *intolerant* Americans . . . tend to be whiter, more highly educated, older, more urban, and more partisan themselves. . . . [W]hite, highly educated people are relatively isolated from political diversity. *They don't routinely talk with people who disagree with them; this isolation makes it easier for them to caricature their ideological opponents. . . .* [P]eople who went to graduate school have the least amount of political disagreement in their lives."[69] Again, unfamiliarity breeds contempt.

Another important aspect of online political discussion is worth noting here: it usually occurs in the presence of unseen observers. The presence of a partly anonymous online audience steers conversation away from learning and toward lobbying. People stop being learners and start acting like professional lobbyists, evaluating news and information not for its contribution to their understanding of an issue but for which "side" of a political fight it helps or hurts. These conversations need not involve lying; rather, participants emphasize certain dimensions of a policy issue and de-emphasize others so as to persuade the audience. And unlike for professional lobbyists, the social distance and anonymity of online settings reduce the reputational risk associated with being wrong. There is far less social pressure online to be cautious, deferential, and civil. To the contrary, in rhetorical battle with other homogenous groups, incivility and extremism may *seem* necessary or advisable.

As participants get used to lobbying a little and as the sense that the cause is urgent grows, it becomes easier to lobby a lot. One way to ramp up outrage about an issue is to show the in-group the worst of the other side. In a series of experiments, the public-policy scholar Chris Bail found that in those rare moments when homogenous online communities are breached by opposing views, those breaches tend to involve particularly extreme versions of those opposing views. This happens in the manner of Rush Limbaugh, wherein extreme stories involving members of the out-group are selected and repackaged to promote ever-more caricatured views of that out-group. As a result of this kind of phenomenon, members of left-leaning bubbles are more likely to know about the plot to kidnap Gov. Gretchen Whitmer than about the plot to assassinate Justice Brett Kavanaugh; in right-leaning bubbles, that order is reversed. Members of conservative bubbles are more likely to have heard (and be upset) about the podcaster Joe Rogan's defense of abortion rights; members of liberal bubbles are more likely to have heard (and be upset) about Rogan's promotion of skepticism about COVID-19 vaccines. Moreover, when these extreme opposing messages penetrate a bubble, community members perceive them as threats to their political identities and react by adopting *more* extreme attitudes.[70] This is the reaction that Saul Alinsky and Roy Cohn predicted. Indeed, it is so predictable and common online that it now has a name: "rage farming."[71]

Cognitive biases also help distort perceptions of the in-group. We project our own values onto political allies. When political opponents confront us with examples of offensive behavior or rhetoric by an ally, we resort to "no true Scotsman" reasoning: that is, we redefine the in-group to exclude those bad actors.[72] This is fairly common in online energy-policy debates: "No *serious* conservative denies the science of human-driven climate change; don't lump those crazies in with us"; "No *serious* energy-transition advocate really favors a 'wind, solar, and batteries only' energy policy; don't lump those crazies in with us." This is another type of attribution error that becomes tempting in the heat of rhetorical battle.

As time goes by within a social media bubble, those who shout in ALL CAPS are not necessarily the most persuasive influencers. Those who bring the group only certain news stories and academic research or who interject selectively to support certain beliefs or evidence and cast doubt on others are often more persuasive over the long run. And once a belief is established within a group, group dynamics will strengthen it and chase away dissenters—either overtly or more gently through the process of self-selection via group entry and exit or by rewarding messages consistent with group orthodoxy with "likes" and punishing dissonant messages with silence. And when dissonant information is presented, it can be brushed aside by casting doubt on the speaker's character or motives. Indeed, ideological media *train* voters to lobby in this way by providing the language of ad hominem dismissal: "leftists," "Marxists," "fascists," "Nazis," "eco-Nazis," "deniers," "doomers," "normies," "SJWs (social justice warriors)," "corporate Democrats," and so on.

In fact, online derision has become a persuasive art form. For example, during the 2021 congressional debates over the particulars of the BBB bill, some progressives on Twitter/X began referring sarcastically to Democrats who raised questions about parts of the bill as "Very Serious People," or "VSPs."[73] Rhetorical devices used to deflect (rather than refute) criticism of the in-group belief become memes. "That's just both siding," or "You're just repeating [our adversary's] talking points."[74] Or one might retweet an adversary's tweet with the derisive rejoinder, "Tell me you don't understand [the subject of the tweet] without saying you don't understand [the subject of the tweet]."[75] Another deflective technique is *whataboutism*, responding to a critical question or assertion with an unrelated counterassertion or criticism.[76] Or one can highlight a single flaw in a long series of legitimate points made by an adversary to suggest that the remainder of the argument is not worth engaging.

The ubiquity of these techniques inculcates the *habit* of dismissing rather than considering counterarguments, particularly when group beliefs are ossified and the persuasive task seems urgent. *If everyone in my online group seems to believe that X is true, then X must be true.*[77] From there, it is a short step to the inference that anyone expressing the contrary view is ignorant, unreasonable, or disingenuous and that their arguments aren't worth considering or engaging. These norms promote orthodoxy over learning and the avoidance of critical examination. The psychologists Barbara Mellers, Philip Tetlock, and Hal Arkes call these processes "self-justifying cycles of reasoning" that make us "progressively more self-righteous and contemptuous of the competence and morality of the other side."[78]

Of course, it ought not to be overlooked that the propaganda machine relies on the very sort of bottleneck industries—delivery platforms—that might once have been regulated as public utilities in a different partisan political environment.[79] Perhaps in another time the online world might not have been as unfriendly to the truth as it is. But modern information platforms have evolved in an era that is more hostile to regulation than the past was, both legally and politically. It is an environment in which socially destructive online behavior only rarely elicits a regulatory response from government. The question of whether or how to regulate the internet is beyond the scope of this book. But given the limits imposed by the First Amendment, the content of the current Supreme Court, and the role individual behavior plays in the dissemination of propaganda, the task of crafting a regulatory regime that will be effective and survive judicial review is a delicate challenge for any government willing to tackle it.

DEFENSES OF THE NEW MEDIA

Of course, lamenting the dangers posed by new communications technologies is a tradition at least as old as the printing press. Twentieth-century writers such as the political journalist Theodore White and the technology writer Neil Postman expressed similar worries about the corrosive effects of television on our political lives.[80] Those observations are not a rejoinder to the analysis here, but there are persuasive, substantive defenses of the new media. Most begin by challenging the suggestion that the old media were in any sense fair or complete. If the old media aspired to objectivity, that aspiration is unimportant because personal or organizational biases inevitably crept into reporting and editorial decisions.[81] One might argue that disclosure of bias is far more important than the old-school quest for objectivity, which was probably futile anyway. The old media were an oligopoly of information gatekeepers who constrained information flows. How can it be a bad thing that modern technology has destroyed that old oligopoly and permitted previously muzzled voices to be heard?

From the right, the populists who now form the base of the GOP view the traditional national news organizations as left-wing outlets worthy of their contempt. That contempt sometimes manifests viscerally in right-wing communities and even more viscerally at Trump political rallies. Populists' view of the mainstream media as biased toward the left is based on research showing that reporters tend to hold left-leaning ideological views as well as the firsthand accounts of bias from conservative reporters who worked for mainstream news organizations. In 2000, the veteran CBS News reporter Bernard Goldberg left CBS for Fox News after charging CBS, NBC, and ABC with left-leaning bias; the ABC News reporter John Stossel and the CBS News anchor Sheryl Attkisson left their positions in 2009 and 2014, respectively, echoing Goldberg's charges. Goldberg and Stossel found Fox News Channel a natural landing point.[82]

The danger to foundational democratic values posed by the (first?) Trump presidency elicited changes in the journalistic practices of mainstream news outlets, changes that fed charges of left bias by conservatives. The *New York Times*, the *Washington Post*, and other such outlets altered their editorial practices to become more openly oppositional to Trump, reasoning that much of the public must have been misunderstanding the nature of the threat he posed to the rule of law, the peaceful resolution of pluralistic conflict, and other liberal-democratic values and institutions. In the words of the *Times* media editor Jim Rutenberg, "You have to throw out the textbook American journalism . . . if you view a Trump presidency as something dangerous." But many Republican voters interpreted this change in editorial policy as a confirmation of their suspicions that mainstream media could not be trusted.[83]

From the left, many progressives see mainstream media outlets as biased toward the status quo and the interests of corporations and the wealthy. Some use the term *corporate media* to refer to both traditional mainstream news sources and Fox News. One of the most persistent critics of corporate media is David Sirota, the former senior adviser and speechwriter for Senator Bernie Sanders. The Sirota-founded online outlet the *Daily Poster* regularly critiques mainstream-media coverage of politics, framing it as the exercise of corporate power. Sirota charged the *New York Times* with "actively working to help . . . corporate [media] owners kill many of the safety net provisions" in the BBB bill, for example.[84] This view follows in the tradition of the late Hunter S. Thompson and Saul Alinski in its focus on power dynamics. Citing Thomas Paine, H. L. Mencken, and Mark Twain, Thompson summarized his own ends-justify-the-means approach this way: "There are a lot of ways to practice the art of journalism, and one of them is to use your art like a hammer to destroy the right people—who are almost always your enemies, for one reason or another, and who usually deserve to be crippled because they are wrong."[85]

Some influential left-leaning writers in the energy and climate space approach their task similarly. The freelance climate writer and podcaster Amy Westervelt frames much of her writing around the idea that oil companies and utilities are so powerful and systematically unscrupulous that it is too late for civility in the climate debate. The energy and climate writer Kate Aronoff's work also portrays corporate political power as the root of the climate problem, but within a more explicitly democratic socialist frame.[86] Her reporting appears in outlets styled as socialist or anticapitalist alternatives to "corporate media," such as *Jacobin, Dissent,* and the *Intercept.*[87] Another climate journalist, the former *Vox* writer David Roberts, runs a Substack site and podcast called *Volts* that educates readers and listeners about energy-transition issues from a progressive point of view. His long-form articles for *Vox* resembled traditional long-form journalism in their explanatory complexity and completeness, and his Volts podcasts are similarly deep and detailed, but his social media presence is often contemptuous of corporations, political moderation, and climate-policy adversaries.

Some defenses of advocacy journalism from both ideological poles invoke the intuition that even the most scrupulous journalist—one dedicated to following the norms of objectivity and completeness—will be influenced by their own subjective sense of what is important for the public to understand and what is missing from the public debate.[88] That sense, in turn, is in part a function of each reporter's individual political leaning or occupational pressures. Therefore, two careful reporters, both aiming for objectivity, can produce significantly different versions of the same story.

Consider, for example, the coverage of grants made by the government under the IIJA's "regional direct air capture [DAC] hubs program" in 2023.[89] The UPI article covering the announcement was mildly positive. It explained that DAC technology removes CO_2 from the ambient air, emphasized how the projects will "help reduce the concentration of carbon dioxide in the atmosphere," and detailed the statutory origins of the grant program. By contrast, the opening paragraphs of the *Washington Post's* coverage of the same announcement used language likely to elicit doubts about the projects, describing them as "giant carbon sucking vacuums," "mammoth projects" consisting of "hulking, costly machinery." Only by reading to the later paragraphs did the reader learn that "mainstream climate scientists . . . no longer see [DAC] as fringe technology" and that "a consensus has emerged at organizations like the International Energy Agency that [DAC] will be an important component to curbing warming."[90] The authors of both stories presumably did their best to tell the public what they believed was important for the public to know within the space they were allotted.

But the existence of that kind of disparity in reporting hardly undermines the value of aspiring to objectivity and completeness. It ought to be evident that, all else being equal, reporters serving an ideologically heterogeneous readership and aspiring to objectivity and completeness will tend to produce fairer, more broadly informative stories even in the presence of unconscious bias. Mainstream journalists must answer to editors who have at least potentially dissimilar views, thereby operating as a potential check on the writer's unconscious bias. By contrast, the domain of advocacy journalists is circumscribed; the set of stories they *might* tell is driven by ideological demands of a narrower, more homogenous audience. In the words of a group of New York University researchers, "Partisan outlets in the conservative media ecosystem are simply not a mirror image of the mainstream news outlets that they often position themselves against. Opinion plays an outsized role in this ecosystem while it is only a part of what mainstream news organizations produce. By the same token, professional journalistic norms are not as widely established in the partisan conservative media, so that conservatives with a taste for both traditionally reported news and congenial opinion may need to sample more widely."[91]

As polarization, tribalism, and the sense of climate urgency grows, this observation can be applied to an increasing share of left-leaning ideological journalism as well. The general problem is that when advocacy journalists frame their coverage so as to nudge their listeners and readers to political conclusions or to portray groups of adversaries as worthy of contempt, they undermine the kind of deep learning that comes from regular engagement with opposing viewpoints.

PARTISAN ASYMMETRY IN ONLINE MEDIA

As with our broader partisan divide, the political distortions of modern information technology do not manifest identically or to the same extent on the ideological right and the ideological left. According to researchers who study the question, there is more right populist messaging online than left populist messaging. Although Fox News and MSNBC were founded the same year, the former has more total viewers and the more popular copycats.[92] There are, of course, left-leaning disinformation purveyors and bots,[93] but research indicates that they are less numerous and widely shared than their right-leaning counterparts.

As suggested by polling data presented in chapter 3, violent, anti-democratic rhetoric has become normalized on conservative broadcast and online media to an extent not seen on left-leaning media. In the words of one media analyst, "The extreme vernacular often flies under the radar, drawing eye rolls from those outside this alternate universe and receiving little media attention. But it shouldn't. Language carries with it serious consequences. And repeatedly conveying to millions of people that their democratically elected leader is a tyrant out to nefariously use the force of government to target and imprison his political opposition carries with it great risk."[94] So when members of Congress referred in early 2024 to convicted January 6 insurrectionists as "hostages," or when former president Donald Trump promised in 2023 to "root out . . . the radical left thugs that live like vermin in our country," they were playing to an audience that has been prepared by right-wing media for that kind of rhetoric. Trump knows that when he says, "I am your justice [and] retribution," he is speaking to voters whose sense of cultural and economic victimhood has been expertly cultivated for more than two decades by those same media outlets.[95]

Some right populists have been openly tactical about disseminating falsehoods. In 2018, Trump adviser Steve Bannon famously said, "Democrats don't matter. The real opposition is the media. And the way to deal with them is to flood the zone with shit." When Trump administration officials promoted "alternative facts" (read: lies), those lies influenced voters' beliefs in part because they were echoed and endorsed by right-wing media.[96] When a partisan voting base is gripped with anger, frustration, fear, and resentment, elected representatives earn support by giving voice to those feelings.[97] Reporters covering Congress during the Trump administration reported that some Republican members were privately aghast by the president's behavior and rhetoric but were unwilling to oppose it publicly.[98] And it was subsequently revealed during litigation that many Fox News hosts and executives were knowingly broadcasting false narratives about fraud in the 2020 election while ridiculing those same narratives in private texts and emails.[99]

But disingenuous leaders can still create sincere belief in their followers. The psychologist Gordon Pennycook and the management scholar David Rand found that repeated exposure to fake-news headlines correlates positively with belief in falsehoods, all else being equal, and that the most partisan users of Twitter/X tend to be more vulnerable to misinformation, regardless of party. But their research also indicates that those who voted for Trump in 2016 were more likely to believe fake news than those who voted for Hillary Clinton and that "right leaning users are . . . more likely [than others] to share misinformation."[100] That may be because there are more false claims in circulation aimed at conservatives. Some conservatives may sense this. According to survey data, conservatives are three times more likely to watch left-leaning news sources than liberals are to watch right-leaning outlets.[101]

A decade or so of social science research has demonstrated that Fox News viewers are systematically less well informed for having watched Fox News Channel.[102] Perhaps not coincidentally, aggregate partisan differences over climate science seem to reflect the effectiveness of anti-climate-science messaging in right-wing media. In 1989, there was virtually no difference between the parties in voter opinions about climate change. In the intervening years, as the climate consensus has solidified in the worldwide scientific community, Democratic but not Republican voter opinion has moved with it. A considerable body of research shows that conservative media have been a driver of that Republican trend. Today, conservative media feature as "experts" people who question the existence of a climate-science consensus.[103]

Right populist messaging often plays to city mouse/country mouse divisions that have plagued U.S. politics throughout the nation's history.[104] For an experienced political consultant such as Roger Ailes, exploiting and fanning those resentments was a simple task, one made easier by left-leaning media outlets that provided fuel for those fires. During the comedian Jon Stewart's first stint as host of *The Daily*

Show (beginning in early 1999), the program had a symbiotic relationship with Fox News. The writer Jesse Bernstein described the dynamic this way:

> [*The Daily Show*] was a cultural touchstone that dealt in mockery and ridicule, as good political comedy should. It parsed the bluster to find the nugget of insincerity that drives selfish politics. But . . . those who counted *The Daily Show* and its even jokier spawn, *The Colbert Report*, as news sources slowly but surely created an echo chamber. The process went something like this: Someone said something on Fox News that mainstream liberalism didn't like; Stewart and/or Colbert aired a sustained critique of the idea and the thinking behind it; liberal internet publications hailed it as the greatest rhetorical victory since Darrow argued for Scopes; liberals' Facebook feeds full of liberal friends filled up with clips of the takedown. *No one learned anything, no one engaged with an idea, and nothing outside of a very specific set of ideas was given any real credence.*[105]

Jon Stewart's presentation was intended as entertainment, not news. It nevertheless provided ammunition for message makers in right-leaning outlets. That dynamic may be one reason why Stewart subsequently later moved into work that focuses more on long-form dialogue and less on point-and-laugh ridicule, and why *The Daily Show* began to diagnose the news a bit more gently in its next iteration.[106]

EXPERTS IN THE MODERN INFORMATION ENVIRONMENT

The internet was supposed to help us access the wisdom of crowds, and sometimes it does. But it also spreads negative, emotional messages farther and faster than positive, factual ones and falsehoods farther and faster than truths.[107] Even in my own social media community of energy-policy wonks, posts that emphasize climate urgency or express contempt for climate villains generate a much more enthusiastic response than posts that raise questions about energy-transition trade-offs, explore opposing views (noncontemptuously), or urge engagement with policy adversaries.

This online environment promotes misunderstanding of climate science, the science of evolution, and genetically modified crops—all science. Researchers emphasize how "insular social networks can be especially ripe for misinformation."[108] For example, one of the more persistent purveyors of climate misinformation is the former Trump environmental adviser Steve Milloy, who told his 123,400 Twitter/X followers in 2023 that "NOAA makes it official. Last 8 years . . . global cooling." What the NOAA's update on the climate in 2023 *actually* said is that "all six major global temperature datasets used for analysis in the report agree that the last eight years (2015–22) were the eight warmest on record."[109]

The political scientist Shanto Iyengar and the sociologist Douglas Massey attribute declining public trust in science to these sorts of dynamics: "Whenever scientific findings clash with a person's or group's political agenda, be it conservative (as with climate science and immigration) or liberal (as with genetically modified foods and vaccination risk), scientists can expect to encounter a targeted campaign of fake news, misinformation and disinformation in response. Under these circumstances, the information is *unlikely to penetrate the cognitive structures of those it threatens*."[110] This explains, for example, how in a few short years the antivaccine movement moved from a disrespected, tiny, bipartisan, science-denying fringe to a "modern political force" that has successfully cultivated vaccine skepticism across a broad swath of society, particularly among Republican voters.[111]

There is some disagreement among scholars over the qualities that make people susceptible to misinformation in the first place. One view is that critical-thinking skills have little effect on gullibility; that is, because emotion and reason work together to shape political beliefs, "people outsource their political positions to their communities," such that their issue positions are virtually unchangeable through reasoned argument.[112] Others believe the ability and willingness to think critically can inoculate people against fake news. In a series of research papers, Pennycook and Rand found that the "disposition to think analytically" correlates negatively with belief in fake news,[113] suggesting that the habit of thinking critically as we consume information may promote resistance to fake news.

Access to the truth *can* be an antidote to false belief online, but research tells us that truth faces an uphill battle. One problem is that truth rarely confronts falsehoods because most of us share information *within* online bubbles rather than *across* them.[114] When scientific truth does confront false belief online, truth tends to prevail *if* a trusted member of the online group understands and embraces that truth and tries to dispel the false belief within the group. Even then, say researchers, the truth may not win out if "social movements or social media elevate the adoption of a particular set of false facts and logic."[115] Thus, social pressure helps attractive falsehoods endure online, and only in-group experts have the credibility to correct mistaken beliefs online.

This tendency suggests an edit of an old axiom: "With ~~great~~ online power comes ~~great~~ online responsibility." That is, experts can use their in-group influence either to support norms of actively open-minded thinking or not to support them. They can feed partisan tribalism or dampen it.[116] To some of us, that power implies a responsibility for experts to be accurate, objective, circumspect, and complete when speaking publicly within the domain of their expertise. There are experts who disagree with the proposition that lobbying ought to take a back seat to education in their online or professional speech.[117] Arguably, when experts speak publicly about such issues, their first duty is to educate, which implies a duty not to mislead. Experts can take to Twitter/X (or YouTube, Facebook, Instagram, an email list, a message board, a podcast, a blog) to place a thumb on the scale of one point of view or the other, but if they do so in ways that omit or misrepresent parts of the full story, they are betraying a trust relationship with the unseen audience.[118]

In their public speech, many experts do promote norms of actively open-minded thinking. But the forces pushing energy and climate experts—writers, pundits, and academics—to "sand the inconvenient edges off the facts" are much stronger today than ever before. Polarized views create a sense of urgency about political outcomes, which is amplified by ideological and social media and then reflected in mainstream media. Some experts lobby carefully and quietly so as to support the truths that (per Bertrand Russell) they "think could have beneficial social effects if [they] were believed" but not the truths that might push the audience away from those beneficial beliefs.[119] Other experts lobby less quietly and join the process of ramping up contempt for an opposing idea, policy, party, or person. Some discuss policy issues online as if venting privately to friends, with sarcasm, mockery, hyperbole, or ad hominem dismissals of opposing views and those who hold them. The examples in table 4.2, many involving harsh criticism of the IRA from the ideological right and left, illustrate the dogmatic and contemptuous tone sometimes taken by online experts in energy-policy discussions.

Most online experts presumably have reasons for communicating as they do.[120] Some, including some scholars, may see their role as providing the intellectual foundation for a social movement and so reject the idea that their duties include the acknowledgment of truths that could be used as ammunition by opponents. Some online experts may believe that their followers understand that they are venting and so will discount their hyperbolic rhetoric accordingly. Or they may believe that the policy adversary deserves their contempt, either as a specific person or as the representative of a contemptible party, ideology, or demographic or economic class. They may choose an entertainingly combative online style to drive traffic to their more substantive treatments of the issues elsewhere. Some may justify their lobbying as necessary to counteract historic power imbalances that bias dominant narratives in favor of a traditionally powerful demographic or other groups. But as the preceding review of the research shows, rhetoric that feeds contempt for others does not have the desired persuasive effects. Today, narratives that impute immorality to an out-group mobilize not only my side but the other side as well. The set of persuadable voters is more likely to be moved by arguments that challenge false narratives directly on their merits.

Wendy Brown, whose essay "Max Weber's Ethical Pedagogy for a Nihilistic Age" (2023) was quoted in the introduction, argues that academic experts can simultaneously acknowledge the power imbalances inherent in the sociopolitical origins of ideas (something she calls "facticity") *and* exercise "self-consciousness, care, and restraint" about their political views in the classroom:

TABLE 4.2 Hyperbole, Sarcasm, and Ridicule by Experts in Climate Debate Online

From the Ideological Left	From the Ideological Right
This [the IRA] is the worst climate bill ever passed.[a]	"The IRA is one of the most corrupt laws in US history. It . . . provides billions of $ for Democrat political machinery disguised as 'climate justice' funding."[b]
"The white men in charge of addressing climate change, who still think it's 2005, really need to fucking go!"[c]	"Every time you see the words 'climate change' replace them with 'gobbledegook' [sic] and you will have a much more useful sentence."[d]
"[Republicans are] going to be maximum assholes at every juncture no matter what Ds do or don't do."[e] "You really should retract all your stupid tweets."[f]	"[Green-energy policies] have nothing to do with common sense. They are all about the politically well-connected draining money from the U.S. taxpayers and indulging the fantasies of climate catastrophists."[g]
"They are literally trying to cover up the effects of their policies by forbidding govt scientists from extending their models past 2050. They are murderers erasing evidence of their crimes."[h]	"The delusional climate apocalypse-mongers will destabilize the economy and worsen the environment."[i]
"Only a washed up water boy for corrupt politicians would celebrate handing our public lands over to the fossil fuel industry for more drilling and fracking as the world burns."[j]	"Stupid westerners are bent on societal suicide via climate idiocy. Thank God, Saudia Arabia wants to make money." [k]

[a] The progressive journalist David Sirota, interviewed by Briahna Joy Gray, "The Worst Climate Bill That Has Ever Passed," *Bad Faith* (podcast), August 2022.

[b] Energy-policy writer Alex Epstein (@AlexEpstein), tweet, Twitter/X, September 14, 2022, https://x .com/AlexEpstein/status/1570078787450159107?s=20. In late 2023, Epstein's Twitter/X account had 188,800 followers.

[c] Climate journalist Amy Westervelt (@AmyWestervelt), tweet, Twitter/X, May 25, 2022, https://x .com/amywestervelt/status/1507498696639856641?s=20. In May 2023, Westervelt's Twitter/X account had 63,700 followers.

[d] Patrick Moore (@EcoSenseNow), tweet, Twitter/X, March 18, 2023, https://x.com/EcoSenseNow /status/1637114120230293504?s=20. Moore is a former president of Greenpeace Canada turned industry consultant. In May 2023, his Twitter/X account had 148,500 followers.

[e] Climate journalist David Roberts (@DrVolts), tweet, Twitter/X, July 13, 2018, since deleted, accessed July 2019. In May 2023, Roberts's Twitter/X account had 197,300 followers.

[f] Stanford engineering professor Mark Jacobson (@MZJacobson), tweet, Twitter/X, sometime between 2016 and 2021, now deleted. Jacobson posted this tweet in response to a tweet showing that solar energy is typically unavailable in the Netherlands when demand for energy from heat pumps is high. In May 2023, Jacobson's Twitter/X account had 40,800 followers.

[g] Manhattan Institute (@ManhattanInst), tweet, Twitter/X, February 9, 2022, https://x.com /ManhattanInst/status/1491532391831289856?s=20. The Manhattan Institute is a conservative think tank. In May 2023, its Twitter/X account had 66,800 followers.

[h] Writer Genevieve Gunther (@DoctorVive), tweet, Twitter/X, May 27, 2019, https://x.com/DoctorVive /status/1133143240083988481?s=20. In October 2023, Gunther's Twitter/X account had 69,200 followers.

[i] Jordan Peterson (@jordanbpeterson), tweet, Twitter/X, March 21, 2023, https://x.com/jordanb peterson/status/1638384062623813632?s=20. Peterson is an academic psychologist and critic of several strains of modern progressivism. In May 2023, his Twitter/X account had 4.2 million followers.

[j] Ana Kasparian (@AnaKasparian), tweet, Twitter/X, July 28, 2022, https://x.com/AnaKasparian /status/1552701867464896512?s=20. Kasparian is a producer of the podcast *TYT* (*The Young Turks*) and was responding to a critic of her earlier criticism of the IRA. In the summer of 2023, she had 530,000 followers on Twitter/X.

[k] Former Trump adviser Steve Milloy (@JunkScience), tweet, Twitter/X, October 17, 2023, https://x .com/JunkScience/status/1714314135884767406?s=20. In October 2023, Milloy's Twitter/X account had 123,400 followers.

Even with the world in an emergency state . . . where we may want every scholarly hand on deck, a moat between academic and political life is essential. *This moat is vital to protecting reflection, imagination, and accountability in knowledge production and dissemination.* It is also vital to protecting an understanding and practice of facticity against the indifference to it generated by nihilism while remaining faithful to the complexity of knowledge formation. It distinguishes the place where values are struggled for from the place where they can be queried and analyzed, doubted, taken apart, reconsidered.[121]

For many people, social media is today's de facto classroom. It may be that online snark and dismissiveness have become an unstoppable societal norm. But that fact ought not stop us from acknowledging that when experts put promotion of a social cause ahead of truth seeking in their public speech, they are misleading their followers,[122] strengthening the centrifugal forces at the center of our political dysfunction and undermining learning. Energy-transition politics would improve if more online experts were to focus on making sure their followers understand the whole truth about policy issues, including the ideas and evidence that challenge their preferred policies or beliefs.

* * *

The internet is not the meritocratic marketplace of ideas that many hoped it would be. Online political discussion is circumscribed, semi-anonymous discussion dominated by intense partisans reacting to ideologically censored news feeds. It is an environment of heightened emotion and continuous invitations to focus our attention on the worst aspects of our policy opponents and their ideas. It facilitates the spread of false belief and is alienating voters from the foundational liberal democratic institutions on which we depend to resolve social conflict peacefully.[123]

Scholars who study the rise and fall of democracies see danger in this trend. The historian Timothy Snyder's best seller *On Tyranny* (2017) urges us to try to recover the norms of the old information system. His recommendations for doing so include multiple admonitions to "separate yourself from the internet" and engage in more face-to-face communication. He urges readers: "Figure things out for yourself. Spend more time with long articles. Subsidize investigative journalism by subscribing to print media. Realize that some of what is on the internet is there to harm you. Learn about sites that investigate propaganda campaigns. . . . *Take responsibility for what you communicate to others.*"[124]

While serving as the U.S. ambassador to the United Nations, Nikki Haley urged the same careful approach to online speech when chastising a group of young Republicans for their habit of trying to "own" liberals online. "I know that it's fun and that it can feel good, but . . . are you persuading anyone? Who are you persuading? . . . [T]*his kind of speech isn't leadership*—it's the exact opposite."[125] When faced with bots, online mercenaries, and other persuaders who mislead for fun or political or financial gain, voters' instincts are to "fight fire with fire," but that is not the best response.

More productive public discussion of the energy transition is possible, but it probably requires acceptance of a proposition with which some readers will disagree; if so, perhaps a second corollary proposition will sound more persuasive.

> Proposition: *There are considerably fewer cartoon villains among the key players in energy-transition debates than some in the climate coalition imagine there to be.*

The Roman stoic Seneca observed that "we suffer more in imagination than in reality."[126] We are too quick to infer that those who oppose our policy objectives are ignorant or evil. Most of the people who populate both sides of the energy-policy debate are neither villains nor saints. They are people who behave and reason in ways that are influenced by the incentives they face. The fundamental attribution error pushes us to believe otherwise.

> Corollary: *Focusing on the villainy of others discourages actively open-minded thinking and obscures important dimensions of the energy-transition task.*

There is now an entire ideological media industry devoted to cultivating the moral case against policy adversaries. It discourages people from engaging others on the substance of the issues at the center of the energy transition. Given the math of majority rule and the magnitude and complexity of the trade-offs involved in the energy transition, members of the climate coalition will have to talk seriously rather than dismissively about energy-transition trade-offs beyond their circle of like-minded friends and colleagues. Those trade-offs and how we discuss them are the subject of the next chapter.

5

FACING ENERGY-TRANSITION TRADE-OFFS

Could you imagine a world without oil? No automobiles. No heat. And polish. No ink. And nylon. No detergents. . . . No polythene. Dry cleaning fluid. And waterproof coats. . . .

—Fictional oil executives, *Local Hero* (Bill Forsyth, 1983)

THE BITTERNESS of modern political debate can make acknowledging the difficulty of the trade-offs at the heart of the energy transition seem like a difficult concession. But it is not. To the contrary, because voters worry about energy trade-offs, we set back the energy transition when we deny its complexity. This chapter explores that complexity and those worries and why experts ought to be patient and scrupulous about acknowledging their importance and about discussing them honestly and transparently.

In the documentary *An Inconvenient Truth* (Davis Guggenheim, 2006), former vice president Al Gore expressed optimism about "Americans'" capacity to tackle the climate challenge, even as he acknowledged the magnitude of the task. His optimism about politics may seem naive today, but at the time he spoke, bipartisanship seemed possible. A year earlier, Senator John McCain's (R–AZ) Climate Stewardship Act was cosponsored in the Senate by two other Republicans, Olympia Snowe (R–ME) and Lincoln Chaffee (R–RI), and by one Republican turned Independent, Jim Jeffords (I–VT), along with thirteen Democrats.[1] Only six years later, though, Chafee had left the GOP, and Snowe had retired from the Senate, citing "hyperpartisanship." The chapter epigraph is from a film from 1983 that Gore has called his favorite movie.[2] It is the story of a fictional proposal for a North Sea oil development in a bucolic seaside village. The story pitted environmental values against economic and development goals (spoiler: environmental values prevail), and the quotation is a colloquy from the film describing how deeply petroleum products are embedded in our daily lives.

Affordable, non-carbon-based substitutes for some of the products mentioned in the quotation have been developed since the film was made, but petroleum remains deeply embedded in the economy. It retains a more than 90 percent market share in the transportation sector, and many fuel and nonfuel products continue to be derived from the petroleum molecule. They include so-called difficult-to-decarbonize products in industries such as cement and steel as well as high-performance materials we place in the "chemicals" sector of the economy—such as Kevlar, or carbon fiber, from which so much military, aerospace, and sporting-goods equipment is made.[3] Finding non-carbon-based substitutes for petroleum products takes time and money, but very few doubt that it is possible. Indeed, for reasons described in previous chapters, this is an economically auspicious moment for the energy transition. But those chapters also explain why it is a politically inauspicious one. The propaganda machine makes it harder to grapple openly with the difficult trade-offs the transition entails. It makes some people too certain that the task will be impossible or impossibly costly. It makes others too certain that the transition will be "easy enough" for most voters. And it makes each group contemptuous and dismissive of the other. All of which breeds more misunderstanding of the transition's particulars.

Historical counterfactuals are always speculative. But it is probably true that our economy's deep reliance on petroleum products is due less to that industry's long tradition of throwing its political weight around than to the attributes of its products.[4] That is not to deny or excuse the immorality of oil titans' complicity in colonial oppression, American political corruption, and funding of misinformation about climate science.[5] Rather, it is simply to acknowledge that fossil fuels offered nineteenth- and twentieth-century Americans better energy services at lower prices, services that they enjoyed relatively unqualifiedly until about fifty years ago. Now most voters want to wean the U.S. economy from energy that produces carbon emissions. They understand that anthropogenic climate change is imposing increasingly serious costs on society, *but* they also worry about the effect of the energy transition on their daily lives. So they are understandably skeptical about rallying rhetoric that dismisses either of those concerns.

Getting to net zero requires policymakers to confront what some scholars call the *energy trilemma*, the question of how to balance social preferences for an energy supply that is simultaneously *reliable*, *affordable*, and *clean*.[6] Each of these objectives subsumes several ideas. For example, an energy supply that people have trouble using or that isn't resilient in the face of a changing climate isn't a reliable one. Likewise, affordability is relative; what is affordable to one person may not be to another. And, of course, clean energy can be measured many ways: carbon emissions versus other emissions, emissions from electricity generation versus life-cycle emissions, and so on. Cognitive biases push experts and laypeople alike to balance these three objectives in ways that are influenced by their respective political philosophies— their views on the relative virtues of markets and regulation, intuitions about the effectiveness of different policy levers, and beliefs about how regulatory politics works.

These biases can affect our judgments (or best guesses) about an uncertain technoeconomic future. But past experience suggests that we ought to be humble about our ability to predict that future. Energy experts were surprised by the high cost of nuclear power in the 1980s, the fracking revolution in the 2000s, the solar revolution in the 2010s, and, more recently, the energy-market disruptions caused by the COVID-19 pandemic and the Ukraine war. We can anticipate *the fact* of technoeconomic change but not the particulars: how much a technology will cost, who will pay, and how the transition will affect the most economically vulnerable. Yet the propaganda machine tempts us to be selectively optimistic about the future affordability or performance of (dis)favored net-zero technologies and policies. But in today's fragmented political environment, "trust me, this will work" assurances are less effective with voters than they once were.

This chapter makes the case for mixing ambition about carbon-emissions goals—the "what" questions—with transparency, caution, and circumspection about the trade-offs inherent in the "how" questions. It suggests *keeping our eyes on the prize:* namely, stabilizing and reducing atmospheric carbon. We are more likely to build *durable* voter support for the transition and to minimize its opportunity costs by leaving all net-zero options open, by discussing trade-offs openly and frankly, and by engaging critical questions rather than dismissing them or attacking the questioner.

RELIABILITY AND THE ENERGY TRANSITION

Before electricity-market restructuring, the management and coordination of power production and power delivery were a mostly intra-utility matter, focused on decisions about how to match supply to predicted variation in demand.[7] IOUs and regulators ensured adequate reserves by building enough power plants to cover anticipated peak demands, and they did so with considerable confidence that those plants would be available when called upon to serve those peaks. Restructuring "externalized" some of these decisions. That is, it replaced a set of informal, intrafirm coordination decisions with a series of arms-length market transactions with third parties. This replacement reduced grid operators' direct leverage over generation plants and their operation.[8]

Across much of the United States, the capacity factors of fossil-fueled generating plants have been declining. Fossil-fueled generators *can* be available for a larger percentage of the year than wind and solar plants can, but grid operators choose to dispatch renewables more often because renewables are cheaper to use when they are available.[9] This increased reliance on cheap, clean wind and solar generation means that there are more frequent weather-driven fluctuations on the supply side than there once were. Therefore, grid operators must increasingly attend to (read: pay for) the availability of resources that can support (read: back up) renewables throughout the day and year. The presence of more wind and solar power on the grid also changes the way planners secure those future reserves. Where they once simply built enough generators to cover projected future needs (with a reserve margin), knowing those generators would likely be available almost all of the time, now they must procure reserves in ways that account for the seasonal and diurnal variation of wind and solar power.

Despite early worries about the effects of these developments on system reliability, grid engineers have met these challenges as renewable generation grows. Their solutions include improved weather forecasting, changes in dispatch and scheduling protocols, improvements in sensing technology and computing power, compensated demand response, and more. They also continue to rely in part on legacy fossil-fueled power plants that can be available when intermittent renewables are not.[10] But there are increasingly affordable "clean-firm" alternatives, the proven and promising zero- or net-zero-carbon technologies that can be available just as (or almost as) reliably as fossil generation: geothermal power, nuclear power, fossil-fueled power with CCS, stored hydroelectric energy, bioenergy with CCS, and certain demand-side resources among them. Right now, most of these clean-firm options tend to cost more, excluding pollution costs, than "dirty"-firm sources. But the IRA ought to spur innovation that will make them cheaper and better.

Decarbonization nevertheless complicates the reliability challenge. In 2023, leading energy modelers characterized the challenge this way: "With the transition towards more variable and uncertain supply resources, operational uncertainty becomes a bigger driver for investment needs, which intersect with planning decisions and long-run uncertainty."[11] Thus, getting to net zero requires affordable clean-firm generation, particularly as we "electrify" activities formerly reliant on direct use of fossil fuels. For better or worse, each clean-firm technology has its partisans. Their views may be sincere but sometimes manifest in the form of "Pollyanna" arguments that downplay uncertainty and minimize trade-off risk or "cry wolf" arguments that exaggerate the downside risks of competing clean-firm technologies.

This sort of lobbying may be the product of a sense of urgency about the transition coupled with worry about the political obstacles. There is a strong temptation to finesse the reliability challenges associated with a net-zero electric grid in order to reassure voters that the challenges can be managed to their satisfaction.[12] There are countless examples of experts being less than circumspect about this issue online. Here are a few:

- An expert on an email list to which I belong suggested that because "renewables are cheaper . . . than fossil energy, and the delivery costs are comparable, . . . the renewable path" will be cheaper than the current system. But we do not know the cost of maintaining current levels of electric-service reliability on a mostly renewables grid.[13]

- An article published in the *Proceedings of the National Academy of Sciences* in 2022 claimed that the capacity factors of existing power (mostly fossil-fueled) plants represent a "direct measurement of the efficacy" of those plants and a proxy for the amount of clean-firm generation that will be needed to back up renewables on the net-zero grid.[14] But those capacity-factor numbers do not exactly represent either of those things because in an unpredictable world a generation asset's broader availability (beyond its actual use) matters. Future clean-firm generation needs will depend on yet to be determined features of the net-zero system.

- In their efforts to rally online support for the transition, some energy-transition thought leaders try to tamp down, mock, or otherwise delegitimize online questions about the intermittency of wind and solar power or questions about pandemic- and war-triggered interruptions of mineral and labor supply for clean-energy production.[15] But these are real issues in need of open discussion if we are to make the transition a reality.

- Similarly, experts are sometimes tempted to imply that because severe weather can disrupt gas- and coal-fired power supplies, "all sources of electricity are 'weather dependent.' "[16] This is technically true but quite misleading.

Energy-transition opponents are certain to raise these questions about how to ensure that the net-zero grid is reliable and affordable. The questions *will* resonate with many voters. Proponents of the transition ought, therefore, to embrace that discussion rather than avoid or dismiss it.

MODELING A RELIABLE, AFFORDABLE NET-ZERO SYSTEM

Those who model the energy future can make highly educated guesses and judgments about these and other questions. For every location in the United States, they know what technologies and fuels currently serve energy demand; how demand has varied hour by hour in the past; what the weather conditions were over those same hours, including how much the sun tends to shine and the wind tends to blow; and various important characteristics of the customer base. Modelers estimate future population growth, the cost trajectories of the various technologies and fuels, and how energy demand will change over time. With all of those assumptions, estimates, and data inputs, they can model how energy supply and demand might adapt to the imposition of carbon-emission constraints over time.

Models also show us *potential* technoeconomic paths to a net-zero economy. Most confirm the importance of clean-firm technologies to ensure reliability.[17] A closer look at three of these studies—the Princeton Net-Zero America study, the National Academy of Sciences Accelerating Decarbonization of the American Energy System, and McKinsey & Company's Navigating America's Net Zero Frontier— help illustrate the nature of the trade-offs between emissions reductions and reliability.[18] All three models emphasize the importance of getting to net zero on the electric grid *before* 2050 because proven zero-emission electric-generation technologies do exist and because we can shift some direct uses of fossil fuels (in driving, cooking, and heating) to electricity relatively cheaply. All three models recognize that replacing fossil and nuclear plants with less frequently available wind and solar power requires building more generating capacity to serve the same amount of demand. And because weather varies regionally, more generating capacity requires some combination of stored renewable energy, new transmission connections, and clean-firm capacity. Therefore, all three models back up wind and solar through some combination of these resources, and all three recognize that these backup requirements can be reduced by assuming more efficient future consumption of electricity.

Table 5.1 summarizes some of their conclusions. The models project a much bigger electric system, at least double the size of today's. The least-cost options selected by the models tend to favor some combination of retaining existing natural gas (with CCS), batteries, or other storage and developing other "green gases" such as hydrogen and renewable methane, as well as nuclear power and biomass facilities.[19] Geothermal power also plays a significant role

TABLE 5.1 Modeling a Net-Zero Electricity Sector

Princeton Net-Zero America Model

Goal: Net Zero by 2050	Electricity Infrastructure at Net Zero
Generating capacity in 2022	~1,300 GW
Generating capacity in 2050	Ranges from 3,800 GW to ~6,200 GW, depending on the scenario
New renewables	Ranges from six to twenty-eight times current capacity
Firm capacity	Most scenarios rely on some natural gas + CCS or with hydrogen blending (500–1,000 GW); some foresee big increases in biomass power plants
Transmission buildout	Ranges from approximately two to five times the current grid

Source: "Net-Zero America: Potential Pathways, Infrastructure and Impacts," Net-Zero America Project, 2021, https://netzeroamerica.princeton.edu/.

National Academy of Sciences Accelerating Decarbonization of the American Energy System

Goal: Net Zero by 2050	Electricity Infrastructure at Net Zero
Generating capacity in 2022	~1,300 GW
Generating capacity in 2050	Not specified
Renewables	Add 600 GW by 2030
Firm capacity	Add 6–11 GW nuclear; 10–60 GW storage; retain natural gas capacity but no new natural gas; add CCS and green gases
Transmission buildout	Increase by 60 percent

Source: "Accelerating Decarbonization of the U.S. Energy System," National Academy of Sciences, 2021, https://doi.org/10.17226/25932.

McKinsey & Company's Navigating America's Net-Zero Frontier

Goal: Net Zero by 2050	Electricity Infrastructure at Net Zero
Generation in 2022	~4,500 terawatt-hours (twh)
Generation in 2050	~10,000 twh
Renewables	Install 40 GW/year 2025–2030; 100 GW/year 2030–2050
Firm capacity	Mostly fossil gas with CCS + green gas (hydrogen or biogas) turbines + smaller shares for nuclear and other clean-firm techs
Transmission buildout	No numbers specified. Assumes buildout to support low-carbon system

Source: "America's Net-Zero Shift," McKinsey & Company, 2022, http://ceros.mckinsey.com/americaco2-2-2-2-2-2-3-1-2-1-2-4-2-1-2-2-1-1-2-2.

in several of the models' scenarios. The models' transmission-buildout projections range from a 60 percent increase up to a four-fold increase in the size of the transmission grid, depending on how much electricity customers will take from the grid under each model scenario.[20] And as explained in chapter 2, that transmission buildout would facilitate investment in hundreds of gigawatts of new wind and solar power plants in the most economically beneficial locations.

We can appreciate the importance of clean-firm power generation in another way—by considering the alternative. The Stanford engineering professor Mark Z. Jacobson and various coauthors have modeled an all-renewable energy system: no nuclear power and no fossil fuels. Consider their modeling for the state of New York. Total generating capacity on the New York ISO grid in 2022 was approximately 40 GW.[21] Under the Jacobson plan, it would be 254 GW and would require (among other things) more than 800 new 50-metawatt (MW) photovoltaic solar installations, twelve thousand 5-MW offshore wind turbines, four thousand onshore wind turbines, and thousands of wave and tidal generators.[22] In 2023, New York State had no commercial wave, tidal, or offshore wind facilities, though several offshore wind projects were in the planning phase. Some researchers contend that the Jacobson model would not provide a sufficiently reliable supply of energy in any event.[23] Even if it would, the construction of that much infrastructure in New York in the reasonably near future seems to assume away the distributional conflicts and delays that are the stuff of regulatory law and politics. Yet the Jacobson model has received much more attention in the popular press than the other, more realistic models presented here.[24]

In addition, the challenge of incentivizing the investment that can complement renewables changes continuously over time and place. For example, the glut of solar power in California has shifted the state's daily net "peak" demand from late afternoon to the early evening, making early-evening supply valuable.[25] Today the technology that serves most of that early-evening peak (gas-fired power) is also available to serve other backup needs, such as diurnal or seasonal wind droughts or extreme-heat events. As planners substitute lithium-ion batteries for gas in that role, they worry about *dunkelflaute*, the rare but periodic droughts of wind (and, to a lesser extent, solar) energy that last longer than a day or two.[26]

Of course, elected politicians of both parties worry about reliability and cost trade-offs, as evidenced by the "out provisions" written into state laws that chart a path to net-zero energy. For example,

- Minnesota's net-zero legislation authorizes the state's PUC to "modify or delay" its implementation "if the commission determines it is in the public interest to do so."[27]
- New York's carbon-free standard authorizes that state's PUC to "temporarily suspend or modify" an obligation under the law after a formal determination that the state program would "impede the provision of safe and adequate electric service."[28]
- New Mexico's net-zero clean-energy standard contains exceptions to its requirements if compliance is not "technically feasible" or makes electric service "unaffordable."[29]

The Obama EPA's CPP included similar out provisions in response to reliability worries expressed by grid operators and regulators.[30] These kinds of escape clauses recognize the high priority that voters and politicians place on ensuring reliability. Energy-transition opponents use these uncertainties to stoke fears that green energy is inherently unreliable, using the hashtag "#BidenBlackouts." When energy-transition experts dismiss those fears, the opponents' message resonates even more strongly.

TECHNOLOGY PARTISANS VERSUS
TECHNOLOGY AGNOSTICS

Most models of a net-zero future *assume* and *optimize*: that is, modelers make (highly) educated guesses about future energy needs and let the model choose the optimal (usually, least-cost) generation mix based on those assumptions. In this sense, the models are technologically agnostic but politically hopeful. Real-life investment decisions are often suboptimal: we will build the energy infrastructure that investors are willing to fund and that can navigate legal and political obstacles successfully.[31] Modelers can account for laws that prohibit particular net-zero technologies but not for the political or social barriers that circumscribe investor choice. Suboptimal choices may make it incrementally more difficult and/or costly to get to net zero. So does policy-instrument partisanship. A carbon tax, a cap-and-trade regime, a net-zero performance standard, emission-based mandates, or even energy subsidies—all can be fashioned to reward or require net-zero energy, whatever its source. Yet policymakers often specify the technologies they want, thereby circumscribing the menu of alternatives from which to optimize.

Some technological partisanship grows out of proponents' differing assumptions about ancillary questions such as "What will/won't be effective, affordable, and so on about each technology in the future?" Some of this partisanship presumably is born of the sort of cognitive dynamics described in chapter 4. In the space-constrained world of social media debate, these beliefs take the form of strong proclamations, phrased in ways that deflect critical examination:

> "Any answer that doesn't include efficiency and carbon sequestration of some kind is . . . not a solution."
> "If your energy plan doesn't include nuclear, you don't have a plan you have an ideology."
> "If your climate policy doesn't include a phase out of fossil-fuel production, it's a sham."

As suggested by these quotations, much technology partisanship concerns fossil fuels and nuclear energy.[32] For example, some members of the climate coalition have objected to oil and gas firms' participation in IRA-subsidized CCS projects, negative-emissions projects, and hydrogen-production projects.[33] Others welcome their participation because well-resourced oil and gas firms can scale and commercialize these nascent technologies or because the least expensive technologies for effectively reducing atmospheric carbon *might* include carbon sequestration or hydrogen.

Those who oppose a role for oil and gas companies in a net-zero future presumably base their opposition on some combination of the following beliefs:

- That geologic carbon sequestration will never be economical or effective;[34]
- that upstream GHG emissions associated with gas production will not be adequately regulated in the future;[35]
- that fossil-fuel firms will exercise political power that subverts the goal of reaching net zero;[36] and
- that the fossil-fuel industry ought to be shut down or nationalized on ethical grounds.[37]

It is fair to say that the online tone of this debate within the climate coalition is sometimes vitriolic. For example, the climate activist and author Genevieve Gunther characterizes some discussion of the costs of decarbonizing as apologia for "genocide" committed by oil and gas companies.[38] And consider a climate journalist's response in 2021 to an ExxonMobil Twitter/X ad touting its carbon-capture research: "These craven psychopaths have fine-tuned their social media ad buys to piggyback carbon capture greenwash onto IPCC tweets."[39] An academic climate scientist's response to the journalist's tweet suggested a different interpretation of the ads: "What if carbon dioxide removal (CDR) isn't some capitalist ideology but just those of us who care about people, creatures, and ecosystems trying our best?"[40]

Given the transferability of their in-house drilling and geological expertise to energy-transition technologies, oil and gas companies will almost certainly be among the firms claiming IRA tax credits for investing in geologic sequestration, geothermal energy, and hydrogen production. Widespread doubts to the contrary notwithstanding, geological sequestration in deep saline aquifers almost certainly offers important advantages over biological sequestration. The U.S. Geological Service estimates that the United States has the capacity to store between 2,400 and 3,700 metric gigatons of CO_2 underground, while the analogous figure for biological sequestration is less than 10 gigatons.[41] And geological sequestration is more secure than biological sequestration, which depends on promises to create or maintain forests and vegetation over decades, promises that often do not survive changes in property ownership or governments, wildfires, and so on.[42] Nevertheless, to those who see the oil and gas industry as the political root of the climate problem, these considerations seem not to resonate.

This schism manifests in technical disputes as well, including fights over whether and how to build carbon-sequestration projects, including the DAC projects discussed in chapter 4, and whether the IRA's subsidies for new hydrogen-production facilities ought to require the use of "hourly matching" when procuring renewable electricity used in the facility.[43] Some researchers favor requiring hourly matching based on their conclusion that it will be sufficiently affordable; others estimate that doing so will be so expensive as to slow the energy transition.[44] Technology partisanship over fossil fuels will presumably continue to drive conflict over the implementation of hourly matching.

Technological partisanship about nuclear power reflects a different kind of split within the climate coalition—one that is a legacy of the past. According to the National Conference of State Legislatures, twelve states retain statutory bans on development of new nuclear power plants within their borders, about half the number that existed during the heyday of antinuclear sentiment. In 2023, all twelve of these states were under Democratic Party control. That is not surprising, given Pew Research polling showing that voters who are most concerned about climate change are also most strongly opposed to nuclear power.[45] This schism is evident among climate activists online. Years ago, I opened my Twitter/X feed to a tweet by a PhD student who was announcing the forthcoming publication of his research on decarbonizing the electric grid. His tweet described the paper as suggesting a role for nuclear power. I was puzzled by a derisive, dismissive response to the tweet from a prominent academic environmental scientist. I responded (I thought politely) that perhaps we should wait to read the study before dismissing it. "That's enough. You're BLOCKED!" was the scientist's response (both to me and to the grad student).

I subsequently learned that some in the climate coalition view proponents of nuclear power with suspicion—referring to them online as "nuclear bros."[46] This label may be a reaction to the messaging of the Breakthrough Institute (BTI), an NGO that advances the idea that reliance on renewables alone will harm the world's poor by slowing economic growth.[47] One of BTI's founders has since become a fierce opponent of wind and solar energy and has split from the organization; the other founder sometimes engages in acrimonious Twitter/X feuds when provoked by critics of BTI.[48] It may also be that for NGOs that have opposed nuclear power assiduously since the 1980s, it may be difficult to reconsider that position now. Some younger activists are pushing environmental NGOs to make just that sort of pivot.[49] Although antinuclear sentiment seems to be waning, some prominent proponents of an all-renewables future (Bernie Sanders, Mark Jacobson) remain opposed to nuclear power.[50]

Unless one has a stake (financial or emotional) in the success or demise of a particular net-zero technology, it ought not to matter which technologies will be a part of a *truly* net-zero energy future. Technology-agnostic paths to net zero will eliminate technologies that cannot compete on performance and/or price and will hold out the prospect of participation in the net-zero future to all. In that way, they leave room for a broader coalition to support the energy transition and for innovations that could make transition trade-offs easier.

RELIABILITY AND PUBLIC-UTILITY REGULATION

Another part of the climate coalition regards electric utilities as the central obstacle to climate progress. This group is challenging fundamental precepts of public-utility law that they say enable IOUs to resist the energy transition. Of course, IOUs have very different functions in competitive electricity markets than in traditionally regulated markets, and sometimes this critique paints IOUs in both situations with the same broad brush. It tends to characterize IOUs as relatively unconcerned about the public interest, in the manner of PG&E's negligence in causing wildfires, and corrupt, in the manner of the FirstEnergy bribery scandal. In this telling, the average IOU is a rent-seeking machine that dominates regulators and regulation for the benefit of shareholders at the expense of the public interest. These critics dismiss ambitious utility pledges to decarbonize as "greenwashing" or industry aberrations.[51] As noted in chapter 1, the political scientist Leah Stokes is a prominent academic proponent of the view that weak climate policies are explained by IOU capture of the policy process. Stokes describes climate politics as "a knife fight" and says that "electric utilities have delayed climate action for 50 years."[52]

Among legal scholars who see IOUs as the major obstacle to climate progress, most tend to focus on how regulatory incentives might be changed to induce IOUs to embrace the energy transition more eagerly. In traditionally regulated markets, IOUs have little incentive to jeopardize the guaranteed returns they earn on old power plants by building or buying cheaper renewable power that could render those plants obsolete. Some states have tried reimbursing IOUs for the cost of decommissioning coal-fired power plants.[53] The legal scholar Joshua Macey and several coauthors have criticized these and other perverse incentives of public-utility regulation in a series of papers. Echoing Stokes, Macey and his colleagues see IOUs as a pernicious influence over competitive wholesale markets and their regulators and argue that public-utility regulation prevents IOU shareholders from internalizing risks the way shareholders in other industries do.[54] These misaligned incentives account for, among other things, ISOs/RTOs' underinvestment in transmission, which in turn threatens the reliability of electricity service and slows development of renewables.[55] This critique is also sometimes dismissive of the reliability challenges associated with the growth of more variable, lower-capacity-factor generation on the grid.[56] In any case, these authors urge changes to the way PUCs regulate IOUs to better align IOU incentives with the public interest.

Another legal scholar, Ari Peskoe, has argued that the set of monopoly rights that states grant to IOUs amounts to a "transmission syndicate," one that, like any other cartel, has a financial incentive to underinvest in new transmission. Competition in transmission, he argues, would attract more investment that connects areas suitable for utility-scale wind and solar projects to demand centers in the cities.[57] Peskoe argues that the state public-utility statutes that restrict transmission development by non-IOUs violate the Constitution's Commerce Clause, and at least one federal circuit court agrees.[58]

As noted in chapter 2, it is evident that underinvestment in transmission has blocked development of some utility-scale wind and solar projects. And in the case of PG&E, the comfort that comes with guaranteed positive returns and monopoly status may have contributed to the deadly wildfires caused by the company's transmission lines. Yet the PG&E example also underscores how our reliance on private capital to supply energy services limits regulators' options. During PG&E's second bankruptcy, a federal court ordered the company not to pay dividends to shareholders until it had complied with tree trimming and other safety rules relating to wildfire risk. Katherine Blunt explains:

> On one level, [the judge's] solution made sense. If the company couldn't fulfill its basic safety commitments, why should investors benefit? But in attempting to address one set of risks, the proposal introduced another. PG&E's financial health after bankruptcy would depend on its ability to make regular dividend payments, a significant factor in attracting more patient investors that . . . would stick around long enough for the company to have a chance to stabilize. . . . Even if the company fell out of compliance on tree work, dividends would help it raise money to make other safety investments.[59]

Government dependence on large amounts of private capital to provide electricity service triggers "too big to fail" incentives in IOUs (per Macey), but it remains to be seen whether changes to PUC oversight can yield a system that allows companies such as PG&E to pursue decarbonization, minimize wildfire risk, and provide reliable, universal electric service—affordably. For its part, FERC is struggling with the question of whether to continue to recognize state-sanctioned monopoly rights for IOUs in FERC's transmission-planning policies.[60] We would presumably have more transmission investment if Congress had delegated to FERC unambiguous power to site interstate transmission, as it has for interstate natural gas pipelines, or if the Department of Energy and FERC used their backstop siting authority for transmission more aggressively.

In contrast to these critiques of traditional regulation are those that advocate a more grid- and utility-centric approach to the energy transition. The legal scholar William Boyd argues that in traditionally regulated states PUCs can use their leverage over IOUs to require the massive investments necessary to make the transition a reality, as California has done.[61] Boyd argues that restructured markets are particularly ill suited to facilitating the transition. In competitive markets, the missing-money problem and behavioral inertia lead to underinvestment in the right mix of clean-energy infrastructure.[62] A rapid transition requires the kind of coordinated effort best mustered *within* an organization (an IOU or government), says Boyd. As noted in chapter 2, economic theory does not suggest that markets always coordinate action more efficiently than intrafirm coordination does; Coase's theory of the firm does not recommend against vertical or horizontal integration in every instance.[63] Boyd sees the market "commodification" of electricity services and the disaggregation of grid management into different market "products" as a singularly inefficient way to manage the energy transition.[64]

In any case, the claim that IOUs have impeded the transition is an imprecise generalization. We do see instances of traditional IOUs embracing the transition today. PG&E has embraced California's aggressive approach to the energy transition, the company's wildfire-liability problems notwithstanding. Minnesota is another state with both traditional retail-rate regulation and aggressive decarbonization goals; its leverage over IOUs may explain the pledges of Xcel Energy to cut its GHG emissions. And the climate activist Bill McKibben has celebrated another example of the Boyd prescription: namely, the PUC of Vermont, which used its leverage over the IOUs to speed the deployment of energy-transition technologies in that state.[65]

Furthermore, what does "efficiency" mean in this context? The transition is a very different proposition in competitive markets than in traditional markets, and economic "efficiency" is an ill-fitting evaluative criterion for thinking about balancing affordability and reliability in a net-zero future. Consider the problem of determining the "value of lost load," a way of estimating the efficient level of service reliability, traditionally expressed in dollar terms. The value most people place on losing electric service for twelve hours is very different than it is for seventy-two hours and very different on a mild day than on a deadly cold or deadly hot one. The cold wave that hit the central United States in December 1989 imposed a freeze on Texas that was no less severe than Winter Storm Uri in 2021. But it fell on an electric system that was managed by vertically integrated IOUs, munies, and co-ops whose prior investment decisions were made with the understanding that revenues would be sufficient to earn a positive return on those investments. The Averch-Johnson effect tells us that the IOUs overinvested in infrastructure. But is that why the outages in 1989 were far less lengthy and extensive than in 2021? The ERCOT market may have saved ratepayers money before February 2021, but whatever "efficiency" gains it realized over the years may have been lost in three days that month.

Another way to understand this debate is by asking whether policymakers can design incentives that will induce good (or good enough) performance over these different situations or must instead have the power to command good performance. IOUs provide a public service. The engineers that dominate the industry will provide that service within whatever constraints policymakers impose on them, including policies favoring more clean energy. Although Boyd's regulatory prescription differs from Macey's and Peskoe's, all three propose regulatory-policy changes that would lower barriers to construction of cheaper, cleaner renewable generation. And of course, all these recommendations depend on state policymakers' willingness to embrace the transition, suggesting that such projects are more likely to be taken up in blue states than in red states, regardless of whether markets in those states are competitive or traditionally regulated.[66]

AFFORDABILITY AND THE ENERGY TRANSITION

Most experts believe that the social net benefits of reducing GHG emissions will be positive and large. Generally speaking, those benefits will tend to flow to economically vulnerable people who would have borne the brunt of climate harms.[67] But to the politicians and voters whose consent is necessary to make the transition happen, the immediate out-of-pocket costs of the transition matter even more. Future beneficiaries seem remote and unidentifiable;[68] by contrast, we can identify those who will pay now to avert those future harms. This difference makes the transition a particularly thorny political problem. It is not that voters don't care about the welfare of others; they do.[69] But they are also reliably risk averse, and their votes are often more strongly determined by the prospect of a decline in their own fortunes than by empathy for unidentified others.

On social media, energy-transition opponents exploit these worries about the cost of the energy transition: "The pursuit of renewable energy will bankrupt America and every American," they say. "The move to renewable energy will bankrupt a lot of people." These concerns become grafted onto the divide over partisan identity. Voters in the lower quartiles of wealth and income may suspect that the transition will leave them even farther behind. They know that many in the climate coalition do not occupy those lower quartiles. They may be unpersuaded by assurances that clean energy will be affordable. They may not trust that the transition will benefit them, because they have previously been on the short end of policy trade-offs.

THE SALIENCE OF PRICES

Part of the reason energy-price risk looms large in people's minds is that most see energy costs as a nondiscretionary expense. This perception may account for some of the unpopularity of a carbon tax, the effect of which voters can easily visualize in the form of higher energy prices.[70] Even if the proceeds of a carbon tax are returned to ratepayers in some form, the payers' loss aversion makes the benefits of the tax seem less salient than the costs. Similarly, voters may sense that they pay an opportunity cost when regulation restricts their energy choices, which may be one reason why polls reveal voter ambivalence about phasing out fossil fuels.[71] By contrast, for members of the climate coalition, the associated costs may seem less worrying and more like a "problem we can solve" or "a small price to pay" for a low-carbon future.

Net-Zero Energy and Energy Burden

This trade-off between carbon emissions and cost is perhaps most salient in consumer products, where the purchase prices of EVs, induction stoves, and heat pumps remain higher (so far) than their fossil-fueled alternatives. With steady improvements in the cost and efficiency of those vehicles and appliances, the trade-offs are becoming easier. But even if the additional out-of-pocket cost of "electrifying everything" is modest, it will be politically significant to some voters. And there *are* features that fossil-fueled appliances and vehicles have that their electric counterparts lack. It takes longer to "refill" a car battery than a gas tank. An all-electric home has no hot water or cooking capability when the grid goes down, unlike a home with a gas water heater or stove. And so on. These are some of the little costs of pursuing the energy transition inefficiently; they may matter politically, especially to economically vulnerable voters.

Many of these voters qualify for federal assistance with their energy bills.[72] But federal low-income energy-assistance programs are routinely underfunded, and state assistance programs vary widely in their ability to help alleviate greater energy burdens. One review of the academic literature confirmed that "after decades of weatherization and bill-payment programs, low-income households still spend a higher percent of their income on electricity and gas bills than any other income group. Their energy burden is not declining, and it remains persistently high in particular geographies such as the South, rural America, and minority communities."[73]

It is intuitive that, all else being equal, energy burden and energy poverty can be higher in rural communities because of disparities between urban and rural lifestyles and incomes.[74] In states whose major cities enjoy the temperature-moderating effects of a nearby ocean, rural voters consume more energy than urban voters, all else being equal. For example, according to researchers at the University of San Diego, energy consumption per square foot in California's inland counties averages more than twice that of its coastal cities, and median incomes are far lower inland.[75] Thus, when groups raise questions about the effect of transition initiatives on their energy burdens, it isn't helpful or justified to dismiss their concerns as utility-industry or fossil-fuel-industry "talking points."[76]

Uncertainty About Net-Zero Energy Costs

The pandemic and the Ukraine war may have interrupted the long decline in prices of labor and raw materials for batteries and renewable generation, and postpandemic inflation and interest-rate increases have added to these price shocks. These forces have altered the balance of supply and demand for critical minerals used in photovoltaic cells, batteries, and wind turbines: silicon, manganese, cadmium, nickel, lithium, and other rare earths as well as copper, used in electrical wiring.[77] They have also reconfigured markets for the skilled, semiskilled, and unskilled labor on which the construction of the clean-energy economy will depend. The possibility of a "Great Resignation"—signaling a shrinking of the labor supply—plagues clean-energy labor markets as well.[78] Cost increases may already be jeopardizing the economic viability of yet unbuilt offshore wind projects in the North Atlantic. And we do not yet know the cost/price effects of incentivizing domestic clean-energy manufacturing—that is, of moving some of the offshore parts of the supply chain onshore, as the IRA aims to do.

All of these factors contributed to increases in the price of clean energy in 2022.[79] Recall the LCOE data described in chapter 2. The leading provider of that data, Lazard, had published its estimates annually, during the fall of the year, for more than a decade, but it declined to publish new estimates in the fall of 2022 as the economy emerged from pandemic. When it finally published new LCOE estimates in April 2023, its estimates confirmed other reporting that costs had increased (see table 5.2).[80] This is apparent on the high end of Lazard's ranges, which increased for almost every electricity-generation technology between the fall of 2021 and the spring of 2023.

However, markets adjust over time; higher prices eventually ought to lead to increased supply, reduced demand, and lower future prices for upstream inputs that are currently in short supply. Furthermore, Lazard's estimates are of *unsubsidized* LCOEs and were calculated without reference to the substantial subsidies contained in the IRA. Those tax and other incentives ought to push the rebalancing of upstream markets in clean-energy investors' favor, all else being equal. One early analysis suggests that IRA subsidies more than compensate for the higher costs of producing critical minerals and manufacturing components in the United States, but time will tell if those projections will hold true.[81] And what costs will the United States incur, if any, from the possibility that IRA subsidies violate World

TABLE 5.2 Change in Lazard LCOE Estimates, 2021–2023[a] ($/mwh)

	LCOE 15.0 (2021)	LCOE 16.0 (2023)
Onshore wind	26–50	24–75
Offshore wind	83[c]	72–140
Utility-scale solar photovoltaics	28–41[d]	24–96[d]
Nuclear power	131–204	115–221
CCNG[b]	45–74	39–101
Coal-fired power	65–152	68–166

[a] Unsubsidized estimates.

[b] Combined-cycle natural gas plant.

[c] Point estimate; no range reported.

[d] Combined range for thin-film and crystalline photovoltaics.

Sources: The 2021 numbers come from Lazard, *Lazard's Levelized Cost of Energy Analysis—Version 15.0* (October 2021), https://www.lazard.com/media/sptlfats/lazards-levelized-cost-of-energy-version-150-vf.pdf. The 2023 numbers come from Lazard, *LCOE* (April 2023), https://www.lazard.com/media/typdgxmm/lazards-lcoeplus-april-2023.pdf.

Trade Organization rules? Will the subsidies provoke retaliatory measures that impose significant costs on Americans?[82] As of late 2023, China has imposed restrictions on the export of high-grade graphite used in EV batteries, and the United States is engaged in delicate negotiations with the European Union over fears that IRA subsidies will divert clean-energy investment from Europe to the United States.

No one knows which, if any, of these downside risks will materialize. By most accounts, investors have remained bullish on clean-energy investments after these pandemic- and war-related shocks.[83] But it makes far more sense for experts to acknowledge and tackle these cost-uncertainty issues transparently than either to react to open discussion of them with disdain or to treat such discussion as an attempt to derail the transition.

HOSTING NEW ENERGY INFRASTRUCTURE: A DIFFERENT SORT OF "COST"

When green-energy infrastructure displaces carbon-emitting energy infrastructure, it reduces pollution costs that tend to fall disproportionately on lower-income people. But even green-energy investment entails unwanted or unintended social costs. *All* new energy infra-structure attracts some sincere and rational local opposition, as well as sincere, rational local support, because new energy projects inevitably impose *some* costs on *some* locals, and *some* of those locals do not capture (or value) the benefits that the projects bring. Indeed, the differing interests of locals and nonlocals explains the dilemma facing the Sierra Club, whose local chapters sometimes oppose clean-energy projects that the national organization favors.[84]

Some locals care more about jobs and economic development than about environmental impacts. The fictional townspeople in *Local Hero* mostly favored the proposed oil terminal because it would make them rich. (In the words of one character, "You can't eat scenery.") Native American tribes such as the Southern Utes and Navajo have earned substantial income exploiting fossil fuels on their lands. Shrinking markets for these products means that those revenue streams must be replaced. Indian lands also contain abundant wind and solar resources, but some reports indicate that tribes have had difficulty exploiting those resources. And some have had trouble obtaining permission to interconnect to the grid, which is a prerequisite to securing IRA subsidies.[85]

Furthermore, although renewable projects can mean revenue for tribes and other communities dependent on old energy technologies, they may not provide the same quality or number of local jobs that fossil-fuel development did. For communities trading a coal mine or a nuclear- or fossil-fueled power station for a wind farm, solar farm, or hydroelectric station, the jobs trade-off looks like a bad deal. Traditional central-station thermal power plants employ a permanent, often unionized, and relatively highly paid workforce. Most employment associated with wind-, solar-, or hydro-generating plants are construction jobs; at the completion of construction, these stations are generally operated remotely from outside the local community.[86] This is one reason why citing job-creation statistics for the clean-energy industry does not resonate in communities losing fossil-fuel or nuclear jobs.

The IRA was designed to address this concern by offering incentives for direct investment in communities that have lost fossil-fuel jobs or are otherwise in need of economic-development help. It includes lucrative tax credits for investments located in "energy communities" or "low income communities."[87] In these ways, the law tries to harmonize the goals of promoting investment in energy-transition technologies, economic development, and environmental justice. But these goals can never be fully harmonized. A solar farm, a wind farm, a hydrogen-production facility, a solar-panel-manufacturing facility, a battery-manufacturing facility, and a carbon-sequestration facility have different physical attributes. The last four will bring more permanent jobs than the first two but will also bring characteristics we associate with industrialization that some locals will dislike.[88] Some members of the community will welcome each investment's particular package of attributes, but others will not. By incentivizing investment in "energy communities" and "low-income communities," the IRA seems to accept (or presume?) that the jobs/environmental impact trade-offs will be made differently in those communities than in wealthier communities.

When communities are split over a project, what is the environmentally just result? A well-established academic literature supports the intuition that industrial infrastructure tends to be sited in poorer communities and that wealthy communities are more adept at leveraging law and the regulatory process to keep such infrastructure out.[89] Indian tribes and communities of color have historically been un- and underrepresented in energy-infrastructure-siting proceedings, leaving some wary of energy projects of all types.[90]

Where NIMBY groups form, the dynamics of local opposition to clean energy mirror the opposition to fossil-energy projects. The development pits the locals who benefit economically from the project against those who do not or who fear threats to their home or cherished places. Although large majorities of voters *say* that they would be comfortable having a wind or solar farm in their community, much of that support vanishes when the question is posed in a way that places the hypothetical project *too close* to home.[91] These local opponents enlist the help of NGOs or business allies to stop projects. They employ data analytics to target audiences on digital and social media platforms and to test the appeal and effectiveness of political messages to specific audiences.[92] That is, they mobilize broader opposition.

They often do so by using risk-based appeals because fear resonates. They fan fears of battery fires to oppose grid-scale battery-storage projects. They stoke fear of "wind turbine syndrome," "the constant noise, flicker, and sound of wind turbines" that opponents allege will "take a toll on your health." They heighten the fear that transmission lines will emit a radio frequency that causes "increased risk of childhood leukemia, adult brain cancer, Lou Gehrig's Disease, and miscarriage."[93] Despite the dubious scientific support for these claims, NIMBY groups can nevertheless cite qualified, dissenting members of the scientific community to support them, just as climate-science skeptics can find dissenters with impressive academic pedigrees.[94] Digital connectedness feeds the emotional intensity of these fights. One clean-energy advocate put it this way: "Every source of renewable energy seems to face an opposition based on a real downside that's blown out of proportion."[95]

This particular approach to mobilizing opposition has slowed all varieties of energy-project development since the 1960s, and now it is slowing development of energy-transition projects.[96] A study by Columbia University scholars concluded that "in nearly every state, local governments have enacted policies to block or restrict renewable energy facilities . . . [resulting] in delay or cancellation of particular projects." Even offshore wind, which is in nobody's backyard, regularly attracts opposition. The presence of sincere local opposition to clean-energy infrastructure is a source of cognitive dissonance for the climate coalition and thus triggers attempts to delegitimate those local opponents. One academic study in 2023 framed opposition to wind farms as "a form of energy privilege" enjoyed by mostly white people at the expense of people of color because large wind farm projects were located in predominantly white areas, wind energy often displaces fossil-fueled energy in the dispatch queue, and the externalities of fossil-fuel combustion fall disproportionately on racial minorities.[97] On social media, it is fairly common for energy-transition proponents to dismiss local opposition as mere "astroturf" activism: phony "grassroots" activism funded by competitors of these projects.

But that dismissal disrespects the sincere local people within that opposition.

Overcoming local opposition may prove particularly difficult for projects designed to increase domestic supplies of upstream raw materials (read: mining and manufacturing) under the IRA's domestic-content provisions. Electrification will impose new demands on lithium and copper markets, and local opposition to new mines for lithium, copper, and other energy-transition minerals in the United States may be sufficiently fierce that weaning clean-energy manufacturing off of raw materials from other nations may be slow or difficult.[98] That may be why Congress crafted the IRA's critical minerals-procurement subsidies for battery manufacturing to favor not only domestically produced minerals but also those produced in nations with which the United States has a free-trade agreement.[99] The Biden administration has even considered financing new mines in Canada as an additional response to this problem.[100]

Experienced developers know that engaging local opposition respectfully is the wiser path. Project proponents and locals can negotiate community-benefit agreements, which attempt to allocate project costs and benefits explicitly in agreed-upon ways within the community. The legal scholar Shelley Welton argues that these arrangements may offer a relatively constructive way to manage siting trade-offs.[101] In any case, they are a more transparent and respectful alternative to litigation, one that recognizes the agency of local communities. At the same time, it is important to acknowledge that it is usually impossible to win over everyone in a community. Therefore, building the low-carbon economy will require more persistent supporters at each stage of the approval process than have materialized in permitting proceedings to date. National environmental NGOs that were organized around *opposition* to development have found it difficult to actively support specific green-energy projects in the face of local opposition. As with the canceled Cape Wind Project in Nantucket Sound, too often the response is "I support this type of project, but just not here." Energy-transition proponents will have to find the will and the resources to support green-energy projects that some locals don't like.[102]

DECENTRALIZATION AND TRADE-OFFS

Other experts argue that we ought to reenvision the energy trilemma in a less supply-centric way. Reliability, they say, is not the responsibility of any particular type of generation or even a responsibility to be met solely by generators as a collective. Rather, it is a value that the system provides.[103] Thus, the problem isn't that a solar farm—or a solar farm paired with a battery—is available to supply power less often than a gas-fired generator. We can achieve our transition objective less expensively and just as reliably, they say, by doing more to incentivize resources that exist (or might exist) behind the meter: rooftop solar, home batteries, and other DERs that can back up grid-based renewables and step up at times of grid need.[104] If we build the right mix of net-zero sources in the right places on both sides of the customer's meter and place more of the responsibility for ensuring reliability on customers, then there is no reason to doubt that a reliable, affordable, net-zero energy near future is possible. And we can do it without all the additional transmission and generation that modelers of a net-zero future say we will need. The advocates of these decentralization arguments are the intellectual descendants of energy-efficiency and conservation advocates of the 1970s, a subset of modern environmentalism pioneered by the physicist Amory Lovins, who remains an active participant in this debate.[105]

VIRTUAL POWER PLANTS AND TIME-OF-USE RATES

Some decentralization advocates propose that aggregations of DERs can act as "virtual power plants," serving the reliability needs of the grid less expensively than central-station generators.[106] That is, they can bid their energy services into the market through an aggregator/agent or by delegating those decisions to their IOU, which will require DER owners to cede control over the use of their energy assets to the aggregator or IOU. Even without aggregation, say decentralization proponents, the right price incentives can make these kinds of transactive markets work. Retail-price signals can tell DER owners when the grid needs their demand reductions, rooftop solar generation, discharges from EV batteries, or energy from other home storage such as the Tesla Powerwall. According to this view, it makes sense for regulators and policymakers to subsidize the installation of smart meters and DERs, to encourage net metering and time-of-use (TOU) or real-time retail rates—all in order to jump-start transactive markets.[107] This approach, say its proponents, can make the energy transition less expensive and more reliable than reliance only on a centralized grid.

Others doubt the case for decentralization. Getting the various financial or behavioral incentives right poses even thornier challenges for transactive markets than for centralized wholesale markets. Monitoring and controlling so many additional generators add another layer of complexity to an already complex system and require much more computing power than existing grid-management algorithms. And there is disagreement among experts over the magnitude of the benefits decentralization can yield. Most customers may be unenthusiastic about this option because they consider the potential gains—saving a few dollars a month on the electric bill—not worth the bother of shifting their electricity-consuming activities to off-peak time periods or investing in new technologies. They may just prefer to pay a premium for rate certainty. According to a study, in 2019 only 14 percent of U.S. utilities offered TOU rates at all; of those, only 3 percent of their customers opted in to those rates. (Since then, a few more states have instituted default TOU rates for certain classes of customers.)[108]

Until 2021, many customers in Texas's competitive retail market had the option to sign up for variable retail rates through a company called "Griddy," but few selected that option. Those who did were presented with exorbitant power bills after Winter Storm Uri in February 2021, thereafter extinguishing customer demand for dynamic retail rates in Texas for the foreseeable future.[109] Utilities and regulators are torn between wanting to protect their customers from retail-price shocks, on the one hand, and wanting to incentivize DER owners to provide services to the grid, on the other. Imposing default TOU rates with large price differentials between peak and off-peak power would tip the balance toward the latter goal and away from the former. But so far that option is not a popular one, suggesting that the future of transactive DER markets may lie almost exclusively with more sophisticated industrial and commercial customers.[110]

Furthermore, to the extent that the case for decentralization implies allowing grid-based reserves to fall below levels sufficient to keep the lights on during severe weather events, it unnerves politicians and regulators—especially given the increasing frequency of power-supply emergencies in Texas and California. If wind, solar, and DERs have sometimes provided more power than expected during recent moments of grid need, might they sometimes provide less?[111] Can we count on customers to be willing to reduce demand or otherwise bear an enhanced role in ensuring service reliability during emergency conditions (extreme heat, extreme cold)? Can we count on the infrastructure-siting process—with its tug-of-war among investors, regulators, and neighbors—to yield those "right investments in the right places" that will maintain supply reliability on a smaller, more decentralized grid?

These are the kinds of questions that deserve transparent discussion. Unfortunately, they often provoke the same sort of hyperbole and ad hominem dismissals discussed in chapter 4. For example, in response to a tweet endorsing net metering as a reduced purchase "from a monopoly," one energy consultant wrote: "That is an inane comment. It's almost as stupid as saying 'don't tax the sun.' You apparently do not understand what is going on with net metering."[112] Another example, from an article explaining utility opposition to net metering, is in the article's title: "Why Your Utility Company Sucks."[113] In this environment, one might never learn that reasonable people disagree over these questions.

HOW WE LIVE

Online debate over the role of individual decisions in contributing to climate change is also frequently hyperbolic because it implicates ethical questions. How much of the blame for carbon emissions should we lay at the feet of individual consumers? How much should we lay at the feet of fossil-fuel companies? Utilities? Or politicians?

Energy-use comparisons between the United States and Europe are fraught in part because of Europe's greater dependence on energy imports. But over many decades and changing relative economic fortunes, U.S. per capita energy consumption has remained substantially higher than Europe's. Some on the right suggest that higher per capita consumption implies a higher quality of life, but most measures of quality of life negate that suggestion. Europeans live less energy-intensive lives (see table 5.3) for geographic and historical reasons. They live in smaller homes on a smaller land mass and are more reliant on public transit than Americans. American cities are spread out and are farther apart, making commuter and intercity rail a more expensive proposition. Consequently, Americans emit more carbon per capita than Europeans.

These differences sometimes trigger expressions of disdain from segments of the climate coalition. One climate-policy opinion leader described the average American as a "sedentary, heart-diseased, fast-food gobbling, car-addicted suburbanite, sitting watching TV in [a] suburban castle."[114] Some ascribe Americans' dependence on

TABLE 5.3 Lifestyle Indicators, United States and Europe

	United States	Europe
Population density (persons/square kilometer)	36	73
Median new home size (square feet)	1,900	1,000
Primary energy consumption per capita (million British thermal units/year)	304	132
Electricity consumption per capita (mwh/year)	12.9	6.6
Automobile ownership per thousand people	890	655
Fossil-fuel consumption per capita (mwh/year)	63.8	28.7

Sources: "Population Density (People per Sq. Km of Land Area)," World Bank, n.d., https://data.worldbank.org/indicator/EN.POP.DNST; "Home Size by Country," World Population Review, https://worldpopulationreview.com/country-rankings/house-size-by-country; "Energy Intensity," U.S. Energy Information Administration, n.d., https://www.eia.gov /international/data/world/other-statistics/energy-intensity-by-gdp-and-population?pd=47 &p=00000000000000000000000000000000000000000000000000002&u=2&f=A&v=line &a=-&i=none&vo=value&t=C&g=none&l=249-ruvvvvvfvtvnvv1vrvvvvfvvvvvvfvvvou20evvvvvvvvvv nvuvs0008&s=1451606400000&e=1546300800000&vb=283&ev=true; "Electric Power Consumption (kWh per Capita)," World Bank, n.d., https://data.worldbank.org/indicator/EG.USE.ELEC.KH.PC; "List of Countries and Territories by Motor Vehicles per Capita," Wikipedia, n.d., https://en.wikipedia.org/wiki/List_of_countries_and_territories_by_motor_vehicles _per_capita; "Fossil Fuel Consumption per Capita 2022," Our World in Data, n.d., https://ourworldindata.org/grapher/fossil-fuels-per-capita?tab=table.

automobiles mainly to the lobbying of the auto and fossil-fuel industries rather than to physical and geographic factors. The automobile and oil industries *have* consistently lobbied for subsidies and less stringent regulatory standards, which make their products cheaper than they otherwise would be.[115] But it is not clear that most Americans would have made substantially different choices about how to live prior to the twenty-first century but for these anticompetitive and lobbying activities.

Transit and Land-Use Choices

Some Americans do emulate Europeans by moving into those city centers that offer good mass-transit service and a more walkable lifestyle. Urbanism, as a philosophy of land use and urban design, is identifying ways to make day-to-day city and village life easier and more efficient through better design choices.[116] Some people (including me) love the ability to access frequent, reliable mass transit and to avoid fighting traffic in cars. But other people prefer rural life or a larger home or simply love driving and the independence from timetables that cars provide.

Certainly, existing land-use design choices tend to push Americans toward automobile use, all else being equal.[117] Housing NIMBYism keeps prices high, thus pricing many people out of more walkable urban communities or places with better public-transit service.[118] And simple unfamiliarity with alternatives to automobiles may make some people reticent about those alternatives—a reticence that might disappear once they experience them. For urbanites, there are, of course, personal mobility alternatives to cars or mass transit. Bicycles, E-bikes, and electric scooters are efficient to operate and independent of mass-transit timetables. But they also expose their users to the vagaries of the weather and to personal safety risks that other options do not.[119] Some people feel safer inside a car than on a bike or scooter. Even in cities with dedicated bike lanes, enforcement of the boundary (keeping cars out of the bike lanes) is often lax, and bicyclists may oppose use of the bike lane by E-bikes and scooters.[120] It will be up to city politicians to change the risk–reward components of mobility decisions in favor of cleaner transportation choices. We can expect them to do so when and where voters reward them for it.

Meanwhile, most Americans will continue to be drivers. Federal legislation offering financial and other incentives for EV adoption will hasten EVs' market penetration, as will other initiatives, such as the Department of Transportation's fuel-economy standards of 2022, the EPA's proposed vehicle standards of 2023, and California's commitment to phase out new gasoline-powered vehicle sales by 2035.[121] But there is a long way to go. EVs composed 7 percent of light-duty vehicle sales in 2022, and the people who adopt EVs tend to be wealthy. This is probably because the sticker price of an EV remains higher than that of comparable gasoline-powered cars, even if the life-cycle cost may not be, which makes an EV purchase a much more comfortable proposition for the rich than for the poor.[122]

Furthermore, the cost and convenience of ownership are different for these two populations. EV owners who live in detached houses can charge their vehicles using a 110-volt outlet in their garages. Residents of multi-unit condo or apartment buildings often lack access to outlets for overnight charging and so must pay commercial (fast) charging providers, usually at higher rates. This is true for the average apartment dweller as well. Apartment dwellers have a relatively high energy burden in part because their median income is about half that of homeowners.[123] All of which makes EV mandates look economically regressive to some observers.

These are the simple, commonsense components of a conversation about climate and transit one might have with a friend or family member: one that acknowledges the concerns of the skeptical and explores how they might be alleviated. Unfortunately, that kind of discussion is less common on social media than scolding tweets such as "How can you drive a car and say you care about climate change?" Of course, few people will be persuaded to change their transportation choices by public shaming.[124] However, consistent with the prescriptions discussed in chapter 6, private reminders that we have more climate-friendly choices available sometimes seem to elicit changes in climate-relevant behavior.[125] Meanwhile, government investment in mass transit, walkable urban design, and alternatives to automobiles can make those choices more numerous and attractive.

Are Individuals Responsible for Their Carbon Emissions?

Some people make the case for strong climate policy by burnishing their personal climate-friendly choices: "I don't own a car," "I don't eat meat," and "I am childless by choice." As with automobiles, we see this logic invoked in its negative forms online fairly regularly:

> You say you care about climate change, but you still eat meat. Sounds like you are the hypocrite.

> If population isn't a concern at this moment in time, then you're not serious about climate change.

There is a difference, of course, between trumpeting one's personal choices and condemning another's or suggesting that one's personal choices ought to become broader social norms. Most of us react defensively to the suggestion that our choices about transport, diet, and procreation are ethically problematic.

But the question remains: Do individuals' choices to use fossil fuels impose on them an ethical responsibility for climate harm or a duty to make different choices? Does the legality of that choice matter? Moral philosophers and ethicists debate this question, but their answers are all over the place.[126] For utilitarians and other consequentialists, the answer may depend on whether the individual's action actually contributes meaningfully to climate change—Is it individually consequential for climate change?[127] By contrast, virtue ethicists and deontological ethicists may see a duty to avoid climate-harming behavior regardless of the action–change correlation, focusing as they do on "good" personal conduct rather than on its consequences.[128] One reason ethicists struggle to reach clear answers to these questions is that questions of individual responsibility are inseparable from the set of social and economic incentives of daily life. Those incentives involve trade-offs. A colleague raised this question to me a few years ago in connection with his ownership of a gasoline-powered car, noting that "we are all caught in a system" in which doing the right thing by the climate costs money and inconvenience. It is yet another cooperation problem: those who spend more in order to pollute less lose out economically, all else being equal.

The same logic applies to the purchase of induction stoves, EVs, heat pumps, and other clean options that cost more than their fossil-fueled counterparts.[129] Businesses are caught in this same cooperation problem, too. When the City of Palo Alto, California, banned the use of gas stoves in new buildings, it made an exception for a celebrity chef who contended that cooking with electricity would "compromise the caliber of [his] cuisine."[130] The city presumably made the exception because it wanted to retain the restaurant within its borders. Likewise, PG&E's pioneering decarbonization efforts in the 2010s brought trade-offs in the form of increased rates and diversion of company resources away from safety operations.[131] Similarly, oil and gas companies could pivot to clean-energy businesses with lower profit margins; but when they do so, they forgo the higher returns associated with producing fossil fuels, which will bring a decline in shareholder price and eventually the request for new leadership. After his term as CEO of BP, Robert Dudley put it this way: "I meet with shareholders and they say 'we would like you to move really quickly into renewables.' I say, 'we can do that, would you like us to cut the dividend?' They go, 'no, no, don't do that.' We've got to find the right balance and pace here."[132]

Do businesses or highly paid people have a greater ethical duty to incur the financial or career costs that produce climate benefits? Is there a personal-wealth threshold above which that greater duty exists? Ethicists have no consensus answers to these questions, either. Some climate activists label Taylor Swift, Jay Z, and other celebrities "climate criminals" for their use of private jets; others call executives who work for or with large oil companies "climate villains."[133] But some businesses engage in voluntary climate-reducing activities that cannot reasonably be dismissed as "greenwashing." Given the set of financial incentives businesses face, an observation by the Stanford University climate scientist Ken Caldeira rings true: "It is surprising . . . how much corporate decarbonization activity is being driven by reputational concerns, customer preference, and the simple desire of people to do good."[134]

Public debates over ethical responsibility for climate harm have been shaped by research that traces twentieth- and twenty-first-century carbon emissions to specific fossil-fuel producers.[135] Scholars, interest groups, and litigators are using that work to ascribe legal or ethical responsibility for climate harm to the companies that extracted those fuels from the ground. Those companies sold those fuels to refiners, electric utilities, manufacturers, vehicle drivers, and others with the knowledge that those buyers would burn it and thus emit carbon. Those sales and the associated combustion were legal, but (arguably) some of them might not have happened but for industry lobbying. Who, then, ought to be morally or legally responsible for the resulting climate harm? The companies who extracted the fuels? Commercial buyers who burned them in their power plants and factories? Individuals who used the energy produced in power plants and burned fossil fuels in their vehicles?

Do the purposes of those sales transactions matter legally? Ethically? The market demand for those products reflects *some* of their social benefits, even if their prices failed to internalize their full social costs. Indeed, when oil prices get too high, it is not uncommon for politicians from both parties to urge oil companies to produce *more*.[136] Is that demand for the product relevant to the question of responsibility? One of the federal judges hearing a climate-liability case, William Alsup, put it this way: "Our industrial revolution and the development of our modern world has [*sic*] literally been fueled by oil and coal. . . . All of us have benefitted. Having reaped the benefit of that historic progress, would it really be fair to now ignore our own responsibility in the use of fossil fuels and place the blame for global warming on those who supplied what we demanded? Is it really fair, in light of those benefits, to say that the sale of fossil fuels was unreasonable?"[137]

In 2017, the legal scholar Eric Biber anticipated that the law would have difficulty with this question of individual responsibility. Noting that climate change is the result of "millions of individual actions," Biber predicted that existing legal doctrines will struggle to respond to the myriad public and private challenges to law that climate change is triggering.[138] But the law will have to adapt regardless, whether as a reaction to these challenges or in anticipation of them.

THE POLITICS OF TRADE-OFFS TODAY

This chapter has only scratched the surface in exploring the complexity of the energy transition and the difficulty of the trade-offs it entails. Today's voters are generally supportive of the energy transition, but they are wary of spin, and they are risk averse about energy security and costs. They deserve transparency and intellectual honesty from experts and opinion leaders.

Experience tells us that the act of raising and then defeating voter expectations is politically costly. Toward the end of the story of the "sad irons" described in chapter 1, Lyndon Johnson's biographer, Robert Caro, suggested that Congressman Johnson risked his political career when he persuaded Depression-era farmers to contribute a few dollars each to the formation of a rural electric cooperative. Caro predicted that if those farmers had remained without electric power at the time of the next election, Johnson would have been voted out of office. When power arrived before the election, his reelection was ensured. Almost ninety years later, Texas regulators did lose their jobs when voters' expectations of reliable, affordable electricity were not met during Winter Storm Uri. And as described in chapter 1, Governor Gray Davis of California met a similar fate for similar reasons in 2001.

The task of the climate coalition is to convince more *voters* to prioritize the energy transition in their voting decisions. That means engaging voters in ways that respect their concerns: not the disingenuous or immovable voters but rather the merely skeptical ones. These persuadable voters exist—perhaps not in large numbers but in large enough numbers. They are the people who may not consider themselves "political" but who worry about climate change even as they also worry about the energy transition. Their ambivalence shows up in poll results and politicians' behavior. They may be suspicious of elites who (they believe) don't understand their lives and needs. But the climate coalition can engage these voters much more productively than it has to date. The particulars of that task are the subject of the next chapter.

6

HOPE AND CONVERSATION

Be curious, not judgmental.

—Ted Lasso

I hate cynicism. It's my least favorite quality,
and it doesn't lead anywhere.

—Conan O'Brien

HYPEREFFICIENT INFORMATION technology amplifies partisan tribalism by making it *harder* for voters to understand complex policy problems, *harder* for experts to explore that complexity publicly, and *easier* for partisan opportunists to manipulate voters and fan their fears and resentments. Constant appeals to moral outrage preach mostly to the choir and do not resonate with swing voters. Worse, those appeals are used to mobilize adversaries *instantly*, enhancing the appeal of vague conspiratorial explanations for unwanted political outcomes. As identity-based group contempt grows to dangerous levels, it weakens the liberal democratic institutions through which we must craft solutions to national problems such as climate change. Those institutions require care and maintenance, which require some minimum threshold amount of respect for pluralism (across social and political groups). Many now worry that we are falling below that threshold.

As someone (who was neither Neils Bohr nor Yogi Berra) once said, "Predictions are difficult, especially about the future."[1] It is not inevitable that this destructive course will continue. Some external shock could disrupt the cycle of contempt. War, escalating political violence, or some other event could conceivably trigger a sharp pivot in voting behavior. But recent history makes that seem unlikely. Partisan polarization and tribalism have only worsened in the face of recent, historic shocks—the largest economic recession since the Great Depression, a pandemic that killed more than one million Americans in less than two years, as well as the ongoing climate crisis. The propaganda machine has framed each new shock in ways that preserve— even magnify—partisan divisions. Consequently, none of these shocks has sparked the kind of unidirectional mobilization of voters that might produce a republican moment for climate policy. Thus, the political task facing the climate coalition is a complex social problem that some mistake for a simple moral choice. When their appeals to others' moral sense fail to generate the desired political response, the propaganda machine invites them to dismiss those others as ignorant or evil. This dynamic manifests online in the myriad ways people have of using ridicule and dismissive rhetoric to avoid engaging opposing views.

While writing this book, I repeatedly encountered a quotation that is used in just that way: "Stupidity is a more dangerous enemy of the good than malice." It comes from the late German theologian Dietrich Bonhoeffer, who openly resisted Naziism and died in a concentration camp in 1945. Interestingly, the letter in which the sentence appears explains that Bonhoeffer was not simply attributing ignorance to Nazis or German citizens. Rather, he was identifying a sociological propaganda problem. The German people, said Bonhoeffer, were "under a spell, blinded, misused and abused."[2] So it is more than a little ironic that his remark is used today in ways that feed tribal enmity. For example, a Twitter/X account called "Changing Climate Times" tweeted the Bonhoeffer quote with the comment that "Dietrich Bonhoeffer has #ClimateChange denialists and their offspring, the delayers, squarely under his microscope." That tweet generated a reply from an account called "Red Barnett": "what he said about stupidity can easily be applied to the climate fools and the U.S. Democrats."[3] And so on.

Of course, today's United States is not Nazi Germany. Nazi propaganda was backed by actual state terror in ways that modern American propaganda is not (yet), leaving open the possibility that American democracy can be repaired. Perhaps regulation of social media

platforms can cure our propaganda problem: either new laws regulating social media or better self-regulation by the platforms.[4] Of course,
even if those proposals would help, the politics of enacting those measures will also be filtered and distorted by the propaganda machine.
Others put their hopes in the replacement of older voters by younger
voters, who currently support strong climate policy in greater percentages than older voters. That process of generational change is slow
and incremental, but even small increments matter in such an evenly
divided electorate. But if that strategy depends on the assumption that
young voters will not be steered toward climate denial or indifference
by the propaganda machine, the strategy may be weak because that
assumption may not hold.

This analysis suggests the need for a different approach to growing the climate coalition, one that strengthens liberal democracy as
it counteracts propaganda. An encouraging sign is that experts from
a variety of disciplines offer strikingly similar prescriptions for doing
so. Their work gets far less public attention than contempt narratives,
perhaps because they recommend turning away from the acrimony
and sharp rhetoric that generates clicks in the first place. They instead
point to *sustained in-person communication across ideological boundaries* as a way to break the spell of contempt and of firm but mistaken
belief. When people get away from the forces that feed negative emotion and false belief, it becomes easier to sustain norms of actively
open-minded thinking and to have conversations that are aimed "not
[at] victory, but [at] progress."[5]

No doubt a persuasive strategy based on iterated, bilateral, in-
person conversations across ideological boundaries sounds slow,
uncomfortable, and even futile to some readers. (Frankly, it *is* uncomfortable; more about that later.) It sounds futile, though, only because
of the caricatured pictures of the political opposition we tend to retain
in our mind's eye. In truth, some of our family, friends, neighbors, and
coworkers are persuadable. The strategy sounds slow, but *slow* is a relative term. We cannot know whether the IRA or some other catalyzing event will transform climate politics in the near term. In an era
of intensifying partisan tribalism, relying on that transformation
seems like a risky bet. Regardless, the prescription discussed in this

chapter makes sense anyway. If prospective members of the climate coalition encounter the increasingly serious disruptions of a changing climate *while* having frank but respectful *ongoing* conversations about climate and energy with people they know and trust, that ought to hasten the growth of the climate coalition.

BELIEF FORMATION: BEING CURIOUS, NOT JUDGMENTAL

The first chapter epigraph is from a fictional television character, Ted Lasso (from the series *Ted Lasso*). It is a deceptively straightforward call to actively open-minded thinking: to uncomfortable truth seeking over comfortable certainty. It echoes Learned Hand's advice from the book's introduction never to be "too sure" that we are right. Philosophers and writers have understood for centuries our urge to judge and the corresponding difficulty of following Ted Lasso's advice. The advice not to judge is implicit in the Confucian ideal of humility and in the tradition of the Stoics, Buddhists, Hindus, and other virtue ethicists who suggest that there is more to be gained by looking inward than by looking outward. Aristotle included in his definition of hubris the idea of a kind of pleasure that comes from shaming others. This idea appears again in ancient Roman literature when Marcus Aurelius advises that "a good man does not spy around for the black spots in others, but presses unswervingly on towards the mark."[6] Thus, these ideas were expounded millennia before Huxley's observation about the temptation to judge being "the most delicious of moral treats" (see chapter 3).

It is particularly important to remember this wisdom today as the propaganda machine continuously provokes our lesser angels.[7] Adopting an actively open-minded thinking mindset means resisting the instinct to judge prematurely, which in turn requires emotional self-awareness and effort. It is uncomfortable to audit our own beliefs or to avoid reacting defensively when they are challenged. But there are other, more important costs associated with ignoring the way emotion distorts our beliefs and actions. One writer describes those costs this way:

Our energies are overwhelmingly directed toward material, scientific, and technical subjects and away from psychological and emotional ones. . . . We devote inordinate hours to learning about tectonic plates and cloud formations, and relatively few fathoming shame and rage. The assumption is that emotional insight might be either unnecessary or in essence unteachable, lying beyond reason or method, an unreproducible phenomenon best abandoned to individual instinct and intuition. We are left to find our own path around our unfeasibly complicated minds—a move as striking (and as wise) as suggesting that each generation should rediscover the laws of physics by themselves.[8]

Because many people recognize the destructive effects of emotion on their own decision making only *after* the fact, it seems worthwhile to work at being curious rather than judgmental *before* deciding and acting, which takes practice.

ENERGY EXAMPLE 1: WITHHOLDING JUDGMENT IS DIFFICULT

In the late 1990s, an American lawyer named Steven Donziger brought a high-profile court case against Chevron on behalf of Ecuadorian villagers. The suit sought damages for environmental harm caused by oil exploration and production. The parties wrangled over preliminary matters for decades, but the case was eventually tried in Ecuadorean court.[9] The plaintiffs charged Chevron with failure to clean up an oil-production site in the jungle. Reading about the pollution left behind—which was nothing short of horrific and a health and environmental tragedy for the Indigenous people who lived in the area—I found myself rooting for the plaintiffs in the case. I was probably also influenced by my prior sense (from talking to people who worked at other major oil companies) that Chevron had a reputation for fighting every lawsuit ferociously to its conclusion regardless of the suit's merits. I was therefore pleased when I heard that the American NGO had won a multi-*billion*-dollar verdict in the Ecuadorian court against Chevron in 2013.[10]

Some years later I read that a federal District Court judge, Lewis Kaplan, had found Donziger and members of his Ecuador litigation team liable for civil violations of an anticorruption statute and that the U.S. court had enjoined Donziger from benefiting financially from enforcement of the Ecuadorian judgment outside of Ecuador.[11] Looking into the history of the case and at the Kaplan opinion, I learned that the case was riddled with bad behavior by both parties and that it had featured an appetite for corruption among some members of the Ecuadorian judiciary.[12] Chevron spent enormous sums trying to smear key members of the plaintiff's team, hiring various public-relations firms and private investigators along the way. But the trial presided over by Judge Kaplan also revealed that Donziger's legal team had bribed the Ecuadorian judge and (furtively) drafted documents putatively authored by the judge—both an environmental report and portions of the judge's final opinion. I began to see Donziger and his team as blameworthy parties.

Still more digging revealed that some of the evidence of ethical violations by the Donziger team came from the previously disqualified Ecuadorian judge, a less than reliable witness in the District Court case who subsequently recanted some of his testimony. Meanwhile, Donziger's supporters took to social media to charge Judge Kaplan with bias. They cited his treatment of plaintiffs in court but also made ad hominem attacks of questionable relevance, pointing to his prior work representing tobacco companies and his ownership of shares in a mutual fund that included oil company stocks. Supporters of the Kaplan verdict responded with their own ad hominem rejoinders, noting that Kaplan was appointed by a Democrat, Bill Clinton. Meanwhile, other courts that examined the case seemed to agree with Kaplan. The Second Circuit Court of Appeals upheld Kaplan's decision. The U.S. Supreme Court refused to hear Donziger's appeal.[13] And courts in Canada, Argentina, and the Hague have rejected the plaintiffs' attempts to enforce the Ecuadorian judgment in their respective jurisdictions. Donziger subsequently went to jail for criminal contempt of court and was disbarred.

I concluded that there probably were no heroes in this case, only victims (the villagers) and bad actors (both litigation teams). At each step of the investigation, my instinct to assign predominant blame to one side or the other turned out to be based on incomplete information. Had I stopped gathering information about the case, that instinct would have misled me. I don't recall whether I expressed any of my premature judgments about the Chevron case to students or others, but I may have. If so, I hope I didn't contribute to their misunderstanding. Indeed, even today two cadres of online partisans continue to battle over the case, each so outraged at the unethical behavior of the other side that neither can talk about much else when engaged on the subject.[14] The result was a tragedy for all concerned. The villagers' injuries were not fully redressed. Donziger lost his career and his reputation. And Chevron spent millions of dollars on lawyers, private investigators, and public-relations firms, money that could have been spent helping vulnerable people and cleaning up the pollution left behind in Ecuador.

One might reasonably ask, "Who has time for all that investigating before making a judgment? Most people can't put that much time and effort into understanding a single issue." True. People are busy. I put in the time only because it was part of my job to do so. No one can be endlessly curious about every important issue. But what we can do is to recognize that there are often devils in the details, unknowns that we may not yet fully understand or appreciate. We can try to be humble about what we believe we know and don't know, to resist certainty, and to avoid moral judgment in the absence of deep understanding.

ENERGY EXAMPLE 2: EMBRACING OPPOSING PERSPECTIVES

In the early 2000s, American public opinion was more evenly divided than it is now on fundamental questions of climate science. A Pew Research Center poll of Americans in 2006 reported that "roughly four-in-ten (41%) believe human activity such as burning fossil fuels is causing global warming, but just as many say either that warming has been caused by natural patterns in the earth's environment (21%), or that there is no solid evidence of global warming (20%)."[15] Teaching energy and environmental law during this era meant addressing this divide, particularly in the state of Texas. Before talking about climate policy in class back then, I asked students to research, develop, and be ready to argue the position on the causes of climate change that conflicted with their own view. I asked them specifically to pretend that they were assigned this contrary position in a competitive debate and to be ready to rebut anticipated counterarguments.

After completing the assignment, both sets of students reported significant changes in their views. Many of those who were predisposed to disbelieve the climate consensus moderated their views considerably. Much of that moderation came from the ease with which (they found that) they could debunk the then current attacks on the climate consensus, which included the idea that climate scientists fudge the data to win grant money and the unfounded allegation that there were methodological flaws in a leading climatologist's work.[16] Through their exposure to these ideas, undertaken alone in the absence of peer pressure or an audience, students shifted their thinking. Similarly, some of those who were predisposed to believe in human-driven climate change found that they had overestimated the uniformity of expert opinion projecting the future impacts of climate change. Some were surprised to learn about the wide variation in estimates of the social cost of carbon and in the projections that some places would see net benefits from climate change.[17] Many of these students became more understanding of climate-science doubters, even if their own positions on the core question remained consistent with the scientific consensus.

ENERGY EXAMPLE 3: BEWARE OF BIAS

For people who want to understand the devil in the details, it is important to seek out sources other than those who want mostly to persuade you. Problematically, the motives of a writer or speaker may not be easy to detect. Expertise alone doesn't remove bias, particularly if experts have an economic or ideological interest in promoting a particular belief. Try to find the people who aspire to objectivity and completeness in their presentations of the problem: people who really understand the problem deeply, at ground level, and/or people whose livelihoods depend on getting to the whole truth. They are the source of the kinds of qualifiers and caveats formerly found in the twentieth paragraph of a news story.

Since 2018, I have taught a law school seminar on the energy transition. For several years, I asked students to read studies commissioned by state governments to help policymakers decide how to compensate rooftop solar owners for the excess power they sent to the grid and whether to move away from net metering. All of the studies ostensibly aimed at estimating the value (in dollars per megawatt hour) of rooftop solar power. I asked students to try to understand how the study authors reached their conclusions by asking the students a long list of questions (too long to reproduce here), including "Did the authors estimate the effect of rooftop solar units on reducing afternoon demand for power from the grid, thereby reducing spot prices and the use of expensive gas-fired peakers?" "Did the authors estimate the effect of DERs on the grid's future investment needs (need for new lines or transformers)? Were those amounts a net positive or a net negative number, and why?" "Did the study place a dollar value on the pollution-reduction benefits of rooftop solar?" "How much of that benefit flows to the ratepayers on the same utility system? How much is captured by people outside of the state?" And so on.

The estimated values of rooftop solar power under the studies' varied wildly across states, from 25 percent of the wholesale rate in one state to 150 percent of the retail rate in another, but none of the analyses was terribly transparent in response to the questions I posed. That opacity may have been by design, to buttress the case for a preferred estimate that the client (government policymakers) wanted all along. I eventually stopped assigning those opaque studies and now assign a single, academic analysis that is more transparent about those subsidiary questions.[18]

CONVERSATION: BEING CURIOUS, NOT JUDGMENTAL

Recall Pete Buttigieg's prescription for actively open-minded conversation from the introduction: "Come at it the way you would approach a conversation with a family member who you care about." To be sure, this advice is difficult to follow for anyone who imagines policy adversaries as a homogenous group whose members are impervious to reason. But no political or ideological grouping is homogenous in that way.

Even the immovable members of the opposition are a heterogeneous group. Some are not impervious to reason; they have simply reached a different conclusion about climate policy. I have academic peers who are conservative regulatory policy scholars. They understand climate science but nevertheless sincerely believe that projections of particular climate-change-induced harms are too speculative to warrant costly mitigative action now. Or they believe that regulation is likely to do more harm than good. These colleagues are already immersed in the energy-transition debate, and some of them see the climate Left as oblivious to its own blind spots about these issues. I wouldn't expect them to be persuaded to change their voting behavior by further climate-policy discussion. If they eventually vote for a candidate who favors the energy transition, it will likely be for reasons other than the candidate's energy-policy positions. Similarly, I also know a few people whom I would call "QAnon adjacent" because they are attracted to conspiracy theories and equate "critical thinking" with reflexively distrusting experts and majority views. When that kind of simplistic contrarianism becomes sufficiently deeply ingrained in one's social or political identity, it may very well be that conversation cannot change it.

However, polling data strongly suggest that there are persuadable people in the electorate, many of whom are not (yet) part of the climate coalition. They include friends, neighbors, family, and coworkers who fall within the 34 percent of voters that the Yale Program on Climate Change Communication classifies as "cautious," "disengaged," or "doubtful" about climate or within the 35 percent of Americans whom the Pew Research Center identifies as the "ambivalent right," the "stressed sideliners," and the "outsider left."[19] These polls suggest that at least a third of voters have views that are not hardened by daily rhetorical battle over politics. They almost certainly include people who may harbor questions and doubts about climate and the energy transition but who are not impervious to careful persuasion. Growing the climate coalition requires engaging those voters—not simply engaging their views but engaging *them*. Engagement is about listening to the *people* who hold those views and trying to understand why they hold them.

EXPOSURE, EMPATHY, AND IMAGINATION

A comprehensive review of the sizable literature on depolarization is beyond the scope of this book, but some lessons from that literature are instructive for the climate coalition. A megastudy organized by a multidisciplinary group of scholars in 2022 examined the effectiveness of more than twenty "interventions" aimed at reducing partisan animosity and strengthening democratic institutions. Most of the studied techniques had some discernible positive effect. Among the most effective were those that sought to evoke empathy for the outgroup by presenting partisans with sympathetic, relatable examples of out-group members or focusing on the aspects of identity that cross partisans have in common.[20] These interventions consisted of little more than ways of getting people to see themselves in another's shoes. That step alone lessened partisan enmity.

This finding is consistent with the work of the political scientist Diana Mutz, who stresses that building cross-partisan empathy does not happen when one is alone in front of a computer screen. Rather, it requires encountering *people* across ideological and partisan boundaries. She puts it this way: "It would advance the cause of hearing the other side if people had more weak ties in their social networks. This is the reason, for example, that those who work outside the home are more exposed to oppositional views than those who do not." Encountering new people in person and on a daily basis improves our understanding of the political world: of policy issues and of each other. When these in-person encounters occur, we are more likely to avoid the sort of preemptive dismissiveness that kills productive conversation before it can begin. "The important skill of citizenship is not so much knowing everything there is to know about all conceivable political issues so one can debate them knowledgeably," states Mutz. "Instead, both informal deliberation and participation involve building and maintaining social and political networks, and both activities inevitably involve practical skills for social interaction."[21] In other words, the kind of engagement that truly persuades others is iterative. It takes time and usually involves frustration and setbacks, even the possibility or actuality of failure.

For those who are willing to try, approaching conversation as an actively open-minded thinker implies the possibility of being influenced by others and of exerting influence. It is about listening, evaluating, and keeping conversation going in the search for understanding and, perhaps, common ground. In the words of the academic philosopher Kwame Appiah,

> Conversations . . . begin with the sort of imaginative engagement you get when you read a novel or watch a movie or attend to a work of art that speaks from some place other than your own. So I'm using the word "conversation" . . . as a metaphor for engagement with the experience and ideas of others. And I stress the role of the imagination here because the encounters, properly conducted, are valuable in themselves. Conversation doesn't have to lead to consensus about anything, especially not values; it's enough that it helps people get used to one another.[22]

The encounters are "valuable in themselves" because conversations that preserve the relationship build trust. They raise the probability that future conversations might reveal mutually acceptable solutions.

Appiah is also describing a version of what communications and conflict-resolution professionals call "active listening." A communications consultant I know, Ray Thompson, likes to say that "active listening is more than waiting for your turn to talk." The United States Institute of Peace, an international conflict-mediation organization, defines it as "a way of listening and responding to another person that improves mutual understanding."[23] It is a conversational style that focuses not on convincing the other person of some predetermined proposition but rather on exploring their wants, needs, and positions in the service of finding common understanding. It avoids statements that close off dialogue and favors questions over argument. It includes both verifying that you understand and hear the points the other person is making as well as validating or empathizing with the emotional content of those points. None of these techniques requires agreeing with the other person or accepting their positions; rather, they are ways of trying to understand and learn from one another.

Every now and then one sees evidence of this sort of iterated discovery of complexity happening online as people's certainty about some aspect of climate or energy policy gives way to open grappling with the reality of trade-offs and the political difficulties they pose. That grappling produces questions such as "Would it be easier and cheaper to fight climate change if we were OK with the occasional blackout?" and "How do we transition to EVs without making inequality worse for apartment dwellers?" These kinds of questions are more typical of in-person communication than of social media exchanges. Nevertheless, posing them online to unseen others online is much more productive and persuasive than grappling with them privately and then simply proclaiming the "right" answer. As in the classroom, questions invite discussion, critical thinking, and therefore learning. They reflect and generate actively open-minded thinking. And as people grapple together with trade-offs, they will generalize the lesson that it is more productive to channel emotional energy into questions than into expressions of contempt for adversaries.

DEEP CANVASSING

A series of studies by the political scientists Joshua Kalla and David Broockman confirm this notion that persuasion is less about being right or having effective arguments and more about building a two-way communication.[24] Kalla and Broockman advocate the use of a political conversational style they call "deep canvassing," a process that involves asking open-ended questions, listening to the answers with sincere interest, and then asking more questions.[25] The follow-up questions might include asking whether the person's view might be different if the propositions they offered in support of that view weren't true. By avoiding *"You're wrong"* statements and instead posing questions, the conversation gives both participants space to think critically about their own views.

Hypothetical 1

Initial conversation:

It sounds like you really don't like that energy-transition legislation. Can you tell me more about why that is? [Open-ended question.]

[After the other person responds]:

I can see why you wouldn't want to see . . . (a) your energy bills go up; (b) something that interferes with the way you live your life; (c) politician X questioning your life choices. I get that. I would feel the same way if I thought that were happening to me.

Later, follow-up conversation:

Would you support energy-transition legislation that (a) meant that you pay less for crop insurance; (b) was structured so as not to increase your energy bill; (c) meant grant money to make your cattle ranch more efficient? Would that affect your position on the legislation?

Even if the conversation ends there, perhaps a seed of doubt has been planted.

Hypothetical 2

PERSON A: What is it about these proposed wind farms that you don't like? [Open-ended question.]

PERSON B: For one thing, they are going to create a noise problem with all the humming and whirring caused by the blades or a problem with shadow flicker, a kind of strobe effect that bothers people nearby and can make them sick], or a problem for farmers by displacing farmland.

PERSON A: I see. That does sound like a problem. Is that something that will affect you? Will you be able to hear the noise from your house? Will you be able to see the shadow flicker from your house?

PERSON B: No, but I care about my neighbors.

PERSON A: Yes! Of course. We have to look out for one another. I wonder how loud those turbines are for the people who live nearby? Do they have a way to measure that? So how does that shadow-flicker problem work? It hits people who live on a straight line between the setting sun and the turbine, right? Are there many people who are in that situation? So does that mean that farmers can't really farm around it? Is the developer trying to put it on farm land against the farmer's will?

In subsequent conversations, persons A and B can explore these questions further together. If they do, it may reveal that person B is under a set of misimpressions about the risks posed by wind farms, for example. Kalla and Broockman studied the use of these rhetorical techniques in conversations between political campaign staff and voters, but anyone can employ these techniques. Indeed, they ought to work more effectively among participants who know and trust each other already or who have more frequent interactions.

Note two things about these hypothetical conversations. First, they employ reactive questions, avoiding contradictions such as "No, you're wrong about that" or presumptuous accusations such as "Oh, then you must not care about X." Second, note that in the second hypothetical person A accepts that she cannot force person B to reverse his opposition to wind developments. All she can do is nudge him toward a more complete picture of the problem. If indeed it is true that some of the people who live near these developments will experience noise pollution or strobe effects from a wind farm, person A may have to accept that there is a certain logic to person B's opposition to the project on those grounds, even if person A disagrees. In that event, the conversation can always continue with new open-ended questions such as "Is there something that can be done to help those people?" and "What's your opinion on coal-fired power?" and "How do your kids feel about that wind farm?"

"BOND, CONNECT, AND INSPIRE"

The climate scientist Katherine Hayhoe has given a great deal of thought to the problem of climate-science communication. While her advice tracks many of the ideas contained in the deep-canvassing approach, her book *Saving Us: A Climate Scientist's Case for Hope and Healing in a Divided World* (2021) develops her model in more descriptive detail and adds elements of optimism and inspiration to the mix. As a mark of that optimism, Hayhoe believes that *most* people are persuadable. She recommends a three-step approach to conversation that she calls "bond, connect, inspire."

Step 1: *Bond*. Hayhoe advises finding some sort of common ground with the other person, something that may seem unrelated to climate or energy. Indeed, this is more than a recommendation; Hayhoe portrays this step as a necessary condition of persuasion. She argues that an atheist, for example, will have a hard time persuading people of faith on climate issues.[26] People have preexisting bonds with family, friends, and some coworkers. We may share with others a household or aspirations or hobbies or passions or a particular skill set. We can bond over these things. With strangers, we may have to search for that common interest or experience. Bonding is about establishing familiarity and trust.

Step 2: *Connect.* The next step is to connect that common interest, experience, or passion to the reasons "why climate change matters to you personally—not the human race in its entirety or the Earth itself, but rather us as individuals."[27] There are as many ways to do this as the number of interests people share. In her book, Hayhoe cites the example of a ski racer worried about how climate change was affecting snowpacks in places she loved to ski. The racer connected with other skiers to form a group called Protect Our Winters. Another of Hayhoe's examples involved a granddaughter who broached the subject of climate change with her grandmother by knitting warming stripes in scarves for their community. Says Hayhoe: "If you're wondering where to start bonding with someone and connecting on climate change, ask yourself[,] 'Because of what we both care about, why might climate change matter to us?' A sense of place is always a key connection. If you both live along low-lying coastlines . . . you're already seeing flooding on sunny days. If you're farmers . . . you've witnessed firsthand how climate change is shifting your seasons and amplifying your natural cycles of drought or flood and hitting you right where it hurts, in the pocketbook."[28]

Making these kinds of connections is enough. One needn't demand agreement or acquiescence from the other person. Rather, it is enough that the conversation helps to fill out the other person's understanding of the issue. It plants a seed that we cannot ever force to bloom but might bloom one day.

Step 3: *Inspire.* This step involves nothing more than talking about what people are already doing to address the climate problem—individuals, communities, and governments: "There are all kinds of solutions," Hayhoe points out, "from cutting our own food waste to powering buses with garbage to using solar energy to transform the lives of some of the poorest people in the world. There are solutions that clean up our air and our water, grow local economies, encourage nature to thrive, and leave us all better off, not worse. Who doesn't want that?"[29]

There are many ways to promote productive dialogue. If you believe that focusing on individual action distracts us from political mobilization, then focus on stories of political mobilization or climate-policy progress in state or local governments. If the momentum created by cascades of individual actions to reduce climate footprints resonates with you, use those stories to inspire action in others.

IDENTITY-BASED PERSUASION

The legal scholar Michael Vandenbergh, whose work on private climate governance was cited in chapter 4, is studying the efficacy of forms of climate persuasion that would leverage the importance of identity to today's voters, specifically conservatives' social identity. Vandenbergh's political analysis is similar to the analysis in this book, and so his working premise is that winning the support of the center-right is required to make real climate progress.

Toward that end, Vandenbergh is studying the scalability of two types of persuasion. The first focuses on correcting conservatives' misimpressions not about climate science or energy-transition trade-offs but rather about the beliefs of their fellow conservatives. Vandenbergh uses the term *pluralistic ignorance* to refer to these mistaken beliefs (or attribution errors) that some Republican voters may hold about their fellow Republicans. The idea here is that people may misperceive the norms of their own social group and so may align their own attitudes and behaviors to these misperceptions. For instance, many Republicans underestimate the percentage of fellow Republicans who accept the basic tenets of climate science.[30] Center-right conservatives' pluralistic ignorance may be exacerbated by the positions taken by elected Republican leaders, who are catering to their ideologically extreme and negatively partisan constituents. Interventions that correct these misperceived norms, therefore, hold the potential for reducing political polarization.

The second type of intervention leverages conservatives' discomfort with (or worries about) government regulation, something Vandenbergh calls *solution aversion*. If some voters deny that a problem exists because they do not like the anticipated solution, then perhaps that sort of solution aversion can be bypassed if conservatives learn about other solutions for which they feel no such aversion. Such solutions might include private-sector (rather than regulatory) climate responses, such as corporate procurement of clean energy, industry efficiency standards, and individual adoption of EVs. Some earlier research indicates that this kind of reassurance about solution aversion can change attitudes.[31] This idea leverages (rather than tries to change) conservatives' aversion to regulatory solutions, so even if it is effective at changing attitudes about the science of climate change, it may not necessarily change attitudes about strong climate policy. Nevertheless, if it yields significant reduction in the carbon intensity of economic activity, all the better.

These two types of intervention complement the identity-based interventions identified in the multiauthor megastudy referenced earlier.[32] So does the American Communities Project, which seeks to identify the roots of the disconnect between real and perceived political and socioeconomic conditions in the United States.[33] But whereas the megastudy and the American Communities Project focus on raising the salience of our common identity across partisan divides, Vandenbergh's work is focused on leveraging *partisan* identity. An encouraging sign is that all three efforts may identify policy interventions and messaging that might be scalable. For example, Vandenbergh is partnering with advocacy groups and the Millions of Conversations organization to explore how to engage Americans at the grassroots level, both online and offline, and to reduce vulnerabilities toward polarizing, "us-versus-them" messaging.[34] If these sorts of interventions prove persuasive, then perhaps they can bring about a broader attitude change through public messaging.

MORE EXAMPLES

The American Psychological Association's Life Tools series includes publications that aim to help people converse with political adversaries. The association stresses the importance of listening and connecting with the other person and of managing one's own emotions as ways of having more productive discussions.[35] Experts recently made this same point in the pages of the *Proceedings of the National Academy of Sciences*: "People believe that facts are essential for earning the respect of political adversaries, but our research shows that this belief is wrong. We find that sharing personal experiences about a political issue—especially experiences involving harm—help to foster respect[,] . . . increasing moral understanding and decreasing political intolerance."[36]

NPR's StoryCorps project has initiated a program called "One Small Step," described as "an effort to remind the country of the humanity in all of us." One Small Step asks individuals with different political views to record and share a fifty-minute conversation. The goal of these conversations is not debate or persuasion but rather understanding one another. They are not focused on any particular policy area or disagreement but rather on the process of bonding and connecting for its own sake.[37]

Another data-driven effort to bridge political divides is Project Home Fire, which is affiliated with the University of Virginia's Center for Politics. Project Home Fire uses polling and other data-analysis techniques to try to identify the roots of political division and thereby to suggest more effective paths forward.[38] This effort is also broader than climate policy but may yield lessons for climate-policy discussion.

A growing number of consultants and NGOs are focused on the urban–rural dimensions of the partisan divide and try to facilitate conversations with and within rural communities on climate and energy issues. Some frame their work in ways that reflect the sense of exclusion from political power that some rural voters feel. One group's website leads with this statement: "We are *unapologetically rural*. We stand up for the family farmer."[39] But these groups also reflect an optimism about energy-transition possibilities in rural areas.

For example, the Institute for Agriculture and Trade Policy runs a program it calls "Rural Climate Dialogues." The institute describes the program's problem- and community-centered approach that emphasizes local control:

The Rural Climate Dialogues use the innovative and time-tested Citizens Jury method for community problem solving and leadership development. This approach, which brings together a microcosm of the community to study an issue in-depth and generate a shared community response, has consistently provided a productive, educational, and inclusive way to address complex or divisive challenges. Each Dialogue focuses on a specific rural community and gathers a randomly selected but demographically representative group of citizens for a three-day moderated study and deliberation forum. They are tasked with creating a shared, community-based response to climate change and extreme weather events. *The panels are completely citizen-driven; no one tells them what to do or what to think.* The panelists have the liberty, information, and resources to produce their own recommendations that respond to community needs, priorities, concerns, and values.[40]

The Rural Reconciliation Project is a parallel effort that touches on climate issues indirectly by addressing land and water issues in rural communities.[41] Another organization, Good Steward Consulting, helps developers of renewable-energy projects gain community acceptance in rural areas. Good Steward principal Mariah Lynne identifies two key drivers of opposition to renewables in rural communities: aesthetics and economic rivalry between neighbors.[42] Her prescription for overcoming resistance emphasizes peer-to-peer communication, echoing Katharine Hayhoe in her emphasis on the importance of the messenger as much as the message and on bilateral conversations rather than ad campaigns, public meetings, or websites. Like Good Steward, the Center for Rural Affairs promotes clean-energy infrastructure (including transmission) in rural areas. Its website includes an interactive "clean-energy map" with which visitors can access stories about rural energy projects throughout the upper Midwest and parts of Canada.

This is just a sampling of the groups working on the kind of dialogue that can advance the energy transition.[43] The IRA and IIJA direct hundreds of millions of dollars to rural and other communities for clean-energy infrastructure development. Groups like these will be well situated to leverage that largesse into local support for the transition by productively engaging voters on climate issues.

IS THERE HOPE FOR ONLINE DIALOGUE?

It seems evident that our politics would be less dysfunctional if people relied less on social media and looked instead for more comprehensive treatments of climate and energy topics from sources that aim to educate rather than persuade them. *If* people sought out coverage by professional journalists and read their work to the last paragraph, *if* they discussed what they read within their existing social networks in ways that engage each other's experience, and *if* it were easier to avoid information sources that try to lobby us, *then* fewer people would be so firmly in the grip of negative partisanship. Yet the technoeconomic forces that shape modern politics seem to be here to stay. They will continue to reward purveyors of simple, moralizing narratives and punish purveyors of more careful, circumspect explanations of political reality.

If we must go online to find and retrieve information, it would improve our politics if more voters treated political discussion on social media as the danger it is and monitored that danger accordingly. We ought to treat our movement through the internet with intellectual and emotional care: get in, get only what we need, and get out. While there, we should move from place to place in the same way that visitors to Yellowstone National Park stick to the boardwalk to avoid falling into deadly geysers. We can try to be more aware of the conditions that tend to distort belief formation. If we have to be online, the best we can do is to watch out for those distortions and their effect on our own perceptions and beliefs and to promote actively open-minded thinking when we do post online.

WHAT TO WATCH OUT FOR

Platforms that permit longer-form communication, such as email or message boards, *can* be more conducive to learning, as are online

environments that eschew anonymity. The email exchanges repro-
duced in appendix F offer examples of experts communicating productively online; not coincidentally, membership in that email list is
moderated, and its rules prohibit anonymity.[44] Those features of the
institutional setting probably allow participants to explore the bases
of their disagreements more fully and with a minimum of vitriol. But
in most online environments, the habits of actively open-minded
thinking are inherently difficult to maintain, even when following
Kwame Appiah's advice about "engagement with the experience and
ideas of others." Not only does the presence of an audience make rhetorical concessions more emotionally costly, but even the most productive, learning-based conversations will be shared and mediated by
messengers who will use them to lobby and breed contempt, thereby
diminishing the educational effects of the conversation. Consider the
following examples.

Example 1: The Presence of an Audience

The presence of an audience distorts conversation, whether online or
offline. Seamus McGraw, who writes about rural communities and
energy, has recounted the story of being invited to speak at a small-
town bookstore "about my own moral ambivalence about the politically charged subject of fracking and climate change." McGraw's prior
expectations were that because the town had recently faced some of
the serious impacts of climate change, his audience would be ame-
nable to a nuanced discussion of the issue.

> At least that was what I thought until about midway through my
> talk, when a member of the audience stood up, and in graphic detail
> related an incident so horrible, so extreme, that it proved, at least in
> that person's mind, that those on the other side of the debate were
> so fundamentally evil that no compromise with them was possible,
> and that no sane person would even consider it.
> The incident, of course, had never happened. If it had, it would
> have been on the front page of every newspaper in the world. . . . But
> I could look into this person's eyes and see that the person was not
> lying to me. The story was related with the same fervent, passionate

faith with which a fundamentalist Christian might recount the story of Noah's flood. . . .

I'm not, by nature, a particularly confrontational person, and so rather than embarrass the person directly, I opted to ask a few probing questions. I made it to the third question, and then I saw a look of panic start to creep across the person's face. I actually felt a twinge of sympathy as the person slowly came to fear that the story didn't hold up under scrutiny. . . . At that moment, the person stood up, marched to the exit, spun around, glared at me, and sputtered, before storming out, "I'm not going to argue with you. I am comfortable in my ignorance!"[45]

It is human nature to want to avoid the embarrassment of a public error. The chances are very good that if McGraw had the very same exchange with that person in private—say, across a kitchen table—it would have gone very differently.

Example 2: Destructive Mediation

Sometimes informative, educational content is repackaged as propaganda. Beware of excerpted material taken out of context and repackaged as evidence supporting proposition X. If the repackaged material seems compelling, go back to the long-form original and find out if someone is manipulating you. As noted in chapter 5, the comedian Jon Stewart offers an example of an opinion leader whose approach to discussion of public issues moved away from contempt-based humor and toward deeper engagement across political boundary lines. As the host of an AppleTV+ public-affairs program in 2023, Stewart had a lengthy and illuminating debate about inflation and monetary policy with former treasury secretary Larry Summers.[46] (The conversation was also tangentially related to climate and energy.)

Summers has developed a reputation among progressives as a particularly objectionable "neoliberal." He earned that reputation by speaking about the relationship between inflation and unemployment in language that seems to reflect a lack of empathy for displaced workers, even an intellectual myopia about that trade-off.[47] In their conversation, Stewart challenged Summers's views on inflation in part by citing data showing that worker wage increases constituted a relatively small part of the inflation problem and that more of the revenue associated with higher prices was flowing to shareholders and corporate officers. Why, then, he asked Summers, do we raise interest rates in response to inflation rather than increase taxes for corporations or executive salaries? Summers's response acknowledged that inequality and lack of worker power were "the most serious problem[s]" the nation faces but argued that the only way monetary policy can address inflation is to manipulate interest rates, thereby affecting unemployment. The colloquy continued, touching on the merits of fiscal-stimulus payments to consumers, worries among low-income people about inflation, and the ethics of charging whatever prices for energy that the market will bear.

It was a fascinating and educational exchange that laid bare fundamental disagreements between the two men over the governance of markets and over the ethics of energy sellers' ability to capture windfall profits and scarcity rents when energy is in short supply. Stewart was troubled by the latter possibility, and Summers ultimately was not. The exchange crystallized contrasting points of view on a complex subject without jargon or nastiness. But unless viewers accessed the original broadcast directly through an AppleTV+ subscription, they would be most likely to encounter it through one of many YouTube links labeled in the familiar online language of rhetorical war: "John Stewart *dismantles* Larry summers," "Jon Stewart *stuns* Larry Summers," "Jon Stewart *shreds* Larry Summers," and so on.[48]

Some of these online messengers went further, deconstructing the conversation so as to present it not as an informative, civil exchange between two human beings trying to understand one another but rather as a battle of good versus evil. For example, consider the YouTube link entitled "Jon Stewart SHREDS Dishonest Moron's Inflation Lies." From the title, one might be surprised to learn that the link comes from a fairly well-established, popular progressive webcast, *The Majority Report w/ Sam Seder*.[49] The hosts of *Majority Report* contextualized the Stewart–Summers exchange for their viewers as they watched it by breaking it into pieces and reframing Summers's side of the discussion:

- "He's just saying this to cover his ass."
- "This is sociopath speak for 'we're going to put people out of work.'"
- "There's just so much bullshit here."
- "This is not about inflation. This is about disciplining labor."

This is recontextualization of an event for lobbying purposes, using the familiar Rush Limbaugh model ("What he really means is . . ."), this time from the ideological left. This approach is extremely common online, and it is part of the reason why private, face-to-face conversations are so much more productive than conversations online, even well-intentioned ones.

Example 3: Two Styles, One Person

Perhaps it is possible to sift online content to access the good and turn a blind eye to the bad. Some online thought leaders engage in more sober analysis of divisive issues in one context but fan the flames of contempt in another. They may use the latter approach out of a sense that they ought to give voice to the anger and resentment of the alienated and frustrated. Perhaps they believe that their own expressions of contempt for others are rarely misdirected. Or maybe they are making a tactical choice about different ways to be persuasive before different audiences.

The former Obama White House staffer Jon Favreau (not the actor-director) is one of the hosts of the left-leaning podcast *Pod Save America*, where he and fellow Obama administration alumni Jon Lovett and Tommy Vietor break down the political news of the day. They are self-described progressives, but theirs is also the perspective of former political professionals, with all the focus on tactics and inside-the-beltway norms that this perspective implies. The *Pod Save America* crew covered the 2021–2022 legislative battles over the IIJA, the BBB, and the IRA recounted in chapter 3. Those twice weekly episodes framed the motives of congressional progressives far more charitably than the motives of Kyrsten Sinema (D–AZ), Joe Manchin (D–WV), House Democrats who opposed portions of that bill, and of course, Republicans.[50] The tone of the podcast is often light-heartedly snarky and tends toward a cynical understanding of legislative politics not uncommon among those who have fought and lost legislative battles in Congress.

In 2021, Favreau started another podcast called *Offline*, focused on "all the ways that our extremely online existence is shaping everything from politics and culture to the how we live, work, and interact with one another."[51] It features longer-form interviews than are found on *Pod Save America*, many with experts who study how being online distorts our perceptions of truth and of each other, making us anxious and angry. *Offline* episodes feature titles that reflect the themes of this book, such as "Why Internet Debates Suck" (July 2022), "Hasan Piker Wants the Left to Persuade, Not Scold" (April 2023, with the left-wing blogger and journalist Hasan Piker), "How to Talk Your Uncle out of QAnon This Thanksgiving" (November 2022), "The Inside Story of How Silicon Valley Rewired Our Brains" (September 2022), and "What Democrats Could Learn from Republicans" (December 2022). *Offline* educates listeners about the pathologies of online communication and offers good advice about the kind of real voter persuasion necessary to build legislative coalitions, advice that is (frankly) not always modeled by the hosts on *Pod Save America*. What listeners will not find much of when listening to *Offline* are actual attempts to put that advice into practice by engaging those with differing political views. Favreau's guests are mostly progressive fellow travelers, not conservatives. But the discussion is more soberly diagnostic and more charitably understanding of policy adversaries.

When it comes to climate and energy-policy podcasts, even the most analytical are like *Offline* in that they almost exclusively feature political allies rather than adversaries. David Roberts, the left-leaning climate and energy journalist, has a podcast called *Volts*. It broadcasts conversations with experts that get into the weeds of energy-transition trade-off problems in ways that make the issues understandable to a broad audience. Chris Nelder's podcast *The Energy Transition Show*, covers similar ground. (Both podcasts represent a nice complement to chapter 5 of this book.) At the same time, neither *Volts* nor *The Energy Transition Show* really engages skeptics in ways that allow those skeptics to speak for themselves; rather, both seem tailored more to exploring trade-offs within the hosts' frames of reference—perhaps a conscious choice on the hosts' part.[52] But their discussions are meatier, more educational explorations of trade-offs than one can find on most social media platforms or in the hosts' respective Twitter feeds.

At the other end of the ideological podcasting spectrum sits conservative media firebrand Ben Shapiro, who is known for his acerbic and frenetic debating style. Shapiro communicates mainly via his own podcast (*The Ben Shapiro Show*), appearances on political debate shows hosted by others, and social media. His statements on the politics of the energy transition seem to accept climate science but reflect the pro-fossil-fuels arguments that are gaining currency in conservative circles. His most caustic and provocative remarks are widely shared by fans and foes alike, and he is not known for offering olive branches across the partisan or ideological divide. At the same time, he is perceptive about identifying attribution errors when those errors are directed at conservatives:

> Everybody who happens to be even slightly right-of-center is tired, sick of being labeled a white supremacist. They're tired of being labeled racist, they're tired of being labeled all the bad words in the universe simply because they disagree with Nancy Pelosi on tax policy and abortion. . . . [T]he Left doesn't understand this.
>
> So when people like me say, you know what, why don't you have a conversation with us? Because we actually agree on white supremacy being evil—we all agree that Nazis suck. We're all on the same page here. The first response of the Left is, "Ah but aren't you a Nazi?"[53]

Shapiro apparently sees no irony in generalizing about "the Left" with a broad brush while simultaneously complaining about generalizations applied to conservatives.[54] But like his left-leaning opposite numbers, he is expressing a sense of resentment that is felt by a broad set of voters.

One way to look at these offerings is to celebrate that there is something for everyone online when it comes to climate and energy policy. You can have a lot of substance on the nitty-gritty details of policy (*Volts*), or you can focus on political tactics (*Pod Save America*). You can have civility and kindness (*Offline*) or provocative, entertaining snark (Ben Shapiro or David Roberts on Twitter). That kind of variety sounds good at first blush. But each of these offerings is a circumscribed version of reality. Readers and listeners who look to Favreau or Roberts or Shapiro for information will glean very different understandings about what is true and what is important to know about the energy transition. They will be invited to admire very different stock heroes and feel contempt for different stock villains. Unfortunately, we are attracted to conflict, simplicity, and moral clarity online. And as suggested by table 6.1, many, many more people see opinion leaders' snarky tweets, which can be accessed quickly and for free, than their longer-form, more substantive discussions of issues in podcasts or articles.[55]

CONSTRUCTIVE PARTICIPATION

Members of the climate coalition can promote the norms of actively open-minded thinking online not only when consuming information, but also when participating in online discussion. As in real life, we can seek out holders of perspectives that differ from our own and engage them with more curiosity and less judgment. We can try to "bond, connect and inspire" and to use deep-canvassing techniques to build empathy and understanding. All of this takes practice, and the journey will be different for each person.

Qualifiers, caveats, open-ended questions, and nuance are good, even online. For example, if what you really *mean* is that "some" people do X or that they do it "sometimes," consider saying precisely *that*. We can all challenge (respectfully) the broad-brush generalizations that don't seem quite right, especially those made by our allies. When we suspect that other members of our community meant to make

TABLE 6.1 Listeners, Readers, Followers: Jon Favreau, David Roberts, Ben Shapiro

Favreau		Roberts		Shapiro	
Pod Save America listeners per episode	Offline subscribers and listeners per episode	Substack subscribers 46,000 listeners per episode (pod)	Twitter followers	The Ben Shapiro Show listeners per episode	Twitter followers
1.1 million[a]	8,000[a]	4,300[a]	197,000	1 million[a]	5.6 million

[a] These data were taken in May 2023 from Rephonic, which tracks listenership for podcasts.

their point in a more careful or precise way, we can help them do so. Better yet, we can *ask* them what they really meant. We can avoid reacting to an ambiguous statement by filling in the blanks in uncharitable ways. We can resist the temptation for the catharsis that comes from scolding others with clever, pithy put-downs. Mostly, we can remember that some of the people seeing our public speech may consider themselves a member of the class that we are tempted to malign.

Meanwhile, we can hope that as the political environment in the United States deteriorates, more people online will tire of bitter rhetorical war. Perhaps more will sense that systematic bias is denying them a more complete understanding of a problem and choose to work harder to counteract those biases. Effective leaders have long understood the value of opinion diversity and the corresponding dangers of unanimity within insular groups. The former General Motors CEO Alfred Sloan once responded to group unanimity this way: "Gentlemen, I take it we are all in agreement on the decision here. Then, I propose we postpone further discussion of this matter until the next meeting to give ourselves time to develop disagreement, and perhaps gain some understanding of what the decision is all about."[56] Energy and climate leaders who choose to be on social media can try to emulate that kind of leadership online by supporting critical thinking and inviting challenges to all points of view (including their own).

THE ENERGY TRANSITION, LIBERAL DEMOCRACY, AND HOPE

ONLY *VOTERS* CAN REPAIR LIBERAL DEMOCRACY

The United States cannot get to net zero without national legislation limiting GHG emissions. The national politicians who might create that legislation respond to electoral risks and rewards, and most of them see little to be gained by changing their existing positions on climate policy. Republican politicians recognize that their conservative constituents view Democrats and the Left as condescending moral scolds who threaten both Republican conservatives' cultural identity and their access to affordable, reliable fossil-fueled energy services.

Democratic politicians know that their constituents see Republicans and the Right as the more or less willing dupes of the corrupt and the wealthy and infer that corruption must be driving disfavored policy outcomes even when we don't observe it. A worrying number of voters now see fundamental political institutions as mere weapons in policy fights rather than as important mechanisms for peaceful conflict resolution worthy of our protection.

American democracy cannot survive in a climate of ever-increasing mutual contempt, and only voters can break the cycle. After the U.S. Department of Justice indicted former president Donald Trump for participation in a conspiracy to use fraudulent electors to overturn the 2020 presidential election, the UCLA law professor Richard Hasen argued in the pages of *Slate* magazine that the case is "perhaps the most important indictment ever handed down to safeguard American democracy" because its resolution will influence the possibility of continued peaceful transfers of power in the United States.[57] The former federal judge J. Michael Luttig, a George W. Bush appointee, joined Hasen in blaming Trump for putting himself in legal jeopardy, as did several conservative legal academics.[58] But the reaction among podcasters, influencers, and many voters on the ideological right mostly ignored the legal merits of the suit, characterized the case as political persecution, and vowed "legal retribution . . . against corrupt Democrats" when the GOP recaptures the presidency.[59] The prevailing cynicism is reflected in the observation made by a prominent newspaper columnist that the government attorneys prosecuting former president Trump must persuade "not only the judges and jurors . . . [but also] the American public, who will decide *whether Trump ultimately has the power to overrule a verdict*."[60]

None of this bodes well for the politics of the energy transition. Voters in the few remaining contestable jurisdictions will determine whether Congress can produce a republican moment for the energy transition.[61] The omnipresence of the propaganda machine drastically reduces the probability that Republican voters will elicit changes in the party's opposition to strong climate policy or that blue-wave elections will sweep large numbers of Democrats into power. It forces politicians who resist the forces of negative partisanship to pay an electoral price for their resistance. GOP voters punish presidential candidates who criticize Donald Trump, just as they punish congressional Republicans who championed carbon taxes and other forms of GHG-emission regulation and reward politicians who embrace fossil fuels.[62]

The bottom-up nature of the political problem is underscored by a description of Donald Trump's relationship with the Republican Party in 2023: "Even if top donors and officials detest the former president, *they cannot afford to anger his devoted base.* Nearly every elected Republican of note and every candidate who is, or is thought to be, seeking the presidency has felt compelled to inveigh against [those investigating Trump for crimes]. Mr. Pence, whom Trump supporters wanted to lynch on January 6th, came to his former boss's defence, calling it 'another politically charged prosecution.' Nikki Haley, a former Trump cabinet member who is running for president, called the prosecution 'more about revenge than it is about justice.' "[63] Today, negative partisans insist that their representatives make decisions that frustrate the objectives of the other side. That is more important to them than good governance. One disturbingly frequent illustration of this trend is the parties' periodic brinksmanship in Congress over extensions of the government-debt ceiling. Defaulting on public debt is the height of fiscal irresponsibility. It does clear, measurable damage to the national economy, which is why wealthy and business constituents oppose it.[64] Yet safe-seat politicians sometimes risk it because it pleases their most ideologically extreme and electorally important constituents. Thus, the members of Congress who voted against raising the debt ceiling in the summer of 2023 tended to be the most ideologically extreme members representing the safest seats. Those representatives were tending neither to the interests of oligarchs nor to the wishes of their average constituent but rather to the more extreme preferences of the average constituent of their own party.

Table 6.2 illustrates these points using the now-familiar DW-NOMINATE measure of congressional member ideology and the *Cook* Partisan Voting Index (PVI) measure of district partisan lean. Congress voted to raise the debt ceiling and avoid a default in the summer of 2023, but there were GOP dissenters who wanted additional spending limits as a condition of approving the extension and Democrat dissenters who opposed the spending limits that were included

TABLE 6.2 Differences Between Congressional Supporters and
Opponents of the 2023 Debt-Ceiling Extension

	Members' Median Conservatism Score[a]		District Median Cook PVI[b]	
	Supporters	Opponents	Supporters	Opponents
House Democrats	−0.37	−0.45	D + 11	D + 20
House Republicans	0.45	0.64	R + 13	R + 15
Senate Democrats	N/A[c]	N/A[c]	N/A[c]	N/A[c]
Senate Republicans	0.37	0.58	R + 10	R + 21

[a] DW-NOMINATE first-dimension score, 2023.

[b] *Cook* PVI score (2023 for House, 2022 for Senate).

[c] No Senate Democrats voted nay.

in the debt-ceiling bill. Both sets of dissenters were free to take the more reckless position in this vote because they knew that they faced no electoral risk in doing so (and that others would vote for passage). Indeed, after the vote, former Trump adviser Steve Bannon suggested that conservative representatives Marjorie Taylor Greene (R–GA) and Jim Jordan (R–OH), who voted for the measure, should face primary challenges from "real MAGA" candidates precisely because they did the fiscally responsible thing.[65]

FACING DIFFICULT REALITY WITH HOPE

It is imperative that this trend of ever-increasing polarization and tribalism be broken. If it continues to escalate, it risks the kind of periodic, identity-based political violence we associate with the sectarian conflicts of Northern Ireland and Israel/Palestine. A similar kind of unrest bubbled in the United States before the Civil War as well. Only voters can change this dynamic peacefully.

I teach grad students, most of whom are in their twenties. Many seem to have an intuitive sense of how the modern information environment is influencing American political life for the worse.[66] Many are unhappy with the status quo and urgently want to change it. Some struggle not to be cynical. If cynicism is critical thinking without hope,[67] then the observation from comedian Conan O'Brien in the second chapter epigraph—that cynicism isn't helpful—is certainly correct. Growing the climate coalition requires critical thinking *and* hope. It requires the climate coalition to remain hopeful *and* to face, perspicaciously and transparently, *both* the difficult trade-offs we must make to get to net zero and the true nature of the political dysfunction that stands in the way of the energy transition. Part of the propaganda machine's effectiveness is that it catches us off guard. If we can learn to recognize its effects, perhaps we can change the way we talk about the politics of the energy transition. If the frog becomes aware that the pot is coming to a boil, maybe it will seek an escape.

Difficult Reality

It is important for the climate coalition to appreciate the danger of political catastrophe as keenly as they do the danger of climate catastrophe. As noted previously, scholars see disturbing parallels between today's American politics and historical transitions away from democracy and toward autocracy. Their analyses are sobering. They warn that the temptation "to think that our democratic heritage automatically protects us against such threats . . . is a misguided reflex." In the presence of that complacency, populism can morph into authoritarianism.[68] Those warnings are *diagnostic*, offered in the service of finding better solutions and averting disaster. Crucially, scholars studying transitions to autocracy stress the importance of engaging political adversaries and of *aiming* for empathy.

For example, Timothy Snyder argues we need to understand why "democracies can fall, ethics can collapse, and ordinary men can find themselves standing over death pits with guns in their hands." Unsurprisingly, part of Snyder's answer lies in the destructive effects that propaganda exerts on belief. Echoing the epigraphs from Russell and Voltaire in the introduction and chapter 4, respectively, Snyder says that we "submit to tyranny when [we] renounce the difference between what [we] *want to hear* and what is actually the case." The way to inoculate ourselves against this risk, says Snyder, is to practice critical thinking and to engage people outside of our respective bubbles. In his words, we should put ourselves "in unfamiliar places with unfamiliar people. Make new friends and march with them."[69] The political scientists Steven Levitsky and Daniel Ziblatt foresee a near future they call "democracy without guardrails," in which negative partisanship continues to further undermine liberal institutions. The best chance for avoiding that descent, they say, is to "preserve, rather than violate, democratic rules and norms."[70]

Ivan Krastev and Stephen Holmes offer another scholarly analysis of the ascendance of nationalist authoritarianism in Europe and the United States, one that takes readers up to the edge of the cliff of hopelessness but closes with this possibility: "We believe that the end of [liberal hegemony in the world] will spell either tragedy or hope depending on how liberals manage to make sense of their post–cold war experience. We can endlessly mourn the globally dominant liberal order that we have lost or we can celebrate our return to a world of perpetually jostling political alternatives, realizing that *chastised liberalism* . . . remains the political idea most at home in the twenty-first century."[71] "Chastised liberalism" sounds a lot like what the legal scholars Joseph Fishkin and William Forbath call a "democracy of opportunity"—one that eschews persistent oligarchy and sustained minority rule and embraces a democratic politics that is more responsive to durable majority opinion and is capable of developing national solutions to national problems, such as climate change.[72]

One more example. In her Pulitzer Prize–winning explanation of why Western democracies are slouching toward authoritarianism, the international-relations writer Anne Applebaum frames her frightening analysis of the problem as a "let's get to work" challenge:

[Maybe those who want a society] where rational debate is possible, where knowledge and expertise are respected, where borders can be crossed with ease represent one of history's cul-de-sacs. We may be doomed, like glittering. multiethnic Habsburg Vienna or creative, decadent Weimar Berlin, to be swept away into irrelevance. . . . Or maybe . . . we will renew and modernize our institutions. . . . Maybe the reality of illness and death will teach people to be suspicious of hucksters, liars and purveyors of disinformation.

Maddeningly, we have to accept that both futures are possible. No political victory is permanent, no definition of "the nation" is guaranteed to last, and no elite of any kind, whether so-called "populist" or so-called "liberal" . . . rules forever.[73]

Again, such warnings are not cynical doomerism. They are wake-up calls.

When people become too cynical, these wake-up calls fall on deaf ears. Cynics look outward and see a situation in which nothing can be done to avert disaster. Were they to look inward, however, they might stop focusing on the contemptibility of adversaries and instead get to work building majority support for the energy transition one voter at a time.

Hope

Even if the road to building a climate majority is long, there are hopeful facts on which to focus. First, we are learning that the most pessimistic of the earlier climate scenarios—those that feed doom narratives—look increasingly unlikely. The Environmental Defense Fund characterized the IPCC's AR6 report of 2023 (see chapter 3) this way: "There's good news on future projections of climate change. A combination of factors—including strengthened commitments—has led to a reduction in the expected warming by at least a degree from a very high emissions scenario. There's a lot of work ahead, but this shows that the future is not set in stone. We can make it safer."[74] Even the writer David Wallace-Wells, a mere three years after he popularized the idea of a climate-change-induced "uninhabitable earth," wrote in an op-ed that we ought to reject "millenarian intuitions of an ecological end of days."[75]

Second, the climate and energy-transition models on which we rely today describe only possible futures. Meanwhile, technological advancement continues, holding out the potential for trade-offs to become easier. Cost-cutting innovations in clean energy will continue, and we will reap some of their benefits even if we can't foresee exactly what those innovations will be. The incentives in the IRA should hasten that kind of technoeconomic progress, assuming Congress doesn't repeal or weaken the statute. As firms compete for contracts to build geothermal-energy projects, hydrogen-production projects, battery projects, CCS projects, wind and solar projects, and so on, their competition will put downward pressure on prices and upward pressure on quality. Innovation will stimulate better, cheaper technologies that ought to make a net-zero future more reliable and affordable. Even without a major technoeconomic breakthrough, utilities and ISOs/RTOs cannot resist forever customer and investor pressure to add inexpensive wind and solar power to their systems, particularly in coal-heavy regional electricity markets that are composed mostly of Democrat-led states—such as the PJM and MISO markets as well as the markets of certain western states. State PUCs may embrace a more transition-focused role. Or perhaps regulators will begin to use their statutory authority more aggressively to facilitate transmission investment over the objections of NIMBY groups.

Third, "net zero by 2050" is an aspirational goal. It is not the do-or-die scientific imperative of worried imagination, even if some climate activists see strategic reasons to treat it that way. The Paris Agreement of 2016 concluded that global warming should be kept "well below" 2°C and that nations ought to "pursue efforts" to keep warming to 1.5°C. The IPCC later concluded that meeting the latter target required getting to net zero by 2050. It is an error to interpret these conclusions as establishing some sort of climate-doomsday threshold. There is a long tradition of unmet but helpful aspirational goals in U.S. environmental law.[76] But the line between ambition and alarmism is a fine one. Ambition can motivate, but alarmism can paralyze people and backfire politically. Climate progress is a continuum, not a cliff. Holding warming to 1.5°C will avert more harm than holding the goal to 2°C; holding warming to 2°C is better than holding it to 2.5°C; and so on. It is a mistake to let the perfect be the enemy of the good. There is progress to be made, and every bit of progress helps. Stepping back and looking at the whole picture can lessen the sense of urgent anxiety that feeds the climate of contempt. That deep breath, in turn, can help sharpen the climate coalition's thinking about the political challenge ahead.

Last, the climate coalition can reasonably hope that the popularity of its political project will pay off in ways that we cannot now foresee. Right now, the politics of the energy transition seems fraught because the future of the U.S. political economy is fraught. Fundamental questions of majority rule, economic freedom, political participation, and whether the U.S. government can still produce collective solutions to problems that markets cannot solve seem to be up in the air. The conservative revolution of the late twentieth century effectively destroyed the New Deal Consensus, hobbling not only regulatory policy but also collective political action generally. Now, elected Republicans pursue a deregulatory, antiredistributive agenda that looks entirely inconsistent with Democrats' policy agenda, including the energy transition.

However ambivalent Americans may be about "the regulatory state" as an idea, they support the individual regulatory regimes that constitute it. Most people want securities laws and antitrust laws that ensure fair competition as well as consumer, health and safety, and environmental laws that protect them from physical and economic harm. They want public goods such as roads, bridges, police, courts, and national defense that markets tend to undersupply. And they want the energy transition, even if its particulars worry them. Even if the New Deal *Consensus* is dead, the New Deal *Majority* isn't—at least among voters. That fact should offer hope to the climate coalition, even if those voters' voting behavior is dominated by affective, negative partisanship. The cynical, resentful nihilism channeled and modeled by Donald Trump remains influential within the Republican Party. It has proven electorally successful in solidly Republican jurisdictions, and so other politicians emulate it. Only voters can stop it by punishing it at the ballot box.

IN CONCLUSION

In the spring of 2023, CNN televised a town hall event featuring former president Donald Trump. Over the course of the evening, Trump insulted one of the women he had previously sexually assaulted, repeated the lies that prompted the January 6 insurrection, and called one of the Black Capitol police offers on duty that day a "thug."[77] The CNN host Anderson Cooper later lamented that Trump supporters at the town hall, "young and old, our fellow citizens, people who love their kids and go to church, laugh[ed] and applaud[ed] his lies."[78] This climate of contempt "horrifies" (to borrow Pete Buttigieg's word) Democrats, but it also feeds a problematic schism in the Democratic Party over the merits of liberal aspirations to objectivity and civility and whether Democrats ought to mirror right populists by channeling voter resentment and demonizing their opponents.

But "organizing hatreds" in that way carries its own dangers. Like any simmering, identity-based feud, each side sees its cause as righteous. Escalation tends mostly to deepen each side's commitment to its cause. The French economist and essayist Frédéric Bastiat may have been thinking of his nation's volatile experience with extremist populism in the early nineteenth century when he warned of the dangers posed by the breakdown of foundational civic norms: "When misguided public opinion honors what is despicable and despises what is honorable, punishes virtue and rewards vice, encourages what is harmful and discourages what is useful, applauds falsehood and smothers truth under indifference or insult, a nation turns its back on progress and can be restored only by the terrible lessons of catastrophe."[79] Bastiat wrote those words about a decade before the American Civil War, the catastrophic "interlude" to which the political scientist Robert Dahl referred in the introduction. That war preserved American liberal democracy the only time it was as ferociously divided as it is today. Avoiding that sort of violence and pain this time around will require repairing democratic norms.

So the cure, or palliative care, for American democracy is the same course of action that will further the cause of getting to net zero: namely, engaging directly those on the other side of the partisan and ideological divide. The remainder of Anderson Cooper's remarks about the CNN town hall echoed Pete Buttigieg: "They are your family members, your friends and neighbors, and they vote. . . . [D]o you think staying in your silo and only listening to people you agree with is going to make [Trump] go away? If we only listen to those we agree with, it may do the opposite."[80] Cooper is echoing a growing chorus of academic voices expressing ideas that are underrepresented in today's hypercompetitive political media landscape: to *put ourselves in unfamiliar places with unfamiliar people, "make new friends and march with them,"* to borrow Timothy Snyder's phrase. It is emotionally uncomfortable outside of our bubbles, but venturing out is worth it. Moving outside our bubbles will facilitate a better understanding of most political issues, including the fundamentals of energy-transition politics and policy. Even though the process is socially uncomfortable, reaching that deeper understanding is satisfying. It can even be exciting outside the bubble. And once we are outside the bubble, the challenge is to avoid drifting back in.

Before the pandemic, I had a conversation with a climate reporter from my original home state of New York. During the conversation, I detected the reporter hinting to me that living in Texas and working for the University of Texas might be biasing my views about energy issues toward the perspective of the fossil-fuel industry. Like most people, the reporter was focused on my biases rather than on the reporter's own. But the suggestion about me was correct, and I had been thinking hard about that issue.

A year or so before that conversation, I was faced with an attractive opportunity to move to another law school in an East Coast city. I ultimately declined the job offer in part *because* I would lose touch with the political and energy-policy influences that come from living in Texas. I am a lifelong liberal Democrat, living in a liberal city (Austin, Texas), and working among a University of Texas law faculty who for the most part sit to the left of the ideological center. A strong majority of my friends and peers outside of Austin are liberal Democrats. I have supported environmental NGOs during most of my adult life, and I am a supporter of the energy transition, as I have made clear throughout this book. But at the University of Texas, I regularly encounter people who are just as likely to be Republicans as Democrats, conservatives as liberals, working in the wind and solar industries *as well as* in the oil and gas industry. All of those influences are in the ether in Austin. I worried that if I lived in Seattle or Boston or Washington, DC, or Los Angeles, I would miss the way those influences broaden my particular frame of reference.

However each of us does so, it is important to break out of the climate of contempt triggered by the propaganda machine. That machine feeds the instinct to use moral suasion and shame as political weapons, but those tools cannot create the net electoral effects—the right changes in the right places—that will lead to durable congressional majorities for the energy transition. The better approach is to resist the "delicious" moral judgments that predominate online and instead to engage people who think differently about climate and energy than we do. Engaging with others—listening to and discussing with them how to build a cleaner energy system *and* keep the lights on *and* make sure we meet the needs of the economically vulnerable along the way—can help us to move beyond the climate of contempt to create a durable, lower-carbon energy future. This is the more hopeful and peaceful path to net zero.

NOTES

INTRODUCTION

1. See, e.g., Bazerman 2022; Prentice 2008. On the hardening of mutually exclusive understandings of American political economy, see appendix G, http://www.ClimateOfContempt.com/Appendices/.
2. Some argue that the word *tribal* should be avoided because it evokes a violent or otherwise pejorative view of African peoples and European colonialism (Lowe 2001). But this argument ignores historians' long-standing application of the term much more broadly to most ethnicity-based social groups, such as the Celts, Slavs, Vikings, Mongols, Franks, Picts, and many other non-African tribes with histories of violent ethnic conflict. The Merriam-Webster dictionary defines *tribalism* as "strong in-group loyalty." In this book, I use the terms *tribal* and *tribalism* in this sense.
3. For readers not familiar with the cultural context of antinuclear activism in the late 1970s, it is worth noting that the Three Mile Island accident occurred less than two weeks after release of the blockbuster Hollywood film *The China Syndrome* (James Bridges, 1979, with Jane Fonda, Jack Lemmon, Michael Douglas), in which owners and operators of a nuclear power plant try to cover up an accident at the plant. Shortly after the real-life accident, many of the popular musicians of the day (Bruce Springsteen, Bonnie Raitt, James Taylor, Jackson Browne, Carly Simon, and Crosby, Stills, and Nash, among others) staged a series of antinuclear concerts in New York City under the banner of an organization called Musicians United for Safe Energy (MUSE). Another film about the nuclear industry, *Silkwood* (Mike Nichols, 1983, with Meryl Streep, Cher), posited that the automobile crash that killed a real-life industry whistleblower was an intentional homicide orchestrated by industry officials to prevent her from disclosing the existence of dangerous corner cutting in the construction of a nuclear power plant.

4. This conflation of "is/ought" questions has long plagued environmental law. See Spence 1995; Kysar and Salzman 2003, 1102 ("despite . . . the maturation of environmental law into distinct fields of study, one still basically sees two warring camps, both politically and ideologically entrenched on opposite sides of the battlefield").

5. Some scholars see an inherent tension between political activism and tolerance of pluralism. See, for example, Mutz 2006, 3 ("The best environment for cultivating political activism is one in which people are surrounded by those who agree with them, people who will reinforce the sense that their own political views are the only right and proper way to proceed"). But John Stuart Mill saw value in activists' myopia: "For our own part, we have a large tolerance for one-eyed men, provided their one eye is a penetrating one: if they saw more, they probably would not see so keenly, nor so eagerly pursue one course of inquiry" (1838, 291). See also Isaiah Berlin's ideas on this subject, including his essay on the fox and hedgehog, in Cherniss and Hardy [2004] 2022, esp. sections 4 and 5.

6. A poll conducted by Pew Research in 2022 found that among Democrats 90 percent favored the United States taking steps to become carbon neutral, while only 44 percent of Republicans supported this goal. However, 67 percent of the youngest Republicans, ages eighteen to twenty-nine, support the United States taking steps to become carbon neutral by 2050 (Tyson, Funk, and Kennedy 2022).

7. Perhaps the best-qualified quasi-dissenter is the climatologist Judith Curry, whose work confirms anthropogenic climate change but whose emphasis on the uncertainty around global-warming projections has led her to question the value of reducing emissions now.

8. The gases I refer to here trap more solar radiation than other elements and compounds found in the atmosphere, which gives rise to the term *greenhouse gases* (GHGs). The largest by volume is CO_2, but methane (natural gas), fluorocarbons, and a few other important compounds are also GHGs. In this book, the terms *carbon emissions* and *atmospheric carbon* will refer to all these GHGs. Each gas has a distinct global-warming potential—that is, each traps heat at a different rate and survives in the atmosphere for a different duration. Therefore, when discussing global-warming potential all numbers are normalized to their CO_2 equivalent (CO_2e). For a digestible explanation of this idea, see "Global Warming Potential," Wikipedia, https://en.wikipedia.org/wiki/Global _warming_potential.

9. "Health Benefits Far Outweigh the Costs of Meeting Climate Change Goals," World Health Organization, December 5, 2018, https://www.who.int/news/item /05-12-2018-health-benefits-far-outweigh-the-costs-of-meeting-climate-change -goals.

10. See "Climate Models Reliably Project Future Conditions," National Academies of Science, August 3, 2023, https://www.nationalacademies.org/based-on -science/climate-models-reliably-project-future-conditions; and Buis 2020.

11. An IPCC report states this conclusion with a "high degree of confidence" (H. Lee, Calvin, Dasgupta, Geden, et al. 2023, 12, 26). RealClimate.org is a good source for primers on the science of so-called climate tipping points, such as the weakening of the Gulf Stream (which is part of the Atlantic Meridional Overturning Circulation), permanent loss of albedo (reflective) capacity associated with loss of sea ice, and release of methane from thawing permafrost.

12. See, e.g., H. Lee, Calvin, Dasgupta, Geden, et al. 2023; and H. Lee Calvin, Dasgupta, Krinner, et al. 2023.

13. Bagri 2017 (describing the massive effort to relocate the village on Isle de Jean Charles, Louisiana, which is being overtaken by the Gulf of Mexico); Waldholz 2017 (describing how thawing of the frozen permafrost underneath the village of Newtok, Alaska, is eroding away land along a river, necessitating villagers' relocation). See also E. Brown 2018, 28–30, and "FAQ: The California Coastal Commission and Sea Level Rise," 2021, https://documents.coastal.ca.gov/assets /slr/CC-SLR-FAQ-Release.pdf.

14. Schulte, Dridge, and Hudgins 2015 (on Tangier); Gewin 2018 (on Maryland).

15. On the Gulf of Mexico and Atlantic coast, see Sweet et al. 2022; Yin 2023; and Dangendorf et al. 2023. On Florida, see "What Climate Change Means for Florida," EPA 430-F-16-011, 2016, https://www.epa.gov/sites/default/files/2016-08 /documents/climate-change-fl.pdf; Flavelle and Mazzei 2021; K. Miller 2020; and Verchick 2023 (chronicling effects of sea-level rise in Miami).

16. Duncan 2021.

17. Berardelli 2019.

18. See, e.g., Cappucci and Samenow 2021; Grullón Paz 2022; Tebor 2021 (warning that the low water levels in the Pacific Northwest are encouraging wildfire spread).

19. "2020 Year-to-Date Temperatures Versus Previous Years," Annual 2020 Global Climate Report, NOAA National Centers for Environmental Information, 2021, https://www.ncei.noaa.gov/access/monitoring/monthly-report/global/202013 /supplemental/page-1.

20. Leonhardt and Wu 2021.

21. Buis 2022.

22. "Extreme Wetness of 2019 Sets Records," NOAA National Centers for Environmental Information, May 7, 2020, https://www.ncei.noaa.gov/news/extreme -wetness-2019-sets-records; Eddy et al. 2021.

23. NOAA National Centers for Environmental Information 2023.

24. Wilkinson 2021; Flavelle 2021.

25. "FEMA Offers More Equitable Flood Insurance Rates Beginning Oct. 1," FEMA press release, 2021, https://www.fema.gov/press-release/20210924/fema-offers -more-equitable-flood-insurance-rates-beginning-oct-1 (noting that by statute most rate increases are capped at 18 percent per year).

26. Diffenbaugh, Davenport, and Burke 2021.

27. Gerson and Goodman 2007, 44–45. This information comes from an account of a classified report leaked to a British newspaper (Townsend and Harris 2004).

28. Lustgarten 2020.

29. See chapter 3 for a fuller discussion of the effect of recent state politics on the energy transition.

30. See Jensen et al. 2012 (finding that party polarization and partisanship were extreme in the late nineteenth century and early twentieth century before decreasing in the mid–twentieth century).

31. This book assumes a basic familiarity with the idea that American democracy is "liberal" democracy in the sense that its basic policymaking structures and rules combine democratic governance with limits on majority control and on the reach of governmental power. This use of the term *liberalism* traces the idea to John Locke and other Enlightenment philosophers. Some scholars use the term differently to signify an antiregulatory *economic* philosophy that arose later, during industrialization (Fawcett 2014; Fishkin and Forbath 2022). As considered here, liberalism is a *political* philosophy that accommodates regulation of markets by democratic governments. It is

distinguished from *neoliberalism* or laissez-faire capitalism in this way. The term *neoliberal* is applied, usually pejoratively, to the political-economic philosophy that advocates for less regulation and more faith in markets to produce social good. Chapter 2 critically examines that philosophy but avoids the term *neoliberal* to prevent confusion between a form of government (liberal democracy) and a particular set of conservative policy preferences (neoliberalism).

32. There is some irony in the fact that Baby Boomers—a generation that energized several left-leaning social movements in the 1960s and 1970s, some of them violent—now face the same charges of apathy, selfishness, or indifference they once leveled at their elders. The left populists of the 1960s applied the term *fascist* liberally to those on their ideological right and produced axioms such as "Never trust anyone over thirty" and "I hope I die before I get old." (Both quotations come from the year 1965: the first from the activist Jack Weinberg and the second from the song "My Generation" by the Who.) For more discussion of Democrats' intraparty divides, see chapters 3–5.

33. See Hayek 1944 (articulating the case against government economic planning in a way that has made him a modern icon of free marketism); Harrington 1989 (articulating an argument for a social democratic version of "socialism" for the United States); Beard 1913 (arguing that the U.S. Constitution was adopted to protect the interests of the wealthy and upper-class members of society); d'Entreves 2022 (on Hannah Arendt, whose political philosophy is not neatly presented in any single work but displays an impatience with the countermajoritarian aspects of liberalism and is more tolerant of revolutionary episodes than are most liberal theorists); Riker 1982 (presenting a rational-choice defense of Lockean liberalism against the populism of Rousseau); Dahl 1956 (analyzing the tensions between republican democracy and majoritarianism); Mills 1956 (arguing that military, corporate, and political leaders share mostly common interests and that they can effectively manipulate the masses in the successful pursuit of those interests); Urofsky 2009 and Murphy 1982 (on Brandeis, who expressed his progressive reform instincts more through his actions than his writings); Hobhouse 1911 (arguing for liberalism's adaptation to the majority's need for protections from the predations of the market in the industrial age); and Marx 1887 (an exhaustive critique of capitalist liberal democracy in the Industrial Age).

34. For a fuller development of this idea, see Spence 2002 and Farber and Frickey 1991, making this same claim before I did.

35. Dahl 1956, 4, 135.

36. Bokat-Lindell 2022. For a summary of polling that suggests declining support for liberal-democratic norms among Americans, see Galston and Kamarck 2022.

37. Snyder 2021.

38. *The American Mind*, a publication of the Claremont Institute, published an essay arguing the government is being destroyed by "progressive tyranny" and describing the Democratic Party as "a party that stands for mob violence, ruthless censorship, and racial grievances, not to mention bureaucratic despotism" (Ellmers 2021). See also Segers 2020.

39. Fuller 2016. At a town hall meeting held by Representative Bob Inglis, Republican from South Carolina, in 2009, a man stood up and told him to "keep your government hands off my Medicare" (qtd. in Krugman 2009).

40. Olya 2021 (highlighting the exploding profits of Amazon, Zoom, and grocery-
     and food-delivery apps); Kinder and Stateler 2020 (comparing the significant
     pandemic wealth increases of Amazon's and Walmart's richest shareholders
     with the limited amount spent on hazard pay for the frontline workers); Gan-
     del 2021 (noting that Zoom paid zero federal taxes in 2020 in part because of
     $580 million in stock compensation paid to mostly executives and including a
     $300 million cash salary paid to CEO Eric Yuan in 2020).
41. See Hobbes [1651] 2005 (arguing that the state of nature is a "war of all against
     all" and that society sets up government to establish peace, order, and
     security).
42. James Madison, *Federalist No. 10*, in Hamilton, Madison, and Jay [1787–1788] n.d.
43. Examples of books making this case include the historian Nancy MacLean's
     *Democracy in Chains: The Deep History of the Radical Right's Stealth Plan for Amer-
     ica* (2017), the journalist Jane Mayer's *Dark Money: The Hidden History of the
     Billionaires Behind the Rise of the Radical Right* (2016), and the science histori-
     ans Naomi Oreskes and Erik Conway's *Merchants of Doubt: How a Handful of
     Scientists Obscured the Truth on Issues from Tobacco Smoke to Global Warming*
     (2010). They stand in contrast to more circumspect accounts of industry
     attempts to influence climate policy, such as *Private Empire: ExxonMobil and
     American Power* (2012), an account by Steve Coll, dean of Columbia University
     School of Journalism, of ExxonMobil's climate lobbying.
44. For a rich and persuasive argument that fights over economic and social equal-
     ity have always been at the heart of U.S. legal and political history, see Fishkin
     and Forbath 2022.
45. The ability of the wealthiest to capture more wealth does not necessarily imply
     that poverty is increasing. However, the trends shown in figure 0.1 are reflected
     in multiple measures, including the Gini index, the Theill index, the Hoover
     index, and the Atkinson index.
46. In the so-called ultimatum game of game theory (a.k.a. the "divide-the-dollar
     game" or the "dictator game"), player one chooses how to divide a sum of money
     between two players. Player two can veto that choice, in which case neither
     player receives any money. Repeated experiments confirm that the second
     player will veto allocations she considers unfair, even though it leaves her eco-
     nomically worse off as a result. Perhaps intuitively understanding this, the first
     player often allocates significant portions of the total to the second player. The
     Wikipedia entry "Dictator Game," https://en.wikipedia.org/wiki/Dictator
     _game, summarizes the experimental literature fairly well.
47. "The Giant Pool of Money," *This American Life*, NPR, 2008, https://www
     .thisamericanlife.org/355/the-giant-pool-of-money. Accounts of both scandals
     depict the systematic way in which the opportunity to earn huge returns over-
     came auditing processes designed to prevent corporate malfeasance. Perhaps
     the best explanation of this phenomenon in the scandals of 2001 is Bethany
     McLean and Peter Elkind's book *The Smartest Guys in the Room: The Amazing
     Rise and Scandalous Fall of Enron* (2003). NPR's brilliant account of the mortgage-
     backed securities crisis in 2008, "The Giant Pool of Money," can be found
     online. Michael Lewis's book *The Big Short: Inside the Doomsday Machine* (2010)
     is another readable explanation of the crisis. Other financial scandals have
     been enabled and worsened by the same sort of motivated reasoning. A more
     recent example is the 1MDB scandal, a story of fraud in the creation and
     management of a Malaysian sovereign-wealth fund, told in Tom Wright and

Bradley Hope's book *Billion Dollar Whale: The Man Who Fooled Wall Street, Hollywood, and the World* (2018).

48. See "Climate Change and Social Vulnerability in the United States: A Focus on Six Impact Sectors," 2021, https://doi.org/10.1163/9789004322714_cclc_2021-0166 -513 (the EPA reporting that the most severe harms from climate change fall disproportionately on vulnerable communities who are least able to prepare for the impacts of climate change and fossil-fuel emissions); Donaghy et al. 2023 (Greenpeace finding that the fossil-fuel industry contributes to public-health harms that disproportionately endanger Black, Brown, Indigenous, and poor communities).

49. A wildfire in 2019 destroyed the town of Paradise, California, a community of people whose incomes were mostly insufficient to afford home ownership in coastal California cities. See Coyle 2019 ("For the nearby university town of Chico, Paradise served as a reservoir of blue-collar workers and laborers [and] for retirees, it was an inexpensive place to make a home, an escape from the absurd price of California real estate").

   The term *energy poverty* is used in two ways. It can refer to lack of access to secure energy supplies, mostly in developing countries. In developed countries, it refers to those who must devote a larger share of their disposable income to paying their energy bills. I am using it in the latter sense here.

50. The psychologist Tom Tyler is widely cited for the idea that the perceived legitimacy of policy outcomes is a function of how people feel about *both* the substantive outcome *and* the fairness of the process that created it. See Tyler 1990.

51. "Congressman DeFazio and Senator Wyden Send Letter to Bureau of Ocean Energy Management on Oregon Coast Offshore Wind Project, U.S. Senator Ron Wyden of Oregon," press release, office of Senator Wyden, September 13, 2023, https://www.wyden.senate.gov/news/press-releases/congressman-defazio-and -senator-wyden-send-letter-to-bureau-of-ocean-energy-management-on -oregon-coast-offshore-wind-project.

52. According to the Pew Research Center, American voters' strong support (67 percent of respondents) for prioritizing development of clean energy is qualified by equally strong (68 percent of respondents) opposition to a rapid abandonment of fossil fuels. That is, voters are worried about the trade-offs associated with getting to net zero. See B. Kennedy, Funk, and Tyson 2023.

53. This higher figure refers to the regular use of the filibuster in recent decades in the U.S. Senate and the sixty-vote requirement for invoking cloture. The filibuster is a procedural rule that the Senate has *chosen* to adopt by majority vote. It has no constitutional standing or claim to status as a foundational democratic norm. To the contrary, the framers of the Constitution disfavored supermajority requirements for legislation. See *Federalist No. 58* (in which James Madison argued that a supermajority requirement for legislation would "empower the minority to screen themselves from equitable sacrifices to the general weal") and *Federalist No. 22* (in which Alexander Hamilton rejected supermajority requirements, arguing that "we forget how much good may be prevented, and how much ill may be produced, by the power of hindering the doing what may be necessary and of keeping affairs in the same unfavorable posture in which they may happen to stand at particular periods") (Hamilton, Madison, and Jay [1787–1788] n.d.).

54. Mark Smith 2000 (empirical analysis concluding that when business is unified in its position on a legislative issue in opposition to the interests of the public,

business tends to lose on that issue because the public tends to be more acti-
vated on the issue, too).

55. The legal scholar James Gray Pope applied the term *republican moments* to
instances in which "normally quiescent citizens" rise up and demand action
(Pope 1990, 310–13). In the 1970s, the economist Anthony Downs described a similar phenomenon he called "the issue attention cycle" (Downs 1972).

56. The term *post-truth* was coined by writer Steve Tesich in an article in *The Nation*
in 1992 about press coverage of the Gulf War.

57. The commission of such errors is sufficiently common that websites dedicated
to explaining them have popped up. See, e.g., the Skeptical Science website at
https://skepticalscience.com/argument.php. The Real Climate website is dedicated to geophysical scientists' much deeper discussion of climate science and
misinformation. It can be accessed at https://www.realclimate.org/.

58. Note that as of late 2022, Twitter was rebranded as X, but most people still
refer to it as Twitter. This book discusses the use of Twitter before its rebrand-
ing and therefore uses the term *tweets* and refers to the platform at "Twitter/X."

59. The ubiquity of the "saving the planet" language in discussions of climate policy may come from either the idea that warming will do "irreparable" damage
to ecosystems on which people depend or will otherwise effect harmful permanent changes or the belief that alarming language will motivate more people to prioritize the energy transition in their votes and political behavior. As
to the first issue, readers who want to make their own judgments about how to
characterize what we know about climate change can look to the IPCC's projections (H. Lee, Calvin, Dasgupta, Geden, et al. 2023; H. Lee, Calvin, Dasgupta,
Krinner, et al. 2023). As to the second issue, part 2 of this book (chapters 4–6)
explains why alarmist rhetoric is ineffective and possibly counterproductive in
today's political environment.

60. Kleinfeld 2021.

61. For an account of the increase in political violence, see Bergengruen 2022
(recounting disturbing incidents of real and threatened violence against sub-
national political and government officials).

62. Gardner 2022; Gardner, Thebault, and Klemko 2022.

63. We associate declining public faith in government institutions with illiberal
philosophies of both the Left (Marxism) and the Right (fascism), but today it is
found between those two extremes. The bipartisan increase in support for political violence is discussed in chapter 3. Anecdotally, in 2023 at the annual meeting of the Federalist Society, a conservative legal organization, conference
attendees struggled to reconcile their view that rule by Democrats is unacceptable with the knowledge that preventing Democrats from controlling the government is unsustainable in a democracy (I. Ward 2023).

64. M. Obama 2016.

65. "Going high" is mocked from the right as hypocrisy by accompanying the quote
with pictures of violent left-wing protests. It is mocked from the left as naive:
e.g., "When they go low, feel free to go lower"; "When they go low, go for the
throat"; or (more profanely) "Fuck going high; I'm going low."

66. See Schroeder 1993; Yadin 2019 (arguing that government should shame firms
that emit carbon because businesses engage in "climate obstruction"); and Jacquet 2015 (arguing that naming and shaming those who oppose strong climate policy will produce a variety of social and political benefits)

67. Halstead quoted in Roston 2016.

68. Arendt 1968, 241.
69. Popper 1998, 64; see also Popper 1945.
70. In the 117th Congress in 2021, Sen. Ed Markey (D–MA) and Rep. Hank Johnson (D–GA) introduced the Judiciary Act in the Senate (S. 1141) and House (H.R. 2584), respectively. The bill would add four new justices to the Court. It is also the objective of an interest group called Demand Justice, https://demandjustice .org/priorities/supreme-court-reform/. On the idea of more senators, see "Pack the Union: A Proposal to Admit New States for the Purpose of Amending the Constitution to Ensure Equal Representation," *Harvard Law Review* 133 (3) (2020): 1049 (proposing to admit 127 Washington, DC, neighborhoods to the union as new states).
71. Bartels 2020; Draper 2022; Thrush 2020. The idea of secession has popped up several times in U.S. history. Northern states twice seriously considered secession—at the Hartford Convention in 1814 and in petitions to Congress by northern abolitionists in the 1840s. Today's Libertarian Party charter affirms the right to secede, as have several conservative states and politicians in the twenty-first century, citing Democratic Party policies or court decisions they deem unacceptable.
72. "TTF22: Opening Keynote: One-on-One with Pete Buttigieg," *Texas Tribune*, 2022, YouTube video, https://www.youtube.com/watch?v=g3iUU3ANB1E, emphasis added.
73. The climate and energy writer David Roberts advocates a strong and persistent morality-based response to policy adversaries on social media: "What we need, from those who value democracy & rule of law, is more polarization and less civility" (David Roberts [@drvolts], tweet, Twitter, June 13, 2023, https://twitter .com/drvolts/status/1668338208722284544). See also Krugman 2023 and Brittenden 2021.
74. Adams 1907, 7.
75. On "what we want," see Tenbrunsel and Messick 2004; Blackburn 2001. For the quotes from *Federalist No. 10*, see Hamilton, Madison, and Jay [1787–1788] n.d.
76. Abrams quoted in Marchese 2019, emphasis added.
77. See Fishkin and Forbath 2022 (contending that the American constitutional tradition requires the fair distribution of economic and political opportunity and is inconsistent with oligarchy); Boyd 2020 (arguing that energy-market pricing is an inherently political process because each system of price formation has foreseeable distributive consequences); Sandel 2020 (arguing that the social adoption of facially neutral merit rules has exacerbated and enshrined inequality); and Eisenberg 2020 (arguing that legal regimes that provide social net benefits nevertheless systematically destroy rural communities). George Orwell was particularly insightful about these sorts of internecine disagreements on the left. Writing about Western nationalism in 1945, he lamented that "a minority of intellectual pacifists" seemed motivated by "hatred of western democracy" and directed their disapproval "almost entirely against Britain and the United States" (Orwell 1945).
78. For an argument that the U.S. Constitution is neutral in this way, see Albert 2021.
79. James Buchan describes the world to which Enlightenment philosophers were responding as a cruel and repressive theocracy in which "to be tolerant was to be lukewarm." Theirs was a "new theory of progress, based on good laws, international commerce and the companionship of men and women, displaced the antique world of valour, loyalty, religion, and the dagger" (2007, 7, 2). See also

Gopnik 2019 (describing the liberal tradition as founded on reform rather than on revolution: a plan to work together to fix the world's ills).

Buchan summarizes the distinction between eighteenth-century Enlightenment theory and practice: "In demanding that experiment not inherited truth define the business of living, the [Enlightenment] philosophers stamped the West with its modern scientific and provisional character. They created a world that tended towards the egalitarian and, within reason, the democratic. . . . Yet they left . . . a paradox[,] . . . [opposing] any but the most gradual political change. . . . With their armory of reason, politeness, patronage and sentiment [they were] as ill equipped to grapple with the French Revolution as they had been with the American" (2007, 336–37).

80. Buchan 2007, 120–21 ("[Adam Smith's] name stands as shorthand for an ideology of unrestricted commerce and blithe social optimism . . . [but b]y the end of his life, [Smith] was expressing the most profound misgivings about the moral complexion of commercial society"). For a fuller treatment of Adam Smith and David Hume's moral philosophy, see Rasmussen 2017. On the Enlightenment influence on the thinking of the framers of the Constitution, see T. Ricks 2020 (describing the influence of the Scottish Enlightenment, by way of Scottish tutors and professors, on the first four presidents of the United States); and Buchan 2007, 2 ("David Hume, Adam Smith, William Robertson, Adam Ferguson and Hugh Blair . . . taught Europe and America how to think and talk about the new mental areas opening to the eighteenth-century view: consciousness, the purposes of civil government, the forces that shape and distinguish society").

81. A. Smith [1759] n.d., 471–74.

82. "We fight for the abolition of capitalism and the creation of a democratically run economy that provides for people's needs" (DSA Political Platform, 2021, https://www.dsausa.org/dsa-political-platform-from-2021-convention/).

83. On Smith and Hume's view of capitalism, see Rasmussen 2019, 60. Hamilton, Jefferson, and Madison had also read James Steuart's *Inquiry Into the Principles of Political Economy* (1767), which makes the case that a market economy and a national currency as a medium of exchange act as a check on despotism (Buchan 2007, 212–16).

84. Some of this semantic confusion is reflected in DSA progressives' adoption of the New Deal as a template because most historians note that "Franklin Roosevelt's New Deal rescued capitalism and the Constitution from their conservative guardians" (Fishkin and Forbath 2022, 16).

85. See, e.g., Aronoff, Dreier, and Kazin 2020, 6–8 (articulating a list of socialist policy priorities shared by many Democrats and [mis]characterizing universal health care—a goal openly pursued by most Democratic Party presidents since World War II—as an idea "considered radical only a few years ago").

86. There is a divide on the left about how to *talk* about capitalism. Rep. Alexandria Ocasio Cortez (D–NY), for example, uses the phrase "late-stage capitalism" fairly regularly and has said that American capitalism is "not redeemable." Other progressives suggest that the progressive agenda is merely about remedying the distortions and defects of unfettered capitalism. Sen. Elizabeth Warren (D–MA), for example, calls herself both a progressive and "a capitalist to my core." For an analysis of divisions within the DSA, see Meyerson 2023 (ascribing to younger DSA members "both the blessings and curses of youth; boundless energy and discomfort with complication and nuance").

Tracking polls from Gallup and Pew Research show that about 60 percent of Americans have a positive view of capitalism and about 40 percent have a positive view of socialism (Newport 2021; "Modest Declines in Positive Views of 'Socialism' and 'Capitalism' in U.S.," Pew Research Center, September 19, 2022, https://www.pewresearch.org/politics/2022/09/19/modest-declines-in-positive-views-of-socialism-and-capitalism-in-u-s/).

87. One strain of recent illiberalism—represented by the political theorist Patrick Deneen and the legal scholar Adrian Vermeule—is associated with religiosity, in particular Catholicism (see Hamid 2018). Another strain is represented by the journalist Glenn Greenwald, who has made common cause with right populists against liberalism, which he views as inherently corruptible (see Chait 2021). On authoritarianism on both the right and the left, see Slade 2022.

88. Thiel 2009. Vermeule offers a more scholarly version of Thiel's view, contending that political liberalism as a theory of governance is dead because it depends on "reasonable pluralism," which Vermeule sees as nonexistent, having been replaced by a "dictatorship of relativism" that uses law to "enforce[] itself by coercive means." He mocks the "endless project of human liberation from the oppression of unchosen constraints, including . . . customary morality, natural and *even biology*" (Vermeule 2024, emphasis in original). His objection to the cultural values of the progressive Left is clearly a driver of his rejection of liberal democracy. As described more fully in chapters 2, 3, and 6, these sorts of rejections of majority rule are especially tempting when one fears that majority rule will impose harm on "my side."

89. E.g., Hartmann 2023 (summarizing these maneuvers and characterizing them as the product of a plan to impose "fascism" by "oligarchs").

90. Hand 1944, emphasis added.

91. The framers believed that the constitutional design "requires a virtuous public and virtuous leaders—or the whole system will fail" (A. White 2020).

92. T. Hall 2021; Sinopoli 1987.

93. See, e.g., Gopnik 2019, 175–76 ("The idea that one should trace the source of an argument backward, to its origins, rather than play it forward to the evidence for its claims is the root doctrine of reaction. . . . [A]n idea is best evaluated . . . by asking what facts support it and what facts might prove it false").

94. Samenow 2012; Kuipers 2012.

95. Nancy MacLean's focus on racial segregation in her indictment of public-choice economics is one example (see chapter 2). The political scientist Matto Mildenberger has criticized the "tragedy of the commons"—a widely cited allegory used to illustrate a particular kind of cooperation problem that environmental regulation tries to solve (see chapter 1)—in part by noting that its popularizer, the neo-Malthusian ecologist Garrett Hardin, was also a proponent of eugenics and various strains of nativism and white nationalism (Mildenberger 2019). For a pointed defense of a focus on merit as a criteria for evaluation against challenges raised by postmodernists, see Farber and Sherry 1997.

96. John James Audubon, the founder of the Audubon Society, and James Muir, the founder of the Sierra Club, both behaved and wrote in ways that revealed an ugly racism and bigotry toward Indigenous Americans and Black people. Aldo Leopold, author of *A Sand County Almanac* (1949), was also a Malthusian who opposed food and medical aid to people in developing nations (see Powell 2015). For some thoughtful reflections on the implications of this information for modern environmentalism, see Kashwan 2020 and Lanham 2021. For

documentation of the overrepresentation of white elites in environmental NGOs, see LeVine 2014; Rothkopf 2014; and Ortiz 2021.

97. Nikole Hannah-Jones's Pulitzer Prize–winning introductory essay to the *New York Times* 1619 Project argues that because of the hypocrisy at the heart of the founders' conception of freedom, the struggles of Black people, from slavery through Jim Crow to the present, have best embodied those founding ideals. See Hannah-Jones 2019. Hannah-Jones erred, however, when in that same essay she argued that a primary reason why the colonists declared independence and took up arms in revolt against Britain was to preserve the institution of slavery. On this point, see Harris 2020.

98. Rakove 1996; Wood 1987.

99. B. Obama 2020.

100. This remark was part of a stirring speech given by Douglass in 1852 called "What to the Slave Is the Fourth of July?"

101. W. Brown 2023a. See also W. Brown 2023b. Thanks to William Boyd for bringing both of these sources to my attention.

102. Ehrlich 1968. The term *Malthusian* refers to the eighteenth-century English economist Thomas Malthus, who is credited with introducing the notion that the earth's capacity to support the human population is limited. See Malthus 1789. For an application of similar ideas to the energy transition, see C. King 2020.

103. The term *doomer* refers to people who are so pessimistic about the prospects for mitigating climate harm that they believe it is futile or pointless to try. The hashtag #ThanosWasRight is a reference to the Marvel Comics supervillain Thanos, whose Malthusian perspective leads him to use his supernatural power to wipe out half of the beings in the universe. The hashtag voices support for depopulation as a solution to overconsumption, and it has trended periodically on social media platforms. The film director James Cameron is apparently among its supporters, calling it "a pretty viable answer" to overpopulation (qtd. in Milheim 2023).

104. For two contrasting and recent discussions of this growth question, see Nordhaus 2020 and Aronoff 2021.

1. REPUBLICAN MOMENTS AND THE CREATION OF THE ENERGY-REGULATORY STATE

1. A thorough account of how the commercial development of oil and gas transformed human life in the late twentieth century can be found in Yergin [1990] 2008.

2. See, e.g., Zingales 2017, especially 123 (arguing for inferring business dominance in the absence of evidence: "to detect the power of corporations we need to look at output"); Zingales 2015, 1338 ("Rich financiers can easily buy their political protection. In fact, this is precisely the problem"); Fishkin and Forbath 2022, 230 ("capitalist wealth has an inevitable tendency to convert economic into political domination"); and Payne 2017.

3. Engstrom 2013, 33.

4. This generalization applies to major regulatory legislation. Other varieties of policy change sometimes happen outside of these republican moments (B. Jones and Baumgartner 2005).

5. David Mayhew (2004) is the most widely cited authority for this proposition.
6. For examples of each of these explanations, respectively, see (1) Krehbiel 1992 (explaining committees as delegates or representatives of the body of each chamber who educate other members on bills); (2) Weingast and Marshall 1988 (explaining committees as providers of distributed goods to members' districts) and Witko 2011 (supporting this idea by showing that companies that contributed more money to federal candidates also received more government contracts); (3) David B. Truman's *The Governmental Process: Political Interests and Public Opinion* (1951) (which argues that interest-group pluralism led to "balanced" policy outcomes) and E. E. Schattschneider's *The Semisovereign People: A Realist's View of Democracy in America* (1960) (which famously observed that the pluralist "heavenly chorus" sings with an "upper class accent" (35); and (4) Grimmer, Westwood, and Messing 2015 (describing how legislators can shape constituents' impressions in pursuit of reelection) as well as Fenno 1978 and Grose, Malhotra, and Van Houweling 2015, all of whom address this sort of perception-shaping behavior.
7. For a summary of the enormous public-choice literature on delegation to agencies, see Spence and Cross 2000, 102–6. For literature on the advantages of smaller, wealthier groups, see, e.g., M. Olson 1965; R. Hardin 1982; Sandler 1992; and Schlozman, Verba, and Brady 2012.
8. M. A. Smith 2000 (finding that when business is unified behind a legislative policy position in opposition to public preferences, the public position tends to prevail over the business position in floor votes in Congress). For a summary of a suite of studies finding little or no effect of campaign contributions on roll-call voting, see Ansolabehere, de Figueiredo, and Snyder 2003, table 1.
9. Wlezien 2004; Soroka and Wlezien 2010; Burstein 2003; Druckman and Jacobs 2006.
10. Gilens and Page 2014, 564 ("Multivariate analysis indicates that economic elites and organized groups representing business interests have substantial independent impacts on U.S. government policy, while average citizens and mass-based interest groups have little or no independent influence"). Other scholars have challenged this conclusion. See Branham, Soroka, and Wlezien 2017 (arguing that the middle class wins almost as much as the rich do); and Enns 2015, 1053 ("even on those issues for which the preferences of the wealthy and those in the middle diverge, policy ends up about where we would expect if policymakers represented the middle class and ignored the affluent").
11. S. Yackee 2022 (documenting this effect).
12. For example, FirstEnergy Corp., an Ohio electric utility, was caught bribing state legislators to secure legislation subsidizing its power plants (Ariza 2023).
13. Stokes 2020, 138.
14. Meckling 2011; Cheon and Urpelainen 2013.
15. D. Levy and Kolk 2002.
16. The political science professors Richard Lau at Rutgers and Adam Bonica at Stanford assert that the association between raising the most money and winning elections has more to do with donors identifying the likely winning candidates than money causing the electoral win. See Koerth 2018 (quoting Lau's phrase "winning attracts money" and Bonica's description of the research literature to the effect that spending "generally" does not affect outcomes); and Ansolabehere, de Fiueiroedo, and Snyder 2003 (concluding that contributing to political campaigns is more of a consumption good, done expressively or to secure access to politicians).

17. Shanor, McDonnell, and Werner 2021.
18. Some research has shown a connection between lax state regulation of campaign contributions, on the one hand, and both weaker redistributive policies and the election of more Republican candidates, on the other. See Flavin 2015 (states with stricter campaign-finance laws devote a larger proportion of their annual budget to public-welfare spending); and Klumpp, Mialon, and Williams 2016.
19. Baumgartner et al. 2009, 268, emphasis added.
20. For a summary of how the wealthiest American billionaires use their wealth politically, see appendix E of this book at https://www.ClimateOfContempt.com/Appendices/.
21. Cline 2012 (noting that Adelson spent $15 million on Newt Gingrich's unsuccessful presidential campaign and more than $20 million on Mitt Romney's unsuccessful presidential campaign); Randall 2012 (noting the Koch brothers pledged $60 million in an effort to defeat President Obama's reelection campaign in 2012).
22. "Why ALEC's Attacks on Renewable Energy Failed Nationwide," *EcoWatch* (blog), November 4, 2013, https://www.ecowatch.com/why-alecs-attacks-on-renewable-energy-failed-nationwide-1881809305.html.
23. See, e.g., *Buckley v. Valeo*, 424 U.S. 1 (1976) (concluding that both governmental restriction of independent expenditures in campaigns and limits on total campaign expenditures violate the First Amendment); and *Citizens United v. FEC*, 558 U.S. 310 (2010) (concluding that corporate funding of independent political broadcasts in candidate elections cannot be limited).
24. The revelation by ProPublica in 2023 that a wealthy Republican Party donor named Harlan Crow lavished gifts on Justice Clarence Thomas—including luxury overseas vacations and payments for property and tuition for Thomas's relatives—makes the Court's already suspect equation between spending and "speech" seem all the more unfair to many people. When members of the Court receive gifts from party activists, it creates the appearance of impropriety and stains the Court's reputation, regardless of whether then existing Court rules prohibited it.
25. S. Schmidt and Grimaldi 2005.
26. On policymakers' need for information from firms, see Potters and van Windon 1992, 270 ("Providing policymakers and legislators with information is often asserted to be one of the most important means by which interest groups influence the policymaking process"); Wagner, Barnes, and Peters 2011, 102 ("business groups . . . benefit from the agencies' need for information that only regulated interests can provide"). On the dampening of the pro-industry bias, see Boehmke, Gailmard, and Patty 2013, 25; Furlong and Kerwin 2005, 353, 356, 361; and Schlozman, Verba and Brady 2012.
27. Kersh 2007, 393–94, emphasis added.
28. Hertel-Fernandez, Mildenberger, and Stokes 2019; R. Hall and Wayman 1990 (donors exercise their influence in committees by motivating donees to actively participate in marking up bills and other committee decisions).
29. On agencies' need for information, see Magat, Krupnick, and Harrington 2013; and Choi 2023. Regarding the inference of injury to the public interest, in their study of executive-branch decisions the political scientists Jason Yackee and Susan Yackee characterize preenactment changes in policy in the direction of business preferences as reflecting a "bias" toward business in the rulemaking process (2006, 128–29).

30. Walters 2019, 186 (suggesting that agencies' initial proposals are sometimes "sandbagging"). See also Coglianese, Zeckhauser, and Parson 2004, 278 ("the best source of information about the risks of products, the behavior of individuals and firms, the costs of remediation or mitigation, or the feasibility of different technologies will be the very firms that the government agency regulates").

31. Wagner 2004.

32. Walters 2019, 187.

33. Choi 2023.

34. Golden 1998; J. Yackee and Yackee 2006.

35. The work of the administrative law scholar Elizabeth Fisher develops more fully the case for the application of deliberative expertise within agencies; see Fisher 2007 and Fisher and Shapiro 2020. See also Rohr 1986; Spence and Cross 2000; and Spence 2001.

36. Zuckert 2018.

37. On liberal democracy as a tool for economic dominance, see Marx 1994, 33 ("a bourgeois republic means the unbridled despotism of one class over all others."); Marx and Engels 2014; Beard 1913 (arguing that the U.S. Constitution was adopted to protect the interests of the wealthy and upper-class members of society); Becker [1909] 2009, 1760–76 (the American Revolution was more a contest for home rule and independence from Britain than it was a contest of who would rule at home and the democratization of American society); and Ollman 2017. On liberal democracy as a tool for racial dominance, see Hannah-Jones 2019 (framing the construction of the Constitution as a way to preserve slavery and make slaveholdings more secure). For a broader discussion on the 1619 Project and historians' responses to it, see Serwer 2019.

38. For an argument that the Constitution embodies ideas of antioligarchy, distributive justice, and social inclusion that are woven through U.S. constitutional history, see Fishkin and Forbath 2022.

39. Michael Cohen, March, and Olsen 1972; Lindblom 1959; Simon 1946.

40. Kingdon 2003, 124–31.

41. Wenner 1982.

42. J. Gordon 1988.

43. Interstate Commerce Act, Pub. L. 49-104, 24 Stat. 379 (February 4, 1887). In the 1960s, revisionist histories of this act argued that railroads supported its passage to avoid ruinous rate competition that destroyed profit margins. See, e.g., Kolko 1965. This is another oversimplification, though. Some railroads did face ruinous competition at the time, but others thrived as monopolists or oligopolists. For a more complete account of the positions of business firms on both sides of the legislative battle, see Purcell 1967, 562–64 (noting that nineteenth-century shippers were exploited by the rail lines in places where a single company provided shipping service), 564–71, 578 ("railroads were not the major advocates behind the [Interstate Commerce Act]"; rather, farm and business interests on both sides of the fight drove the debate), and 572 (noting the bitter opposition by railroad president Charles Perkins as well as the opposition by the lines owned by the Vanderbilt family and Jay Gould). See also A. Martin 1974, 339 (calling the idea that "railroad corporations . . . supported [the Interstate Commerce Act] as being in their own best interests" a "historically invalid" notion).

44. Yergin [1990] 2008, 25–35.

45. Chernow 1998, 129–55, 135–42; Yergin [1990] 2008, 41.

46. On creative destruction, see Schumpeter [1942] 1987, 81–86; on market stability and the benevolent monopolist, see Chernow 1998, 168, 144 (quotes), and Yergin [1990] 2008, 42–43.

47. Chernow 1998, 537–59; Yergin [1990] 2008, 81–98.

48. Sherman Antitrust Act, Ch. 647, 26 Stat. 209 (1890) (codified as amended at 15 U.S.C. §§1–7 (2006)) (in the words of a leading antitrust scholar, members of Congress were motivated not by economic-efficiency concerns "but rather [by] the distributive goal of preventing monopolists from transferring wealth away from consumers" [Hovenkamp 1994, 50]). See also 15 U.S.C. §§1–2.

49. The articles in *McClure's* became a best-selling book, *The History of the Standard Oil Company* (Tarbell [1904] 1966), presenting a detailed narrative of the history of Standard Oil. For the articles' effects, see the Hepburn Act, 34 Stat. 584 (June 29, 1906); the Mann-Elkins Act, 36 Stat. 539 (June 18, 1910); *Standard Oil Co. of New Jersey v. U.S.*, 221 U.S. 1, 81–82 (1911).

50. Chernow 1998, 617; Clayton Act, Ch. 323, 38 Stat. 730 (1914) (codified as amended at 15 U.S.C. §§12–27 (2006) and 29 U.S.C. §§52–53 (2006)); Federal Trade Commission Act, Ch. 311, 38 Stat. 717 (1914) (current version at 15 U.S.C. §§41, 58 (1950)).

51. *Barnard v. Monongahela Natural Gas Co.*, 65 A. 801, 802–3 (Pa. 1907). For an analysis of the rule of capture and its effects, see generally B. Kramer and Anderson 2005.

52. McDonald 1971, 36–38, n. 27. The process of managing the rights of multiple owners of a single oilfield involves prorating production and sharing revenues. For a brief history of the early proration orders issued by the Texas and Oklahoma oil and gas commissions, see McDonald 1971, 36–37. For a good discussion of the state commissions' various approaches to this task, see generally R. Pierce 1987.

53. *Champlin Ref. Co. v. Corp. Comm'n of Okla.*, 286 U.S. 210, 232–34 (1932); *Cities Serv. Gas Co. v. Peerless Oil & Gas Co.*, 340 U.S. 179, 186–89 (1950).

54. Hofstadter 1955, 304 ("the New Deal episode marks the first in the history of reform movements when a leader of the reform party took the reins of a government confronted above all by the problems of a sick economy").

55. Securities Act, Pub. L. No. 73-22, 48 Stat. 74 (1933); Banking Act, Pub. L. No. 73-66, 48 Stat. 162 (1933); Securities Act, Pub. L. No. 73-291, 48 Stat. 881 (1934); Communications Act, Pub. L. No. 73-416, 48 Stat. 1064 (1934); Civil Aeronautics Act, Pub. L. No. 75-706, 52 Stat. 973 (1938); Agricultural Adjustment Act, Pub. L. No. 73-10, 48 Stat. 31 (1933); Soil Conservation Act, Pub. L. No. 74-461, 49 Stat. 1148 (1935); Bankhead-Jones Farm Tenant Act, Pub. L. No. 75-210, 50 Stat. 522 (1937).

56. Yergin [1990] 2008, 251–54; Johnsen 1991, 184; Crane 2006, 3–5. Independent producers can be distinguished from the so-called majors or supermajors, whose vertically integrated operations included their own storage and refining capacity. The independents tended to compete only in the production segment of the industry and depended on third parties to get their oil to market.

57. National Industrial Recovery Act, Ch. 90, 48 Stat. 195 (1933); *Panama Ref. Co. v. Ryan*, 293 U.S. 388, 432–33 (1935). That same year, Congress approved the formation of an interstate compact among oil-producing states through which the members voluntarily coordinated their oil production to try to reduce waste and stabilize prices. The compact still exists. See "Interstate Oil and Gas Compact Commission Charter," August 11, 2023, https://iogcc.ok.gov/charter.

58. *United States v. Socony-Vacuum Oil Co.*, 310 U.S. 150, 210–31 (1940).

59. Yergin [1990] 2008, 589–609 (discussing the Nixon administration's price-control implementation and OPEC's response) and 659–60 ("The politics and intense

pressures of the time gave rise to an awesome Rube Goldberg system of price controls, entitlements, and allocations that made the mandatory oil import program of the 1960s appear, by comparison, to have the simplicity of a haiku").

60. "Oil Supply Security: Emergency Response of IEA Countries," International Energy Agency, 2007, 50, https://www.iea.org/reports/oil-supply-security -emergency-response-of-iea-countries-2007 (showing a sharp trend away from oil-fired generation after the oil crises of the 1970s).

61. "The Oil and Gas Industry in Energy Transitions," International Energy Agency, 2020, 24, https://www.iea.org/reports/the-oil-and-gas-industry-in-energy -transitions (attributing 13 percent of global crude-oil production to the seven majors). The International Energy Agency classifies the largest privately owned oil and gas companies as "majors": BP, Chevron, ExxonMobil, Shell, Total, ConocoPhillips, and Eni. The majors held 12 percent of the world's oil reserves in 2018. See "The Oil and Gas Industry in Energy Transitions," 17–20.

62. "Unlike oil's first century, over the last 20 years no single nation, government, cartel or corporation has controlled its fate. Markets have now determined prices and investment" (Bower 2009, xv–xvi).

63. Bonneville Project Act, Pub. L. No. 75-329, 50 Stat. 731 (1937); Tennessee Valley Authority, Pub. L. No. 108-447, 48 Stat. 58 (1933). In 1940, there was a sufficient number of municipal electric utilities to trigger the formation of a trade group, the American Public Power Association.

64. The first state PUC, the Massachusetts Board of Gas and Electric Light Commissioners, was created in the late nineteenth century (Forstall 1900, 329). The trade association of state commissioners, the National Association of Regulatory Utility Commissioners, was established in 1889, evincing the existence of multiple state commissions by that point.

65. *Public Utilities Commission of Rhode Island v. Attleboro Steam and Electric Co.*, 273 U.S. 83, 89–90 (1927) (prohibiting state regulation of rates for a wholesale sale of electricity across the Massachusetts–Rhode Island border), abrogated by *Ark. Elec. Coop. Coop. v. Ark. Pub. Serv. Comm'n*, 461 U.S. 375, 393 (1983); Federal Power Act, Pub. L. No. 74-333, Ch. 687, 49 Stat. 803 (1935) (codified at 16 U.S.C. §§79–79z (2006)). The portions of the Public Utility Holding Company Act relevant to this analysis were repealed by the Energy Policy Act, Pub. L. No. 109-58, §1263, 119 Stat. 594 (2005).

66. Natural Gas Act, Pub. L. No. 76-88, Ch. 556, 52 Stat. 821, 821-22 (1938) (codified as amended at 15 U.S.C. §717 (2006)); FPA, Ch. 687, pt. 2, 49 Stat. 803, 847–48 (1935) (codified as amended at 16 U.S.C. §824 (b) (1) (2006)). The FPC and FERC are one and the same agency: the FPC's name was changed to "Federal Energy Regulatory Commission" in 1977. See Department of Energy Organization Act, Pub. L. No. 95-91, §§401–2, 91 Stat. 565, 582–85 (1977) (codified as amended at 42 U.S.C. §§7171–72 (2006)).

67. The primary aim of the NGA, for example, was to "protect consumers against exploitation at the hands of natural gas companies." See *FPC v. Hope Nat. Gas Co.*, 320 U.S. 591, 610 (1944) (but also articulating the rights of firms to fair rates). The legislative fight over the Public Utility Holding Company Act was particularly fierce, but it was a fight the utilities lost. See Neufeld 2016, 147–52. On Samuel Insull, see Funigiello 1973, 19; Wasik 2006, 103 (recounting how during the 1910s Insull "was constantly worried about the public takeover of his utilities"); and Neufeld 2016, 61 (recounting a speech by Insull in 1898 endorsing utility commission regulation of electric utilities as preferable to government ownership).

68. In the words of the legal scholars Sharon Jacobs and Dave Owen, "The holding company form enabled the capital accumulation required to construct large networked systems" (2023, 259).

69. Rural Electrification Act, Pub. L. No. 74-605, 49. Stat. 1363. (1936). Modern electric-transmission systems became possible only after George Westinghouse and Nikola Tesla prevailed over Thomas Edison in the "war of the currents," triggering the alternating-current transmission system we have today. See Klein 2008, 329–30.

70. This requirement is found in sections 205 and 206 of the FPA, 16 U.S.C. §§824d–e (2006), and the NGA, 15 U.S.C. §§717c–d (2006). The public-utility codes of every state contain similar requirements.

71. A common way of describing the rate-making process is to say that in rate cases PUCs typically make rate decisions using the following equation: $R = Br + O$, where R represents the company's total revenue requirement, B the value of capital deployed to provide energy services (the "rate base"), r the permissible rate of return on investment, and O the permissible operating expenses. Assets used and useful for supplying electric service are includable within the rate base, and the company is guaranteed a fair return on those assets.

72. *Fed. Power Comm'n v. Hope Natural Gas Co.*, 320 U.S. 591, 617–18 (1944).

73. That power is found in section 7 of the NGA, at 15 U.S.C. §717f (2006). For a richer exploration of the political drivers of these decisions to leave siting authority with the federal government rather than with state governments, see Klass and Meinhardt 2015.

74. "Economic Dispatch of Electric Generation Capacity: A Report to Congress and the States Pursuant to Sections 1234 and 1832 of the Energy Policy Act of 2005," U.S. Department of Energy, 2007, https://www.energy.gov/oe/articles/economic -dispatch-electric-generation-capacity.

75. That is, in order to keep the lights on, the American alternating-current grid must be kept at a frequency of 60 Hz; if it deviates too far from this target, it fails. This is a feature of all alternating-current grids, although many grids outside the United States are balanced at 50 Hz.

76. Rome 2003, 527 (citing the "explosive growth of concern about the environment" in the 1960s and the growth of Sierra Club membership around that time).

77. For the ecological approach, see Rachel Carson's classic *Silent Spring* (1962), which documented the ecological harm caused by widespread use of pesticides; for a summary of the early approaches, see Spence 1995; for the moral and religious appeals, see Nelson 2012; for the Gaia Hypothesis, see Lovelock and Margulis 1974; for the moral philosophy approach, see Sandel 1997 (arguing that pollution has a properly associated moral stigma and that pollution-related fines convey community judgment that the polluter has done something wrong).

78. Blumm and Schwartz 2021 (summarizing the history of the public-trust doctrine and its resurgence following the publication of Professor Joseph Sax's famous article "The Public Trust Doctrine in Natural Resource Law" in 1970); Cameron and Abouchar 1991 (on the precautionary principle); and Stone 1972 (on legal protection of natural resources).

79. G. Hardin 1968, 1247.

80. See, e.g., Axelrod 1984 and R. Hardin 1982.

81. Pigou 1929 (developing the concept of externalities as costs imposed or benefits conferred on others and arguing that the existence of externalities is sufficient justification for government intervention); Baumol and Oates 1988. On

market-based incentives, see Tietenberg 1992, 51–68, 360–86; and Varian 1990, 555–56.

82. National Environmental Policy Act, Pub. L. No. 91-190, 83 Stat. 852 (1969).

83. Clean Air Act, Pub. L. No. 91-604, 84 Stat. 1676 (1970); Clean Water Act, Pub. L. No. 92-500, 86 Stat. 816 (1972); Resource Conservation and Recovery Act, Pub. L. No. 94-580, 90 Stat. 2795 (1976); Comprehensive Environmental Response, Compensation, and Liability Act, Pub. L. No. 96-510, 94. Stat. 2767 (1980).

84. Coastal Zone Management Act, Pub. L. No. 92-583, 86. Stat. 1280 (1972).

85. 42 U.S.C §7412 (2006); 42 U.S.C. §6921 (2006).

86. Mine Safety and Health Act, Pub. L. No. 95-164, 91 Stat. 1290 (1977); Occupational Safety and Health Act, Pub. L. No. 91-596, 84 Stat. 1590 (1970); Toxic Substances Control Act, 15 U.S.C. §2604 (1976); Surface Mining Claims and Reclamation Act, 30 U.S.C. §§1231–45, 1258 (1977).

87. Public Utility Regulatory Policies Act, Pub. L. No. 95-617, 92 Stat. 3117 (1978) (codified as amended in scattered sections of 7 U.S.C., 15 U.S.C., 16 U.S.C., 42 U.S.C., and 43 U.S.C. (2006)). PURPA defined "alternative"-energy facilities to include various forms of renewable energy, such as solar, wind, and geothermal, as well as small hydroelectric facilities and cogeneration plants (16 U.S.C. §824a–3 (2006)).

88. 16 U.S.C. §824a–3(b) (2006); 18 C.F.R. § 292.304(e) (2020).

89. For up-to-date information about state RPSs, see the Database of State Incentives for Renewable Energy & Efficiency at http://www.dsireusa.org.

90. Reorganization Plan No. 3 of 1970, 35 Fed. Reg. 15,623 (July 9, 1970), reprinted in 42 U.S.C. §4321 (2010) and in 84 Stat. 2086 (1970).

91. Clean Air Act Amendments, Pub. L. No. 101-549, 104 Stat. 2468 (1990). On Bush's campaign, see L. D. Feldman and Perotti 2002, 8.

92. Actions—H.R.1, 100th Congress (1987–1988): Water Quality Act of 1987, https://www.congress.gov/bill/100th-congress/house-bill/1/all-actions?overview=closed&q=%7B%22roll-call-vote%22%3A%22all%22%7D, accessed February 17, 2023.

93. Fischman 2005, 180; Buzbee 2005; Schapiro 2005, 316.

94. See Coastal Zone Management Act, Pub. L. No. 92-583, 86 Stat. 1280. (1972). This act gives states a veto (though an overridable one) over federal agency decisions to authorize energy projects that could directly affect their coastal zones.

95. Buhlman-Pozen and Gerken 2009 (describing how states use regulatory power conferred by the government to resist federal policy).

96. Clean Air Act, 42 U.S.C. §7604 (1990)); Clean Water Act, 33 U.S.C. §1365 (1982); Endangered Species Act, 16 U.S.C. §1540(g) (1973); Resource Conservation and Recovery Act, 42 U.S.C. §6972 (2015); Surface Mining Claims and Reclamation Act, 30 U.S.C. §1270 (1977); Comprehensive Environmental Response, Compensation, and Liability Act, 42 U.S.C. §9659 (1980). For a discussion of the role citizen suits can play in the enforcement of multiple environmental regulations, see Fadil 1985.

97. As an example of conservative judges' discomfort with citizen suits, see *Lujan v. Nat'l Wildlife Fed'n.*, 497 U.S. 871 (1990), and *Bennett v. Spear*, 520 U.S. 154 (1997). On the Supreme Court and citizen suits, see Sunstein 1992 (discussing the standing doctrine and how Justice Scalia's *Lujan* opinion largely restricted the role of citizen suits in environmental and regulatory law); and Spence 2001, 941–44 (exploring later internecine Supreme Court battles over standing)

98. Endangered Species Act, 16 U.S.C. §1538 (1988) (making it unlawful for any person to take a listed endangered species), and §1532(19) (1988) (defining "take" as "to . . . harm") (internal quotations omitted).

99. Sweeney et al. 2012 (by 2007, the cap-and-trade program established by the 1990 Clean Air Amendments had led to a 43 percent reduction in SO_2 emissions from 1990 levels).

100. "Health and Environmental Effects of Particulate Matter (PM)," Overviews and Factsheets, EPA, April 26, 2016, https://www.epa.gov/pm-pollution/health-and -environmental-effects-particulate-matter-pm.

101. P. Epstein et al. 2011; Muller, Mendelsohn, and Nordhaus 2011.

102. The exception is the State of Hawai'i, which has long imported most of its energy and as of 2023 relies on oil combustion for two-thirds of its electricity.

103. For good descriptions of these developments, see G. Zuckerman 2013 and Gold 2014.

104. Clean Air Act, §109(b), 42 U.S.C. §7409(b) (1977).

105. Clean Air Act, §110, 42 U.S.C. §7410.

106. Clean Air Act, 42 U.S.C. § 7411(d).

107. 40 C.F.R. Part 63, Subpart UUUUU (by 2017, mercury emissions had dropped 86 percent since the Mercury and Air Toxics Rule was implemented).

108. The EPA and the Obama administration introduced the Clean Power Plan on August 3, 2015 (see chapter 3). It was stayed by the courts before it was implemented and then eventually repealed by the Trump administration.

109. Casey, Fisher, and Kleveno 1965.

110. On U.S. rivers and lakes, see Semple 2022; on the Bald Eagle, see "Bald Eagle (*Haliaeetus leucocephalus*)," U.S. Fish & Wildlife Service, August 13, 2023, https:// www.fws.gov/species/bald-eagle-haliaeetus-leucocephalus.

111. 33 U.S.C. §1251(a)(1) (1987) ("it is the national goal that the discharge of pollutants into the navigable waters be eliminated by 1985").

112. D. S. Brown 2006 (summarizing the origins and essence of Hofstadter's "New Deal consensus"). Some dispute the consensus. See, e.g., Fishkin and Forbath 2022, 19, 427 (arguing that conservatives "never agreed" to the "settlement" that liberals imagine). But readers who doubt the existence of post–World War II cross-party support for a more robust governmental presence in the market should browse GOP presidential platforms from 1948 to 1976 and political scientists' measurements of the ideological makeup of the parties in Congress (at https://www.voteview.com).

113. Livermore 2014.

114. Averch and Johnson 1962.

115. For examples of environmental laws imposing liability in this way, see Spence 1999a, 2001.

116. The legal scholar William Buzbee (2003) conceives of a "regulatory tragedy of the commons" in which jurisdictional gaps can be exploited by firms. The regulatory anticommons involves jurisdictional overlap producing too many veto rights over a regulated activity. See Kosnik 2010; Bellantuono 2014; Heller 1998. The legal scholars Hari Osofsky and Hannah Wiseman (2014) call the problem of multiple levels of approval "hybrid energy governance" and propose a way of thinking about regulatory commons and anticommons problems in the energy sector.

117. See, e.g., "Memorandum of Agreement Regarding Mitigation Under CWA Section 404(b)(1) Guidelines," U.S. EPA, February 6, 1990, https://www.epa.gov/sites

/default/files/2019-05/documents/1990_army-epa_mitigation_moa.pdf; and "Memorandum of Understanding Between the Federal Energy Regulatory Commission (FERC) and the Commodity Futures Trading Commission (CFTC) Regarding Information Sharing and Treatment of Proprietary Trading and Other Information," FERC, CFTC, October 12, 2005, https://www.cftc.gov/sites /default/files/files/opa/opacftcfercmou.pdf.

118. For discussions of federal preemption and state preemption regimes in energy law, see, respectively, Spence 2013, 468–77, and Spence 2014.

119. Federal Water Power Act, 41 Stat. 1077 (1920); Atomic Energy Act, Pub. L. No. 83-703, 68 Stat. 919 (1954).

120. Spence 1999b.

121. Federal Water Power Act, 16 U.S.C. §821 (1920) (expressing the congressional purpose to leave state laws governing water rights undisturbed by the act); *Pac. Gas & Elec. Co. v. State Energy Res. Conserv'n & Dev. Comm'n*, 461 U.S. 190, 191, 213–16 (1983) (upholding a California statute regulating nuclear-waste storage because the statute had an "economic rather than safety purpose" and therefore was not preempted by the Atomic Energy Act).

122. 33 U.S.C. §1341 (1977).

123. Klass and Rossi 2017, 425–26, 427; Everly 2018; Malik 2017.

124. See appendix A for this book at https://www.ClimateOfContempt.com /Appendices/.

125. At one point during the New Deal, Democratic Party *margins* were 244 seats (333–89) in the House and 60 seats (76–16) in the Senate. The late Progressive Era statutes listed in table 1.3 were also enacted by majority parties with control of all the policymaking branches and clear legislative margins as well, ranging between 7 and 26 seats in the Senate and between 29 and 163 seats in the House.

126. The House passed the conference version of Dodd-Frank in 2009 (H.R. 4173, 111th Cong.) with the support of 234 Democrats and 3 Republicans; 173 Republicans and 19 Democrats opposed it. Most Democrats who opposed the bill represented a moderate or conservative district. The bill passed the Senate with the support of 57 Democrats and 3 Republicans; 38 Republicans and 1 Democrat voted no. In 2010, the House and Senate passed the Affordable Care Act (H.R. 3590, 111th Cong.) without the support of a single Republican.

127. For accounts of the weakening of the Affordable Care Act and Dodd-Frank, see, respectively, Gluck, Regan, and Turret 2020; and A. Levin and Macey 2018.

2. IDEOLOGICAL CONSERVATISM AND DEREGULATION

1. See L. Davis and Wolfram 2012; Slocum 2007, 2–4.

2. The DW-NOMINATE data set can be found at https://www.voteview.com. The scale runs from −1 (the left-wing pole) to +1 (the right-wing pole), so that higher scores represent higher levels of ideological conservatism. In other words, we can imagine members of each party (in each Congress) distributed along the two-point ideological scale around the individual senator or representative whose ideological score represents the median of their party.

3. For the regulatory-policy dimension, see Carroll et al. 2015 ("The first dimension can be interpreted in most periods as government intervention in the economy or liberal-conservative in the modern era").

2. IDEOLOGICAL CONSERVATISM AND DEREGULATION 261

4. Fiorina and Abrams 2009, 5–7; Desilver 2022 (discussing DW-NOMINATE data, the political parties' ideological cohesion, and the decline of moderate Democrats and Republicans in Congress). The absence of overlap is very recent; see Geiger 2014 ("Today, 92% of Republicans are to the right of the median Democrat, and 94% of Democrats are to the left of the median Republican.").

5. F. Lee 2015, 268–71 (explaining how Congress changed as parties became more polarized); see also generally Eilperin 2007 (arguing that American voters' wishes are not reflected in Congress as political parties fight for power).

6. M. Barber and McCarty 2015, 39. For more on why polarization begets gridlock in Congress, see appendix B of this book at https://www.ClimateOfContempt.com/Appendices/.

7. Rohac, Kennedy, and Singh 2018, 6 ("In the past . . . the policy positions of major candidates were almost indistinguishable, suggesting that political parties lacked any firm principles. That view was in line with the canonical result of public choice theory, which predicts that political parties focus their efforts on competing for the median voter, moving their platforms towards the center"); D. A. Brown 1996, 179–80 (explaining public-choice theory).

8. Spence 2017, 993–94; A. Smith [1776] 1850, 129–30 (containing the oft-quoted language about the "invisible hand" of the market); Hayek 1944, 27, and 1948, 169–70 (critiquing public-utility regulation as wasteful central planning).

9. Rothbard [1982] 2003, 71–72 (arguing that it is unjust for a government to tax or regulate an oil field if the property is private property).

10. Hayek 1944, 54 ("Since legislators as well as those to whom the administration of law is intrusted are fallible men, the essential point [is] that the discretion left to the executive organs wielding coercive power should be reduced as much as possible"); Hayek 1948, 169–70 (critiquing public-utility regulation as wasteful central planning).

11. Others before Hayek had described the idea of spontaneous order. The Enlightenment scholar Adam Ferguson (1996) wrote of the concept in slightly different language in 1767, Adam Smith's day, and the economist Michael Polanyi coined the term a few years before Hayek discussed it in print (see Struan Jacobs 1997). On the application of Hayek's framework to energy markets, see Kiesling 2009 (conceptualizing electricity markets as complex adaptive systems in which price signals will stimulate innovation and create value).

12. Nixon captured almost 60 percent of the popular vote to McGovern's 37.5 percent and 541 electoral votes to McGovern's 17. For a summary of the deregulatory efforts during a Democratic administration, see Dudley 2023.

13. Bill Clinton signed into law legislation deregulating portions of the financial-derivatives market, thereby creating regulatory loopholes that eventually affected energy markets. See the Commodity Future Modernization Act, Pub. L. No. 106-554, 114 Stat. 2763 (2000). Those loopholes were mostly closed more than a decade later with the passage of the Dodd-Frank Wall Street Reform and Consumer Protection Act, Pub. L. No. 111-203, 124 Stat. 1376 (2010).

14. For a more nuanced account of the spread of public-choice ideas, see McGarity 2013. The work of Timothy Werner and his coauthors has shed considerable light on the circumstances in which firms try to use dark money. See, e.g., Shanor, McDonnell, and Werner 2021, 154 ("the traceability of money creates a concrete limit on the ability of corporate actors to influence politics," pushing firms that are most concerned about their reputations toward "less traceable forms of political activity"); Skaife and Werner 2020 (finding a mixed

relationship between levels of corporate political activity and shareholder returns); Wei et al. 2022 (finding that the gradual erosion of political institutions in advanced democracies from rising populism generates regulatory risks for firms); and Skocpol and Hertel-Fernandez 2016, 684–87 (explaining the evolution of the Koch network and its reach in political advocacy).

Regarding the push toward a greater conservative direction in academic scholarship, my employer, the University of Texas, offers an illustrative example. Conservative donors funded a center at the McCombs School of Business called the Salem Center for Policy. More recently, conservative donors and Texas politicians have worked to create a university-wide center—initially called the Liberty Institute and later changed to the Civitas Institute—over the objections of most faculty. Both centers are explicitly ideological, based on the false premise that students cannot otherwise be exposed to conservative thought on campus. For example, the Salem Center's limited programming on climate policy *invariably* features prominent dissenters from the consensus positions described in chapter 1, such as the political scientist Bjorn Lomborg and the physicist Steve Koonin.

15. Rakove 2017. For another critical evaluation of MacLean's thesis, see Fleury and Marciano 2018.
16. Arrow 1951 (arguing that no social choice theorem can satisfy all democratic conditions and simultaneously have a transitive outcome); Stigler 1971; Peltzman 1976.
17. For a summary of public-choice scholarship's effects on antitrust law, see Hovenkamp 1994, 61–64.
18. Battistoni and Britton-Purdy 2020; Shughart and McChesney 2010, 386–88 (explaining how public-choice theory made antitrust law less protective of consumers); and Philippon 2019.
19. Three examples of public-choice examinations of antitrust doctrine by scholars who became prominent federal judges are Bork 1978, Easterbrook 1984, and Posner 1977, 309–48.
20. Hovenkamp 1994, 61 (calling the public-choice "revolution . . . a full assault on the New Deal . . . conception of the frailty of markets and the appropriate scope of antitrust intervention" but characterizing the courts as stopping short of full adoption of public-choice ideas).
21. For a deeper dive into the historical and theoretical origins of this methodological bias, see appendix C at https://www.ClimateOfContempt.com/Appendices/C.
22. Yost 2010.
23. Martorana 2007.
24. For more on how this assumption biases public-choice analyses and how it has influenced energy law and regulation, see Spence 2017 and Boyd 2020.
25. Hicks 1975, 310 ("The 'Pareto optimum' has gone into the textbooks. Because of the opportunities it offers for mathematical manipulation, great castles of theory have been built upon it"); Boyd 2014, 1657 ("comparing an ideal view of markets to real-world regulation was never going to go in regulation's favor").
26. On capture theory generally, see Niskanen 1971; Peltzman 1976; Stigler 1971; and Kalt and Zupan 1990.
27. The first version of capture theory posits that after an initial burst of interest in regulation, the general public loses interest in agency policymaking, leaving only regulated interest groups to participate in the process. See Balla 1998;

S. Gordon and Rashin 2021; Hempling 2014; and Wagner 2010. The second version is the classic conception of capture first articulated by George Stigler, who argued that "as a rule, regulation is acquired by the industry and is designed and operated primarily for its benefit" (1971, 3). See also R. Ripley 1975, 324–27; Cater 1964; and J. L. Freeman 1965. Some theorists argue that this strong version of capture involves the complicity of congressional committees via "iron triangles."

28. Scott Pruitt's reign at the EPA in 2017–2018 evidenced levels of a pro-business bias that many described as corruption. See, e.g., Milman and Rushe 2017. Justice Samuel Alito failed to report a luxury fishing trip funded by GOP donors Paul Singer and Robin Arkley II, both of whom were involved with later cases before the Court. Justice Clarence Thomas failed to report a series of lavish gifts from GOP donor Harlan Crow. For a summary of these ethical lapses, see Bazail-Eimil and Berg 2023. For a description of gifts that justices have reported receiving, see Romoser 2023.

29. The most prominent example of the use of capture theory by a public-choice scholar is Kolko 1965; for its use among revisionist historians, see Mayer 2016 and MacLean 2017. Many of my friends and peers in the energy law academy see regulatory capture as a primary impediment to the energy transition. See, e.g., Welton 2021, 212 (discussing "structural corporate domination" of the governance of the electric grid); Payne 2017 (concluding that the outcome of utility ratemaking proceedings is the product of regulatory capture); Eisen and Payne forthcoming ("utilities agree to hortatory goals, but then undercut progress or make it difficult to achieve [and] cozy up to state legislators . . . in shady ways"). Nevertheless, although some regulators and IOUs actively resist the transition through their influence over grid-governance institutions, the remainder of this book explains why regulatory capture fails as a generalization about energy regulators and why it is far from the most important obstacle to the energy transition.

30. J. Zuckerman 2021 (explaining how FirstEnergy funded $60 million into a political nonprofit to secretly influence a state bill with a $1.3 billion bailout package); Zekeria and Legum 2021 (exposing Southern Company for donating nearly $40,000 to Georgia state legislators who sponsored certain bills). Readers interested in a concrete, detailed example of such misapplication can find one in appendix F at https://www.ClimateOfContempt.com/Appendices/.

31. See Libgober 2020, 642 (finding that agency rulemaking is characterized by neither "extreme public interest zealotry" nor "strong capture").

32. Spence 1999b.

33. This priority ranking is built into the security-constrained economic dispatch principle described in chapter 1. Courts infer it from the statutory requirement that gas and electric rates be "just and reasonable." See *Grand Council of Crees (of Quebec) v. Fed. Energy Regul. Comm'n*, 198 F.3d 950, 957 (D.C. Cir. 2000). But see Davis Noll and Unel 2019, 2 (seeing "no impediment" to FERC using its FPA authority to require internalization of GHG emissions); and Weissman and Webb 2014, 36 (arguing that FERC can approve carbon adders under its existing authority).

34. Carpenter and Moss 2014, 22.

35. Stokes 2020; Teske 2004 (focusing on deregulatory policies).

36. Carrigan and Coglianese 2016.

37. Moss and Carpenter 2014, 451–52 ("the old Stiglerian notion of a fully captured regulator is mostly likely a rarity, if it exists at all).

38. Carpenter 2014. See also, generally, Boyd 2014 (challenging the capture hypothesis as applied to PUCs); and Spence and Cross 2000 (challenging the evidentiary support for capture theory).

39. McGarity and Wagner 2023 (arguing that interference with the discretion of agency careerists is most harmful to good policymaking when that interference limits the agency's ability to gather information to its decision).

40. Administrative Procedures Act, Pub. L. 79-404, 60 Stat. 237 (1946). Despite the findings of Paul Eric Teske's study on regulation (Teske 2004), we can imagine a potential inverse relationship between the salience of an agency's policy choice and the probability that industry can push the agency away from the public interest (i.e., "capture" it). If that intuition is right, then capture ought to be easier in state government because voters pay closer attention to the policy choices made in national and local governments than to those made in state governments. The demise of local newspaper coverage of state legislatures may contribute to this effect.

41. Fares 2017.

42. S. Yackee 2022 (finding that interest-group participants in forty-seven U.S. Food and Drug Administration rulemaking proceedings tended selectively to characterize the outcomes as regulatory capture, depending on whether their positions prevailed in the agency's final decisions).

43. Schoenbrod 1995 (conceiving of regulation, including Clean Air Act regulation, in starkly public-choice terms as the product of rent seeking); Bradley 2008, 162–67 (describing energy regulation in public-choice terms); Joskow, Bohi, and Gollop 1989, 128 (discussing the likely consequences of rate regulation and evaluating their underlying public policies); R. Pierce 1986, 1187 (proposing partial deregulation of the electricity industry through the provision of equal access to transmission facilities, deregulation of bulk-power sales, privatization of state-owned facilities, and a conditional federal preemption of state authority to regulate bulk-power transactions); Stigler and Friedland 1962, 12 ("The theory of price regulation must, in fact, be based upon the tacit assumption that in its absence a monopoly has exorbitant power. . . . The electrical utilities do not provide such a possibility"); Demsetz 1968, 55 (making the economist's case for restructuring); Williamson 1976, 73–74 (arguing for a loosening of regulation).

    This critique of regulation extended beyond the public-choice community. See Breyer 1979, 551, 609 (providing a basic framework for analyzing regulation and concluding that the energy market is a good candidate for "less restrictive alternatives" to regulation).

44. S. Shapiro and Tomain 2003, 20–21 (describing a move away from regulation in general and noting the effect on the natural gas and electricity industries); Spence 2008, 770–74 (describing the "unbundling" of energy production and distribution as a result of changing economic and political views of regulation in the United States and Europe during the 1980s); Demsetz 1968, 65; Williamson 1976, 73–76.

45. The precise economic definition of *monopsony* is "one buyer"; *monopoly* means "one seller." Antitrust law tends to apply the term *monopoly power* more broadly to any firm that has the power to influence the market price.

46. *Phillips Petroleum Co. v. Wisconsin*, 347 U.S. 672, 685 (1954).

47. The dissent in *Phillips* predicted this result. See Opinion of Justice Douglas (dissenting), 347 U.S. at 687–90.

48. R. Pierce 1988, 8–9 (on the reduced incentive). In the early 1970s, U.S. proven reserves of natural gas had fallen to a little more than 200 trillion cubic feet. At that time, American consumption was in the neighborhood of 20 trillion cubic feet a year, leading some analysts to state that the United States had only ten years' worth of natural gas supply and reserve. See Federal Power Commission, "Annual Report," 1971, https://hdl.handle.net/2027/hvd.hl363p?urlappend=%3Bseq=6.

49. Natural Gas Policy Act, Pub. L. No. 95-621, 92 Stat. 3352 (1978) (as codified at 15 U.S.C. §§3301–432 (2006)). For a description of the early effects of the NGPA, see generally R. Pierce 1983. For a description of the strange and unpredictable trajectory of natural gas prices during the slow deregulation process under the NGPA, see J. Griffin and Steele 1986, 301–3.

50. FERC Order 436 set the standards the agency applied to this practice. See Regulation of Natural Gas Pipelines After Partial Wellhead Decontrol, Order No. 436, 50 Fed. Reg. 42,408 (Oct. 18, 1985) (to be codified at 18 C.F.R. pts. 2, 157, 250, 284, 375, and 381).

51. Regulations Governing Blanket Marketer Sales Certificates, 57 Fed. Reg. 57,952, 57,953 n. 4 (Dec. 8, 1992) (to be codified at 18 C.F.R. pt. 284); Natural Gas Wellhead Decontrol Act, Pub. L. 101-60, 103 Stat. 157 (1989).

52. Pipeline Service Obligations and Revisions to Regulations Governing Self-Implementing Transportation Under Part 284 and Regulation of Natural Gas Pipelines After Partial Wellhead Decontrol, Order No. 636-C, 57 Fed. Reg. 13,267, 13,270 (Apr. 16, 1992) (to be codified at 18 C.F.R. pt. 284); Regulation of Natural Gas Pipelines After Partial Wellhead Decontrol, Order Denying Rehearing and Clarifying, Order Nos. 636 and 636-A, 57 Fed. Reg. 57,911, 57,914 (Nov. 27, 1992).

53. See Regulation of Natural Gas Pipelines After Partial Wellhead Decontrol, Order Denying Rehearing and Clarifying, Order Nos. 636 and 636-A, 57 Fed. Reg. 57,911, 57,914 (Nov. 27, 1992).

54. For good histories of the development of fracking as a production method, see G. Zuckerman 2013, 376, and Gold 2014.

55. "Sources of Greenhouse Gas Emissions," U.S. EPA, Overviews and Factsheets, December 29, 2015, https://www.epa.gov/ghgemissions/sources-greenhouse-gas-emissions.

56. For a full description of natural gas trade flows and market centers in the United States, see "Natural Gas Market Centers: A 2008 Update," U.S. Energy Information Administration, 2009, 1, 7, fig. 3, https://www.eia.gov/naturalgas/archive/ngmarketcenter.pdf.

57. Energy Policy Act, Pub. L. 102-486, 106 Stat. 2776 (1992), §§711 (repealed 2005), 712, 721, 106 Stat. 2776, 2905-11, 2915 (codified as amended at 16 U.S.C. §§824j, 2621 (Supp. III 2011)) (requiring open access to transmission lines).

58. Promoting Wholesale Competition Through Open Access Non-discriminatory Transmission Services by Public Utilities, Order No. 888, 61 Fed. Reg. 21,540 (May 10, 1996) (to be codified at 18 CFR pts. 35, 385; Recovery of Stranded Costs by Public Utilities and Transmitting Utilities, 61 Fed. Reg. 21,540, 21,541–43 (May 10, 1996) (to be codified at 18 C.F.R. pt. 37) (requiring transmission-line owners to file so-called open-access tariffs offering nondiscriminatory transmission services and to "functionally unbundle" transmission from electricity sales); Open Access Same-Time Information System (Formerly Real-Time Information Networks) and Standards of Conduct, Order No. 889, 61 Fed. Reg. 21,737, 21,740–41 (Apr. 24, 1996) (to be codified at 18 C.F.R. pt. 37) (mandating

transparency in transmission services by requiring all takers of transmission services—including affiliates of the transmission owner—to take such services using an open-access posting system).

59. See, e.g., Entergy Services, Inc., 58 FERC, ¶61,234 (1992) (authorizing electricity sales at market-based rates).

60. See "The Changing Structure of the Electric Power Industry: An Update," U.S. Department of Energy, 2000, U.S. DOE/EIA-0562(96), 434430, 74–77, https://doi .org/10.2172/434430.

61. In these states, residential consumers can enter their zip code into a website and choose from among a selection of electricity-supply contacts offered by different sellers at different terms and prices.

62. Order No. 888 encouraged ISOs. Order No. 2000 encouraged RTOs. See Regional Transmission Organizations, Order No. 2000, 89 FERC, ¶61,285 (1999).

63. For a description of the status of electricity-trading hubs at the turn of the century, see "The Changing Structure of the Electric Power Industry," U.S. Department of Energy, 74–78.

64. Coase 1937.

65. See A. Moore and Lynch 2001.

66. As has been widely reported, electric capacity in California declined during the 1990s, while demand grew by more than 10 percent (see "Subsequent Events—California's Energy Crisis," 2023, U.S. Energy Information Administration, Office of Coal, Nuclear, Electric, and Alternate Fuels, Washington, DC, https:// www.eia.gov/electricity/policies/legislation/california/subsequentevents .html). The supply interruptions included a drought-induced shortage of hydropower in the Pacific Northwest and unusual interruptions in the supply of natural gas to feed gas-fired generators in southern California. Natural gas prices in California were high as the crisis began and steadily increased to unprecedented levels as generators ran nonstop to take advantage of high wholesale electricity prices. See, e.g., "What Can Be Learned from California's Electricity Crisis?," Public Policy Institution of California, 2003, 1–2, https://www .ppic.org/wp-content/uploads/content/pubs/rb/RB_103CWRB.pdf.

     Regarding bottlenecks, Path 15 is the major north–south transmission line in California. On it, see "ISO Board of Governor's Approves Path 15 Upgrade: Board Finds Project Cost Effective and Good for the Grid," 2002, https://www .caiso.com/Documents/ISOBoard-Governor'sApprovesPath15UpgradeBoardFi ndsProjectCostEffectiveandGood_theGrid.pdf. At the time of the crisis, Path 15's capacity narrowed to two 500 kV lines in central California, which was insufficient to handle the necessary load. The line later expanded to three 500 kV lines ("ISO Board of Governor's Approves Path 15 Upgrade").

67. In the initial phases of the restructured California market, the California Public Utilities Commission did not permit use of long-term or futures contracts. See "Causes and Lessons of the California Electricity Crisis," U.S. Congressional Budget Office, 2001, 21–22, https://www.cbo.gov/sites/default/files/107th -congress-2001-2002/reports/californiaenergy.pdf.

68. On scarcity rents, see Gelinas 2003. The term *scarcity rents* (or *economic rents*) refers to profits over and above those that sellers could earn in a competitive market because of the relative scarcity of the product sold; see, e.g., Varian 1990, 384–87. On fraud and manipulation, see Massey and Brownell 2003, 1–2.

69. Subsequent FERC investigations confirmed that holders of generation scheduled unplanned outages to create this kind of scarcity. See Gelinas 2003, 6:54–55.

70. Gelinas 2003, 6:26–30.
71. Gelinas 2003, 7:1–16.
72. Enron had circulated memos explaining several of the more popular techniques for gaming the California market. These memos are viewable at FERC's webpage dedicated to the California energy crisis. See also Gelinas 2003.
73. "Largest Fines, Penalties, and Refunds Ordered by Federal and State Authorities Against Corporations for Manipulation of the West Coast Energy Market and Natural Gas Price Index Manipulation," Public Citizen, n.d., https://www .citizen.org/wp-content/uploads/camarketfines.pdf.
74. 16 U.S.C. §824v (2005) (prohibiting energy-market manipulation in the FPA); 15 U.S.C. §717c-1 (2005) (prohibiting energy-market manipulation in the NGA).
75. W. Hogan 2005, 6–8 (explaining the idealized energy-only model); "PUC Rulemaking to Amend PUC Subst. R. 25.505, Relating to Resource Adequacy in the Electric Reliability Council of Texas Power Region," Public Utility Commission of Texas, 2012 (providing information and documents), https://www.puc.texas .gov/agency/rulesnlaws/subrules/electric/25.505/40268adt.pdf.
76. Cramton and Stoft 2006, 8–11 (describing the missing-money problem); Joskow 2008, 159 (arguing that the missing-money problem can never be fully ameliorated, even with freely floating prices); and see generally Spence 2008 (questioning whether politicians can credibly commit to letting the price signal work).
77. As of 2023, PJM, the New England ISO, and the New York ISO run some form of capacity auction. For the criticism, see, e.g., Bushnell, Flagg, and Mansur 2017, 49–50.
78. The polar vortex of 2014 affected 200 million people in the United States and Canada and cost an estimated cost $5 billion (James 2014). PJM used to refer to "Pennsylvania–New Jersey–Maryland," but this ISO is now known only by the abbreviation.
79. For example, a retailer buying 10 MW of spot market power per hour during the crisis would have paid $6.48 million ($9,000 × 72 × 10); buying 10 MW of power per hour for the remaining 8,688 hours of the year would cost $4.34 million ($50 × 8,688 × 10).
80. Smeltzer 2021.
81. Svitek 2022.
82. Federal Regulatory Commission and North American Electric Reliability Corporation 2011; Kuckro 2015; North American Electricity Reliability Corporation 2022.
83. Arbaje 2023.
84. On these grid-stress events in general, see Von Kaenel 2022; Deliso 2022; and Watkins 2022. On the California event, see "Summer Market Performance Report: Sept. 2022," CAISO, 2022, 12, https://www.caiso.com/Documents/Sum merMarketPerformanceReportforSeptember2022.pdf ("The prolonged heat event precipitated an unprecedented number of calls for consumer conservation . . . [including] 10 consecutive days of voluntary Flex Alerts"). On the Texas event, see Dey and Ferman 2022 ("Texans avoided rolling blackouts . . . after the Electric Reliability Council of Texas requested that they cut back on their energy use").
85. Jayashankar et al. 2023.
86. These bilateral arrangements are usually called "reliability must run" or "reliability unit commitment" contracts. Texas regulators call their requirement a "performance credit mechanism." See Foxhall and Ford 2023.

87. For example, see Joskow 1988, 105 (characterizing freely floating spot prices as an "unsatisfactory governance mechanism for inducing the parties to make the specific investments necessary"); and Spence 2008, 811 (if politicians cannot protect vulnerable consumers against price spikes without distorting price signals, then "markets will continue to struggle with shortages").

88. Borenstein and Bushnell 2015, 437 ("In reality, the electricity rate changes since restructuring have been driven more by exogenous factors—such as generation technology advances and natural gas price fluctuations—than by efforts of restructuring"); MacKay and Mercadal 2021 (attributing the failure of competition to reduce electricity prices to the exercise of market power by generators).

89. Ramirez 2022.

90. Boyd 2022.

91. "U.S. Federal Power Program: The PMAs and TVA," American Public Power Association, 2023, https://www.publicpower.org/system/files/documents/70%20 2023%20PMC%20Issue%20Briefs_U.S.%20Federal%20Power%20Program _FINAL.pdf. Power for Tomorrow's website is at powerfortomorrow.org.

92. Kiesling 2009 (making a Hayekian argument for market competition in the electricity sector); Macey 2020 (critiquing the traditional justifications for utility regulation); Macey and Salovaara 2020 (critiquing the use of capacity markets to assure adequate reserves); Mays et al. 2021, 369; Klass et al. 2022 (making the case for changes in grid-governance rules as the grid decarbonizes); Hayek 1944, 29; "Alternative Energy Tax Incentives: The Effect of Short-Term Extensions on Clean Energy Investment, Domestic Manufacturing, and Job Creation," Subcommittee on Energy, Natural Resources, and Infrastructure of the Committee on Finance, U.S. Senate, 2011, https://www.finance.senate.gov/imo/media /doc/77605.pdf.

93. For readers wishing to know more about state RPSs or clean-energy standards, the National Council of State Legislatures maintains a compendium of state clean-energy policies at www.dsireusa.org.

94. "Alternative Energy Tax Incentives," U.S. Senate, 2011, statement of Molly Sherlock, analyst, Congressional Research Service.

95. "Alternative Energy Tax Incentives," Sherlock statement.

96. Energy Policy Act, Pub. L. 109-58, 119 Stat. 594 (2005) (codified in scattered section of 42 U.S.C.); Energy Independence and Security Act, Pub. L. 110-140, 121 Stat. 1492 (2007) (codified as 42 U.S.C. §§17001-386); American Recovery and Reinvestment Act, Pub. L. 111-5, 123 Stat. 115 (2009).

97. Integration of Variable Energy Resources, Order No. 764, 139 FERC, ¶61,246 (2012) (requiring competitive wholesale markets to remove barriers to entry for wind and solar generators); Demand Response Compensation in Organized Markets, Order No. 745, 134 FERC, ¶61,187 (2011) (requiring competitive wholesale markets to compensate providers of demand-response services at the spot wholesale price); Electric Storage Participation in Markets Operated by Regional Transmission Organizations and Independent System Operators, 83 Fed. Reg. 9,580 (2018) (to be codified at 18 C.F.R. pt. 35); Wiser et al. 2016, 13 (on commissioners' resistance).

98. Fares 2016. The LCOE is a fraction: the numerator is the present value of the total costs of building and operating the project over its useful life; the denominator is the number of hours a project is expected to operate over its life. So the LCOE can be thought of as the average price the project must command for its electricity in order to break even. The United States has never seen

sustained average wholesale power prices of $600 per mwh, so the availability of tax subsidies and policy-driven markets have been important to wind power's early development. It should be noted that the (actual and expected) profitability of a specific project depends on other factors besides the LCOE, such as the market value of the power sold by the project because power prices vary by time and place.

99. In 2023, the interconnection application queues at ISOs/RTOs and state PUCs— requests from new or pending projects for permission to connect to the grid— were several years long, filled mostly with solar and wind projects. In the fall of 2023, FERC finalized a rule aimed at reducing these backlogs. See Improvements to Generator Interconnection Procedures and Agreements, 88 Fed. Reg. 61,014 (2023) (to be codified at 18 C.F.R. pt. 35).

100. Caperton and Kasper 2011 (detailing that the United States needs to invest at least $298 billion to upgrade by 2030); Fox-Penner 2010, 89–92 (describing plans for a transmission "superhighway"); Wald 2009 (describing the possibility for a new system of high-voltage lines controlled by state-of-the-art transmission centers); and *Grid 2030* 2003, iv.

101. "Energy Infrastructure Update for 2023," FERC, September 21, 2023, 6, https:// cms.ferc.gov/media/energy-infrastructure-update-january-2023-0; see also R. Kessler 2023. The transmission system comprises the higher-voltage lines (up to 765 kV) used to send power over longer distances, whereas distribution lines are the lower-voltage lines used to bring power to end users. But neither the Federal Power Act nor FERC has established any voltage or other numerical bright-line test to distinguish one from the other. Rather, FERC uses a functional test to distinguish the two, such that a 69-kV line may serve a transmission function in one setting and a distribution function in another.

102. For an analysis of the political barriers to siting energy infrastructure, including transmission, see Spence 2017. For analyses of the legal barriers to siting transmission lines, see A. Brown and Rossi 2010 (discussing how recent developments have challenged the definition of "public interest") and Robertson 2001, 73 (arguing that proper transmission policy "requires greater federal power"—namely, Congress rather than the courts).

103. State laws favoring incumbent utilities may violate the Commerce Clause of the Constitution. This issue is discussed in, e.g., Peskoe 2021 and *Nextera Capital Holdings v. Lake*, 48 F.4th 306 (5th Cir. 2022) (holding that a Texas statute granting incumbent utilities exclusive right to build new transmission lines violates the Commerce Clause). For a compelling account of the formidable political and legal obstacles faced by nonutility developers of transmission projects, see Gold 2019.

104. As of 2023, Rep. Scott Peters (D–CA) and Sen. John Hickenlooper (D–CO) have introduced into the 118th Congress a bill (S. 2827, Building Integrated Grids with Inter-regional Energy Supply Act, or the Big WIRES Act) that would mandate the construction of new transmission between regional grids, thereby expanding markets for inexpensive renewable power. Section 1221 of Energy Policy Act of 2005 authorizes three or more contiguous states to enter into an interstate compact that establishes regional siting agencies to carry out those states' siting responsibilities (16 U.S.C. § 824p(i) (2021)). On "backstop authority," see Energy Policy Act, 6 U.S.C. § 824p(a)-(b) (2021).

105. On the court cases, see *Piedmont Env't Council v. FERC*, 558 F.3d 304 (4th Cir. 2009) (finding multiple problems with the rules); *Calif. Wilderness Coal. v. U.S. Dep't. of Energy*, 631 F.3d 1072 (9th Cir. 2011) (overturning the rules for failure to

comply with the NEPA). For the IIJA, see Infrastructure Investment and Jobs Act, Pub. L. 117-58, 135 Stat. 429 (2021) (amending the backstop-siting provision to remove the obstacle created by the court in the *Piedmont* decision).

106. On FERC not using its backstop authority, see "Joint Statement from Chairman Glick & Commissioner Clements on Building Transmission for the Future," FERC, July 15, 2021, https://www.ferc.gov/news-events/news/joint-statement -chairman-glick-commissioner-clements-building-transmission-future. On the designation of transmission corridors, see U.S. Department of Energy Grid Deployment Office, "Transmission Siting and Permitting Efforts," n.d., https:// www.energy.gov/gdo/transmission-siting-and-permitting-efforts.

107. For a fuller description of the positive-externality problem and its role in under-supplying high-voltage transmission and energy-network infrastructure generally, see Spence 2017, 1017–23.

108. M. H. Brown and Sedano 2004.

109. *Illinois Com. Comm'n v. FERC*, 576 F.3d 470, 479 (7th Cir. 2009) (Cudahy, J., dissenting), emphasis added.

110. Promoting Transmission Investment Through Pricing Reform, 71 Fed. Reg. 43,293 (2006) (to be codified at 18 C.F.R. pt. 35); Transmission Planning and Cost Allocation by Transmission Owning and Operating Public Utilities, 76 Fed. Reg. 49,841 (2012) (to be codified at 18 C.F.R. pt. 35) (authorizing transmission utilities to allocate costs to users who reap reliability benefits and to consider public policies such as RPSs in determining the distribution of benefits and encouraging regional planning).

111. See S.B. 20, 79th Leg. §3(g)(3) (Tex. 2005).

112. Brinkman et al. 2020.

113. Participation of Distributed Energy Resource Aggregations in Markets Operated by Regional Transmission Organizations and Independent System Operators, 86 Fed. Reg. 33,853 (2021) (to be codified at 18 C.F.R. pt. 35).

114. See Burger et al. 2019, 16 (for a nuanced review of the case against net metering); and Lacey 2014 (describing dynamics of the "spiral" in Europe and the United States).

115. Welton 2017, 576 (arguing for policies that facilitate the participation by less wealthy customers in ownership of clean DERs rather than abandonment of net metering); Welton and Eisen 2019 (detailing reforms that might facilitate broader participation in the benefits of clean DERs); Rule 2015 (arguing that utility rates are replete with cross subsidies); Welton 2017 as well as Kim and Fischer 2021 (on the benefits of DERs).

116. State of Nevada Public Utilities Commission, "Net Metering in Nevada," n.d., https://puc.nv.gov/Renewable_Energy/Net_Metering/; Delgado 2022; California Public Utilities Commission, "Customer-Sited Renewable Energy Generation," n.d., https://www.cpuc.ca.gov/industries-and-topics/electrical-energy/demand -side-management/net-energy-metering; R. Kennedy 2022.

117. California, which has the highest rooftop solar penetration rates in the nation, has floated a proposal for a fixed grid-access charge that varies with income. The proposal has met with stiff resistance among solar owners, some of whom have threatened to exit the grid. For most rooftop solar owners, these threats are probably empty, but they are reminiscent of public-utility economists' recommendation that rates for industrial customers should be kept low enough to prevent their exit from the grid (an approach called "Ramsey pricing"). Canary Media has covered the progress of the California net-metering proposal

at https://www.cpuc.ca.gov/industries-and-topics/electrical-energy/demand-side-management/customer-generation.

118. Kiesling 2009. The mathematician Eric Gimon (2022), the legal scholar Joshua Macey (Mays et al. 2022), and the economist Ahmad Faruqui (Faruqui and Palmer 2011) are (or have been) among the other prominent proponents of this vision.

119. My employer, the University of Texas, has a microgrid. It is connected to the local utility, Austin Energy, but gets its power from an on-campus gas-fired combined heat-and-power plant. Microgrids at universities, military bases, and other large institutions have been part of the electricity landscape for decades.

120. Westwick 2019; Roberts 2019; Atleework 2018; Penn 2021; Penn and Eavis 2023; Shah 2023.

121. An early proponent of dynamic-pricing regimes for customers, Ahmad Faruqui has expressed frustration with the "glacial speed" of their rollout. See his statements in Behr 2022.

122. New York Public Service Commission, Case 14-M-0101, Proceeding on Motion of the Commission in Regard to Reforming the Energy Vision, Order Adopting Regulatory Policy Framework and Implementation Plan (2015), https://nyrevconnect.com/rev-briefings/track-one-defining-rev-ecosystem/.

123. Brand and Ostadan 2023.

124. Trabish 2018; Wash 2023.

125. Participation of Distributed Energy Resource Aggregations in Markets Operated by Regional Transmission Organizations and Independent System Operators, 85 Fed. Reg. 67,094 (2020) (to be codified at 18 C.F.R. pt. 35).

126. One analysis estimated that these sorts of downward price pressures from renewable generators saved Texas ratepayers more than $27 billion between 2010 and August 2022 (Rhodes 2022).

127. A bill before the Texas Legislature in 2023, SB 624, would have imposed additional fee and environmental-review requirements on renewable generators, but the bill failed to pass.

128. The writer Adam Gopnik makes the same point this way: "Let's be clear . . . that a philosophy of right wing politics . . . exists that is not merely paid hate literature. . . . Many . . . assume that conservative ideas are not much more than a series of sham apologies in which well-paid scribes write whatever their well-paid bosses at Fox News and Koch Industries want them to write" (2019, 84).

129. Daniel Cole (2023) describes a range of "libertarian" perspectives, from opposition to all government regulation as tyranny to a preference for market-based regulatory instruments such as carbon taxes and cap-and-trade regulation. Mandates such as clean-energy standards, says Cole, are unacceptable to libertarians.

3. PARTISAN TRIBALISM AND CLIMATE POLICY

1. J. Brown and Enos 2021, 1005–6.

2. See Pearson 2015 on greater party unity and discipline. For sophisticated explanations of how polarization induces legislative gridlock, see Binder 2003; Krehbiel 1998; J. Bond, Fleisher, and Cohen 2015; and Theriault 2015.

3. American Clean Energy and Security Act (a.k.a. Waxman-Markey bill), H.R. 2454, 111th Cong. (2009); Build Back Better Act, H.R. 5376, 117th Cong. (as passed

by the House, November 19, 2021). For accounts of the congressional politics that doomed Waxman-Markey in the Senate, see Weiss 2010 and Cassidy 2021.

4. Fourier theorized that some solar energy reaching the earth must be captured by the earth's atmosphere; Foote conducted experiments that demonstrated the heat-trapping properties of moist air; and Tyndall identified CO_2's heat-trapping qualities through a series of laboratory experiments.

5. S. Solomon et al. 2007; IPCC, "History," August 15, 2023, https://www.ipcc.ch /about/history/.

6. On the Chafee hearings, see *Ozone Depletion, the Greenhouse Effect, and Climate Change* 1986. On the reference to climate effects in the Clean Air Act, see Clean Air Act, 42 U.S.C. §7602(h) (1990). The directive to the EPA was part of the Clean Air Act Amendments, Pub. L. 101-549, §821 (Nov. 15, 1990) (42 U.S.C. §7651k (1990)).

7. Mayer 2016; Oreskes and Conway 2010 (elaborating this explanation). For a more nuanced view of how (and how successfully) ExxonMobil participated in climate and environmental politics, see Coll 2012.

8. This claim about oil companies' understanding of the problem is based on research conducted at Stanford University for the American Petroleum Institute in the 1960s, internal Exxon research in the 1970s, and research by a Royal Dutch Shell subsidiary in the 1980s (Franta 2018).

9. The issue was on the U.S. international-relations agenda before the turn of the twenty-first century. The United States participated in international meetings on climate, including the Rio Summit in 1992 and the Kyoto Protocol in 1997, which it signed but never ratified. For an account of thinking on climate science within the National Academy of Sciences in the late twentieth century, see Nierenberg, Tschinkel, and Tschinkel 2010, 318.

10. In AR1, the IPCC concluded that "the size of this warming is broadly consistent with predictions of climate models, but it is also of the same magnitude as natural climate variability. Thus the observed increase could be largely due to this natural variability, alternatively this variability and other human factors could have offset a still larger human-induced greenhouse warming" (IPCC 1992, xii). In AR2, the IPCC noted a "discernible human influence" on global climate change (Houghton, Meira Filho, et al. 1996, 4–5).

11. See *Global Environmental Change* 1999, 293–357 (chapter 7, "Human Dimensions of Global Environmental Change").

12. Houghton, Ying, et al. 2001, 10 ("[M]ost of the observed warming over the last 50 years is likely to have been due to the increase in greenhouse gas concentrations").

13. For AR4, see Pachauri and Reisinger 2007, 10; for AR5, see IPCC 2014, 4; for the special report, see IPCC 2019.

14. IPCC 2023.

15. On the carbon-trading scheme, see Ellerman and Buchner 2007, 66. On the scheme as a constraint on emissions, see Bayer and Aklin 2020 and R. Martin, Muûls, and Wagner 2016. On other nations' regulations, see World Bank 2022, 19.

16. Hibbard et al. 2018; Larsen 2022.

17. At least one California utility, PG&E, followed the state's lead in embracing carbon-emissions reductions in 2006. See Blunt 2022, 96 ("At the time the climate change debate was mostly limited to scientists and policymakers awakening to the consequences of burning fossil fuels with abandon"). On the California–Canada trading market, see Agreement Between the California Air Resources Board and the Government du Quebec Concerning the

Harmonization of Cap-and-Trade Programs for Reducing Greenhouse Gas Emissions, September 22, 2017.

18. See Washington's cap-and-invest program, Washington Department of Ecology, at https://ecology.wa.gov/Air-Climate/Climate-Commitment-Act/Cap-and-invest.

19. The political history of the effort against acid rain is described in Conniff 2009.

20. Clean Air Act Amendments, Pub. L. 101-549, 104 Stat. 2399 (1990), Title IV.

21. Naomi Oreskes published her seminal article "The Scientific Consensus on Climate Change" in *Science* in 2004, between AR3 and AR4. The scientists she identifies as "merchants of doubt" lent credibility to the efforts by conservative media and conservative politicians to sow doubt in climate science. But it is speculation to credit those scientists' efforts with preventing policy change. Oreskes claims that they, most notably the physicist Fred Singer, exerted a distorting effect over IPCC reports followed (by several years) of mirror-image allegations that individual scientists had tampered with earlier IPCC reports to overstate climate risks. And national GHG limits continue to elude us even though most voters understand climate science today.
RINO is "Republican in name only," and DINO is "Democrat in name only." As the parties became more ideologically homogenous and divergent, these terms referred to members of each party whose ideology was at the center-facing edge of their own party's ideological distribution.

22. Climate Stewardship Act of 2003, S. 139, 108th Cong. (2003); Climate Stewardship and Innovation Act, S. 1151, 109th Cong. (2005); Climate Stewardship and Innovation Act, S. 280, 110th Cong. (2007).

23. American Clean Energy and Security Act, H.R. 2454, 111th Cong. (2009); Clean Energy Jobs and American Power Act, S. 1733, 111th Cong. (2009).

24. The U.S. Climate Action Partnership was an ad hoc lobbying group that supported the Waxman-Markey cap-and-trade regime, triggering sharp criticism from fossil-fuel companies.

25. On Kerry-Boxer not being brought to a vote, see McGarity 2014 and MacNeil 2012; on green groups' opposition to it, see, e.g., "Greenpeace Opposes Waxman-Markey," *Greenpeace USA* (blog), July 6, 2010, https://www.greenpeace.org/usa/news/greenpeace-opposes-waxman-mark/. It is possible that the bill would have failed to command a majority in the Senate regardless of the filibuster. Sen. Max Baucus (D–MT), Jay Rockefeller (D–WV), Evan Bayh (D–IN), and George Voinovich (D–OH) expressed opposition to the bill on behalf of their states' coal industries. Ben Nelson (D–NE) may have been representing other rural Democrats when he opposed the bill because of worries about its effects on energy prices. Significantly, *all* of the seats these Senate Democrats held in 2010 are now held by Republicans.

26. Weigel 2014 (quoting the vendor of a "coal-rolling retrofit" kit who ascribed the trend to dislike of President Obama and the desire do the opposite of what Obama advised or preferred). Rolling coal predates climate-policy battles, and its use to target Prius drivers is just a more recent expression of partisan contempt.

27. For the Supreme Court case, see *Massachusetts v. EPA*, 549 U.S. 497 (2007), 532. The requirement of a finding that the pollutant endangers public health and welfare is found at 42 U.S.C. §7408(a)(1)(1998).

28. Light-Duty Vehicle Greenhouse Gas Emission Standards and Corporate Average Fuel Economy Standards, 75 Fed. Reg. 25,323 (May 7, 2010) (codified at 40 C.F.R. pts. 85, 86, 600 and at 49 C.F.R. 531, 533, 536, 537, 538); Reconsideration of

Interpretation of Regulations That Determine Pollutants Covered by Clean Air Act Permitting Programs, 75 Fed. Reg. 17,003 (Apr. 2, 2010) (codified at 40 C.F.R. pts. 50, 51, 70, 71); and Prevention of Significant Deterioration and Title V Greenhouse Gas Tailoring Rule, 75 Fed. Reg. 31,513 (June 3, 2010) (codified at 40 C.F.R. pts. 51, 52, 70, 71) (exempting smaller sources but otherwise applying the Clean Air Act's technology-based permitting standards to GHGs at new and modified sources).

29. *Utility Air Regulatory Group v. EPA*, 573 U.S. 302, 314–34 (2014), 323–24.

30. In 2013, the EPA regulated GHG emissions from new power plants under the New Source Performance Standard program, which covers only new or modified fossil-fueled power plants. See Standards of Performance for Greenhouse Gas Emissions for New Stationary Sources: Electric Utility Generating Units, 80 Fed. Reg. 64,509 (Oct. 23, 2015) (codified at 40 C.F.R. pts. 60, 70, 71, 98), http://www.epa.gov/airquality/cpp/cps-final-rule.pdf. In June 2014, the EPA proposed regulation of emission from existing plants under the CPP and finalized it in August 2015. See Carbon Pollution Emission Guidelines for Existing Stationary Sources: Electric Utility Generating Units, 80 Fed. Reg. 64,566 (Oct. 23, 2015) (codified at 40 C.F.R. 60).

31. 42 U.S.C. §7411(a)(1) (1990).

32. Spence 2022, 977–82.

33. Environmental Protection Agency, Carbon Pollution Emission Guidelines for Existing Stationary Sources: Electric Utility Generating Units, 80 Fed. Reg. 64,661 (Oct. 23, 2015) (codified at 40 C.F.R. 60).

34. On the fierce opposition, see Richardson 2015, 247; on Manchin in particular, see Wing 2017.

35. Repeal of the Clean Power Plan; Emission Guidelines for Greenhouse Gas Emissions from Existing Electric Utility Generating Units; Revisions to Emission Guidelines Implementing Regulations, 84 Fed. Reg. 32,520 (July 8, 2019) (codified at 40 C.F.R. 60). For an analysis of the role of party politics in litigation against the CPP, see Adelman and Spence 2017, 401–10.

36. *West Virginia v. EPA*, 142 S. Ct. 2587 (2022), 2610. Many observers were surprised that the Court took this case because the rule in question was no longer in effect, and the case sought resolution of an academic or hypothetical legal question (Jody Freeman 2022).

37. Appendix D contains a selection of these bills in the 112th through 115th Congresses, 2011–2018, at https://www.ClimateOfContempt.com/Appendices/. At least one Republican joined in Democrats' attempts to strengthen GHG regulation. In the 115th Congress, Florida Republican representative Carlos Curbelo introduced H.R. 6463, a bill to impose a carbon tax on GHG emitters. One Democrat joined Republican attempts to stop GHG regulation. In the 114th Congress, Sen. Joe Manchin (D–WV) introduced S.1905, the Electricity Security and Affordability Act, which proposed to prevent the imposition of GHG emissions limits on fossil-fueled power plants.

38. On emission-cap bills, see Climate Solutions Act of 2015, H.R.1971(Ted Lieu [D–CA 33]); Climate Protection and Justice Act of 2015, S.2399 (Bernard Sanders [I–VT]); American Energy Innovation Act, S.2089 (Maria Cantwell [D–WA]); Climate Solutions Act of 2017, H.R.2958 (Ted Lieu [D–CA 33].

On carbon taxes and fees, see American Opportunity Carbon Fee Act, S.2940 (Sheldon Whitehouse [D–RI]); American Opportunity Carbon Fee Act of 2015, S.1548 (Sheldon Whitehouse [D–RI]); American Opportunity Carbon Fee Act of 2015, S.1548 (Sheldon Whitehouse [D–RI]); American Opportunity Carbon Fee

Act of 2017, H.R.3420 (Earl Blumenauer ([D–OR 3]); American Opportunity Carbon Fee Act of 2017, S.1639 (Sheldon Whitehouse [D–RI]); American Opportunity Carbon Fee Act of 2018, H.R.4926 (Earl Blumenauer [D–OR 3]; American Opportunity Carbon Fee Act of 2018, S.2368 (Sheldon Whitehouse [D–RI]); Healthy Climate and Family Security Act of 2018, S.2352 (Chris Van Hollen ([D–MD); Healthy Climate and Family Security Act of 2018, H.R.4889 (Donald S. Beyer Jr. [D–VA 8] ; Energy Innovation and Carbon Dividend Act of 2018, H.R.7173 (Theodore E. Deutch [D–FL 22).

On supporting the clean-energy export industry, see Climate Protection Act of 2013, S.332 (Bernard Sanders [I–VT]). And on local green-energy investment, see "A Bill to Amend Title 31, United States Code, to Provide for the Issuance of Green Bonds and to Establish the United States Green Bank, and for Other Purposes," S.3382 (Christopher Murphy [D–CT]); "A Bill to amend Title 31, United States Code, to Provide for the Issuance of Green Bonds and to Establish the United States Green Bank, and for Other Purposes," S.1406 (Christopher Murphy [D–CT]); "A Bill to Amend Title 31, United States Code, to Provide for the Issuance of Green Bonds and to Establish the United States Green Bank, and for Other Purposes," H.R.2995 (Elizabeth H. Esty [D–CT 5]).

39. Schwartz 2017 (on the Climate Leadership Council); Roston 2016 (on the Congressional Climate Solutions Caucus); Meyer 2018 (on the GOP's loss of "its climate moderates").

40. This rejuvenated support for government-led industrial policy was an idea associated with the late Michael Harrington, DSA founder. His ideas influenced the Great Society programs of the 1960s.

41. Stolberg 2019; Fandos 2020; House 2019.

42. On the two-point DW-NOMINATE ideological scale, in 2018–2019 the median New Democrat (–0.30) sat 0.14 points to the right of the median progressive (–0.44) in the House and 0.49 points to the left of the most liberal House Republican (0.19). In the summer of 2019, two senior staffers to Rep. Ocasio-Cortez abruptly left her congressional office after voicing criticism of moderate Democrats. Her former chief of staff and Justice Democrats founder Saikat Chakrabarti tweeted that New Democrats "seem hell bent to do to black and brown people today what the old Southern Democrats did in the 40s" and that Rep. Sharice Davids (D–KS), a Native American, "votes to enable a racist system" (qtd. in Bresnahan 2019). Communications Director Corbin Trent had threatened Democrats who sided with Republicans on votes by saying that they are "going on a list," presumably one associated with challenges to election (qtd. in Debonis 2019).

The feelings of being condescended to were precipitated by House Speaker Nancy Pelosi's interview in the summer of 2019 in which she spoke disparagingly of the Twitter followings of the new House progressives and by the lecturing tone taken by the late Senator Diane Feinstein when she spoke to Sunrise Movement protestors in her office earlier that same year.

43. IPCC 2019, 15 ("Pathways limiting global warming to 1.5°C with no or limited overshoot would require rapid and far-reaching transitions in energy, land, urban and infrastructure [sic] (including transport and buildings), and industrial systems (high confidence)"), bracketed insertions in the original.

44. Thunberg's statements regarding her protests can be found in her Twitter/X posts in 2018, @GretaThunberg.

45. Lipsitz 2022; "About the Sunrise Movement," *Sunrise Movement* (blog), August 15, 2023, https://www.sunrisemovement.org/about/; Taylor 2020.

46. Recognizing the Duty of the Federal Government to Create a Green New Deal, H.Res. 109, 116th Cong. (2019).
47. "Bernie Sanders Wants to Change Your Mind," *New York Times*, January 13, 2020, https://www.nytimes.com/interactive/2020/01/13/opinion/bernie-sanders -nytimes-interview.html.
48. See Cillizza 2021; Herndon 2020; Bade and Werner 2020.
49. The partisan lean number estimates the expected breakdown of vote by party in the absence of candidate-specific factors. The *Cook Political Report* explains its partisan lean measures in "The Cook Partisan Voting Index (Cook PVI℠)," n.d., https://www.cookpolitical.com/cook-pvi. According to Pew, the set of Democrat voters who feel alienated from the Democratic Party (what Pew calls the "Progressive Left" and the "Outsider Left") constitutes 28 percent of the party's voters. See "Beyond Red vs. Blue: The Political Typology," Pew Research Center, November 9, 2021, https://www.pewresearch.org/politics/2021/11/09 /beyond-red-vs-blue-the-political-typology-2/.
50. Frey 2021.
51. Roose 2021.
52. Tully-McManus 2020; Rosenberg 2021; Knutson 2020.
53. Warren and Gangel 2021; J. Martin and Burns 2021.
54. Scott 2022.
55. Yourish, Buchanan, and Lu 2021. Gallup's poll found that 62 percent of Americans polled said the outcome of the election was swayed by misinformation (J. Jones 2020). Rasmussen Reports found that 47 percent of Americans believe it is "likely" Democrats stole votes or destroyed Trump ballots (Bleau 2020).
56. Build Back Better Act, H.R. 5376, 117th Cong. (2021–2022). The original Green New Deal price tag was estimated at more than $16 trillion (Briedman 2019).
57. A. Lawson 2021.
58. In the 117th Congress, Manchin (−0.06) and Sinema (−0.105) were the most conservative Senate Democrats on the DW-NOMINATE measure. Another measure of congressional ideology from a group called ProgressivePunch also listed the two senators as the most conservative Democrats in the Senate. See the ProgressivePunch website at https://www.progressivepunch.org.
59. Brownstein 2022.
60. The Infrastructure Investment and Jobs Act, Pub. L. No. 117-58, 135 Stat. 429 (2021).
61. McCarter 2010.
62. See "The 2021 Cook Partisan Voting Index (Cook PVI℠)," *Cook Political Report*, 2021, https://www.cookpolitical.com/cook-pvi/2021-partisan-voting-index. Donald Trump carried West Virginia by about forty points in both the 2016 and 2020 elections.
63. Metzger 2021; "Sen. Manchin Wants You to Know He Is Not a Liberal #shorts," YouTube, 2021, https://www.youtube.com/shorts/7c-RFGVctTU.
64. On credits to developers, see Inflation Reduction Act, Pub. L. 117-169, 136 Stat. 1818 (2022), §§13101 (Extension and Modification of Credit for Electricity Produced from Certain Renewable Sources), 13102 (Extension and Modification of Energy Credit), 13701 (Clean Energy Production Credit), and 13702 (Clean Electricity Investment Credit); Treasury Department and the Internal Revenue Service, Notice 2023-38: Domestic Content Bonus Credit Guidance Under Sections 45, 45Y, 48, and 48E (2023).
    On benefits to wages, see IRA, Pub. L. 117-169, 136 Stat. 1818 (2022), §§13101 (Extension and Modification of Credit for Electricity Produced from Certain

Renewable Sources), 13102 (Extension and Modification of Energy Credit), 13104 (Extension and Modification of Credit for Carbon Oxide Sequestration), 13105 (Zero-Emission Nuclear Power Production Credit), 13204 (Clean Hydrogen), 13303 (Energy Efficient Commercial Buildings Deduction), 13304 (Extension, Increase, and Modifications of New Energy Efficient Home Credit), 13404 (Alternative Fuel Refueling Property Credit), 13501 (Extension of the Advanced Energy Project Credit), 13702 (Clean Electricity Investment Credit), and 13704 (Clean Production Credit).

On benefits to energy communities, see IRA, Pub. L. 117-169, 136 Stat. 1818 (2022), §§13101 (Extension and Modification of Credit for Electricity Produced from Certain Renewable Sources), 13102 (Extension and Modification of Energy Credit), 13701 (Clean Energy Production Credit), and 13702 (Clean Electricity Investment Credit).

On benefits to low-income communities, see IRA, Pub. L. 117-169, 136 Stat. 1818 (2022), §§13103 (Increase in Energy Credit for Solar and Wind Facilities Placed in Service in Connection with Low-Income Communities) and 13702 (Clean Electricity Investment Credit).

65. Lakhani 2022; L. Friedman 2022.

66. Wallace-Wells 2022b.

67. Krebs 2023. One account, from an academic in contact with congressional staffers, credits the IRA's passage to the lobbying by industries and groups about which Manchin cared most: the United Mine Workers, "carbon capture, nuclear power, hydrogen and advanced manufacturing" (J. Jenkins 2023).

68. "Manchin Supports Inflation Reduction Act of 2022," U.S. Senator Joe Manchin of West Virginia, July 27, 2022, https://www.manchin.senate.gov/newsroom /press-releases/manchin-supports-inflation-reduction-act-of-2022.

69. The name "Inflation Reduction Act" can be read as an ideological statement, reflecting Manchin's belief that inflation imposes burdens on the poor and working class, and an implied refutation of progressive macroeconomic philosophies such as modern monetary theory. The theory's proponents argue that (a) because U.S. debt is denominated in U.S. dollars, the United States can pay down that debt by expanding the money supply without jeopardizing its credit; (b) traditional macroeconomics overstates the risk of inflation associated with rapid expansions of the money supply; and (c) in any case, inflation reduces the value of debt, thereby transferring wealth from lenders (who tend to be richer) to borrowers (who tend to be poorer). See, e.g., Horsley 2019 and Kelton 2020.

70. See Aronoff 2022a.

71. In 2002, the Union of Concerned Scientists called PURPA "the most effective single measure in promoting renewable energy," crediting it with incentivizing development of 12 GW of nonhydrorenewable generation. See Union of Concerned Scientists, "Public Utility Regulatory Policies Act," 2002, https://www .ucsusa.org/resources/public-utility-regulatory-policy-act.

72. On support for nuclear power, see Energy Policy Act, H.R. 6, 109th Cong. (2005), and Stolte 2006. On energy efficiency, see American Recovery and Reinvestment Act, H.R. 1, 111th Cong. (2009); Carley, Nicholson-Crotty, and Fisher 2015; and Aldy 2011.

73. The IRA creates a new tax credit for the production of hydrogen and defines "qualified clean hydrogen" as hydrogen that is produced through a process that results in a life-cycle GHG emissions rate of not greater than 4 kilograms of CO_2e per kilogram of hydrogen. On direct payments to claimants, see IRA,

§13204. On direct payments, see IRA, §13801, 26 U.S. Code §6417 (2022). On qualifying munies and other public entities, see 26 U.S.C. §§45Q–45Z (2022).

74. The EPA estimates that the IRA will speed the transition sufficiently quickly that 76 percent of net electricity generation in 2040 will be from zero-emission sources. See U.S. EPA, "Proposed Rule: New Source Performance Standards for Greenhouse Gas Emissions from New, Modified, and Reconstructed Fossil Fuel–Fired Electric Generating Units; Emission Guidelines for Greenhouse Gas Emissions from Existing Fossil Fuel–Fired Electric Generating Units; and Repeal of the Affordable Clean Energy Rule," 88 Fed. Reg. 33,240, 33,253 (May 23, 2023). This number is only slightly higher than the numbers predicted by other prominent models.

   For an analysis of the uncertainty and potential-effects scenarios, see Bistline, Mehrotra, and Wolfram 2023 (predicting higher implementation costs and lost revenues than the Congressional Budget Office predicted). For another projection of the statute's impact, see J. Jenkins 2022 (predicting that the IRA will put emissions reductions on a trajectory that is much closer to a net-zero pathway than the status quo).

75. Levi 2012; Kaufman et al. 2020.

76. Penrod 2023.

77. U.S. EPA, New Source Performance Standards for Greenhouse Gas Emissions from New, Modified, and Reconstructed Fossil Fuel–Fired Electric Generating Units; Emission Guidelines for Greenhouse Gas Emissions from Existing Fossil Fuel–Fired Electric Generating Units; and Repeal of the Affordable Clean Energy Rule, 88 Fed. Reg. 39,390 (2023).

78. Cal. Pub. Util. Code §399.11 (2019); Cal. Pub. Util. Code §399.15 (2019); Cal. Pub. Util. Code §399.30 (2019).

79. Haw. Rev. Stat. §269–92 (2020).

80. N.Y. Env't. Conserv. Law §75-0103 (McKinney) (2020).

81. Mich. SB 271 (Nov. 8, 2023).

82. Wash. Rev. Code Ann. §19.285.040 (2021).

83. Energy Transition Act, S.B. 489, 54th Leg., 1st sess. (N.M. 2019).

84. Minn. Stat. §216H.02 (2023).

85. Van Horn and Hitt 2019.

86. Several major investor-owned utilities have recently pledged to rapidly reduce their reliance on fossil fuels: Xcel Energy, serving parts of Minnesota and Colorado, has pledged to rely only on generation that emits no carbon dioxide at all (100 percent emission reduction) by 2050. See, e.g., Novachek 2019.

87. Pyper 2017 (describing exponential growth in demand recently); Gardiner 2017 (describing the prevalence of clean-energy goals among major manufacturers). On the survey, see "Global Warming's Six Americas," *Yale Program on Climate Change Communication* (blog), August 16, 2018, https://climatecommunication.yale.edu/about/projects/global-warmings-six-americas/.

88. On the earlier favorable attitude toward the wind turbines, see Slattery et al. 2012; on the cooling of that attitude, see Eller and Hardy 2017 and Mensching 2017. Farmers have been less favorably disposed to hosting solar farms. See Bryce 2021, explaining farmers' worries that solar panels will reduce farm income. But also see Hanley 2020, explaining how "agrovoltaics" can assuage farmers' worries about solar's effect on farming.

89. Rhodes 2023.

90. Logan and Kaur 2022; Tamborrino and Siegel 2023.

91. Breetz, Mildenberger, and Stokes 2018 (offering a policy-as-constituent-building explanation of the politics of the energy transition). The idea that tangible benefits build political durability into new regulatory or social programs can be traced back to Otto von Bismarck and the creation of one of the first social insurance regimes in Germany. See also J. Walker 1991 (teasing out in theoretical and empirical detail a general explanation of how policies create constituencies and political momentum). However, issue appeals are not driving differential turnout advantages for Democrats, nor are they converting GOP voters to the Democratic Party. See Hartig et al. 2023.
92. Ferman 2022; Basiouny 2022; Gelles 2022.
93. The IRA passed the Senate 51–50, with the vice president casting the tie-breaking vote. It passed the House 220–213 on a straight party-line vote, with one Democrat and one Republican abstaining.
94. On blaming wind and solar generators for the power failures in Texas, see Mena 2021 and "Governor Abbott Directs Public Utility Commission to Take Immediate Action to Improve Electric Reliability," Office of the Texas Governor, Greg Abbott, July 6, 2021, https://gov.texas.gov/news/post/governor-abbott-directs -public-utility-commission-to-take-immediate-action-to-improve-electric -reliability. On favoritism toward dispatchable power plants, see Breed 2023. For a list of such anti-renewable-energy bills in the Texas Legislature, see Pahwa 2023.
95. Mattison 2022.
96. Minn. HF 7, 93rd Leg. (2023–2024); Teirstein 2023.
97. Michelson 2023.
98. Infrastructure Investment and Jobs Act, Pub. L. No. 117-58, 135 Stat. 429 (2021) ; Ferris 2023.
99. Michael Smith 2023 (quoting DeSantis on gas stoves); Wolman 2022 (quoting West Virginia's treasurer saying that "this is going to escalate [and w]e are going full throttle once we get to 2023"); Vanderford 2022 (quoting DeSantis saying, "We are protecting Floridians from woke capital and asserting the authority of our constitutional system over ideological corporate power").
100. The axiom that "all politics is local" is regularly credited to former Speaker of the House Thomas "Tip" O'Neill, but he did not originate the phrase. On the nationalization of politics, see Hopkins 2018 (explaining how the nationalization of politics can incentivize state politicians to be more responsive to the national party and less responsive to local interests).
101. *West Virginia v. EPA*, 142 S.Ct. 2626 (2022) (Kagan, J., dissenting).
102. The EPA expects that by the time the new rule's mandates take effect, the IRA will have made CCS and hydrogen co-firing (with natural gas) less expensive and therefore "adequately demonstrated . . . considering costs." See U.S. EPA, Proposed Rule: New Source Performance Standards for Greenhouse Gas Emissions from New, Modified, and Reconstructed Fossil Fuel–Fired Electric Generating Units; Emission Guidelines for Greenhouse Gas Emissions from Existing Fossil Fuel–Fired Electric Generating Units; and Repeal of the Affordable Clean Energy Rule, 88 Fed. Reg. 33,240, 33,247 (May 23, 2023).
103. This argument apparently relies on section 135(a)(6) of the IRA, which appropriated to the EPA "for fiscal year 2022" $18 million "to ensure that reductions in greenhouse gas emissions are achieved through use of the existing authorities of this Act" (Pub. L. 117-169, 136 Stat. 1818, §135(a)(6) (2022)). But one wonders if the Supreme Court will see this appropriation provision as the kind of clear

statement delegation it now requires under *West Virginia*, especially given its oft-quoted observation in an earlier major-questions case that Congress does not "hide elephants in mouseholes" (*FDA v. Brown & Williamson Tobacco Corp.*, 529 U.S. 120, 159–60 (2000)).

104. Spence 2022, 982–87.
105. Specifically, Justices Thomas, Alito, Gorsuch, Kavanaugh, and Barrett were confirmed by senators whose states represent a minority of the American population; of those five, all but Thomas were also nominated by a president who received fewer votes than his opponent in the presidential election.
106. Rural, mostly Republican voters are systematically overrepresented in U.S. Senate elections. See Silver 2020 and Drutman 2020.
107. Abramowitz, Alexander, and Gunning 2006; Mayhew 1974; Kustoff et al. 2021.
108. Jody Freeman and Spence 2014, 7; Kenny et al. 2023. See also Poole and Rosenthal 2007, 301–5; Theriault 2008, 11–42; Fiorina and Abrams 2008 (highlighting a divergence between elite polarization and mass polarization); Fiorina 1999 (discussing possible explanations for increasing polarization between candidates); and Bishop 2009 (on urban/rural sorting of liberals and conservatives).
109. Wasserman 2023 (concluding that "Democrats fared slightly better than they would have under old maps thanks to their own gerrymanders in Illinois, Nevada, New Mexico and Oregon and a temporary court-drawn map in North Carolina [because] Republicans focused on locking in as many safe GOP seats as possible"). But my colleague Steve Vladeck has estimated that the Supreme Court's shadow-docket decisions to uphold redistricting maps ruled illegal by state courts in four states moved at least four House seats from "lean/likely Democrat" to "lean/likely Republican," potentially flipping the House to Republican control during the 118th Congress in 2024 (cited in Okun 2023).
110. In any case, voters tell pollsters that environmental issues are relatively low on their list of voting priorities. See Fingerhut 2016; "Economy Remains the Public's Top Policy Priority; COVID-19 Concerns Decline Again," Pew Research Center, February 6, 2023, https://www.pewresearch.org/politics/2023/02/06/economy-remains-the-publics-top-policy-priority-covid-19-concerns-decline-again/.
111. Aldrich 2000, 644 (concluding that "the attempt to keep an illiberal social institution [slavery] embedded in a putatively democratic polity . . . required that the development of democratic institutions be stunted to the point of failure to achieve the required results").
112. Mason 2016 (exploring the convergence of social and political identities as part of American voter polarization).
113. "The Partisan Divide on Political Values Grows Even Wider," Pew Research Center, October 5, 2017, https://www.pewresearch.org/politics/2017/10/05/the-partisan-divide-on-political-values-grows-even-wider/.
114. "As Partisan Hostility Grows, Signs of Frustration with the Two-Party System," Pew Research Center, August 9, 2022, https://www.pewresearch.org/politics/2022/08/09/as-partisan-hostility-grows-signs-of-frustration-with-the-two-party-system/.
115. Enten 2021 (discussing the National Election Study data showing a sharp increase in animosity toward members of the other party from the 1970s to 2022). But see also Sanders 2022 (arguing that Americans are "at least as motivated by the passion they have for their own party").
116. Geiger 2014.
117. McLaughlin 2022.
118. Colton 2022 (quoting various Democrats).

119. Agiesta and Edwards-Levy 2021.
120. Vance 2016; Hochschild 2016. In 2016, conservatives trying to explain Trump-ism to Democrats urged them to "take Trump seriously, not literally" (qtd. in Zito 2016). That admonition lost much of its force after the January 6 insurrection.
121. Sandel 2020; Fishkin and Forbath 2022. Some other social scientists also see antipluralism and racism as drivers of negative polarization. See, e.g., Dawkins and Hanson 2022 (crediting a "racialized conception of American identity" among white Americans as a driver of polarization).
122. "Competing Visions of America: An Evolving Identity or a Culture Under Attack? Findings from the 2021 American Values Survey," *PRRI* (blog), November 1, 2021, https://www.prri.org/research/competing-visions-of-america-an-evolving -identity-or-a-culture-under-attack/.
123. Burga 2023 (on De Santis and Disney); G. Lopez 2023 (on Abbott and DeSantis bussing asylum seekers to other states). On the killing of the Black Lives Mat-ter protestor, see Chappell 2023. On the weakening of state universities, see Mazzei 2023; Fausset 2015; and "University of Texas Regents Approve Creation of New College to House Civitas Institute at UT Austin," Texas Public Radio, May 4, 2023, https://www.tpr.org/news/2023-05-04/university-of-texas-regents -approve-creation-of-new-college-to-house-civitas-institute-at-ut-austin.
124. Lerer and Herndon 2021; Barron-Lopez and Conciatori 2022; Saric 2022.
125. The final manuscript for this book was submitted to the publisher in late 2023, before either the nomination process or the prosecutions had gotten underway.
126. Huckabee made the remark quoted in his TBN television show *Huckabee* in Sep-tember 2023. At a GOP meeting in August 2023, Lake said: "If you want to get to President Trump, you are going to have to go through me, and you are going to have to go through 75 million Americans just like me. And I'm going to tell you, most of us are card carrying members of the N.R.A." (qtd. in Pengelly 2023a). Palin, speaking to Newsmax, said in August 2023: "I think those who are con-ducting this travesty, . . . I want to ask them: What the heck? Do you want us to be in civil war? Because that's what's going to happen" (qtd. in Pengelly 2023b). The language of some conservative media hosts actively urges violent insurrec-tion, perhaps most prominently Fox News host Greg Gutfeld (Tandanpolie 2023). For a sampling, see M. Schmidt et al. 2023.
127. Mark Twain and H. L. Mencken embodied this tradition. In the words of one writer, "They share the honors of having brought into American satire those saline and salutary qualities of corrosiveness and vigorous ridicule that pre-serve satire from dying of anemia" (Francis 1950, 33).
128. Alinsky 1971, 126–30.
129. Alinsky 1971, 24–47.
130. Famously, *Rules for Radicals* inspired Barack Obama's career as a young com-munity organizer in Chicago and was the subject of Hillary Clinton's under-graduate thesis at Wellesley College. For the book's influence on conservatives, see, e.g., Coller and Libit 2009 (" 'Rules for Radicals' . . . has been among Ama-zon's top 100 sellers for the past month, put there in part by people who 'also bought' books by Michelle Malkin, Glenn Beck, and South Carolina Republi-can Sen. Jim DeMint"). See also Merrell 2010 and Leahy and Loudon 2009, which adapt Alinsky's ideas to conservative activism.
131. Research supports the idea that *both* party switching (what political scientists call "conversion") *and* mobilization of new voters contributed to the New Deal

partisan realignment that subsequently begat the New Deal Consensus. See J. Campbell 1985, 357–76. For the definitive examination of parties and partisan realignments, see Aldrich 2011.

On twentieth-century social science research, see Downs 1957 (describing his median-voter theorem); Arnold 1990, 40–47, 72–76 (fleshing out his model of "retrospective voting," which suggests that politicians' behavior creates a sort of ideological brand that helps voters decide for whom to vote by helping them anticipate candidates' future policy positions); and the trust-based models described in Bianco 1994 and Fenno 1978.

132. Garzia and Ferreira da Silva 2022 (analyzing negative, affective partisanship as a driver of votes). To be fair, this is not a new idea. See A. Campbell et al. 1960, 134–35 (asserting a local- and culture-driven theory of partisan attachment). Rather, what changes over time is the *relative* sway of affective drivers versus issue-based drivers of voting behavior.

133. The percentage of young Republicans who say the seriousness of global warming is generally exaggerated has grown from 46 percent in the first decade of the twenty-first century to 53 percent in 2021 (Teirstein 2021). Alex Epstein has several books arguing that the costs of transition to a net-zero future exceed the benefits, including *Fossil Fuels Improve the Planet* (A. Epstein and Dennis 2013); *The Moral Case for Fossil Fuels* (2014); and *Fossil Future: Why Global Human Flourishing Requires More Oil, Coal, and Natural Gas—Not Less* (2022). Epstein's position runs counter to the weight of expert opinion, which acknowledges the trade-offs (see chapter 5) but views them as reconcilable with the transition. See Jody Freeman 2015 and A. Epstein 2017.

A Pew Research Center poll in 2021 found that 82 percent of Republican respondents believed that the Biden administration was taking the country in "the wrong direction" on climate policy; 79 percent of Democrats reported that it was taking the country "in the right direction" (B. Kennedy, Tyson, and Funk 2022).

134. Andris et al. 2015, emphasis added.

135. Most people resist the notion that they are influenced by negative partisanship. In 2022, when I observed to a reporter that Texas Republicans' opposition to some aspects of the energy transition was a response to voters' negative partisanship (see Clifford 2022), that observation provoked some of the angriest reactions I have ever received in response to a quoted remark I made. Those reactions included the voicemail message, "You are the epitome of the failure of the American educational system. . . . I can only imagine what students are learning in your . . . class. It's incredible to me that a dunce like you would be teaching people about . . . law," and the email message, "You sir are a clown, so in the immortal words of Logan Roy, 'Fuck Off.' I am only a small investor but you can bet your last dollar that I intend to fully divest of any Blackrock funds in my portfolio." Politicians know that people who are sufficiently motivated to leave such messages are probably sufficiently motivated to vote.

136. A well-known representative of the first strain's view is the Danish political scientist Bjorn Lomborg, a former climate-change-science denier who more recently has argued that there are "a lot of positives" about climate change and that resources devoted to mitigation are better spent elsewhere (Lomborg 2020). On the second strain, see Ben Shapiro (@benshapiro), tweets, Twitter/X, 2019, and Lomborg 2020. For a discussion of the third strain of Republicans' opposition to climate policy, see Collomb 2014 (ascribing some opposition to "a strong

ideological commitment . . . to *laissez-faire* and . . . defence of the American way of life, defined by high consumption").

137. Luttig 2023; Snyder 2017, 30.
138. On GOP tribalism, see Davie and Oliphant 2019. On Republicans against Trump's lies, see Beck et al. 2016. On the GOP's future, in 2013 Governor Bobby Jindal of Louisiana warned Republicans to "stop being the stupid party [and to] talk like adults" (qtd. in Chait 2018, which also notes Jindal's subsequent accommodation to hyperbolic populism). On "never Trumpers," see V. Friedman 2021 and Brooks 2023. And on lining up behind Trump, see Dunn 2021.
139. Kalmoe and Mason 2022 (supporting this general proposition that political violence is not exclusively Republican); D. Cox 2021 (suggesting a bipartisan increase in support for violence); Diamond et al. 2020 (showing bipartisan support for violent resistance to victory by the other side, though that support declined in later polling). But also see Westwood et al. 2022 (challenging these studies' conclusions as artifacts of the survey instruments used and other circumstances of their administration). On the poll in 2023, see "Voice of the Voter Survey," UVA Center for Politics, October 2023, https://centerforpolitics.org/crystalball/wp-content/uploads/2023/10/VoV-Presentation-FINAL.pdf.
140. At the time of Bork's confirmation hearings, his extensive writings as a judge, commentator, and academic included some incendiary ideas, including praise for the Chilean dictator Augusto Pinochet, virulent criticism of modern social and sexual norms, and opposition to desegregation laws. But senators who opposed him cited mainly his originalist judicial philosophy, an approach that is now fairly common in the federal judiciary, even if it has never gained much support in the legal academy. However, it should be noted that Bork was accorded a vote of the full Senate, while Garland was denied that vote.
141. Hickman 2021, 2022; Adler and Walker 2020; Adler 2022a, 2022b; C. Walker 2022; Barnett and Walker 2017.
142. Battistoni and Britton-Purdy 2020 (noting that progressives seek climate policy via more democracy).

4. THE PROPAGANDA MACHINE

1. On this point, see Jody Freeman and Stephenson 2022; Squitieri 2021; and Richardson 2023.
2. One meta-analysis in 2021 found that "a range of experts have concluded that social media does contribute to polarization" and that "widespread use of [social media] platforms has exacerbated partisan hatred" (Barrett, Hendrix, and Sims 2021, 3, 6).
3. Russell 2009, 121.
4. Baron 2019, 11. Baron's text on belief formation is *Thinking and Deciding* (2008).
5. Finkel et al. 2020, 533.
6. *The Turner Diaries* (W. Pierce 1978) is a bigoted novel depicting the overthrow of the U.S. government and the extermination of nonwhite races. Modern white-supremacist terrorists, including the Oklahoma City bomber of 1993, have cited it as an inspiration. *The Jewish Peril: Protocols of the Elders of Zion* (1903) is a book riddled with falsehoods and antisemitism that purports to detail a plan for Jewish domination of the world.
7. "Taylor Lorenz on Why All Culture Is Internet Culture," *Offline with Jon Favreau* (podcast), March 20, 2022, https://crooked.com/podcast/taylor-lorenz-on-why-all

-culture-is-internet-culture/. Lorenz is a columnist and media analyst for the *Washington Post*.

8. G. King, Schneer, and White 2017, 779 ("Given the tremendous power media out-lets have to set the agenda for public discussion, the ideological and policy perspectives of those who own media outlets [have] considerable importance for the nature of American democracy and public policy").

9. Geiger 2014.

10. Gladwell 2000; Druckman, Levendusky, and McLain 2018.

11. Tokita, Guess, and Tarnita 2021.

12. The Engaging News Project explores the effects of different kinds of "clickbait" headlines. Its website can be accessed at https://mediaengagement.org/wp-content/uploads/2016/08/ENP-Investigating-the-Influence-of-Clickbait-News-Headlines.pdf.

13. Drexler 2020 (on the hunger for big stories); B. Smith 2023, 11 (on viral stories); Pilkington 2020 (quoting the *New Yorker* editor Michael Luo in defending the reporter Ronan Farrow against charges of sloppy reporting).

14. B. Smith 2023; Marshall Cohen 2021; O'Dowd 2023. Asked about the decision, Smith responded, "I continue to think that was the right call" (qtd. in O'Dowd 2023). When pressed if the decision was influenced by the desire for clicks, he pointed to a disclaimer on the Buzzfeed website that most people who read the dossier never saw.

15. Strong 2021.

16. Jurkowitz and Gottfried 2022.

17. Haidt quoted in Tavernise and Cohn 2019.

18. For accessible summaries of their voluminous work, see Bruckmaier et al. 2021, 1; Kahneman 2011; Kahneman and Tversky 1979, 1984; Jolls, Sunstein, and Thaler 1998; Thaler and Sunstein 2009. To give credit where credit is due, other legal scholars imported behavioral ideas into their work before 1998. See Hanson and Kysar 1999; Prentice and Roszkowski 1992, 291. For early applications of behavioralism to environmental law, see Rachlinski 1996, 1998, 2000; Vandenbergh 2005; Mark Cohen and Vandenbergh 2008.

19. Herbert Simon's notion of "satisficing" predated Kahneman and Tversky's work by at least a decade. Simon's observation that "a wealth of information creates a poverty of attention" now seems particularly prescient (1984, 297). After World War II, many researchers tried to understand how the citizens of a European democracy could rationalize their embrace of fascism and commit or tolerate the cruelties of the Holocaust. See, e.g., Milgram 1963; Asch 1951; and Janis 1972.

20. See, e.g., Festinger 1957.

21. For a thorough account of the origins of confirmation-bias research within the field of psychology, see Nickerson 1998.

22. Lewis 2017, 255–56. In truth, many economists understood the limits of *homo economicus* as a description of reality but valued it nevertheless for its theory-building utility.

23. The Wikipedia entry "List of Cognitive Biases" (https://en.wikipedia.org/wiki/List_of_cognitive_biases) describes more than 120 cognitive biases and more than 40 additional "social" biases. The two types are not mutually exclusive; indeed, many offer overlapping explanations for the same behavior. The so-called replication crisis in social psychology has brought into question some of these biases. But this chapter focuses on a few well-established logical falla-cies and biases that affect how we ascribe beliefs and intentions to others.

24. Elkins and McKitrick 1993, 4, 290–91 (describing the enmity between Hamilton and Jefferson and their quarrels while both worked in Washington's cabinet).

25. Arieli, Amit, and Mentser 2019 (literature review).

26. The vast majority of people vote for either the Democratic Party or the Republican Party. Thanks to the workings of Duverger's Law, American democracy tends strongly toward two dominant parties for structural reasons. When third parties arise, they tend to be ephemeral, eventually absorbed or displaced as the system returns to two dominant parties. That we refer to new parties as "third parties" is a testament to the strength of the generalization.

27. Fiske and Taylor 2021.

28. Barasz, Kim, and Evangelidis 2019, 96.

29. G. Cox and Redden 2021.

30. Alinsky 1971, 32; Safire 1986, quoting a personal conversation with Cohn. More recently, the conservative activist Matt Walsh echoed Alinsky's Rule No. 13 ("pick a target") on Twitter/X: "We don't need to [boycott every woke company]. Pick a few strategic targets. Make them pay dearly. That's enough to make wokeness a lot less appealing to the corporate world. Stop trying to bring down the whole line of dominos at once. Start with one, and then the next" (Matt Walsh [@MattWalshBlog], tweet, Twitter/X, May 23, 2023, https://x.com/MattWalshBlog/status/1661438131365707798?s=20).

31. For a colorful account of the hyperpartisan newspaper "journalism" of the early American republic, see Lepore 2007. Jill Lepore recounts how Hamilton considered Jefferson a "crafty, fanatical, 'contemptible hypocrite'" and how Federalist newspapers focused on Jefferson's alleged atheism. Republican papers focused on Hamilton's extramarital affair. For his part, Jefferson considered Hamilton "not only a monarchist, but for a monarchy bottomed in corruption" (Jefferson [1818] n.d.).

32. See Bazerman and Tenbrunsel 2011, 98–99 (describing how "the want self" dominates "the should self" in human decision making). The communications professor John Daly, my University of Texas colleague, likes to say that "a good story beats data every time."

33. Snyder 2017.

34. For a more comprehensive treatment of this topic, see Snyder 2017 and Wolfe et al. 2004.

35. Nickerson 1998, 175 (calling confirmation bias "strong and pervasive"); Belsky and Gilovich 1999 (on psychologists' description of confirmation bias: Thomas Gilovich is an academic psychologist; Gary Belsky is a writer).

36. On recalling evidence, see Perkins, Allen, and Hafner 1983; Perkins, Farady, and Bushey 1991. On the amount of supportive evidence needed, see Pyszczynski and Greenberg 1987. On the experiment concerning the death penalty, see Lord, Ross, and Lepper 1979, 2108. On biased subjectivity, see Pitz, Downing, and Reinhold 1967.

37. Pitz, Downing, and Reinhold 1967. See also Nickerson 1998, 177 ("once one has taken a position on an issue, one's primary purpose becomes that of defending or justifying that position").

38. Kahan, Braman, Monahan, et al. 2010, 122; Kahan, Jenkins-Smith, and Braman 2011, 149. Dan Kahan, Hank Jenkins-Smith, and Donald Braman note that this phenomenon does not imply duplicity but rather the same kind of unconscious case building described by Nickerson, albeit for a slightly different reason (2011, 149).

39. Irving Janis describes groupthink as "a mode of thinking that people engage in when they are deeply involved in a cohesive in-group, and members' strivings for unanimity override their motivation to realistically appraise alternative courses of action" (1972, 9). See also Dawes 2019, 152; Lord, Ross, and Lepper 1979; and Sunstein 2000.
40. Inglis interviewed in Breslow 2012.
41. Del Vicario et al. 2016; Boorman et al. 2013; Faraji-Rad, Samuelsen, and Warlop 2015; Faraji-Rad, Warlop, and Samuelsen 2012, 682–83; Schilbach et al. 2013; Marks et al. 2019 (citing research by Jonathan Haidt); Chait 2020. The New York University law professor Richard Epstein is an example of how the democratization of expertise online undermines scientific literacy. Epstein is an expert on the law but not on epidemiology, yet he famously predicted (on Stanford's Hoover Institution website) that the COVID-19 pandemic would kill only 5,000 Americans (an estimate he later revised to 50,000). As of the summer of 2023 , the World Health Organization put the U.S. death toll at 1,118,800 ("Number of COVID-19 Deaths Reported to WHO (Cumulative Total) United States of America," updated monthly, https://data.who.int/dashboards/covid19/deaths?m49 =840&n=c). Indeed, monthly death totals continued to exceed Epstein's original cumulative deaths estimate throughout 2023.
42. Kahan, Braman, Slovic, et al. 2007 (on gun control); Ellsworth and Gross 1994 and Gross 1998 (on the death penalty); Kahan, Braman, Slovic, et al. 2007, 5 (on nuclear power). Dan Kahan and his colleagues use a two-dimensional test to identify political ideology of experimental subjects: one dimension measures preference for hierarchy rather than egalitarianism, and the other measures preference for individualism rather than communitarianism. Hierarchical individualists tend to be conservatives; egalitarian communitarians tend to be liberals (Kahan, Braman, Monahan, et al. 2010). See also Douglas and Wildavsky 1982, exploring this phenomenon.
43. Kahan, Braman, Slovic, et al. 2007, 4–6. These propositions were selected because the National Academy of Sciences had issued reports supporting both (Kahan, Braman, Slovic, et al. 2007, 3–6).
44. On seeing things as either "objective" or "biased," see Kahan, Jenkins-Smith, and Braman 2011, 164. Raymond Nickerson calls this "reification" ("Given the existence of a taxonomy, no matter how arbitrary, there is a tendency to view the world in terms of the categories it provides" [1998, 183–84]). These kinds of associations are often a function of how the human brain stores and recalls information (Buonomano 2011).
45. Kahan, Jenkins-Smith, and Braman 2011, 170. The political economy scholar Tim Kuran (1995) uses the term *preference falsification* to describe how we tailor our choices to conform to what is socially acceptable within our group.
46. For a literature review of the academic research examining how the changing media environment affects climate-change coverage, see Schäfer and Painter 2021.
47. Researchers found that Gen Z, millennial, and Gen X readers are more likely to be confident in their ability to identify misinformation, though members of Gen Z nevertheless seem to be susceptible to the same traps of misinformation that have plagued earlier generations (Breakstone et al. 2021).
48. The "Fairness Doctrine was created by the FCC in 1949, and imposed certain fairness rules on broadcast licensees' discussion of public issues" (*In the Matter of Editorializing by Broadcast Licensees*, 13 FCC Rept. 146 (1949)). It was repealed in 1987 in a case called *In Re Complaint of Syracuse Peach Council against*

Television Station WTVH Syracuse, New York, 2 FCC Rcd 5043 (1987). The doctrine never applied to cable and satellite TV providers, and one wonders if it might be given the current Supreme Court's view of constitutionally protected speech (J. Kessler and Pozen 2018).

49. The decline of newspaper readership has been thoroughly documented (see, e.g., "Newspapers Fact Sheet," Pew Research Center, June 29, 2021, https://www.pewresearch.org/journalism/fact-sheet/newspapers/).
50. Snyder 2017, 61.
51. Schäfer and Painter 2021, 13.
52. "Newspapers Fact Sheet"; "Network TV: Evening News Ratings Over Time by Network," Pew Research Center, July 9, 2015, https://www.pewresearch.org/journalism/chart/network-tv-evening-news-ratings-over-time-by-network/.
53. See Jamieson and Cappella 2008 (on Ailes, Fox, and Limbaugh—Ailes had previously been executive producer of Limbaugh's television show) and Hemmer 2022, 13 (quote). See also Sherman 2018.
54. See Barker 2002, demonstrating how Limbaugh "primed" conservative values in especially persuasive ways.
55. For example, in 2023 a Fox News chyron labeled President Biden a "wannabe dictator." For a broader flavor of how Fox uses its chyron to influence viewers, see LaFrance 2019.
56. From Fox News's creation in 1996 until 2002, it trailed CNN in total viewership. In January 2002, though, it passed CNN in total viewers and has held its lead since then. See "State of the News Media 2004," Pew Research Center, 2004, https://www.pewresearch.org/journalism/state-of-the-news-media-report-2004-final/. On talk radio from the right, see Rosenwald 2019. On former Fox host Tucker Carlson's promotion of the theory of the destruction of white Christian culture, see Hemmer 2021.
57. Mastrangelo 2022 (citing Nielsen ratings).
58. One America's viewership surged immediately after the insurrection and attack on the U.S. Capitol on January 6, 2001, when right-populist viewers deemed Fox News coverage insufficiently loyal to Donald Trump (Schiffman 2021).
59. The most popular media-bias-rating organizations, such as Media Bias/Fact Check (MBFC), AllSides.com, and Ad Fontes Media, rate the bias and/or accuracy of various media outlets. Their ratings provoke strong disagreement among active partisans about both their respective methodologies and their conclusions. But their bias ratings (which should be distinguished from accuracy or reliability ratings) are in agreement more than one might expect, and I have found them to be a helpful check on drivers of my own biases. All three ratings sites place NPR and the three traditional broadcast networks (NBC, ABC, CBS) only slightly to the left of center, Reuters in the ideological center, Fox News to the far right of center, and MSNBC to the far left. They tend to disagree about other media outlets near the ideological center. For example, Ad Fontes and MBFC place *The Economist* in the ideological center, whereas AllSides (which was founded by conservative social scientists) puts it slightly left of center. When I disagree with the bias-rating organizations' consensus ratings, I try to resist the instinct to find fault with their methods and instead take disagreement as a cue to audit my own sense of why I see particular outlets differently than they do.
60. Carr 2008.
61. Pariser 2011 (outlining the filter-bubble concept and discussing how we click on stories we want to read or see); Cinelli et al. 2021, 5 ("users online tend to

prefer information adhering to their worldviews, ignore dissenting information, and form polarized groups . . . [causing] the aggregation of homophilic clusters"); R. Levy 2021 (on algorithms); Samantray and Pin 2019 (on self-censoring through clicks).

62. Douglas 2003, 1351.

63. On this point, see Mutz 2006, 2 ("despite the tremendous negative publicity that currently plagues American businesses, the American workplace is inadvertently performing an important public service by establishing a social context in which diverse groups of people are forced into daily interactions with one another").

64. Peck 2019 (on Fox's understanding of viewers' emotions); Goldstein 2006 and Dickinson 2011 (both describing the top-down process by which Fox News editors push anchors to frame the news ideologically).

65. "Brooks and Capehart on CPAC and the Future of the Republican Party," *NewsHour*, PBS, March 3, 2023, https://www.pbs.org/newshour/show/brooks-and-capehart-on-cpac-and-the-future-of-the-republican-party.

66. "*The Young Turks*," Young Turks (website), May 16, 2023, https://tyt.com/home; "About This Podcast," *Pod Save America* (podcast), n.d., https://crooked.com/podcast-series/pod-save-america/; *The Majority Report*, n.d., https://majorityreportradio.com/.

67. Tokita et al. 2021, 2–4 (describing how social media algorithms contribute to the "fusion" of political and social identities). See also Tufekci 2018 and Albright 2018, both describing how YouTube algorithms feed ever more polarizing content to users.

68. Eady et al. 2019, 18–19, emphasis added.

69. A. Ripley, Tenjarla, and He 2019, emphasis added.

70. Bail 2021. See also Marcus 2023 (illustrating how ideas are repackaged and caricatured on the social media site Rumble).

71. See "Rage Farming," Wikipedia, https://en.wikipedia.org/wiki/Rage_farming, which describes the term's etymology and meaning.

72. For more on this logical fallacy, see "No True Scotsman," Wikipedia, https://en.wikipedia.org/wiki/No_true_Scotsman.

73. "Very Serious People: Did you know we're shoveling $ to the elderly w Social Security and MEdicare even though they have more $ on average?" (@JamesGLeckie, tweet, Twitter/X, May 15, 2023, https://x.com/JamesGLeckie/status/1658167073002905608?s=20); "Who are these VSPs & where can we read their very (in)accurate & (un)important position papers so we can know what's (not) really happening" (@kerrforjeffco, tweet, Twitter/X, October 20, 2022, https://x.com/kerrforjeffco/status/1583258687581274112?s=20); and "I remember back in the 2010s, one of the signature VSP pundit moves was to blame Al Gore for polarizing climate change" (David Roberts, @drvolts, tweet, Twitter/X, October 3, 2022, https://x.com/drvolts/status/1577055008117620736?s=20).

74. Basu 2017 ("That's just both siding," tying this technique to populist autocrats).

75. "Tell me you don't understand climate change without telling me you don't understand climate change" (@sundog723, tweet, Twitter/X, February 25, 2023, https://x.com/aprincipe1/status/1621896071965282307?s=20); and "Tell me you don't understand energy economics without saying you don't understand energy economics" (@GovDunleavy, tweet, Twitter/X, November 1, 2022, https://x.com/GovDunleavy/status/1587479699345014789?s=20).

76. See Zimmer 2017 (tying the technique of whataboutism to Soviet disinformation training administered to KGB agents in the Soviet era and "the Troubles"

in Northern Ireland); and "Whataboutism: Come Again Comrade?," *The Economist*, January 31, 2008, https://www.economist.com/europe/2008/01/31/whataboutism (tracing similar origins).

77. We are more willing to search for and consider new information about an issue when (*a*) the emotional and opportunity costs of the search are low and (*b*) we feel less confident in our beliefs about the issue. But ideologically homogenous online groups bring us to higher levels of confidence about the dominant group beliefs more quickly and increase the emotional cost of searching for information that might conflict with that belief. See Baron 2019, 10–11.

    Even in the absence of social media, people tend to overestimate the extent to which others share their views. See, e.g., Lee Ross, Greene, and House 1977 and Mullen et al. 1985.

78. Mellers, Tetlock, and Arkes 2019, 20.

79. There is an extensive legal scholarship literature on network neutrality and how the law ought to treat modern information technology platforms. For an overview, see M. Ricks et al. 2022, chaps. 19–23.

80. Theodore H. White's *Making of the President* books revolutionized and personalized coverage of presidential campaigns. See T. White 1961, 1969. But White eventually came to lament the combination of that personalizing approach with television coverage of campaigns. See Porch 2015. Neil Postman's critique of modern communications technology went well beyond politics. See, e.g., Postman 2006.

81. The most conservative of the three media-bias-ratings sites, AllSides.com, prefaces each media-bias rating with this statement: "Everyone is biased—and that's okay. There's no such thing as unbiased news. But hidden bias misleads, manipulates and divides us."

82. On left-leaning reporters, see Dautrich and Hartley 1999; Weaver and Wilhoit 1986. On Goldberg's exit from CBS, see Goldberg 2001. For Stossel's and Attkisson's accounts, see Stossel 2003 and Attkisson 2014.

83. Rutenberg 2016; Boyer 2019.

84. Sirota 2021.

85. Thompson 1994, 10.

86. Heglar and Westervelt 2021 makes the case for alarmism and confrontation in climate activism. Aronoff has written two books presenting the climate problem in these terms (see Aronoff 2021 and Aronoff et al. 2019). For a fuller sense of the democratic-socialist environmental movement, see Aronoff, Dreier, and Kazin 2020.

87. *Jacobin* describes itself as a voice offering socialist perspectives (https://jacobin.com/about); *Dissent* magazine describes itself as democratic socialist since 1954 (https://twitter.com/DissentMag); and the *Intercept* does not describe itself as "socialist" (https://theintercept.com/about/) but publishes writers who describe themselves that way.

88. Indeed, almost everything written with the intention of educating an audience—including this book—is influenced by the writer's sense of what is important for people to understand and where the gaps in public understanding lie. But when experts put pen to paper, it is important for them to aspire to present all dimensions of an issue in a fair way.

89. Infrastructure Investment and Jobs Act, Pub. L. 117-58, 135 Stat. 429 (2021), §40308(a) (2021).

90. For the UPI article, see A. Lee 2023. For the *Washington Post* article, see Halper 2023. See also Meyer 2023 (expressing concern that one of the DAC hubs would

be operated by an oil company, arguing that "the Biden team cannot ensure" that the company's "heart . . . will remain pure").

91. Eady et al. 2019, 9.
92. On the amount of rightist versus leftist messaging, see Nikolov, Flammini, and Menczer 2021 and DeVerna et al. 2022. According to media-bias-ratings agencies, there are as many left-leaning outlets as right-leaning outlets these days. However, there are more far-right broadcast outlets on cable TV systems. One America News and Newsmax, for example, are included in some cable television packages.
93. Frenkel and Wakabayashi 2018.
94. Darcy 2023 (citing numerous examples of violent incitement in support of the claim that "rhetoric . . . once reserved for tyrants and dictators has become commonplace on right wing media"). See also Benkler, Faris, and Roberts 2018 (documenting and explaining the asymmetry of partisan misinformation online); and Bouie 2023 (chronicling the praise of four different vigilantes by Marjorie Taylor Green, Greg Abbott, Tucker Carlson, Greg Gutfeld, and the 2020 Republican National Convention).
95. For the reference to "hostages," see "Elise Stefanik Calls Jan. 6 Defendants 'Hostages,'" *Politico* video, January 26, 2024, https://www.politico.com/video /2024/01/26/elise-stefanik-calls-jan-6-defendants-hostages-1198580. Trump made the reference to "retribution" in a speech to the Conservative Political Action Committee in March 2023 and at a rally in New Hampshire on November 11, 2023.
96. Lewis 2018 (quoting Bannon); "Conway: Press Secretary Gave 'Alternative Facts,'" *Meet the Press*, NBC News, January 22, 2017, https://www.nbcnews.com /meet-the-press/video/conway-press-secretary-gave-alternative-facts-860142 147643. Insider accounts confirm that a surprising number of veteran Republican strategists and leaders have abandoned their own ethical standards of professional conduct in the Trump era. The party strategist Tim Miller's (2022) account of why cites a mix of psychological needs (e.g., to feel important), calculated ambition, and the simple realization that the use of propaganda will help the party succeed. The veteran Republican political operative Stuart Stevens (2020) tells a similar story of cynical ambition driving unusual levels of disregard for truth among party professionals.
97. In 2023, a freshman representative reported to his constituents that the most outraged members of Congress are "faking it . . . for the cameras" ("Most of the Angry Voices in Congress Are Faking," Rep. Jeff Jackson, video statement to constituents, YouTube, https://www.youtube.com/watch?v= _PEo9U6UwdY).
98. Burns, Haberman, and Martin 2016; Karni 2019; Daugherty 2018.
99. The discovery phase of this lawsuit revealed that multiple Fox News executives privately doubted Trump's claims of election fraud and mocked them. See Timm, Terkel, and Gregorian 2023 and Quinn 2023.
100. Pennycook, Cannon, and Rand 2018; Pennycook and Rand 2019, 41. On the greater tendency to share misinformation, see Nikolov, Flammini, and Menczer 2021, 5. See also M. Lawson and Kakkar 2021 (finding that less conscientious conservatives are more likely to share fake news and ascribing that tendency to a greater "desire for chaos") and DeVerna et al. 2022 (finding that conservatives are more likely to spread rumors both before and after misinformation is corrected, regardless of the ideological content of the rumor).

101. Garrett and Bond 2021; Eady et al. 2019.
102. Broockman and Kalla 2002; Cassino, Woolley, and Jenkins 2012 ("people learn most from NPR, Sunday Morning Shows, 'The Daily Show'"). See also L. P. Feldman 2007, 406–27, and Bauder 2004.
103. Carmichael, Brulle, and Huxster 2017; Brulle, Carmichael, and Jenkins 2012, 169 (demonstrating that elite cues play an important role in shaping aggregate opinion about climate change); L. P. Feldman, Hart, and Milosevic 2017, 481 (noting the way partisan media create echo chambers that reinforce dominant opinion); Guber 2013, 93, and McCright and Dunlap 2011 (both matching partisan polarization to diverging opinions about climate); A. Epstein 2014, 2022 (on "experts" used in conservative media).
104. This colloquialism comes from Aesop's fable "The Town Mouse and the Country Mouse," available online at https://read.gov/aesop/004.html.
105. Bernstein 2016, emphasis added.
106. Stewart subsequently created *The Problem, with Jon Stewart*, an Apple TV interview show focused on policy issues. *The Daily Show*'s next host, Trevor Noah, steered it away from its focus on mocking Fox News.
107. On the speed of emotional messages, see Stieglitz and Linh 2013 and Frimer et al. 2019. On the speed of falsehoods, see Vosoughi, Roy, and Aral 2018 (showing falsehoods are 70 percent more likely to be shared on Twitter/X) and Ahmed et al. 2020 (using Twitter/X data to show that "fake news websites were the most popular web source shared by users" during the pandemic).
108. Scheufele and Krause 2019, 7665.
109. Steve Milloy (@junkscience), tweet, Twitter/X, January 13, 2023, since deleted, accessed in January 2023; "Reporting on the State of the Climate 2022," NOAA National Centers for Environmental Information, September 6, 2023, https://www.ncei.noaa.gov/news/reporting-state-climate-2022.
110. Iyengar and Massey 2019, 7660, emphasis added. Before the pandemic, antivaccination campaigners were at least as likely to express left-leaning views as right-leaning ones. The pandemic may have changed that distribution. As if to underscore the continuing bipartisan nature of this phenomenon, the climate campaigner Robert F. Kennedy Jr. was deplatformed by Facebook in 2021 for spreading antivaccine propaganda during the COVID-19 pandemic (S. Bond 2021).
111. Piper 2023; Shepard 2023.
112. Sloman and Rabb 2019, 2. See also Selezneva 2021 (priming subjects to be cautious about the news did not reduce receptivity to fake news about critical race theory).
113. Pennycook and Rand 2019, 47; Martel, and Pennycook, and Rand 2020, 15 ("momentary emotion . . . is predictive of increased belief in fake news").
114. Conover et al. 2012.
115. Friedkin and Bullo 2017, 11384.
116. Wilson, Parker, and Feinberg 2020, 227 ("Rising institutional polarization (among elites, media and social media) selectively amplif[ies] the worse the other side has to offer, which can feed directly into rising false polarization among the electorate . . . via basic psychological processes . . . [and] can intensify out-group dislike").
117. In 2022, the polling analyst Nate Silver tweeted his views that "academia and journalism should be scrupulously truth-seeking" and that the question "'how could this [fact] be weaponized politically' should be a second-order concern

at best" (@NateSilver538, tweet, Twitter/X, August 21, 2022, https://x.com /NateSilver538/status/1561456857306349571?s=20). Although many of his followers supported the sentiment, some experts thought it naive. The historian Naomi Oreskes wrote, "Of course I am an activist. It's irrational and immoral to be passive in the face of imminent danger" (@Naomi Oreskes, tweet, Twitter/X, October 5, 2022, https://x.com/NaomiOreskes/status/157781493766 5150976?s=20).

118. I don't know if the instinct for circumspection is correlated with age and experience, but it is for me. I recall what a heady thing it was to develop expertise when I was younger. In retrospect, I was much too certain then about beliefs that I later amended with experience. I have no idea whether my trajectory is typical or if I was more hubristic than the average young expert. But George Orwell's famous observation about the inherent subjectivity of our perceptions applies to me: "Each generation imagines itself to be more intelligent than the one that went before it, and wiser than the one that comes after it" (1968).

119. Russell 1959.

120. The climate journalist David Roberts and the academic psychologist Jordan Peterson took hiatuses from the online rhetorical battle because of what each described as mental strain. See Roberts 2013 ("I am burnt the fuck out . . . responding to an incoming torrent of tweets. . . . I'm never disconnected. It's doing things to my brain"); B. Ward 2013 (on Roberts's break); Beyerstein 2020 (on Peterson's break).

121. W. Brown 2023a, emphasis added.

122. For example, in 2020 a bipartisan group of incumbent House members released a letter to the House leadership expressing concern about the size of the national debt. "Arrington, Peters Pen Bipartisan Letter on Need for Budget Reform, Debt Reduction," U.S. Representative Jodey Arrington, press release, June 1, 2020, https://arrington.house.gov/news/documentsingle.aspx?Docum entID=326. One climate journalist posted a tweet calling the letter's signatories the "Bipartisan Climate Denier Caucus," alongside a trashcan emoji (Kate Aronoff [@KateAronoff], tweet, Twitter/X, June 10, 2020, https://x.com/Kate Aronoff/status/1270706274032922625?s=20). But of the thirty Democrats who signed the letter, most had strong environmental and climate credentials; their average lifetime environmentalism "score" from the League of Conservation Voters was 93/100. Four of the Democrat signers were running in toss-up districts, and another twelve represented districts that favored the Republican candidate, according to the *Cook Political Report* (my summary of the data given in these two sources in general). Among the nine (of twelve) who survived the 2020 election, all voted for the Build Back Better bill.

123. According to the *Cook Political Report*, third-party voters probably denied Hillary Clinton the presidency in 2016, and "many of these voters . . . want to disrupt the two-party system, not simply keep the current political structure in place" (Walter 2023).

124. Snyder 2017, 59, 71–79, emphasis added.

125. Haley quoted in Blake 2018, emphasis added.

126. Seneca, "Thirteenth Letter (on Groundless Fears)," Wikisource, https://en .wikisource.org/wiki/Moral_letters_to_Lucilius/Letter_13. See also Mastroianni 2023 (crediting cognitive bias for persistent belief in society's moral decline across the political spectrum even though "people are wrong about this decline").

5. FACING ENERGY-TRANSITION TRADE-OFFS

1. Climate Stewardship Act of 2005, S342, 109th Cong. (died in committee). The bill would have established a marketable permit program for carbon emissions from sources in "the electric power, industrial or commercial sectors" of the economy, including the oil and gas sector. Its companion bill in the House had fifteen Republican cosponsors. See appendix D, https://www.ClimateOfCon tempt.com/Appendices/.

2. Gerstenzang 2000 (Gore responded *Local Hero* when asked his favorite movie).

3. On the transportation sector, see "Energy, Water, and Carbon Informatics, 2021 Energy Flow Diagram," Lawrence Livermore National Laboratory, July 26, 2023, https://flowcharts.llnl.gov/. Regarding the cement and steel industries, see Krishnan et al. 2022 (singling out steel and cement, among industry sectors). Even in these sectors, lower-carbon alternatives such as carbon-*negative* cement are being developed. Whether they will be part of the most affordable path to net zero is an open question. Modern wind turbines typically contain steel, lubricating oils, plastic, and carbon fiber in the blades, which has made them lighter and more efficient. Researchers and manufacturers are already working on nonpetroleum substitutes for all these inputs. See, e.g., Upadhyayula et al. 2022.

   Regarding the phrase "difficult to decarbonize," some climate-policy advocates voice objections online to it and its companion "hard to abate." One venture capitalist tweeted that " 'hard to abate' = just another set of whiny excuse words" (Rob Majteles [@RobMajteles], tweet, Twitter/X, January 3, 2023, https://x .com/RobMajteles/status/1610324742724276224?s=20). The Princeton professor Jesse Jenkins argued on Twitter/X that we should stop using the phrase because we just haven't yet "worked hard enough" on decarbonizing yet (@JesseJenkins, tweet, Twitter/X, January 3, 2023, https://x.com/JesseJenkins/status/16102969 45037250561?s=20). Based on current knowledge, some sectors are indeed more difficult to decarbonize (harder to abate) than others. See Krishnan et al. 2022. Therefore, I use this phrase when describing this reality.

4. Perhaps the best (though very long) account of the process by which petroleum embedded itself into the world economy is provided in Daniel Yergin's book *The Prize: The Epic Quest for Oil, Money, and Power* ([1990] 2008), especially 371–542. Petroleum's biggest market advantage is its relatively high energy density, which of course is nevertheless far lower than that of uranium. See Fischer, Werber, and Schwartz 2009.

5. On oil companies' complicity in oppression, see Yergin [1990] 2008. Some observers see continuing "colonialism" in the modern "oil curse" (or "the resource curse"), a set of economic, political, and social distortions experienced by developing countries with valuable natural-resource endowments, including oil reserves; see, e.g., M. Ross 2012. For good, readable accounts of political corruption and fossil fuels, see Chernow 1998 (detailing John D. Rockefeller Sr.'s support for Republican politicians); McCartney 2009 (detailing the political corruption at the heart of the Teapot Dome scandal of the 1920s); and Coll 2012 (detailing ExxonMobil's modern relationship to Congress). On the funding of misinformation, see Coll 2012 (detailing the misinformation activities of the Heartland Institute).

6. Sautter, Landis, and Dworkin 2009, 478.

7. Stein 2016; Klass et al. 2022.

8. To underscore the context-specific nature of the make-or-buy decision, recall from chapter 2 that restructuring of natural gas services led to an increase in reliability by incentivizing production. In electricity, it seemed to have the opposite effect in some places.

9. Capacity factor is a simple fraction. Its numerator is the number of megawatt hours the plant dispatches to the grid each year. Its denominator is the plant's nameplate capacity (in megawatts) × 8,760 (the number of hours in a year).

   One of the ways (but not the only one) regulators try to measure the availability value of a generation technology is through the concept of Effective Load Carrying Capacity, which focuses on the *potential* use of different generation resources during the periods of anticipated peak daily and seasonal loads (read: demand). For example, in the ERCOT region, solar power is predicted to be available at 81 percent of its capacity during summer peaks but only 11 percent of its capacity during winter peaks. The Effective Load Carrying Capacity numbers for fossil generators hover at or a little more than 90 percent across all the system peaks. Thus, while regulators and grid operators have gotten very good at predicting the availability of wind and solar power, these energy sources' higher levels of seasonal and weather dependence make their availability significantly lower than for traditionally dispatchable generating plants. See Carden, Dombrowsky, and Amitava 2022.

10. "Legacy" plants are those that were built before restructuring and under a set of financial incentives that entailed far less risk for investors.

11. T. Levin et al. 2023, 1203.

12. Several of my academic energy-law colleagues recently suggested that a high-renewables grid would be more reliable than the alternative because it would necessarily entail building more high-voltage transmission, which enhances system reliability. See Klass et al. 2022, 978 ("the only way to secure a reliable grid under conditions of climate change is to rapidly engage in a clean-energy transition in the electricity sector"). Alexandra Klass and her colleagues' article contains valuable insights about improving grid governance, but it may suggest to some readers that renewable-energy growth enhances grid reliability, all else equal, which it does not. Building more transmission enhances reliability, as does adding supply redundancy, such as backup generation and storage. But given renewable electricity's lower capacity potential, there is nothing inherently more reliable about it.

    In a conversation with the Harvard law professor Ari Peskoe in 2018, Phil Sharp, former congressman (D–IN) and Resources for the Future president, referred to reliability concerns as "the last refuge of scoundrels" (quoting Samuel Johnson on the use of the term *patriotism* in 1775). The full conversation reflects a more sophisticated understanding of the energy security/environment trade-offs, but that statement paints with too broad a brush. See "Phil Sharp and Ari Peskoe Celebrate PURPA's 40th Birthday," *Soundcloud* (podcast), 2018, https://soundcloud.com/user-995691545/phil-sharp-and-ari-peskoe-cele brate-purpas-40th-birthday.

13. Post by an electricity-policy expert on the Electricity Brain Trust email list, June 13, 2023, access restricted. The public-policy scholar Robert Idel has constructed a measure of the LCOE that includes the costs of relative intermittency and dispatchability, something he calls "levelized full-system cost of energy." Idel's levelized full-system cost point estimates for wind and solar are $483/mwh and $1,380/mwh, respectively, many multiples of his estimates for fossil-fueled sources (Idel 2022). Nevertheless, these estimates do not imply that a

net-zero grid will necessarily be unaffordable, but they represent one attempt to demonstrate why low LCOE for wind and solar do not imply that the net-zero grid will necessarily be less expensive than the current system.

14. Bolson, Prieto, and Patzek 2022.

15. Critics charge that the claim about intermittency is an unnecessary statement of the obvious, is (more or less) accounted for in energy modeling, and/or is a disingenuous attempt to raise worries about renewable energy. For example, the climate writer David Roberts responded to the statement this way: 'When you say dumb shit like 'the wind doesn't always blow,' the experts laugh at you. They know that. . . . Just because you're a dumbass doesn't mean they are" (@ drvolts, tweet, Twitter/X, December 24, 2022, https://x.com/drvolts/status /1606479052990459907?s=20). For an example of dismissiveness toward worries about interruptions to supply and labor, see Michael Liebreich (@Mliebreich), tweet, Twitter/X, July 1, 2021, https://x.com/Mliebreich/status/1410482332117 704704?s=20.

16. Off-Grid Tech (@OffGridTech_net), tweet, Twitter/X, May 21, 2023, https://x.com /OffGridTech_net/status/1660310852648706049?s=20.

17. H. Lee, Calvin, Dasgupta, Geden, et al. 2023, 60 ("Global net zero CO_2 or GHG emissions can be achieved even if some sectors and regions are net emitters, provided that others reach net negative emissions").

18. "Net-Zero America: Potential Pathways, Infrastructure, and Impacts," Net-Zero America Project, 2021, https://netzeroamerica.princeton.edu/; "Accelerating Decarbonization of the U.S. Energy System," National Academies of Science, 2021, https://doi.org/10.17226/25932; "Net-Zero United States: A Business Guide," McKinsey & Company, May 5, 2022, https://www.mckinsey.com/capabilities /sustainability/our-insights/navigating-americas-net-zero-frontier-a-guide-for -business-leaders; and "America's Net-Zero Shift," McKinsey & Company, 2022, http://ceros.mckinsey.com/americaco2-2-2-2-2-2-3-1-2-1-2-4-2-1-2-2-1-1-2-2.

19. Most hydrogen is currently made from fossil fuels using a steam reforming process. This so-called gray hydrogen is not a green gas. The IRA subsidies most clearly apply to "green hydrogen" production, which uses zero-emission electricity and water to produce hydrogen from electrolysis.

20. That is, if we assume that households will have their own batteries, backup generators, or efficiency devices, they will need less grid-based electricity, and the grid will be smaller than if households continue to rely on the grid for all their electricity needs. Similarly, if we assume that nonelectric, net-zero alternatives can be found for fossil fuels used currently in manufacturing, transportation, and buildings, the grid will be smaller than if those sectors must be electrified.

21. See "NYISO Gold Book: Load and Capacity Data 2022," New York Independent System Operator, Inc., 2022, tables III-a and III-b, https://www.nyiso.com /documents/20142/2226333/2022-Gold-Book-Final-Public.pdf.

22. Jacobson et al. 2013.

23. See, e.g., Clack et al. 2017.

24. In May 2023, a search for newspaper articles about the Jacobson model and the Princeton Net-Zero America model returned more than 3,600 articles about the former and a little more than 200 articles about the latter.

25. This is California's famous "duck curve," so named because a daily graph of system demand slopes sharply upward after the sun goes down and people come home from work, and the curve supposedly looks like a duck's neck. That need, which requires more than a doubling of system generation in less than

three hours, is filled now mostly by gas-fired generators. For a look at the daily net demand curve, go to the CAISO website at http://www.CAISO.com.

26. Wikipedia provides a clear and relatively complete description of this phenomenon, also known in meteorology as "anticyclonic gloom," in its entry "Dunkelflaute," https://en.wikipedia.org/wiki/Dunkelflaute.

27. Minn. Stat. §216B.1691 (2022), Subd. 2b. The statute directs the commission to consider factors such as the impact of the standard on customers' utility costs and the reliability of the electric system (Subd. 2b(1) and (2)).

28. N.Y. Pub. Serv. L. §66-p(4) (2023).

29. N.M. Stat. Ann. § 62-15-34A(3)(c) (2021).

30. See National Emission Standards for Hazardous Air Pollutants from Coal and Oil-Fired Electric Utility Steam Generating Units and Standards of Performance for Fossil-Fuel-Fired Electric Utility, Industrial-Commercial-Institutional, and Small Industrial-Commercial-Institutional Steam Generating Units, 76 Fed. Reg. 24,976 (proposed May 3, 2011); Carbon Pollution Emission Guidelines for Existing Stationary Sources: Electric Utility Generating Units, 79 Fed. Reg. 34,830 (2011). For a fuller discussion of these objections, see Adelman and Spence 2017, 360–74. In general, comments on proposed rules can be skewed toward the negative because people are more likely to object to losses than to support gains. This is the loss-aversion bias. That bias indicates that we experience a smaller increase in utility from a gain of $X than the decrease in utility we experience from losing $X. This is a very robust experimental result. See Kahneman and Tversky 1979.

31. Russell Gold's account of the rise and fall of Clean Line Energy illustrates the practical difficulty of realizing even the most sensible ambitions. Clean Line was created by the entrepreneur Michael Skelly to build high-voltage transmission lines connecting the windy rural Midwest to cities. Despite the existence of a clear economic opportunity, Clean Line ultimately failed in the face of daunting legal and political opposition (Gold 2019).

32. A group called the Climate Justice Alliance opposed both the IIJA and the BBB because the bills included support for CCS and nuclear power, failed to promote a shift toward "relocalize[d] . . . production and consumption," and failed to "divorc[e] ourselves from the comforts of empire" (qtd. in Chait 2022).

33. Steve Jurvetson (@FutureJurvetson), tweet, Twitter/X, August 12, 2021, https://x .com/FutureJurvetson/status/1425954725254492160?s=20 (calling green hydrogen a "marketing façade for oil companies"); SC MacAlpine (@Applied-Coastal), tweet, Twitter/X, April 9, 2019, https://x.com/AppliedCoastal/status /1115641438488813569?s=20 ("sequestration and extraction are opposite actions, yet the industry wants us to believe they can do both?"); Greenpeace International (@Greenpeace), tweet, Twitter/X, February 3, 2020, https://x.com /Greenpeace/status/1224305825436651520?s=20 ("Oil companies . . . think carbon capture technologies and billions of trees will clean up their mess. But this won't work").

34. Hauter 2022 ("There is no real evidence that carbon capture can or will do what its optimistic name suggests"); Drugmand and Muffett 2021, 2 ("The unproven scalability of CCS technologies and their prohibitive costs mean they cannot play any significant role in the rapid reduction of global emissions necessary to limit warming to 1.5°C").

35. Rabe 2023 and Donaghy et al. 2023, assuming away the possibility that a net-zero future can include oil and gas production without dangerous or harmful emissions.

36. Nichols 2023, quoting Secretary-General Antonio Guterres of the United Nations ("Fossil fuel companies must also cease and desist influence peddling and legal threats designed to knee-cap progress. I am thinking particularly of recent attempts to subvert net-zero alliances, invoking anti-trust legislation").

37. This is the position of Robert Pullin, an economist at the University of Massachusetts Amherst. See Pollin 2022. See also Arkush and Braman 2024 (arguing for compulsory conversion of fossil-fuel companies to public-benefit corporations). The group Stop Ecocide International is lobbying governments to make "ecocide"—or the "wanton" emission of pollutants with knowledge that they will cause severe, long-term damage—an international crime. See its webpage "Making Ecocide a Crime," Stop Ecocide International, n.d., https://www.stopecocide.earth/making-ecocide-a-crime. The climate journalist Kate Aronoff urges prosecuting fossil-fuel executives for "crimes against humanity." See Aronoff 2019 ("It isn't hyperbole to say that fossil fuel executives are mass murderers").

38. In a series of tweets, some of which have been deleted, Gunther accused CNN of covering for "business-as-usual interests who are . . . willing to commit genocide for money." She characterized the failure of newspapers to feature an IPCC report on their homepages as "a form of authoritarian disinformation that aids and abets genocide" (Genevieve Gunther (@DoctorVive), tweet, Twitter/X, October 8, 2018, https://x.com/DoctorVive/status/10494402 94805090305?s=20). A year later, Gunther characterized Royal Dutch Shell's explanation of its ongoing oil production to serve a market need as "the voice of genocide for money," adding, "FUCK YOU, you sociopathic murderer" (@DoctorVive, tweet, Twitter/X, October 15, 2019, https://x.com/Doc torVive/status/1183928587822551046?s=20). Gunther has been featured on CNN and in *The New Yorker* and as of late 2023 had more than 68,000 Twitter/X followers.

39. Amy Westervelt (@AmyWestervelt), tweet, Twitter/X, August 9, 2021, https://x .com/amywestervelt/status/1424774950192238592?s=20.

40. David Ho (@_david_ho_), tweet, Twitter/X, August 2, 2022, since deleted, accessed August 2022.

41. See "How Much Carbon Dioxide Can the United States Store Via Geologic Sequestration?," U.S. Geological Survey, July 27, 2023, https://www.usgs.gov/faqs /how-much-carbon-dioxide-can-united-states-store-geologic-sequestration. The analogous figure for biological sequestration is probably considerably less than 10 gigatons. For a sampling of the literature estimating this number, see "The Potential for Carbon Sequestration in the United States," U.S. Congressional Budget Office, 2007, n. 6, https://www.cbo.gov/publication/19138.

42. For a comparison of geological and biological sequestration, see, e.g., Hill 2021 and "Understanding the Differences Between Carbon Capture & Carbon Dioxide Removal," Environmental Defense Fund, 2022, https://www.edf.org/sites /default/files/documents/carbon%20removal%20vs.%20carbon%20cap- ture%20fact%20sheet_FINAL.pdf (noting that a "vast majority of captured carbon will need to be secured . . . in [deep] saline formations"). On promises to create or maintain forests and vegetation, see Morita and Matsumoto 2023. On the survival of such promises, see Massarella et al. 2018.

    California Redwoods are often cited as the best trees for carbon sequestration; see Fimrite 2020. However, these same ecosystems can be destroyed by wildfires; see George 2023 and "Fire & Redwoods—What Does the Future Hold for This Ancient Species?," U.S. National Park Service, July 17, 2022, https://www

.nps.gov/articles/000/fire-redwoods-what-does-the-future-hold-for-this
-ancient-species.htm.

43. For a good discussion of the debate over carbon-sequestration projects, see
Buck 2023. Hourly matching requires that the facility procure its zero-carbon
electricity by way of contracts that purchase renewable-energy credits (see chapter 2) in amounts representing its electricity consumption hour by hour rather
than day by day, week by week, month by month, or year by year. The former
method will spur more new renewable-energy investment by bidding up the
price of renewable-energy credits during evening and nighttime operating
hours or during periods of low wind.

44. Wilson Ricks, Qingyu Xu, and Jesse Jenkins (2023) estimate that hourly matching adds less than $1 per kilogram to hydrogen prices. See also Stokes 2023. The
consultancy Wood McKenzie concluded that hourly matching will add $2–3.5
per kilogram to the price of hydrogen compared to annual matching (Vargas,
McNutt, and Seiple 2023). E3, another consultancy, concludes that for "all but
the most flexible" purchasers of electricity, hourly matching is "prohibitively
expensive" (A. Olson et al. 2023).

45. "States Restrictions on New Nuclear Power Facility Construction," National
Conference of State Legislatures, 2021, https://www.ncsl.org/environment-and
-natural-resources/states-restrictions-on-new-nuclear-power-facility-construc-
tion; "State Partisan Composition," National Conference of State Legislatures,
2023, https://www.ncsl.org/about-state-legislatures/state-partisan-composition.
On the connection between climate-change and nuclear-power concerns, see
B. Kennedy, Funk, and Tyson 2023.

46. Osaka 2022.

47. Ted Nordhaus and others associated with the pro-nuclear BTI consistently
articulate this view. See, e.g., Nordhaus 2021 and Gilbert 2020.

48. Michael Shellenberger, a cofounder of the BTI (with Ted Nordhaus), later broke
away from it to form the NGO Environmental Progress. See, e.g., Shellenberger
2019. In response to a tweet from Dr. Genevieve Gunther mocking a BTI analysis of energy and pollution in Bangladesh, Nordhaus called Gunther "a rich lady
from the upper East side" who doesn't "actually give a fig about air pollution
deaths in poor countries" (Ted Nordhaus (@TedNordhaus), tweet, Twitter/X,
August 30, 2023, https://x.com/TedNordhaus/status/1696989134890348700?s=20).

49. Wikipedia lists more than fifty antinuclear NGOs in the United States ("Antinuclear Groups in the United States," Wikipedia, https://en.wikipedia.org/wiki
/Anti-nuclear_groups_in_the_United_States). Both the original Green New
Deal resolution and Sen. Bernie Sanders's energy plan omitted nuclear power
as well as fossil fuels. See "Bernie Sanders on Energy Policy," Feel the Bern,
2020, https://feelthebern.org/bernie-sanders-on-energy-policy/.On the reconsideration of nuclear power, see Horton 2023.

50. See Mark Jacobson's "wind, water and sun" model of an all-renewables future
(Jacobson et al. 2013). See also Howarth 2013 ("We do not need nuclear power
as we move forward in the 21st Century. Renewables such as wind and solar will
do just fine to replace fossil fuels").

51. Some ascribe failures of regulatory governance in part to the revolving door
between IOUs and public-utility companies (Heern 2023; see also Roth 2023).
For a more nuanced discussion of the revolving-door problem, see appendix F,
https://www.ClimateOfContempt.com/Apendices/.

    In 2023, the EPA highlighted the efforts of "GHG reduction commit-
ments" of ten of the nation's largest electric utilities, "many with emission

reduction targets of at least 80 percent." See the EPA's power plant proposed rule (described in chapter 3), 88 Fed. Reg. 33262–33263. That group included three of the top-ten largest utilities by revenue and four of the top ten by number of customers. "Greenwashing" occurs when a business makes misleading claims about the environmental benefits of its activities or products.

52. Stokes quoted in Davenport 2022. A profile in the *Santa Barbara Independent* describes the qualities that make Stokes a persuasive advocate: "As a public speaker, she's commanding, fluid and accessible; there is no know-it-all arrogance to her delivery. Little wonder her op-eds run with such frequency in the pages of the *New York Times* and other media outlets. On top of that, Stokes does a regular podcast—*A Matter of Degrees*[, which is devoted] . . . to climate change" (Welsh 2023). As noted in chapter 1, the idea that utilities capture state politics and regulation is a central thesis of Stokes's book *Short Circuiting Policy* (2020). See also Williams et al. 2022 (to which Stokes is a contributor), citing industry contributions to trade associations and other lobbying groups that in the past promoted the denial of climate science.

53. State of Wisconsin Clean Energy Plan, Executive Budget, GTFCC Tier 2 #50, Wis. Stat. Ann. §196.027 (2022); Energy Transition Act, N.M. Stat. Ann., §§62–64.2, 4.3 (2019); State of Michigan, *In the Matter of Application of CONSUMER ENERGY COMPANY for a Financing Order Approving the Securitization of Qualified Costs*, Case No. U-20889 (2020).

It is difficult to persuade IOUs and state public-utility companies to retire a fossil-fuel-generation system that has some remaining useful life and is part of an IOU's rate base. Some states have therefore begun to explore securitized compensation of the IOU for retiring those assets. Securitization refers to lump-sum compensation paid by the issuance of long-term bonds that ratepayers or taxpayers pay off over time. See Fong and Mardell 2021.

54. Macey 2020 (critiquing the traditional justifications for utility regulation); Macey and Salovaara 2020 (critiquing the use of capacity markets to assure adequate reserves); Mays et al. 2021; Klass et al. 2022 (making the case for changes in grid-governance rules as the grid decarbonizes); Walters and Kleit 2023 (arguing that RTO governance is an outdated "corporatist" system that omits important stakeholders from regulatory policymaking).

55. Kovvali and Macey 2023, 574.

56. See Macey, Welton, and Wiseman 2023, 172. The journalist David Wallace-Wells has traced how the primary strategy for slowing progress on climate change has shifted in recent years from denial to delay as climate impacts become impossible to ignore. An emerging throughline in this dilatory rhetoric is to emphasize the threats that a rapid clean-energy transition poses to grid reliability.

57. Peskoe 2021. See also Gearino 2023 ("Energy analysts and economists who have studied this issue are mostly critical of [the] right-of-first-refusal laws" that enable the transmission syndicate).

58. *NextEra Energy Capital Holdings, Ltd. v. Lake*, 48 F.4th 306 (5th Cir. 2022) (overturning a Texas law granting IOUs a "right of first refusal" to build new transmission in the state as being in violation of the dormant Commerce Clause).

59. Blunt 2022, 210. See also Blunt, Frosch, and Carlton 2023 (offering a similar explanation for the relative lack of attention Hawaiian Electric Co. paid to known wildfire risks in its service territory).

60. Building for the Future Through Electric Regional Transmission Planning and Cost Allocation and Generator Interconnection, 179 FERC ¶61,028 (issued April 21, 2022) (18 C.F.R. Pt 35).

61. Boyd 2014. See also Monast 2022 (making the case for public-utility companies to focus on risk, including climate risk, in their rate making and regulation of IOUs).

62. Boyd 2022. Focusing more narrowly on ensuring a reliable, affordable supply, Commissioner Mark Christie of FERC, a Republican, has echoed some of William Boyd's critique on failures of market pricing, particularly as managed by RTOs. See Christie 2023.

63. Coase 1937.

64. Boyd 2022.

65. McKibben 2015 (celebrating the way Green Mountain Power, a Vermont IOU, embraced innovative, greener solutions to supplying its customers with power).

66. Some attribute red state policymaking to regulatory capture by IOUs. See, e.g., Harrison and Welton 2021 (providing examples of utility industries infiltrating state legislatures and regulatory commissions to promote changes) and Peskoe 2021 ("Public utility laws arose in-part out of the interests of incumbent IOUs in protecting their industry from competition"). Regardless, courts treat traditional public-utility regulation and the monopoly rights it confers as a legitimate state policy choice. See, e.g., *TEC Cogen, Inc. v. Florida Power & Light*, 76 F.3d 1560 (11th Cir. 1996), and *North Carolina Util. Comm'n v. N.C. WARN*, 805 S.E.2d 712 (N.C.Ct. App. 2017).

67. Budolfson et al. 2021.

68. Although majorities of the American public worry about global warming, accept the basic science, and agree that it affects others now and in the future, only a minority of Americans believe it will affect them personally. See the Yale Climate Maps at https://climatecommunication.yale.edu/visualizations-data/ycom-us/.

69. In the words of Adam Smith, "[However] selfish man may be supposed, there are evidently some principles in his nature, which interest him in the fortune of others, and render their happiness necessary to him, though he derives nothing from it, except the pleasure of seeing it" ([1759] n.d., 1). For a summary of the modern social science literature establishing this point, see Spence 2017, 1001–5.

70. Of course, all GHG regulation imposes compliance costs, many of which are passed on to consumers. But other regulatory instruments do so much less transparently than a carbon tax. For a comparison of different regulatory approaches by cost per ton of emissions abated, see Gillingham and Stock 2018.

71. According to the Pew Research Center, despite widespread support for the energy transition, only 31 percent of Americans favor phasing out fossil fuels altogether, and 40 percent favor phasing out gasoline-powered vehicles (B. Kennedy, Funk, and Tyson 2023).

72. The Low Income Home Energy Assistance Program, established in 1981, provides annual grants to aid low-income households with their home energy needs, including heating and cooling costs, crisis assistance, and weatherization. Households with incomes at or below 150 percent of the poverty level or at 60 percent of state median income, whichever is higher, are federally eligible for assistance from the program, although states can set lower income limits. See Perl 2018.

73. M. Brown et al. 2020, 1. See also Memmott et al. 2021 (finding that energy insecurity is "highly prevalent among households at or below 200% of the federal poverty line," is more likely to affect minority households and households with young children, and has been exacerbated by the COVID-19 pandemic).

74. Lauren Ross, Drehobl, and Stickles 2018; Low Income Energy Affordability Data (LEAD) Tool, U.S. Department of Energy, https://www.energy.gov/scep/slsc/low-income-energy-affordability-data-lead-tool; Energy Burden Calculator, Sierra Club, n.d., https://www.sierraclub.org/energy-burden-calculator.

75. "Quality of Life Dashboard: Residential Energy Use," University of San Diego Nonprofit Institute, July 31, 2023, https://www.sandiego.edu/soles/centers-and-institutes/nonprofit-institute/what-we-do/create-and-share-knowledge/dashboard/electricity.php.

76. "Calling for National Utility Reform and Elimination of Inflated Fixed Rates, with Special Consideration of the Tennessee Valley Authority (TVA) Service Area," NAACP, 2019, https://naacp.org/resources/calling-national-utility-reform-and-elimination-inflated-fixed-rates-special.

77. Crooks et al. 2023 (discussing the massive increases in the supply of copper, nickel, and other minerals that will be required to get to net zero and exploring the mining-development challenge these increases present).

78. On labor shortages and challenges in the U.S. solar industry, see DiGangi 2023. A study by the National Bureau of Economic Research indicates a 2.3 percent drop in the labor-force participation rate and a 4.6 percent decrease in desired work hours across all individuals from February 2020 to the end of 2021. See Faberman, Mueller, and Şahin 2022.

79. "Overview and Key Findings—World Energy Investment 2022—Analysis," International Energy Agency, n.d., https://www.iea.org/reports/world-energy-investment-2022/overview-and-key-findings.

80. "Levelized Cost of Energy 16.0," Lazard, April 2023, https://www.lazard.com/research-insights/levelized-cost-of-energyplus/. See also Zeitlin 2023b ("Up and down the East Coast . . ., offshore wind projects have been delayed or even cancelled thanks to costs rising faster than expected") and Marcacci 2023.

81. Bistline, Mehrotra, and Wolfram 2023; J. Jenkins et al. 2023; Min et al. 2023, 12–14 (projecting increases in the demand for labor and materials related to constructing renewable-energy sources).

82. See the podcast discussion of this World Trade Organization issue between Jason Furman of Harvard and Jason Bordoff of Columbia in "The Economics of Green Industrial Policy," *Columbia Energy Exchange*, June 6, 2023, https://www.energypolicy.columbia.edu/the-economics-of-green-industrial-policy/. The indirect costs (if any) of trade protectionism are difficult to predict. Proponents of post–World War II free-trade regimes saw such regimes as a tool for promoting cross-border understanding and interdependence, thereby incentivizing peaceful conflict resolution. The founders of the European Union envisioned a united and peaceful Europe through economic and political integration. See "Founding Fathers," Council of Europe, July 31, 2023, https://www.coe.int/en/web/about-us/founding-fathers.

83. "The Inflation Reduction Act Took U.S. Climate Action Global," *Time*, August 16, 2023, https://time.com/6305001/inflation-reduction-act-what-happens-next/; Penrod 2023.

84. Sierra Club's California/Nevada Desert Committee, a local chapter, broke with the national organization to oppose renewable projects in the Mojave Desert,

citing threats to the desert tortoise and other species (Owens 2016). The Northern Pass Transmission Project, which would have brought hydroelectric power to New England, provoked a similar split between the national organization and its local chapters in New Hampshire (Corkery 2015).

85. "Exploring the Energy Transition on Tribal Lands, with Pilar Thomas," *Resources Radio* (podcast), hosted by Daniel Raimi, May 4, 2021, https://www.resources.org/resources-radio/exploring-the-energy-transition-on-tribal-lands-with-pilar-thomas/; Johnson 2023; Barringer 2021; Volcovici 2023.

86. And for solar farms on flat properties, robots can now do some of that construction work.

87. The statute defines energy communities as either a brownfields site (as defined in the federal Superfund law) or metropolitan areas with particularly high levels of fossil-fuel-related employment or census tracts in which a coal mine closed since 1999 or a coal-fired power plant closed since 2009. See 26 U.S.C. §45(b)(11)(B) (2023), See also Treasury Notice 2023-09 (2023) (further defining "energy communities"). For "low-income communities," see 26 U.S.C. §48(e) (2023) and Treasury Notice 2023-29 (2023).

88. For a summary of the rich academic literature on intra- and cross-jurisdictional political conflict over siting and pollution externalities, see Spence 2014, 384–97. These externalities might include pipelines (CCS and hydrogen production), chemical uses (battery and solar manufacturing), manufacturing, truck traffic, industrial buildings, and so on.

89. For a relatively recent treatment of this issue, see Spence 2019. See also Buckman 2011 and Sutcliffe 2008.

90. "Pursuing Energy Justice: A Conversation with Shalanda Baker," Case Western Reserve University School of Law, September 15, 2023, https://case.edu/law/our-school/events-lectures/pursuing-energy-justice-conversation-shalanda-baker.

91. On what voters say, see Chiu, Guskin, and Clement 2023. On how voters actually respond, see Harold et al. 2021. This study revealed that local acceptance of wind and solar farms in the United States was high—89 and 92 percent, respectively—if the project was located in the community but more than five kilometers from their home; it fell to 17 and 24 percent, respectively, when the project was located within one kilometer of their home. Acceptance of biomass facilities mirrored that of coal-fired power plants in this survey.

92. Karpf 2016.

93. On opposition to battery-storage projects, see G. Barber 2023; on "wind-turbine syndrome," see Fight the Wind's Facebook page and T. Jones 2011; on the dangers of transmission lines, see the Hope for the Hills website at http://www.hopeforthehills.org/.

94. On these claims' dubious science, see J. Schmidt and Klokker 2014; "Wind Farms and Health," Australian Medical Association position statement, 2014, https://www.ama.com.au/position-statement/wind-farms-and-health-2014; *Possible Health Effects of Exposure to Residential Electric and Magnetic Fields* 1997; World Health Organization 2007; Porsius et al. 2014. Some scholars ascribe these claims to the "nocebo effect," a phenomenon in which subjects experience expected symptoms after exposure to a stimulus or attribute existing symptoms to a suggested stimulus. See Chapman et al. 2013 (discussing the role of nocebo effects in complaints about wind farms) and Enck and Häuser 2012 (explaining research into side effects experienced by drug-trial patients taking placebos and asserting that "expectations can also do harm").

Regarding qualified dissenters, for example, the work of Dr. Nina Pierpont, a pediatrician, and Dr. David O. Carpenter, a health sciences academic, is frequently cited by opponents of wind farms, smart meters, and transmission lines. See Spence 2019.

95. Zeitlin 2023a.

96. It is not uncommon for clean-energy projects to be delayed by litigation (Bennon and Wilson 2023). Scholars disagree over the extent to which environmental laws are significant sources of delay for energy infrastructure (see, e.g., Coleman 2022 and Adelman 2023).

97. On energy privilege, see Stokes, Franzblau, Lovering, and Miljanic 2023. For the Columbia study, see Aidun et al. 2022. On opposition to offshore wind projects, see, e.g., Storrow 2023a and Plaven 2023.

98. On new raw-material demands, see Khan 2023. Proposals for new U.S. lithium mines are mired in litigation (Cough and Semuels 2023; Sonner 2023). In 2023, the U.S. Department of the Interior banned mining in northeastern Minnesota on environmental grounds, preventing renewal of historic copper-mining activities there (Scheyder 2023).

99. Inflation Reduction Act, Pub. L. No. 117-169, §3401(e)(1)(A)(i)(II) (2022).

100. It may attempt to do so under the Defense Production Act, P.L. 81-774, 64 Stat. 798 (1950). See Holzman 2022.

101. Welton 2023. For a review of these agreements in the clean-energy context in the United Kingdom, see Paddock and Greenblum 2016.

102. For a good (and entertaining) chronicle of this sort of opposition to the Cape Wind Project, see the documentary film *Cape Spin: An American Power Struggle* (Robbie Gemel, John Kirby, 2011). Most law schools have environmental law "clinics" that do traditional environmental litigation work, usually in opposition to some sort of development. Only one that I know of, Columbia Law School, has a program dedicated to actively supporting renewable-energy projects, the Renewable Energy Legal Defense Initiative.

103. Eric Gimon and his colleagues at Energy Innovation make this point: "It is important to remember reliability is a system attribute—replacement renewable portfolios need not bear sole responsibility for replacing the reliability services of individual coal plants" (quoted in M. Solomon et al. 2023, 2–3).

104. M. Hogan 2023 (calling customer-demand response "the untapped mother lode" and urging retail dynamic pricing to tap it).

105. As early as the mid-1970s, Lovins advocated a "soft energy path" characterized by more efficient consumption and more reliance on renewables. He later founded the Rocky Mountain Institute, whose research and advocacy continue to support that vision in today's energy-policy debates.

106. Hledik and Peters 2023.

107. Faruqui and Palmer 2011; Faruqui, Hledik, and Sergici 2019; Gimon 2022; Kiesling 2009.

108. On opting in to TOU rates, see, e.g., Faruqui, Hledik, and Sergici 2019. On default TOU rates, see Trabish 2023 and "New Time-of-Use Rate Plan Will Support Cleaner, More Reliable Grid and Enhance Choice and Control for PG&E Customers," *Business Wire*, January 8, 2018, https://www.businesswire.com/news/home/20180108006733/en/New-Time-of-Use-Rate-Plan-Will-Support-Cleaner-More-Reliable-Grid-and-Enhance-Choice-and-Control-for-PGE-Customers.

109. McDonnell Nieto del Rio, Bogel-Burroughs, and Penn 2021; Hawkins 2021.

110. Transactive DER markets are sometimes limited because of these factors. See Faruqui and Trewn 2017; Vadari 2018, 118–28.

111. See e.g., Storrow 2023b and Nilsen 2022.
112. Robert Borlick (@BorlickRobert), tweet, Twitter/X, October 10, 2022, https://twitter.com/BorlickRobert/status/1579655505303465984. Borlick is an energy consultant, but as of September 2023 he had only 169 followers on Twitter/X.
113. Aronoff 2022b.
114. This colorful phrase comes from a since deleted tweet by the climate writer David Roberts on November 1, 2018, expressing frustration over the lack of voter outrage about the inhumane treatment of refugees at southern U.S. border. In response to criticism of his phrasing, Roberts explained in a later (also deleted) tweet that his characterization of "suburbanites" was intended as a reference to "suburban and small-town Trump voters raging about lazy, handout-seeking immigrants" despite living "lives of [comparatively] absurd luxury & overindulgence" (David Roberts, @drvolts, tweet, Twitter/X, November 3, 2018).
115. In the mid–twentieth century, a consortium of automotive and oil industry firms worked to convert city mass-transit systems from electric streetcars to buses. Some of its members were convicted of conspiring to monopolize the sale of buses to local transit companies. For a good explanation of what these conspirators did and didn't do, see "National City Lines," Wikipedia, https://en.wikipedia.org/wiki/National_City_Lines, and "General Motors Streetcar Conspiracy," Wikipedia, https://en.wikipedia.org/wiki/General_Motors_streetcar_conspiracy.
116. See Forsyth, Salomon, and Smead 2017; Fields and Renne 2021.
117. See Boarnet and Crane 2001.
118. See Holleran 2022 (discussing the consequences of housing NIMBYism and younger generations' (millennials') reactions to it); A. Kramer 2018 (analyzing whether those who are most likely to ride public transit in North American cities can afford to live near it); and Geller 2010 (analyzing form-based zoning codes and detailing their impact on housing in walkable developments).
119. Rix et al. 2021.
120. Sorrel 2017.
121. For the Transportation Department's fuel-economy standards, see Exec. Order No. 13,990, 86 FR 7038 (2021). On the EPA's proposed vehicle standards, see "Multi-pollutant Emissions Standards for Model Years 2027 and Later Light-Duty and Medium-Duty Vehicles," 40 CFR Parts 85, 86, 600, 1036, 1037, and 1066, *Federal Register* 88, no. 87 (May 5, 2023): 29184–446, https://www.govinfo.gov/content/pkg/FR-2023-05-05/pdf/2023-07974.pdf. Under its Clean Air Act authority, the EPA is proposing new, more stringent emissions standards for criteria pollutants and GHGs for light-duty vehicles and Class 2b and 3 ("medium-duty") vehicles that would phase in over model years 2027 through 2032. For California's commitment to phasing out gas-powered new cars, see California Exec. Order No. N-79-02 (2020).
122. On the proportion of EV vehicle sales and who buys them, see Osaka 2022 and N. Lopez 2023 (67 percent of households that own an electric vehicle make more than $100,000 per year), respectively. On gas vehicles' and EVs' life-cycle costs, see Furch, Konečný, and Krobot 2022 (a mathematical model of life-cycle costs for traditional cars and EVs shows that the life-cycle cost of an EV is the lowest). In late 2023, the Hyundai Kona EV MSRP started at $33,550, and the gas model at $22,140 (Hyundai, "Kona," 2024, https://www.hyundaiusa.com/us/en/vehicles/kona). The Chevrolet Blazer EV MSRO started at $44,995, and the gas model at $35,100; the Chevrolet Equinox EV MSRP started at $30,000, and the gas model at $26,600 (see https://www.chevrolet.com/).

123. Drehobl, Ross, and Ayala 2020; "As Electric Vehicles Become More Popular, Home Renters Face a Charging Dilemma," NPR, October 25, 2022, https://www.npr.org/2022/10/25/1131369881/electric-vehicles-home-apartment-renters-charging-evs; Desilver 2021.

124. "Shaming People Into Fighting Climate Change Won't Work, Says Scientist," CBC Radio, August 19, 2019, https://www.cbc.ca/radio/thecurrent/the-current-for-august-19-2019-1.5251826/shaming-people-into-fighting-climate-change-won-t-work-says-scientist-1.5251832 (quoting the climate communicator Katherine Hayhoe); "People Reject Popular Opinions If They Already Hold Opposing Views, Study Finds," *ScienceDaily*, August 2010, https://www.sciencedaily.com/releases/2010/08/100802125819.htm. For a contrary opinion, see Reid 2019. For an analysis comparing these views, see Fredericks 2021.

125. Thaler and Cass 2009; Carrico and Riemer 2011.

126. Some people find it helpful to categorize moral philosophies this way: (1) those that look to some higher authority such as God or natural law to identify "good" or "right" behavior; (2) consequentialism, as followed by the utilitarians Jeremy Bentham and J. S. Mill, who base their definitions of good behavior on how that behavior affects others; (3) so-called deontological theories, such as those associated with Immanuel Kant and John Rawls, who define good behavior based on universal duties that we owe to one another (e.g., the Golden Rule); and (4) virtue ethics of the kind we associate with Buddhism or Hinduism, which focus on the good behavior as a personal journey or an exercise in perfecting oneself.

127. Consequentialists are people whose definitions of right behavior depend on the consequences of that behavior. Jeremy Bentham's utilitarianism is perhaps the most well-known consequentialist philosophy.

128. Virtue ethicists focus on perfecting one's own character, developing personal ethical standards of behavior irrespective of the situation or consequences. Deontological approaches, from the Greek word for "obligation" or "duty," focus not on the consequences of behavior but on the inherent rightness or wrongness of action, in particular its adherence to ex ante ethical rules. For a review of the literature on the philosophies or ethics behind the decision to use or not use fossil fuels, see Lenzi 2022.

129. McDevitt 2022.

130. Coggins 2023.

131. Katherine Blunt ascribes this problem to both PG&E and the California Public Utilities Commission. She says that PG&E's aggressive acquisition of renewable power was one of the drivers of increases in its retail rates by "an inflation-adjusted 9 percent between 2004 and 2010" and that the "years long focus on renewable energy had diverted the attention of . . . the company [away from safety]" (2022, 127, 185). As for the commission, Blunt writes that its "intense focus on climate policy came at the expense of one of its core responsibilities: holding the utilities accountable on safety" (2022, 133).

132. Dudley quoted in Crowley 2020.

133. G. Wright, Olenick, and Westervelt 2021.

134. Ken Caldeira (@KenCaldeira), tweet, Twitter/X, February 21, 2023, https://x.com/KenCaldeira/status/1628176915571032065?s=20.

135. This research produced the Climate Accountability Institute's "carbon majors database." See P. Griffin 2017.

136. See, e.g., Baker and Krauss 2022 (quoting President Biden urging oil companies to produce more oil to reduce gasoline prices that had spiked after Russia's invasion of Ukraine). See also *Gasoline Prices, Oil Company Profits, and*

the American Consumer: Hearing Before the Subcomm. on Oversight & Investigations of the H. Comm. on Energy & Commerce, 110th Cong., 1st sess., May 22, 2007.

137. City of Oakland v. BP, PLC, Order Granting Motion to Dismiss Amended Complaints (Aslup, J.) (N.D. CA, June 25, 2018), at http://climatecasechart.com/wp-content/uploads/sites/16/case-documents/2018/20180625_docket-317-cv-06011_order-2.pdf. See also O'Neill 2023 (arguing for developing climate policy using conception of risk rather than anticipated climate harm).

138. Biber 2017.

6. HOPE AND CONVERSATION

1. Both men are regularly credited with making this observation—as is Mark Twain. But all these attributions are wrong. The origin of the quote is apparently unknown. The increasing frequency of this kind of "Churchillian Drift"—the rapid spread of pithy quotes falsely attributed to famous people—is yet another type of misinformation accelerated by the internet age.

2. Bonhoeffer 2010, 43–44. A Google search of the quotation in question returned more than 168,000 results in September 2023. Bonhoeffer apparently used a German word that has gentler connotations than the English word *stupidity*. For an interesting online message board discussion of this translation issue by anonymous participants, see the thread on the *Hacker News* message board, https://news.ycombinator.com/item?id=28888996.

3. @TimesClimate, tweet, Twitter/X, December 5, 2019, https://x.com/TimesClimate/status/1206340514129297408?s=20; @yehezkell, tweet, Twitter/X, December 15, 2019, https://x.com/yehezkell/status/1206342586992091140?s=20. A search revealed many of these examples, invoking the "stupidity" remark to denigrate "climate change alarmists," "COVIDiots," "anti-vax" people, people who "deny COVID or even climate change," and so on.

4. E.g., Barrett, Hendrix, and Sims 2021, 2 (offering a list of such recommendations); and Dvoskin 2023 (recommending regulation that reorders social media algorithms to promote diversity or underrepresented opinions).

5. "The aim of argument, or of discussion, should not be victory, but progress" (Joseph Joubert, Pensées de J. Joubert [1848], in Oxford Essential Quotations, 4th ed., online [Oxford: Oxford University Press, 2016], https://www.oxfordreference.com//display/10.1093/acref/9780191826719.001.0001/q-oro-ed4-00018440).

6. For a modern summary of these traditions, see the entry "Modesty and Humility" in The Stanford Encyclopedia of Philosophy (Bommarito 2018). For the quote from Marcus Aurelius, see Meditations, book 4, passage 18.

7. Another modern comedian cum philosopher puts it this way: "Disposition is more important than position. . . . How you are in the world is much more important than how the world is" (Jimmy Carr in a conversation with Stuart Goldsmith at the Savoy Theater, London, October 2021, viewable at https://www.youtube.com/watch?v=TTFRMAcaxIM&t=414s).

8. Botton 2020, 1.

9. The Business & Human Rights Centre maintains a website documenting the history of this case at https://www.business-humanrights.org/en/latest-news/texacochevron-lawsuits-re-ecuador-1/.

10. The original verdict was reduced from $18 billion to $9 billion by Ecuador's highest court (Romero and Kraus 2011).
11. *Chevron Corp. v. Donziger*, 833 F. 3d 74, 80 (2d Cir. 2016).
12. The disqualification of an earlier judge on corruption grounds in the Ecuadorian case is detailed in Barrett 2014, chaps. 15–18. Paul Barrett describes the Ecuadorian case as a "kidney-punching, shin-kicking contest" (199).
13. *Chevron Corp. v. Donziger*, 833 F.3d 74 (2d Cir. 2016), cert. denied, 137 S. Ct. 2268 (2017). See also *Chevron Corp. v. Donziger* (2d. Cir. 2021) (denying various other challenges raised by Donziger to the particulars of the District Court's judgment).
14. For Donziger, see, e.g., Brockovich 2022. Against Donziger, see, e.g., Porter 2022.
15. "Little Consensus on Global Warming," Pew Research Center, July 12, 2006, https://www.pewresearch.org/politics/2006/07/12/little-consensus-on-global-warming/.
16. The RealClimate.org website contains thorough rebuttals to all of the various (and mostly specious) arguments attacking the climate consensus. These attacks continued for many years. The controversies they spawned are succinctly but comprehensively described in "Michael Mann," Wikipedia, https://en.wikipedia.org/wiki/Michael_E._Mann.
17. On estimates of the social cost of carbon, see Tol 2005. On the projections of net benefits from climate change, see T. Moore 1996; Herring 2020; and "Carbon Dioxide Benefits the World: See for Yourself," CO2 Coalition, n.d., https://www.commerce.senate.gov/services/files/FC7C4946-11A3-4967-BF28-8D0386608D3E.
18. Burger et al. 2019.
19. "Global Warming's Six Americas," *Yale Program on Climate Change Communication* (blog), August 16, 2023, https://climatecommunication.yale.edu/about/projects/global-warmings-six-americas/; "Beyond Red vs. Blue: The Political Typology," Pew Research Center, November 9, 2021, emphasis added, https://www.pewresearch.org/politics/2021/11/09/beyond-red-vs-blue-the-political-typology-2/.
20. Voelkel et al. 2022.
21. Mutz 2006, 145–50, quote on 150.
22. Appiah 2007, 6.
23. "What Is Active Listening?," United States Institute of Peace, n.d., https://www.usip.org/public-education-new/what-active-listening. See also P. Cohen 2023.
24. Kalla and Broockman 2018.
25. These findings were made in connection with political campaigns that aimed to reduce transphobic attitudes and negative attitudes toward undocumented immigrants. See Broockman and Kalla 2016; Kalla and Broockman 2020.
26. Hayhoe 2021, 31.
27. Hayhoe 2021, 10.
28. Hayhoe 2021, 25, 29, 229. Warming stripes are colored horizontal bands depicting annual temperature changes over time at different locations on a map.
29. Hayhoe 2021, 11.
30. Van Boven, Ehret, and Sherman 2018.
31. Gillis et al. 2021.
32. Voelkel et al. 2022. See also Levendusky 2018 (suggesting that focusing on common national identity can reduce affective partisanship).
33. American Communities Project, https://www.americancommunities.org.
34. Millions of Conversations, https://millionsofconversations.com/.

35. See, e.g., Israel 2020.
36. Kubin et al. 2021.
37. See the website One Small Step, StoryCorps, https://storycorps.org/discover/onesmallstep/.
38. Project Home Fire, https://www.ProjectHomeFire.com.
39. Center for Rural Affairs, https://www.cfra.org/, emphasis added.
40. "About the Rural Climate Dialogues," Institute for Agriculture and Trade Policy, n.d., https://www.iatp.org/about-rural-climate-dialogues, emphasis added.
41. Rural Reconciliation Project, https://www.ruralreconcile.org; "Land & Water: Rural Resources, Rural Lives," Rural Reconciliation Project, n.d., https://www.ruralreconcile.org/programs/landwater.
42. "About," Good Steward Consulting, n.d., https://www.goodstewardconsulting.com/about; Hopman and Ennis 2022.
43. Solar United Neighbors of Virginia has worked with member-owners of the Shenandoah Valley Electric Cooperative to help them push for expanded solar options and is working with member-owners of the Rappahannock Electric Cooperative to support a campaign called Repower REC to bring democracy and transparency back to their cooperative; see "Rural Electric Cooperatives," Solar United Neighbors, September 18, 2017, https://www.solarunitedneighbors.org/learn-the-issues/rural-electric-cooperatives/. See also "Electric Co-Op Facts & Figures," NRECA, April 13, 2023, https://www.electric.coop/electric-cooperative-fact-sheet.
44. See appendix F at https://www.ClimateOfContempt.com/Appendices/.
45. McGraw 2015, 23–24.
46. This conversation occurred on Stewart's program *The Problem, with Jon Stewart* in the episode "The Inflation Blame Game" on March 17, 2023. The clip can be found on the program's YouTube channel at https://youtu.be/tU3rGFyN5uQ.
47. See the *New York Times* editorial board's opposition to Summers's candidacy to lead the Federal Reserve in 2013, charging Summers with "indifference to the effect of economic decisions on ordinary people" ("The Federal Reserve Nomination," *New York Times*, September 6, 2013, https://www.nytimes.com/2013/09/06/opinion/the-federal-reserve-nomination.html).
48. This sort of mediation is common on YouTube and other platforms, particularly among the devoted followers of prominent, rhetorically combative champions of a political ideology.
49. See "Jon Stewart SHREDS Dishonest Moron's Inflation Lies," *The Majority Report with Sam Seder*, March 17, 2023, https://www.youtube.com/watch?v=MV7d6PaXkcM&t=349s. At the time of this broadcast, the *Majority Report* YouTube channel had more than 1.2 million subscribers and is distributed as a podcast on various other platforms. The show was briefly broadcast over NBC's Peacock streaming service in 2020 and 2021 and has won five People's Choice Podcast Awards, according to *"The Majority Report with Sam Seder,"* Wikipedia, https://en.wikipedia.org/wiki/The_Majority_Report_with_Sam_Seder.
50. For example, see "The Fun Part," *Pod Save America* (podcast), September 30, 2021, https://crooked.com/podcast/the-fun-part/ (e.g., "Not a single Republican wants to help a single person," and "Sinema . . . what the fuck is she doing?").
51. *"Offline with Jon Favreau,"* Apple Podcasts Preview, n.d., https://podcasts.apple.com/us/podcast/offline-with-jon-favreau/id1610392666.
52. On Twitter, Roberts periodically brings the full force of his gift for language to expressions of contempt for Republicans, conservatives, industry, moderate Democrats, and others. On Joe Manchin: "Asshole" (multiple tweets by Roberts

in 2022 and 2023). On Democrats worried about the debt ceiling fight: "Every single Democrat quoted in this piece needs to immediately go fuck themselves. Losers, committed to losing" (David Roberts [@drvolts], tweet, Twitter/X, April 21, 2023, https://x.com/drvolts/status/1649517098941693953?s=20). A few days after the 2020 presidential election: "Fuck healing. Fuck moving on" (David Roberts [@drvolts], tweet, November 6, 2020, https://x.com/drvolts/status /1324821501430755330?s=20).

53. B. Shapiro 2019.

54. Shapiro's calls for "reason and civility" may ring hollow to viewers who watched him once defend his position in a heated debate by saying that "I will comfort myself tonight by sleeping on my bed made of money" (from a debate between Shapiro and Malcolm Nance on HBO's *Real Time with Bill Maher* in 2021).

55. As for the disparity between listener numbers for Jon Favreau's two podcasts, it is difficult to know how much of it is due to the relatively snarkier tone of *Pod Save America* versus the fact that *Offline* is much newer.

56. Quoted in "Alfred Sloan," *The Economist*, January 31, 2008, https://www .economist.com/europe/2008/01/31/whataboutism.

57. Hasen 2023.

58. J. Michael Luttig (@judgeluttig), tweet, Twitter/X, August 2, 2023, https://x.com /judgeluttig/status/1686733788133617664?s=20; Bravender and Cama 2023.

59. Darcy 2023; Charlie Kirk (@charliekirk11), tweet, August 1, 2023, https://x.com /charliekirk11/status/1686889467729305600?s=20. Charlie Kirk had 2.4 million Twitter followers at the time of his quoted tweet. The podcaster Joe Rogan agreed, saying that the case makes the United States look like a banana republic. *The Rubin Report* podcast included speculation that the Biden administration would suspend the 2024 presidential elections in order to cover up its own criminality. Rogan reaches an estimated 11 million listeners per episode, and the Rubin podcast has about 2 million subscribers. Laura Ingraham's Fox News evening show echoed the Charlie Kirk vow of retribution and at the time had about 1.7 million viewers.

60. Leonhardt 2023, emphasis added.

61. According to the *Cook Political Report*, in 2022 the median Senate seat had a PVI of R + 3, and the median House seat had a PVI of R + 1. By *Cook*'s measures, the number of swing seats (PVI between R + 5 and D + 5) is the lowest since 1994, and the number of "hypercompetitive" seats (PVI between R + 3 and D + 3) the lowest ever (Wasserman 2022).

62. "GOP Presidential Candidates Face Popularity Drop for Criticizing Trump: Quinnipiac Poll," *Esquire*, August 28, 2023, https://www.todaysesquire.com/gop -presidential-candidates-face-popularity-drop-for-criticizing-trump-quinnipia c-poll/, shows that GOP presidential candidates who criticize Trump lose support. The conservative writer Niall Ferguson made this point in 2023 about the issues on which GOP voters meted out punishments and rewards when he said, "Soon I expect the internal combustion engine to join the gun and the Bible as a physical expression of American conservatism" (Niall Ferguson [@ nfergus], tweet, Twitter/X June 4, 2023, https://x.com/nfergus/status/1665364 543889981440?s=20).

63. "The Cases Against Donald Trump Are Piling Up," *The Economist*, March 23, 2023, emphasis added, https://www.economist.com/united-states/2023/03/23/the -cases-against-donald-trump-are-piling-up.

64. Chun and Balasaygun 2023; see also "The Potential Economic Impacts of Various Debt Ceiling Scenarios," White House, May 3, 2023, https://www.whitehouse

.gov/cea/written-materials/2023/05/03/debt-ceiling-scenarios/. After the first fight in Congress over the debt-ceiling extension in 2023, the credit-rating agency Fitch downgraded the U.S. government's credit rating from AAA to AA+, citing "fiscal deterioration over the next three years and repeated down-the-wire debt ceiling negotiations that threaten the government's ability to pay its bills" (Barbuscia 2023).

65. Bannon posted this statement on the social media app GETTR on June 1, 2023.
66. Steele 2022 ("the percentage of college students who believe the political and social climate on their campus prevents people from freely expressing themselves rose from 54.7 percent in 2019 to 63.5 percent in 2021").
67. Popova 2015.
68. Snyder 2017, 13. On populism and authoritarianism, see Buhlman-Pozen and Seifter 2022, summarizing the various state legislative initiatives designed to subvert democratic election outcomes.
69. Snyder 2017, 12, 83.
70. Levitsky and Ziblatt 2019, 208, 217–18.
71. Krastev and Holmes 2020, 205, emphasis added.
72. See Fishkin and Forbath 2022.
73. Applebaum 2020, 186–87.
74. Alpert 2023.
75. Wallace-Wells 2022a.
76. For example, we continue to permit discharges of pollution into waterways despite the Clean Water Act's stated goal of eliminating such discharges by 1985 (33 U.S.C. §1251(a)(1) (1987)).
77. "Fact-Checking Trump's CNN Town Hall in New Hampshire," CNN, May 11, 2023, https://www.cnn.com/2023/05/10/politics/fact-check-donald-trump-town-hall/index.html.
78. "Anderson Cooper 360 Degrees," CNN, May 11, 2023, https://transcripts.cnn.com/show/acd/date/2023-05-11/segment/01.
79. Bastiat 1964.
80. "Anderson Cooper 360 Degrees," May 11, 2023.

REFERENCES

Abramowitz, Alan I., Brad Alexander, and Matthew Gunning. 2006. "Incumbency, Redistricting, and the Decline of Competition in U.S. House Elections." *Journal of Politics* 68 (1): 75–88. https://doi.org/10.1111/j.1468-2508.2006.00371.x.

Adams, Henry. 1907. *The Education of Henry Adams.* Boston: Houghton Mifflin.

Adelman, David E. 2023. "Permitting Reform's False Choice." SSRN Scholarly Paper. https://doi.org/10.2139/ssrn.4540734.

Adelman, David E., and David B. Spence. 2017. "Ideology vs. Interest Group Politics in U.S. Energy Policy." *North Carolina Law Review* 95 (2): 339–411.

Adler, Jonathan H. 2022a. "A 'Step Zero' for Delegations." In *The Administrative State Before the Supreme Court: Perspectives on the Nondelegation Doctrine*, edited by Peter J. Wallison and John Yoo, 161–94. Washington, DC: American Enterprise Institute.

——. 2022b. "West Virginia v. EPA: Some Answers About Major Questions." In *Cato Supreme Court Review, 2021–2022*, 37–67. Washington, DC: Cato Institute.

Adler, Jonathan H., and Christopher J. Walker. 2020. "Delegation and Time." *Iowa Law Review* 105 (5): 1931–93.

Agiesta, Jennifer, and Ariel Edwards-Levy. 2021. "CNN Poll: Most Americans Feel Democracy Is Under Attack in the US." CNN, September 15. https://www.cnn.com/2021/09/15/politics/cnn-poll-most-americans-democracy-under-attack/index.html.

Ahmed, Wasim, Josep Vidal-Alaball, Joseph Downing, and Francesc López Seguí. 2020. "COVID-19 and the 5G Conspiracy Theory: Social Network Analysis of Twitter Data." *Journal of Medical Internet Research* 22 (5): 1–9. https://doi.org/10.2196/19458.

Aidun, Hillary, Jacob Elkin, Radhika Goyal, Kate Marsh, Neely McKee, Maris Welch, Leah Adelman, et al. 2022. "Opposition to Renewable Energy Facilities in the United States: March 2022 Edition." Sabin Center for Climate Change Law, Columbia School of Law. https://scholarship.law.columbia.edu/sabin_climate_change/186.

Albert, Richard. 2021. "America's Amoral Constitution." *American University Law Review* 70 (3): 773–827.

Albright, Jonathan. 2018. "Untrue-Tube: Monetizing Misery and Disinformation." *Medium* (blog), March 2. https://d1gi.medium.com/untrue-tube-monetizing-misery-and-disinformation-388c4786cc3d.

Aldrich, John H. 2000. "Presidential Address: Southern Parties in State and Nation." *Journal of Politics* 62 (3): 643–70.

——. 2011. *Why Parties? A Second Look*. Chicago: University of Chicago Press.

Aldy, Joseph E. 2011. "A Preliminary Review of the American Recovery and Reinvestment Act's Clean Energy Package." IDEAS Working Paper Series from RePEc. https://search.proquest.com/docview/1698260160.

Alinsky, Saul. 1971. *Rules for Radicals: A Pragmatic Primer for Realistic Radicals*. New York: Random House.

Alpert, Alice. 2023. "5 Hopeful Takeaways from the Latest International Climate Report." *Environmental Defense Fund* (blog), March 20. https://www.edf.org/article/5-hopeful-takeaways-latest-international-climate-report.

Andris, Clio, David Lee, Marcus J. Hamilton, Mauro Martino, Christian E. Gunning, and John Armistead Selden. 2015. "The Rise of Partisanship and Super-cooperators in the U.S. House of Representatives." *PLOS One* 10 (4): art. e0123507. https://doi.org/10.1371/journal.pone.0123507.

Ansolabehere, Stephen, John M. de Figueiredo, and James M. Snyder Jr. 2003. "Why Is There so Little Money in U.S. Politics?" *Journal of Economic Perspectives* 17 (1): 105–30. https://doi.org/10.1257/089533003321164976.

Appiah, Kwame. 2007. *Cosmopolitanism: Ethics in a World of Strangers*. New York: Norton.

Applebaum, Anne. 2020. *Twilight of Democracy: The Seductive Lure of Authoritarianism*. New York: Doubleday.

Arbaje, Paul. 2023. "Storm Elliott Knocked Out Fossil-Fuel Power. We've Been Here Before." *The Equation* (blog), January 24. https://blog.ucsusa.org/paul-arbaje/storm-elliott-knocked-out-fossil-fuel-power-weve-been-here-before/.

Arendt, Hannah. 1968. *Between Past and Future: Eight Exercises in Political Thought*. New York: Viking.

Arieli, Sharon, Adi Amit, and Sari Mentser. 2019. "Identity-Motivated Reasoning: Biased Judgments Regarding Political Leaders." *Cognition* 188:64–73. https://doi.org/10.1016/j.cognition.2018.12.009.

Ariza, Mario. 2023. "Ohio Republicans Accused of Taking $60m in Bribes as Corruption Trial Opens." *The Guardian*, January 24. https://www.theguardian.com/us-news/2023/jan/23/ohio-republican-larry-householder-corruption-trial.

Arkush, David, and Donald Braman. 2024. "Climate Homicide: Prosecuting Big Oil for Climate Deaths." *Harvard Environmental Law Review* 48 (1). https://doi.org/10.2139/ssrn.4335779.

Arnold, R. Douglas. 1990. *The Logic of Congressional Action*. New Haven, CT: Yale University Press.

Aronoff, Kate. 2019. "It's Time to Try Fossil-Fuel Executives for Crimes Against Humanity." *Jacobin*, February 5. https://jacobin.com/2019/02/fossil-fuels-climate-change-crimes-against-humanity.

——. 2021. *Overheated: How Capitalism Broke the Planet—and How We Fight Back*. New York: Bold Type.

——. 2022a. "The Bitter Triumph of the Inflation Reduction Act." *New Republic*, August 8. https://newrepublic.com/article/167337/bitter-triumph-inflation-reduction-act.

——. 2022b. "Why Your Utility Company Sucks." *New Republic*, May 19. https://newrepublic.com/article/166541/utility-company-energy-transition.

Aronoff, Kate, Alyssa Battistoni, Daniel Aldana Cohen, and Thea Riofrancos. 2019. *A Planet to Win: Why We Need a Green New Deal*. New York: Verso.

Aronoff, Kate, Peter Dreier, and Michael Kazin. 2020. Introduction to *We Own the Future: Democratic Socialism—American Style*, edited by Kate Aronoff, Peter Dreier, and Michael Kazin, 5–14. New York: New Press.

Arrow, Kenneth J. 1951. *Social Choice and Individual Values*. New Haven, CT: Yale University Press.

Asch, Solomon E. 1951. "Effects of Group Pressure Upon the Modification and Distortion of Judgments." In *Groups, Leadership, and Men: Research in Human Relations*, edited by Harold Steere Guetzkow, 177–90. Pittsburgh: Carnegie Mellon University Press.

Atleework, Kendra. 2018. "Power Lines Are Burning the West." *The Atlantic*, May 25. https://www.theatlantic.com/technology/archive/2018/05/power-lines-are-burning-the-west/561212/.

Attkisson, Sharyl. 2014. *Stonewalled: My Fight for Truth Against the Forces of Obstruction, Intimidation, and Harassment in Obama's Washington*. Reprint ed. New York: Harper Paperbacks.

Averch, Harvey, and Leland L. Johnson. 1962. "Behavior of the Firm Under Regulatory Constraint." *American Economic Review* 52 (5): 1052–69.

Axelrod, Robert M. 1984. *The Evolution of Cooperation*. New York: Basic.

Bade, Rachael, and Erica Werner. 2020. "Centrist House Democrats Lash Out at Liberal Colleagues, Blame Far-Left Views for Costing the Party Seats." *Washington Post*, November 6. https://www.washingtonpost.com/politics/house-democrats-pelosi-election/2020/11/05/1ddae5ca-1f6e-11eb-90dd-abd0f7086a91_story.html.

Bagri, Neha Thirani. 2017. "The US Is Relocating an Entire Town Because of Climate Change. And This Is Just the Beginning." *Quartz*, June 5. https://qz.com/994459/the-us-is-relocating-an-entire-town-because-of-climate-change-and-this-is-just-the-beginning.

Bail, Christopher. 2021. *Breaking the Social Media Prism: How to Make Our Platforms Less Polarizing*. Princeton, NJ: Princeton University Press.

Baker, Peter, and Clifford Krauss. 2022. "Biden Accuses Oil Companies of 'War Profiteering' and Threatens Windfall Tax." *New York Times*, October 31. https://www.nytimes.com/2022/10/31/us/politics/biden-oil-windfall-tax.html.

Balla, Steven J. 1998. "Administrative Procedures and Political Control of the Bureaucracy." *American Political Science Review* 92 (3): 663–73. https://doi.org/10.2307/2585488.

Barasz, Kate, Tami Kim, and Ioannis Evangelidis. 2019. "I Know Why You Voted for Trump: (Over)Inferring Motives Based on Choice." *Cognition* 188:85–97. https://doi.org/10.1016/j.cognition.2018.05.004.

Barber, Gregory. 2023. "Big Batteries Are Booming. So Are Fears They'll Catch Fire." *Wired*, September 8. https://www.wired.com/story/big-grid-batteries-are-booming-so-are-fears-fire/.

Barber, Michael J., and Nolan McCarty. 2015. "Causes and Consequences of Polarization." In *Solutions to Polarization in America*, edited by Nathaniel Persily, 15–58. Cambridge: Cambridge University Press.

Barbuscia, Davide. 2023. "Fitch Cuts U.S. Credit Rating to AA+; Treasury Calls It 'Arbitrary.'" Reuters, August 2. https://www.reuters.com/markets/us/fitch-cuts-us-governments-aaa-credit-rating-by-one-notch-2023-08-01/.

Barker, David C. 2002. *Rushed to Judgment: Talk Radio, Persuasion, and American Political Behavior* New York: Columbia University Press.

Barnett, Kent, and Christopher Walker. 2017. "Short-Circuiting the New Major Questions Doctrine." *Scholarly Works* 70 (January): 147–63.

Baron, Jonathan. 2008. *Thinking and Deciding*. 4th ed. Cambridge: Cambridge University Press.

——. 2019. "Actively Open-Minded Thinking in Politics." *Cognition* 188:8–18. https://doi.org/10.1016/j.cognition.2018.10.004.

Barrett, Paul M. 2014. *Law of the Jungle: The $19 Billion Legal Battle Over Oil in the Rain Forest and the Lawyer Who'd Stop at Nothing to Win*. New York: Crown.

Barrett, Paul M., Justin Hendrix, and J. Grant Sims. 2021. "Fueling the Fire: How Social Media Intensifies U.S. Political Polarization—and What Can Be Done About It." New York University Stern Center for Business and Human Rights. https://static1.squarespace.com/static/5b6df958f8370af3217d4178/t/613a4d4cc86b9d3810eb35aa/1631210832122/NYU+CBHR+Fueling+The+Fire_FINAL+ONLINE+REVISED+Sep7.pdf.

Barringer, Felicity. 2021. "What It May Take to Harness Solar Energy on Native Lands." *Stanford Earth Matters Magazine*, May 6. https://earth.stanford.edu/news/what-it-may-take-harness-solar-energy-native-lands.

Barron-Lopez, Laura, and Tess Conciatori. 2022. "How Some Members of the Republican Party Have Normalized the Use of Violent Rhetoric." *NewsHour*, PBS, July 18. https://www.pbs.org/newshour/show/how-some-members-of-the-republican-party-have-normalized-the-use-of-violent-rhetoric.

Bartels, Larry M. 2020. "Ethnic Antagonism Erodes Republicans' Commitment to Democracy." *Proceedings of the National Academy of Sciences* 117 (37): 22752–59. https://doi.org/10.1073/pnas.2007747117.

Basiouny, Angie. 2022. "Texas Fought Against ESG. Here's What It Cost." *Knowledge at Wharton* (blog), July 12. https://knowledge.wharton.upenn.edu/podcast/knowledge-at-wharton-podcast/texas-fought-against-esg-heres-what-it-cost/.

Bastiat, Frédéric. 1964. *Economic Harmonies* (1850). Edited by George B. De Huszar. Translated by W. Hayden Boyers. New York: Foundation for Economic Education.

Basu, Shumita. 2017. "The History of Blaming 'Both Sides' and Why Language Matters." WNYC, August 16. https://www.wnyc.org/story/history-blaming-both-sides-language-charlottesville-trump/.

Battistoni, Alyssa, and Jedediah Britton-Purdy. 2020. "After Carbon Democracy." *Dissent Magazine* (blog), Winter. https://www.dissentmagazine.org/article/after-carbon-democracy/.

Bauder, David. 2004. "Young Get News from Comedy Central." CBS News, March 1. https://www.cbsnews.com/news/young-get-news-from-comedy-central/.

Baumgartner, Frank R., Jeffrey M. Berry, Marie Hojnacki, Beth L. Leech, and David C. Kimball. 2009. *Lobbying and Policy Change: Who Wins, Who Loses, and Why*. Chicago: University of Chicago Press.

Baumol, William J., and Wallace E. Oates. 1988. *The Theory of Environmental Policy*. 2nd ed. Cambridge: Cambridge University Press.

Bayer, Patrick, and Michaël Aklin. 2020. "The European Union Emissions Trading System Reduced CO_2 Emissions Despite Low Prices." *Proceedings of the National Academy of Sciences* 117 (16): 8804–12. https://doi.org/10.1073/pnas.1918128117.

Bazail-Eimil, Eric, and Matt Berg. 2023. "Justice Samuel Alito Faces Scrutiny Over Trips with GOP Donor, Pens Defensive Op-Ed." *Politico*, June 21. https://www.politico.com/news/2023/06/21/alito-singer-propublica-oped-00102874.

Bazerman, Max H. 2022. *Complicit: How We Enable the Unethical and How to Stop.* Princeton, NJ: Princeton University Press.

Bazerman, Max H., and Ann E. Tenbrunsel. 2011. *Blind Spots: Why We Fail to Do What's Right and What to Do About It.* Princeton, NJ: Princeton University Press.

Beard, Charles A. 1913. *An Economic Interpretation of the Constitution of the United States.* New York: Macmillan.

Beck, Glenn, David Boaz, L. Brent Bozell III, Mona Charen, Ben Domenech, Erick Erickson, Steven F. Hayward, et al. 2016. "Conservatives Against Trump." *National Review* (blog), January 21. https://www.nationalreview.com/2016/01/donald-trump-conservatives-oppose-nomination/.

Becker, Carl Lotus. [1909] 2009. *The History of Political Parties in the Province of New York, 1760–1776.* Reprint. Ithaca, NY: Cornell University Library.

Behr, Peter. 2022. "How a Smarter Grid Can Prevent Blackouts." *E&E News*, March 16. https://www.eenews.net/articles/how-a-smarter-grid-can-prevent-blackouts/.

Bellantuono, Giuseppe. 2014. "The Regulatory Anticommons of Green Infrastructures." *European Journal of Law and Economics* 37 (2): 325–54. https://doi.org/10.1007/s10657-012-9298-3.

Belsky, Gary, and Thomas Gilovich. 1999. *Why Smart People Make Big Money Mistakes—and How to Correct Them: Lessons from the New Science of Behavioral Economics.* New York: Simon & Schuster.

Benkler, Yochai, Robert Faris, and Hal Roberts. 2018, *Network Propaganda: Manipulation, Disinformation, and Radicalization in American Politics.* New York: Oxford University Press.

Bennon, Michael, and Devon Wilson. 2023. "NEPA Litigation Over Large Energy and Transport Infrastructure Projects." *Environmental Law Reporter* 53:10836–59.

Berardelli, Jeff. 2019. "How Climate Change Is Making Hurricanes More Dangerous." Yale Climate Connections, July 9. http://yaleclimateconnections.org/2019/07/how-climate-change-is-making-hurricanes-more-dangerous/.

Bergengruen, Vera. 2022. "The United States of Political Violence." *Time*, November 4. https://time.com/6227754/political-violence-us-states-midterms-2022/.

Bernstein, Jesse. 2016. "How Jon Stewart's Culture of Ridicule Left America Unprepared for Donald Trump." *Tablet Magazine*, August 9. https://www.tabletmag.com/sections/news/articles/how-jon-stewarts-culture-of-ridicule-left-america-unprepared-for-donald-trump.

Beyerstein, Lindsay. 2020. "What Happened to Jordan Peterson?" *New Republic*, March 10. https://newrepublic.com/article/156829/happened-jordan-peterson.

Bianco, William T. 1994. *Trust: Representatives and Constituents.* Ann Arbor: University of Michigan Press.

Biber, Eric. 2017. "Law in the Anthropocene Epoch." *Georgetown Law Journal* 106 (1): 1–68.

Binder, Sarah A. 2003. *Stalemate: Causes and Consequences of Legislative Gridlock.* Washington, DC: Brookings Institution Press.

Bishop, Bill. 2009. *The Big Sort: Why the Clustering of Like-Minded America Is Tearing Us Apart.* Boston: Mariner.

Bistline, John, Neil R. Mehrotra, and Catherine Wolfram. 2023. "Economic Implications of the Climate Provisions of the Inflation Reduction Act." Brookings Papers of Economic Activity, March. https://www.brookings.edu/wp-content/uploads/2023/03/BPEA_Spring2023_Bistline-et-al_unembargoedUpdated.pdf.

Blackburn, Simon. 2001. *Being Good: A Short Introduction to Ethics.* Oxford: Oxford University Press.

Blake, Aaron. 2018. "Nikki Haley Warns Against 'Owning the Libs.' That's Basically Trump's Entire Political Strategy." *Washington Post*, July 24.

Bleau, Hannah. 2020. "Poll: 47% of Americans Say Dems 'Likely' Stole Votes or Destroyed Trump Ballots." *Breitbart*, December 8. https://www.breitbart.com/2020 -election/2020/12/08/poll-47-americans-believe-it-is-likely-democrats-stole-votes -destroyed-trump-ballots/.

Blumm, Michael C., and Zach Schwartz. 2021. "The Public Trust Doctrine Fifty Years After *Sax* and Some Thoughts on Its Future." *Public Land & Resources Law Review* 44 (June): 1–48. https://doi.org/10.2139/ssrn.3567536.

Blunt, Katherine. 2022. *California Burning: The Fall of Pacific Gas and Electric—and What It Means for America's Power Grid*. New York: Portfolio/Penguin.

Blunt, Katherine, Dan Frosch, and Jim Carlton. 2023. "Hawaiian Electric Knew Wild-fires in Maui Were a Growing Risk, but Waited Years to Act." *Wall Street Journal*, August 17. https://www.wsj.com/us-news/wildfire-risk-maui-hawaiian-electric -7beed21e.

Boarnet, Marlon Gary, and Randall Crane. 2001. *Travel by Design: The Influence of Urban Form on Travel*. Oxford: Oxford University Press.

Boehmke, Frederick J., Sean Gailmard, and John W. Patty. 2013. "Business as Usual: Interest Group Access and Representation Across Policy-Making Venues." *Journal of Public Policy* 33 (1): 3–33. https://doi.org/10.1017/S0143814X12000207.

Bokat-Lindell, Spencer. 2022. "Is Liberal Democracy Dying?" *New York Times*, September 28. https://www.nytimes.com/2022/09/28/opinion/italy-meloni-democracy-au thoritarianism.html.

Bolson, Natanael, Pedro Prieto, and Tadeusz Patzek. 2022. "Capacity Factors for Elec-trical Power Generation from Renewable and Nonrenewable Sources." *Proceed-ings of the National Academy of Sciences* 119 (52): 1–6. https://doi.org/10.1073/pnas .2205429119.

Bommarito, Nicolas. 2018. "Modesty and Humility." In *The Stanford Encyclopedia of Philosophy*, edited by Edward N. Zalta, Winter ed. Stanford, CA: Stanford Univer-sity. https://plato.stanford.edu/entries/modesty-humility/.

Bond, Jon R., Richard Fleisher, and Jeffrey E. Cohen. 2015. "Presidential–Congressional Relations in an Era of Polarized Parties and a 60-Vote Senate." In *American Gridlock: The Sources, Character, and Impact of Political Polarization*, edited by James A. Thurber and Antoine Yoshinaka, 133–51. Cambridge: Cam-bridge University Press.

Bond, Shannon. 2021. "Just 12 People Are Behind Most Vaccine Hoaxes on Social Media, Research Shows." NPR, May 14. https://www.npr.org/2021/05/13/996570855 /disinformation-dozen-test-facebooks-twitters-ability-to-curb-vaccine-hoaxes.

Bonhoeffer, Dietrich. 2010. "On Stupidity." In *Letters and Papers from Prison*, edited by John W. de Gruchy, translated by Isabel Best, Lisa E. Dahill, Reinhard Krauss, and Nancy Lukens, vol. 8 of *Dietrich Bonhoeffer Works*, 37–54. Minneapolis: For-tress Press.

Boorman, Erie D., John P. O'Doherty, Ralph Adolphs, and Antonio Rangel. 2013. "The Behavioral and Neural Mechanisms Underlying the Tracking of Expertise." *Neu-ron* 80 (6): 1558–71. https://doi.org/10.1016/j.neuron.2013.10.024.

Borenstein, Severin, and James Bushnell. 2015. *The U.S. Electricity Industry After 20 Years of Restructuring*. National Bureau of Economic Research (NBER) Work-ing Paper no. W21113. Cambridge, MA: NBER.

Bork, Robert H. 1978. *The Antitrust Paradox: A Policy at War with Itself*. New York: Basic.

Botton, Alain de. 2020. *The School of Life: An Emotional Education*. London: School of Life.

Bouie, Jamelle. 2023. "The Republican Embrace of Vigilantism Is No Accident." *New York Times*, May 16. https://www.nytimes.com/2023/05/16/opinion/neely-penny-perry-rittenhouse-desantis.html.

Bower, Tom. 2009. *Oil: Money, Politics, and Power in the 21st Century*. New York: Grand Central.

Boyd, William. 2014. "Public Utility and the Low-Carbon Future." *UCLA Law Review* 61 (6): 1614–710.

——. 2020. "Ways of Price Making and the Challenge of Market Governance in U.S. Energy Law." *Minnesota Law Review* 105 (2): 739–830.

——. 2022. "Energy Price Shocks and the Failures of Neoliberalism." *Law & Political Economy Project* (blog), December 1. https://lpeproject.org/blog/energy-price-shocks-and-the-failures-of-neoliberalism/.

Boyer, Peter J. 2019. "Donald Trump Changed 'The New York Times.' Is It Forever?" *Esquire*, March 19. https://www.esquire.com/news-politics/a26454551/donald-trump-interview-new-york-times-media-objectivity/.

Bradley, Robert L., Jr. 2008. *Capitalism at Work: Business, Government, and Energy*. Salem, MA: M&M Scrivener Press.

Brand, David, and Bahar Ostadan. 2023. "Energy Company's Plan to Place 150-Ton Batteries on Williamsburg Rooftop Ignites Tenants' Fears." *Gothamist*, August 15. https://www.gothamist.com/news/energy-companys-plan-to-place-%20150-ton-batteries-on-williamsburg-rooftop-ignites-tenants-fears.

Branham, J. Alexander, Stuart N. Soroka, and Christopher Wlezien. 2017. "When Do the Rich Win?" *Political Science Quarterly* 132 (1): 43–62. https://doi.org/10.1002/polq.12577.

Bravender, Robin, and Timothy Cama. 2023. "Legal Expert: Trump Indictment 'Bad News' for Jeff Clark." *E&E News*, August 2. https://www.eenews.net/articles/legal-expert-trump-indictment-bad-news-for-jeff-clark/.

Breakstone, Joel, Mark Smith, Sam Wineburg, Amie Rapaport, Jill Carle, Marshall Garland, and Anna Saavedra. 2021. "Students' Civic Online Reasoning: A National Portrait." *Educational Researcher* 50 (8): 505–15. https://doi.org/10.3102/0013189X211017495.

Breed, Ellie. 2023. "Public Utility Commission of Texas Unanimously Adopts Performance Credit Mechanism Reliability Service." Public Utility Commission of Texas. https://www.puc.texas.gov/agency/resources/pubs/news/2023/puct_adopts_performance_credit_mechanism_reliability_service.pdf.

Breetz, Hanna, Matto Mildenberger, and Leah Stokes. 2018. "The Political Logics of Clean Energy Transitions." *Business and Politics* 20 (4): 492–522. https://doi.org/10.1017/bap.2018.14.

Breslow, Jason M. 2012. "Bob Inglis: Climate Change and the Republican Party." *Frontline*, interview, PBS, October 23.

Bresnahan, John. 2019. "Alexandria Ocasio-Cortez's Chief of Staff, Spokesman Leave Her Office." *Politico*, August 2. https://www.politico.com/story/2019/08/02/aoc-staff-saikat-chakrabarti-climate-1445478.

Breyer, Stephen. 1979. "Analyzing Regulatory Failure: Mismatches, Less Restrictive Alternatives, and Reform." *Harvard Law Review* 92 (3): 547–609. https://doi.org/10.2307/1340395.

Brinkman, Gregory, Joshua Novacheck, Aaron Bloom, and James McCalley. 2020. "Interconnections Seam Study." National Renewable Energy Laboratory, October.

Brittenden, Miriam. 2021. "Renewing American Democracy? We Need More, Not Less, Populism." *LSE Blog*, January 22. https://blogs.lse.ac.uk/religionglobalsociety/2021/01/renewing-american-democracy-we-need-more-not-less-populism/.

Brockovich, Erin. 2022. "This Lawyer Should Be World-Famous for His Battle with Chevron—but He's in Jail." *The Guardian*, February 8. https://www.theguardian.com/commentisfree/2022/feb/08/chevron-amazon-ecuador-steven-donziger-erin-brockovich.

Broockman, David, and Joshua Kalla. 2016. "Durably Reducing Transphobia: A Field Experiment on Door-to-Door Canvassing." *Science* 352 (6282): 220–24. https://doi.org/10.1126/science.aad9713.

——. 2022. "Consuming Cross-Cutting Media Causes Learning and Moderates Attitudes: A Field Experiment with Fox News Viewers." OSF Preprints. https://doi.org/10.31219/osf.io/jrw26.

Brooks, David. 2023. "What If We're the Bad Guys Here?" *New York Times*, August 2. https://www.nytimes.com/2023/08/02/opinion/trump-meritocracy-educated.html.

Brown, Ashley C., and Jim Rossi. 2010. "Siting Transmission Lines in a Changed Milieu: Evolving Notions of the 'Public Interest' in Balancing State and Regional Considerations." *University of Colorado Law Review* 81 (3): 705–70.

Brown, David S. 2006. *Richard Hofstadter: An Intellectual Biography*. Chicago: University of Chicago Press.

Brown, Dorothy A. 1996. "The Invisibility Factor: The Limits of Public Choice Theory and Public Institutions." *Washington University Law Review* 74 (1): 179–222.

Brown, Edmund G. 2018. "Residential Adaptation Policy Guidance." California Coastal Commission.

Brown, Jacob R., and Ryan D. Enos. 2021. "The Measurement of Partisan Sorting for 180 Million Voters." *Nature Human Behaviour* 5 (8): 998–1008. https://doi.org/10.1038/s41562-021-01066-z.

Brown, Marilyn A., Anmol Soni, Melissa V. Lapsa, Katie Southworth, and Matt Cox. 2020. "High Energy Burden and Low-Income Energy Affordability: Conclusions from a Literature Review." *Progress in Energy* 2 (4): 1–36. https://doi.org/10.1088/2516-1083/abb954.

Brown, Matthew H., and Richard P. Sedano. 2004. *Electricity Transmission: A Primer*. Denver, CO: National Council on Electricity Policy.

Brown, Wendy. 2023a. "Max Weber's Ethical Pedagogy for a Nihilistic Age." *Chronicle of Higher Education*, May. https://www-chronicle-com.ezproxy.lib.utexas.edu/article/max-webers-ethical-pedagogy-for-a-nihilistic-age.

——. 2023b. *Nihilistic Times: Thinking with Max Weber*. Cambridge, MA: Belknap Press of Harvard University Press.

Brownstein, Ronald. 2022. "How Manchin and Sinema Completed a Conservative Vision." *The Atlantic*, January 17. https://www.theatlantic.com/politics/archive/2022/01/manchin-sinema-filibuster-voting-rights/621271/.

Bruckmaier, Georg, Stefan Krauss, Karin Binder, Sven Hilbert, and Martin Brunner. 2021. "Tversky and Kahneman's Cognitive Illusions: Who Can Solve Them, and Why?" *Frontiers in Psychology* 12:1–25. https://doi.org/10.3389/fpsyg.2021.584689.

Brulle, Robert J., Jason Carmichael, and J. Craig Jenkins. 2012. "Shifting Public Opinion on Climate Change: An Empirical Assessment of Factors Influencing Concern Over Climate Change in the U.S., 2002–2010." *Climatic Change* 114 (2): 169–88. https://doi.org/10.1007/s10584-012-0403-y.

Bryce, Robert. 2021. "Build It and They Won't Come—an Iowa Farmer Explains Backlash Against Big Solar." *Forbes*, December 22. https://www.forbes.com/sites/robertbryce/2021/12/22/build-it-and-they-wont-come--an-iowa-farmer-explains-backlash-against-big-solar/.

Buchan, James. 2007. *Capital of the Mind: How Edinburgh Changed the World*. Edinburgh: Birlinn.

Buck, Holly Jean. 2023. "The Carbon Capture Distraction." *Dissent Magazine* (blog), July 12. https://www.dissentmagazine.org/article/the-carbon-capture-distraction/.

Buckman, Stephen T. 2011. "Upper Middle Class NIMBY in Phoenix: The Community Dynamics of the Development Process in the Arcadia Neighborhood." *Journal of Community Practice* 19 (3): 308–25. https://doi.org/10.1080/10705422.2011.595306.

Budolfson, Mark, Francis Dennig, Frank Errickson, Simon Feindt, Maddalena Ferranna, Marc Fleurbaey, David Klenert, et al. 2021. "Climate Action with Revenue Recycling Has Benefits for Poverty, Inequality, and Well-Being." *Nature Climate Change* 11 (12): 1111–16. https://doi.org/10.1038/s41558-021-01217-0.

Buhlman-Pozen, Jessica, and Heather K. Gerken. 2009. "Uncooperative Federalism." *Yale Law Journal* 118 (7): 1256–310.

Bulman-Pozen, Jessica, and Miriam Seifter. 2022. "Countering the New Election Subversion: The Democracy Principle and the Role of State Courts." *Wisconsin Law Review* 2022:1337–65. https://scholarship.law.columbia.edu/faculty_scholarship/3883.

Buis, Alan. 2020. "Study Confirms Climate Models Are Getting Future Warming Projections Right." Climate Change: Vital Signs of the Planet, NASA, January 9. https://climate.nasa.gov/news/2943/study-confirms-climate-models-are-getting-future-warming-projections-right.

——. 2022. "Too Hot to Handle: How Climate Change May Make Some Places Too Hot to Live." Climate Change: Vital Signs of the Planet, NASA, March 9. https://climate.nasa.gov/explore/ask-nasa-climate/3151/too-hot-to-handle-how-climate-change-may-make-some-places-too-hot-to-live/.

Buonomano, Dean. 2011. *Brain Bugs: How the Brain's Flaws Shape Our Lives*. New York: Norton.

Burga, Solcyre. 2023. "Where the Disney v. DeSantis Case Stands." *Time*, May 21. https://time.com/6281591/disney-desantis-timeline-case/.

Burger, Scott P., Jesse D. Jenkins, Samuel C. Huntington, and Ignacio J. Perez-Arriaga. 2019. "Why Distributed? A Critical Review of the Tradeoffs Between Centralized and Decentralized Resources." *IEEE Power and Energy Magazine* 17 (2): 16–24. https://doi.org/10.1109/MPE.2018.2885203.

Burns, Alexander, Maggie Haberman, and Jonathan Martin. 2016. "Inside the Republican Party's Desperate Mission to Stop Donald Trump." *New York Times*, February 27. https://www.nytimes.com/2016/02/28/us/politics/donald-trump-republican-party.html.

Burstein, Paul. 2003. "The Impact of Public Opinion on Public Policy: A Review and an Agenda." *Political Research Quarterly* 56 (1): 29–40. https://doi.org/10.1177/106591290305600103.

Bushnell, James, Michaela Flagg, and Erin Mansur. 2017. "Capacity Markets at a Crossroads." Energy Institute at Haas School of Business, University of California, Berkeley.

Buzbee, William W. 2003. "Recognizing the Regulatory Commons: A Theory of Regulatory Gaps." *Iowa Law Review* 89 (1): 1–64.

——. 2005. "Contextual Environmental Federalism." *New York University Environmental Law Journal* 14 (1): 108–29.

Cameron, James, and Juli Abouchar. 1991. "The Precautionary Principle: A Fundamental Principle of Law and Policy for the Protection of the Global Environment." *Boston College International and Comparative Law Review* 14 (1): 1–27.

Campbell, Angus, Philip E. Converse, Warren E. Miller, and Donald E. Stokes. 1960. *The American Voter*. Chicago: University of Chicago Press.

Campbell, James E. 1985. "Sources of the New Deal Realignment: The Contributions of Conversion and Mobilization to Partisan Change." *Western Political Quarterly* 38 (3): 357–76. https://doi.org/10.2307/448520.

Caperton, Richard W., and Matt Kasper. 2011. "Re-energize Regional Economies with New Electric Transmission Lines." *Center for American Progress* (blog), December 15. https://www.americanprogress.org/article/re-energize-regional-economies-with-new-electric-transmission-lines/.

Cappucci, Matthew, and Jason Samenow. 2021. "Pacific Northwest in the Grips of Another Heat Wave Amid Worsening Drought." *Washington Post*, July 30. https://www.washingtonpost.com/weather/2021/07/30/pacific-northwest-heat-wave-drought/.

Carden, Kevin, Alex Dombrowsky, and Rajaz Amitava. 2022. "Effective Load Carrying Capability Study: Final Report." Astrape Consulting, December 9. https://www.ercot.com/files/docs/2022/12/09/2022-ERCOT-ELCC-Study-Final-Report-12-9-2022.pdf.

Carley, Sanya, Sean Nicholson-Crotty, and Eric J. Fisher. 2015. "Capacity, Guidance, and the Implementation of the American Recovery and Reinvestment Act." *Public Administration Review* 75 (1): 113–25. https://doi.org/10.1111/puar.12294.

Carmichael, Jason T., Robert J. Brulle, and Joanna K. Huxster. 2017. "The Great Divide: Understanding the Role of Media and Other Drivers of the Partisan Divide in Public Concern Over Climate Change in the USA, 2001–2014." *Climatic Change* 141 (4): 599–612. https://doi.org/10.1007/s10584-017-1908-1.

Caro, Robert A. 1990. *The Path to Power*. Vol. 1 of *The Years of Lyndon Johnson*. New York: Vintage.

Carpenter, Daniel. 2014. "Detecting and Measuring Capture." In *Preventing Regulatory Capture: Special Interest Influence and How to Limit It*, edited by Daniel Carpenter and David A. Moss, 57–68. New York: Cambridge University Press.

Carpenter, Daniel, and David A. Moss. 2014. Introduction to *Preventing Regulatory Capture: Special Interest Influence and How to Limit It*, edited by Daniel Carpenter and David A. Moss, 1–22. New York: Cambridge University Press.

Carr, Nicholas. 2008. "Is Google Making Us Stupid?" *The Atlantic*, August.

Carrico, Amanda R., and Manuel Riemer. 2011. "Motivating Energy Conservation in the Workplace: An Evaluation of the Use of Group-Level Feedback and Peer Education." *Journal of Environmental Psychology* 31 (1): 1–13. https://doi.org/10.1016/j.jenvp.2010.11.004.

Carrigan, Christopher, and Cary Coglianese. 2016. "Capturing Regulatory Reality: Stigler's 'The Theory of Economic Regulation.' " University of Pennsylvania Institute for Law and Economic Research Paper No. 16-15, posted July 7. https://doi.org/10.2139/ssrn.2805153.

Carroll, Royce, Jeff Lewis, James Lo, Nolan McCarty, Keith Poole, and Howard Rosenthal. 2015. "DW-NOMINATE Scores with Bootstrapped Standard Errors." Vote View, last updated September 17. https://legacy.voteview.com/dwnomin.htm.

Carson, Rachel. 1962. *Silent Spring*. Boston: Houghton Mifflin.

Casey, Donald J., William Fisher, and Conrad O. Kleveno. 1965. "Lake Ontario Environmental Summary 1965." U.S. Environmental Protection Agency. https://nepis.epa.gov/Exe/ZyPDF.cgi/9101NY9G.PDF?Dockey=9101NY9G.PDF.

Cassidy, John. 2021. "Joe Manchin Kills the Build Back Better Bill." *The New Yorker*, December 19. https://www.newyorker.com/news/our-columnists/joe-manchin-kills-the-build-back-better-bill.

Cassino, Dan, Peter Woolley, and Krista Jenkins. 2012. "What You Know Depends on What You Watch: Current Events Knowledge Across Popular News Sources." Public Mind Poll, Fairleigh Dickinson University. http://publicmind.fdu.edu/2012/confirmed/final.pdf.

Cater, Douglass. 1964. *Power in Washington: A Critical Look at Today's Struggle to Govern in the Nation's Capital.* New York: Random House.

Chait, Jonathan. 2018. "Bobby 'Stop Being the Stupid Party' Jindal Now Says GOP Isn't Stupid Enough." *New York*, February 15. https://nymag.com/intelligencer/2018/02/bobby-stop-being-the-stupid-party-jindal-is-now-pro-stupid.html.

——. 2020. "Richard Epstein Can't Stop Being Wrong About the Coronavirus." *New York*, April 21. https://nymag.com/intelligencer/2020/04/richard-epstein-coronavirus-500-5000-deaths.html.

——. 2021. "Why Glenn Greenwald Says Tucker Carlson Is a True Socialist." *Intelligencer*, March 4. https://nymag.com/intelligencer/2021/03/why-glenn-greenwald-says-tucker-carlson-is-a-true-socialist.html.

——. 2022. "The Climate-Justice Movement Is Helping Neither the Climate nor Justice." *Intelligencer*, October 13. https://nymag.com/intelligencer/2022/10/the-climate-justice-movement-is-bad-for-climate-and-justice.html.

Chapman, Simon, Alexis St. George, Karen Waller, and Vince Cakic. 2013. "The Pattern of Complaints About Australian Wind Farms Does Not Match the Establishment and Distribution of Turbines: Support for the Psychogenic, 'Communicated Disease' Hypothesis." *PLOS One* 8 (10): art. e76584. https://doi.org/10.1371/journal.pone.0076584.

Chappell, Bill. 2023. "What to Know as Gov. Abbott Pushes to Pardon a Man Who Was Just Convicted of Murder." NPR, April 10. https://www.npr.org/2023/04/10/1168974403/texas-greg-abbott-pardon-daniel-perry.

Cheon, Andrew, and Johannes Urpelainen. 2013. "How Do Competing Interest Groups Influence Environmental Policy? The Case of Renewable Electricity in Industrialized Democracies, 1989–2007." *Political Studies* 61 (4): 874–97.

Cherniss, Joshua, and Henry Hardy. [2004] 2022. "Isaiah Berlin." In *The Stanford Encyclopedia of Philosophy*, edited by Edward N. Zalta and Uri Nodelman, Fall ed. Stanford, CA: Stanford University. https://plato.stanford.edu/entries/berlin/#LibePlur.

Chernow, Ron. 1998. *Titan: The Life of John D. Rockefeller, Sr.* New York: Random House.

Chiu, Allyson, Emily Guskin, and Scott Clement. 2023. "Americans Don't Hate Living near Solar and Wind Farms as Much as You Might Think." *Washington Post*, October 3. https://www.washingtonpost.com/climate-solutions/2023/10/03/solar-panels-wind-turbines-nimby/.

Choi, Dayhun. 2023. "Teaming Up Across Political Divides: Evidence from Climate Regulations." Paper presentation at McCombs School of Business, Austin, TX, November 10. On file with the author.

Christie, Mark C. 2023. "It's Time to Reconsider Single-Clearing Price Mechanisms in U.S. Energy Markets." *Energy Law Journal* 44:1–30.

Chun, Carolyn, and Kaitlin Balasaygun. 2023. "With Debt Ceiling, Default Threat, These Are Banking Moves Every Small Business Should Be Making." CNBC, May 26. https://www.cnbc.com/2023/05/26/the-message-for-small-business-economy-in-debt-ceiling-default-scare.html.

Cillizza, Chris. 2021. "Even Democrats Are Now Admitting 'Defund the Police' Was a Massive Mistake." CNN, November 5. https://www.cnn.com/2021/11/05/politics/defund-the-police-democrats/index.html.

Cinelli, Matteo, Gianmarco De Francisci Morales, Alessandro Galeazzi, Walter Quattrociocchi, and Michele Starnini. 2021. "The Echo Chamber Effect on Social Media." *Proceedings of the National Academy of Sciences* 118 (9): art. e2023301118. https://doi.org/10.1073/pnas.2023301118.

Clack, Christopher T. M., Staffan A. Qvist, Jay Apt, Morgan Bazilian, Adam R. Brandt, Ken Caldeira, Steven J. Davis, et al. 2017. "Evaluation of a Proposal for Reliable Low-Cost Grid Power with 100% Wind, Water, and Solar." *Proceedings of the National Academy of Sciences* 114 (26): 6722–27. https://doi.org/10.1073/pnas.1610381114.

Clifford, Catherine. 2022. "Texas Accuses 10 Financial Companies, Including Black-Rock, of 'Boycotting' Energy Companies and Orders State Pension Funds to Divest from Holdings." CNBC, August 25. https://www.cnbc.com/2022/08/25/texas-says-10-companies-including-blackrock-boycotting-energy-.html.

Cline, Seth. 2012. "Sheldon Adelson Spent $150 Million on Election." *US News & World Report*, December 3. https://www.usnews.com/news/articles/2012/12/03/sheldon-adelson-ended-up-spending-150-million.

Coase, Ronald H. 1937. "The Nature of the Firm." *Economica* 4 (16): 386–405. https://doi.org/10.1111/j.1468-0335.1937.tb00002.x.

Coggins, Madeline. 2023. "Gas Stove Exception for Celebrity Chef José Andrés Rankles Local Restaurant Owners: 'California Crazy.' " Fox News, May 19. https://www.foxnews.com/media/gas-stove-exception-celebrity-chef-jose-andres-rankles-local-restaurant-owners-california-crazy.

Coglianese, Cary, Richard J. Zeckhauser, and Edward Parson. 2004. "Seeking Truth for Power: Informational Strategy and Regulatory Policymaking." *Minnesota Law Review* 89 (2): 277–341.

Cohen, Mark A., and Michael P. Vandenbergh. 2008. "Consumption, Happiness, and Climate Change." *Environmental Law Reporter* 38 (12): 10834–37.

Cohen, Marshall. 2021. "The Steele Dossier: A Reckoning." CNN, November 18. https://www.cnn.com/2021/11/18/politics/steele-dossier-reckoning/index.html.

Cohen, Michael D., James G. March, and Johan P. Olsen. 1972. "A Garbage Can Model of Organizational Choice." *Administrative Science Quarterly* 17 (1): 1–25. https://doi.org/10.2307/2392088.

Cohen, Paula Marantz. 2023. *Talking Cure: An Essay on the Civilizing Power of Conversation*. Princeton, NJ: Princeton University Press.

Cole, Daniel. 2023. "Do Libertarians Have Anything Useful to Contribute to Climate Change Policy?" In *Climate Liberalism: Perspectives on Liberty, Property, and Pollution*, edited by Jonathan H. Adler, 53–78. Cham, Switzerland: Palgrave Macmillan.

Coleman, James W. 2022. "Overcoming Local Roadblocks to Energy Transport and a Cleaner New Energy System." American Enterprise Institute, August 18. https://www.aei.org/research-products/report/overcoming-local-roadblocks-to-energy-transport-and-a-cleaner-new-energy-system/.

Coll, Steve. 2012. *Private Empire: ExxonMobil and American Power*. New York: Penguin.

Coller, Andie, and Daniel Libit. 2009. "Conservatives Use Liberal Playbook." *Politico*, September 18. https://www.politico.com/story/2009/09/conservatives-use-liberal-playbook-027285.

Collomb, Jean-Daniel. 2014. "The Ideology of Climate Change Denial in the United States." *European Journal of American Studies* 9 (1). https://doi.org/10.4000/ejas.10305.

Colton, Emma. 2022. "Biden's Condemnation of Violent Rhetoric on the Right Ignores These Incendiary Comments from His Own Party." Fox News, November 6. https://www.foxnews.com/politics/bidens-condemnation-violent-rhetoric-the-right-ignores-these-incendiary-comments-his-own-party.

Conniff, Richard. 2009. "The Political History of Cap and Trade." *Smithsonian*, August. https://www.smithsonianmag.com/science-nature/the-political-history-of-cap-and-trade-34711212/.

Conover, Michael D., Bruno Gonçalves, Alessandro Flammini, and Filippo Menczer. 2012. "Partisan Asymmetries in Online Political Activity." *EPJ Data Science* 1 (1): 1–19. https://doi.org/10.1140/epjds6.

Corkery, Catherine. 2015. "Northern Pass: A Burden Too Heavy for New Hampshire." *Laconia Citizen*, November 13. Reprinted on the Sierra Club New Hampshire website. https://www.sierraclub.org/new-hampshire/northern-pass-editorial.

Cough, Kate, and Alana Semuels. 2023. "A Remarkable Discovery in Maine's Wilderness Sparks a Debate Over the Risks and Rewards of Mining." *Maine Monitor* , July 17. https://themainemonitor.org/a-remarkable-discovery-in-maines-wilderness-sparks-a-debate-over-the-risks-and-rewards-of-mining/.

Cox, Daniel A. 2021. "Support for Political Violence Among Americans Is on the Rise. It's a Grim Warning About America's Political Future." *American Enterprise Institute* (blog), March 26. https://www.aei.org/op-eds/support-for-political-violence-among-americans-is-on-the-rise-its-a-grim-warning-about-americas-political-future/.

Cox, Gary, and Jonathan Redden. 2021. "Demonization as an Electoral Strategy." Stanford University Working Paper.

Coyle, Michael J. 2019. "Like We Weren't Worth Saving." *Social Justice: A Journal of Crime, Conflict & World Order*, January. http://www.socialjusticejournal.org/like-we-werent-worth-saving/.

Cramton, Peter C., and Steven Stoft. 2006. *The Convergence of Market Designs for Adequate Generating Capacity: With Special Attention to the CAISO's Resource Adequacy Problem*. Cambridge, MA: MIT Center for Energy and Environmental Policy Research.

Crane, Daniel A. 2006. "The Story of *United States v. Socony-Vacuum*: Hot Oil and Antitrust in the Two New Deals." Jacob Burns Institute for Advanced Legal Studies. https://papers.ssrn.com/abstract=945455.

Crooks, Scott, Jonathan Lindley, Dawid Lipus, Harry Robinson, Eugéne Smit, and Jessica Vardy. 2023. "Regulatory Efficiency Will Be Essential for the Energy Transition." *McKinsey Report*, June 16. https://www.mckinsey.com/industries/metals-and-mining/our-insights/regulatory-efficiency-will-be-essential-for-the-energy-transition.

Crowley, Kevin. 2020. "BP CEO Warns of Pitfalls of Moving Too Fast on Climate Change." *Houston Chronicle*, January 27. https://www.houstonchronicle.com/business/article/Outgoing-BP-CEO-Warns-of-Moving-Too-Fast-on-15010736.php.

Dahl, Robert A. 1956. *A Preface to Democratic Theory*. Chicago: University of Chicago Press.

Dangendorf, Sönke, Noah Hendricks, Qiang Sun, John Klinck, Tal Ezer, Thomas Frederikse, Francisco M. Calafat, et al. 2023. "Acceleration of U.S. Southeast and Gulf Coast Sea-Level Rise Amplified by Internal Climate Variability." *Nature Communications* 14 (1): 1–11. https://doi.org/10.1038/s41467-023-37649-9.

Darcy, Oliver. 2023. "Dark and Sinister Rhetoric Drenches Right-Wing Media Amid Trump Indictments." CNN, August 3. https://www.cnn.com/2023/08/03/media/right-wing-media-rhetoric-reliable-sources/index.html.

Daugherty, Owen. 2018. "McCaskill: GOP Senators Privately Say Trump Is 'Nuts.'" *The Hill* (blog), December 24. https://thehill.com/homenews/senate/422765-mccaskill -gop-senators-privately-say-trump-is-nuts/.

Dautrich, Kenneth, and Thomas H. Hartley. 1999. *How the News Media Fail American Voters: Causes, Consequences, and Remedies.* New York: Columbia University Press.

Davenport, Coral. 2022. "Court Decision Leaves Biden with Few Tools to Combat Climate Change." *New York Times*, June 30. https://www.nytimes.com/2022/06/30 /climate/biden-climate-action-epa.html.

Davie, Haley, and J. Baxter Oliphant. 2019. "More Republicans Say Stricter Environmental Regulations Are 'Worth the Cost.'" Pew Research Center, February 7. https://www.pewresearch.org/short-reads/2019/02/07/more-republicans-say -stricter-environmental-regulations-are-worth-the-cost/.

Davis, Lucas W., and Catherine Wolfram. 2012. "Deregulation, Consolidation, and Efficiency: Evidence from US Nuclear Power." *American Economic Journal: Applied Economics* 4 (4): 194–225. https://doi.org/10.1257/app.4.4.194.

Davis Noll, Bethany A., and Burcin Unel. 2019. "Markets, Externalities, and the Federal Power Act: The Federal Energy Regulatory Commission's Authority to Price Carbon Dioxide Emissions." *New York University Environmental Law Journal* 27 (1): 1–56.

Dawes, Robyn. 2019. *Everyday Irrationality: How Pseudo-scientists, Lunatics, and the Rest of Us Systematically Fail to Think Rationally.* London: Taylor and Francis.

Dawkins, Ryan, and Abigail Hanson. 2022. "'American' Is the Eye of the Beholder: American Identity, Racial Sorting, and Affective Polarization Among White Americans." *Political Behavior*, December. https://doi.org/10.1007/s11109-022-09834-x.

Debonis, Mike. 2019. "House Democrats Explode in Recriminations as Liberals Lash Out at Moderates." *Washington Post*, March 1. https://www.washingtonpost.com /powerpost/house-democrats-explode-in-recriminations-as-liberals-lash-out-at -moderates/2019/02/28/c3d163fe-3b87-11e9-a06c-3ec8ed509d15_story.html.

Delgado, Jason. 2022. "Gov. DeSantis Vetoes Net Metering Bill." *Florida Politics— Campaigns & Elections, Lobbying & Government* (blog), April 27. https:// floridapolitics.com/archives/520090-gov-desantis-vetoes-net-metering-bill/.

Deliso, Meredith. 2022. "Why California Has Blackouts: A Look at the Power Grid." ABC News, September 9. https://abcnews.go.com/US/california-blackouts-power -grid/story?id=89460998.

Del Vicario, Michela, Alessandro Bessi, Fabiana Zollo, Fabio Petroni, Antonio Scala, Guido Caldarelli, H. Eugene Stanley, et al. 2016. "The Spreading of Misinformation Online." *Proceedings of the National Academy of Sciences* 113 (3): 554–59. https:// doi.org/10.1073/pnas.1517441113.

Demsetz, Harold. 1968. "Why Regulate Utilities?" *Journal of Law & Economics* 11 (1): 55–65.

D'Entreves, Maurizio Passerin. 2022. "Hannah Arendt." In *The Stanford Encyclopedia of Philosophy*, edited by Edward N. Zalta and Uri Nodelman, Fall ed. Stanford, CA: Stanford University. https://plato.stanford.edu/archives/fall2022/entries/arendt/.

Desilver, Drew. 2021. "As National Eviction Ban Expires, a Look at Who Rents and Who Owns in the U.S." Pew Research Center, August 2. https://www.pewresearch .org/short-reads/2021/08/02/as-national-eviction-ban-expires-a-look-at-who-rents -and-who-owns-in-the-u-s/.

——. 2022. "The Polarization in Today's Congress Has Roots That Go Back Decades." Pew Research Center, March 10. https://www.pewresearch.org/short-reads/2022/03 /10/the-polarization-in-todays-congress-has-roots-that-go-back-decades/.

DeVerna, Matthew R., Andrew M. Guess, Adam J. Berinsky, Joshua A. Tucker, and John T. Jost. 2022. "Rumors in Retweet: Ideological Asymmetry in the Failure to Correct Misinformation." *Personality & Social Psychology Bulletin* 50 (1). https://doi.org/10.1177/01461672221114222.

Dey, Sneha, and Mitchell Ferman. 2022. "Texas Grid Operator Urges Electricity Conservation as Heat Wave Drives Up Demand." *Texas Tribune*, July 11. https://www.texastribune.org/2022/07/10/texas-blackouts-power-ercot/.

Diamond, Larry, Lee Drutman, Tod Lindberg, Nathan P. Kalmoe, and Lilliana Mason. 2020. "Americans Increasingly Believe Violence Is Justified If the Other Side Wins." *Politico*, October 1, updated October 9. https://www.politico.com/news/magazine/2020/10/01/political-violence-424157.

Dickinson, Tim. 2011. "How Roger Ailes Built the Fox News Fear Factory." *Rolling Stone*, May 25. https://www.rollingstone.com/politics/politics-news/how-roger-ailes-built-the-fox-news-fear-factory-244652/.

Diffenbaugh, Noah S., Frances V. Davenport, and Marshall Burke. 2021. "Historical Warming Has Increased U.S. Crop Insurance Losses." *Environmental Research Letters* 16 (8). https://doi.org/10.1088/1748-9326/ac1223.

DiGangi, Diana. 2023. "Young Workers Are Flocking to Renewable Jobs, but the Sector Remains Short on Labor, Report Shows." *Utility Dive*, August 1. https://www.utilitydive.com/news/workers-gen-z-renewable-energy-industry-solar-workforce/689271/.

Donaghy, Timothy Q., Noel Healy, Charles Y. Jiang, and Colette Pichon Battle. 2023. "Fossil Fuel Racism in the United States: How Phasing Out Coal, Oil, and Gas Can Protect Communities." *Energy Research & Social Science* 100. https://doi.org/10.1016/j.erss.2023.103104.

Douglas, Mary. 2003. "Being Fair to Hierarchists." *University of Pennsylvania Law Review* 151 (4): 1349–70. https://doi.org/10.2307/3312933.

Douglas, Mary, and Aaron Wildavsky. 1982. *Risk and Culture: An Essay on the Selection of Technical and Environmental Dangers*. Berkeley: University of California Press.

Downs, Anthony. 1957. *An Economic Theory of Democracy*. New York: Harper.

——. 1972. "Up and Down with Ecology—the 'Issue-Attention Cycle.'" *National Affairs*, Summer. https://www.nationalaffairs.com/public_interest/detail/up-and-down-with-ecologythe-issue-attention-cycle.

Draper, Robert. 2022. "The Arizona Republican Party's Anti-democracy Experiment." *New York Times Magazine*, August 15. https://www.nytimes.com/2022/08/15/magazine/arizona-republicans-democracy.html.

Drehobl, Ariel, Lauren Ross, and Roxana Ayala. 2020. "An Assessment of National and Metropolitan Energy Burden Across the United States." https://www.aceee.org/sites/default/files/pdfs/u2006.pdf.

Drexler, Peggy. 2020. "What the Ronan Farrow Controversy Says About Us." CNN.com, May 22. https://www.cnn.com/2020/05/21/opinions/ronan-farrow-isnt-synonymous-with-metoo-drexler/index.html.

Druckman, James N., and Lawrence R. Jacobs. 2006. "Lumpers and Splitters: The Public Opinion Information That Politicians Collect and Use." *Public Opinion Quarterly* 70 (4): 453–76. https://doi.org/10.1093/poq/nfl020.

Druckman, James N., Matthew S. Levendusky, and Audrey McLain. 2018. "No Need to Watch: How the Effects of Partisan Media Can Spread Via Interpersonal Discussions." *American Journal of Political Science* 62 (1): 99–112. https://doi.org/10.1111/ajps.12325.

Drugmand, Dana, and Carroll Muffett. 2021. "Confronting the Myth of Carbon-Free Fossil Fuels: Why Carbon Capture Is Not a Climate Solution." Center for International Environmental Law (CIEL), July 31. https://www.ciel.org/wp-content/uploads/2021/07/Confronting-the-Myth-of-Carbon-Free-Fossil-Fuels.pdf.

Drutman, Lee. 2020. "The Senate Has Always Favored Smaller States. It Just Didn't Help Republicans Until Now." *FiveThirtyEight* (blog), July 29. https://fivethirtyeight.com/features/the-senate-has-always-favored-smaller-states-it-just-didnt-help-republicans-until-now/.

Dudley, Susan. 2023. "Jimmy Carter, the Great Deregulator." *Regulatory Review*, March 6. https://www.theregreview.org/2023/03/06/dudley-jimmy-carter-the-great-deregulator/.

Duncan, Charles. 2021. "Rising Oceans Part 2: What Does Sea-Level Rise Mean for the Future of N.C. Coast?" Spectrum News 1, May 26. https://spectrumlocalnews.com/nc/charlotte/news/2021/05/26/what-does-the-future-of-sea-level-rise-mean-for-north-carolina-outer-banks-.

Dunn, Amina. 2021. "Two-Thirds of Republicans Want Trump to Retain Major Political Role; 44% Want Him to Run Again in 2024." Pew Research Center, October 6. https://www.pewresearch.org/short-reads/2021/10/06/two-thirds-of-republicans-want-trump-to-retain-major-political-role-44-want-him-to-run-again-in-2024/.

Dvoskin, Brenda. 2023. "The Illusion of Inclusion: The Perils of the New Governance Project for Content Moderation." Working paper. On file with the author.

Eady, Gregory, Jonathan Nagler, Andy Guess, Jan Zilinsky, and Joshua A. Tucker. 2019. "How Many People Live in Political Bubbles on Social Media? Evidence from Linked Survey and Twitter Data." *SAGE Open* 9 (1). https://doi.org/10.1177/2158244019832705.

Easterbrook, Frank H. 1984. "Limits of Antitrust." *Texas Law Review*, occasional papers from the University of Chicago Law School, 63:1–40.

Eddy, Melissa, Megan Specia, Steven Erlanger, Jack Ewing, Thomas Erdbrink, and Henry Fountain. 2021. "Flooding in Europe: Europe Flooding Deaths Pass 125, and Scientists See Fingerprints of Climate Change." *New York Times*, July 16. https://www.nytimes.com/live/2021/07/16/world/europe-flooding-germany.

Ehrlich, Paul. 1968. *The Population Bomb*. New York: Ballantine.

Eilperin, Juliet. 2007. *Fight Club Politics: How Partisanship Is Poisoning the U.S. House of Representatives*. Illus. ed. New York: Rowman & Littlefield.

Eisen, Joel B., and Heather Payne. Forthcoming. "Utilities with Purpose." *Florida Law Review* 76. https://papers.ssrn.com/sol3/papers.cfm?abstract_id=4571183.

Eisenberg, Ann M. 2020. "Distributive Justice and Rural America." *Boston College Law Review* 61 (1): 189–251.

Elkins, Stanley M., and Eric McKitrick. 1993. *The Age of Federalism*. New York: Oxford University Press.

Eller, Donnelle, and Kevin Hardy. 2017. "Is Wind Power Saving Rural Iowa or Wrecking It?" *Des Moines Register*, April 20, updated April 24. https://www.desmoinesregister.com/story/tech/science/environment/2017/04/20/wind-power-saving-rural-iowa-wrecking/99789758/.

Ellerman, A. Denny, and Barbara K. Buchner. 2007. "The European Union Emissions Trading Scheme: Origins, Allocation, and Early Results." *Review of Environmental Economics and Policy* 1 (1): 66–87. https://doi.org/10.1093/reep/rem003.

Ellmers, Glen. 2021. " 'Conservatism' Is No Longer Enough." *The American Mind*, March 24. https://americanmind.org/salvo/why-the-claremont-institute-is-not-conservative-and-you-shouldnt-be-either/.

Ellsworth, Phoebe C., and Samuel R. Gross. 1994. "Hardening of the Attitudes: Americans' Views on the Death Penalty." *Journal of Social Issues* 50 (2): 19–52. https://doi.org/10.1111/j.1540-4560.1994.tb02409.x.

Enck, Paul, and Winfried Häuser. 2012. "Beware the Nocebo Effect." *New York Times*, August 10. https://www.nytimes.com/2012/08/12/opinion/sunday/beware-the-nocebo-effect.html.

Engstrom, David Freeman. 2013. "Corralling Capture." *Harvard Journal of Law & Public Policy* 36:31–39.

Enns, Peter K. 2015. "Relative Policy Support and Coincidental Representation." *Perspectives on Politics* 13 (4): 1053–62. https://doi.org/10.1017/S1537592715002315.

Enten, Harry. 2021. "Statistically, Democrats and Republicans Hate Each Other More Than Ever." CNN, November 20. https://www.cnn.com/2021/11/20/politics/democrat-republican-hate-tribalism/index.html.

Epstein, Alex. 2014. *The Moral Case for Fossil Fuels*. New York: Portfolio.

———. 2017. "A Straw Man Attack on the Moral Case for Fossil Fuels." *Energy Law Journal* 38:79–94.

———. 2022. *Fossil Future: Why Global Human Flourishing Requires More Oil, Coal, and Natural Gas—Not Less*. New York: Portfolio/Penguin.

Epstein, Alex, and Eric M. Dennis. 2013. *Fossil Fuels Improve the Planet*. San Diego: Center for Industrial Progress.

Epstein, Paul R., Jonathan J. Buonocore, Kevin Eckerle, Michael Hendryx, Benjamin M. Stout III, Richard Heinberg, Richard W. Clapp, et al. 2011. "Full Cost Accounting for the Life Cycle of Coal." *Annals of the New York Academy of Sciences* 1219 (1): 73–98. https://doi.org/10.1111/j.1749-6632.2010.05890.x.

Everly, Steve. 2018. "Why Natural Gas from Putin's Russia Has to Be Imported to New England." *Washington Examiner*, March 24. https://www.washingtonexaminer.com/opinion/op-eds/why-natural-gas-from-putins-russia-has-to-be-imported-to-new-england.

Faberman, R. Jason, Andreas I. Mueller, and Ayşegül Şahin. 2022. "Has the Willingness to Work Fallen During the COVID Pandemic?" *Labour Economics* 79:1–16. https://doi.org/10.1016/j.labeco.2022.102275.

Fadil, Adeeb. 1985. "Citizen Suits Against Polluters: Picking Up the Pace." *Harvard Environmental Law Review* 9:23–82.

Fandos, Nicholas. 2020. "Cori Bush Defeats William Lacy Clay in a Show of Progressive Might." *New York Times*, August 5. https://www.nytimes.com/2020/08/05/us/politics/cori-bush-missouri-william-lacy-clay.html.

Faraji-Rad, Ali, Bendik M. Samuelsen, and Luk Warlop. 2015. "On the Persuasiveness of Similar Others: The Role of Mentalizing and the Feeling of Certainty." *Journal of Consumer Research* 42 (3): 458–71. https://doi.org/10.1093/jcr/ucv032.

Faraji-Rad, Ali, Luk Warlop, and Bendik Samuelsen. 2012. "When the Message 'Feels Right': When and How Does Source Similarity Enhance Message Persuasiveness?" *Advances in Consumer Research* 40:682–83.

Farber, Daniel A., and Philip P. Frickey. 1991. *Law and Public Choice: A Critical Introduction*. Chicago: University of Chicago Press.

Farber, Daniel A., and Suzanna Sherry. 1997. *Beyond All Reason: The Radical Assault on Truth in American Law*. New York: Oxford University Press.

Fares, Robert. 2016. "Wind Energy Experts See Lower Costs, Bigger Turbines on the Horizon." *Scientific American Blog Network* (blog), November 29. https://blogs.scientificamerican.com/plugged-in/wind-energy-experts-see-lower-costs-bigger-turbines-on-the-horizon/.

——. 2017. "Energy Secretary Rick Perry Proposes New Regulation to Prop Up Coal, Nuclear Plants." *Scientific American Blog Network*, October 30. https://blogs .scientificamerican.com/plugged-in/energy-secretary-rick-perry-proposes-new -regulation-to-prop-up-coal-nuclear-plants/.

Faruqui, Ahmad, Ryan Hledik, and Sanem Sergici. 2019. *A Survey of Residential Time-of-Use (TOU) Rates*. Boston: Brattle Group. https://www.brattle.com/wp-content /uploads/2021/05/17904_a_survey_of_residential_time-of-use_tou_rates.pdf.

Faruqui, Ahmad, and Jennifer Palmer. 2011. "Dynamic Pricing and Its Discontents." *Regulation* 34:16–22.

Faruqui, Ahmad, and Henna Trewn. 2017. "Enhancing Customer-Centricity." *Public Utilities Fortnightly* 155 (8). https://www.fortnightly.com/fortnightly/2017/08 /enhancing-customer-centricity.

Fausset, Richard. 2015. "University of North Carolina Board Closes 3 Centers." *New York Times*, February 27. https://www.nytimes.com/2015/02/28/us/university-of -north-carolina-board-closes-3-academic-centers.html.

Fawcett, Edmund. 2014. *Liberalism: The Life of an Idea*. Princeton, NJ: Princeton University Press.

Federal Regulatory Commission (FERC) and North American Electric Reliability Corporation (NERC). 2011. *Report on Outages and Curtailments During the Southwest Weather Event of February 1–5, 2011*. Washington, DC: FERC, NERC. https://www .ferc.gov/sites/default/files/2020-04/08-16-11-report.pdf.

Feldman, Lauren P. 2007. "The News About Comedy: Young Audiences, *The Daily Show*, and Evolving Notions of Journalism." *Journalism* 8 (4): 406–27. https://doi .org/10.1177/1464884907078655.

Feldman, Lauren P., Sol Hart, and Tijana Milosevic. 2017. "Polarizing News? Representations of Threat and Efficacy in Leading US Newspapers' Coverage of Climate Change." *Public Understanding of Science* 26 (4): 481–97. https://doi.org/10.1177 /0963662515595348.

Feldman, Leslie Dale, and Rosanna Perotti. 2002. *Honor and Loyalty: Inside the Politics of the George H. W. Bush White House*. Westport, CT: Greenwood Press.

Fenno, Richard F. 1978. *Home Style: House Members in Their Districts*. Boston: Little, Brown.

Ferguson, Adam. 1996. *An Essay on the History of Civil Society* (1767). Edited by Fania Oz-Salzberger. Cambridge: Cambridge University Press.

Ferman, Mitchell. 2022. "Texas Bans Local, State Government Entities from Doing Business with Firms That 'Boycott' Fossil Fuels." *Texas Tribune*, August 24. https:// www.texastribune.org/2022/08/24/texas-boycott-companies-fossil-fuels/.

Ferris, David. 2023. "Why Wyoming Won't Build Biden's EV Chargers." *Energywire* (blog), January 31. https://www.eenews.net/articles/why-wyoming-wont-build -bidens-ev-chargers/.

Festinger, Leon. 1957. *A Theory of Cognitive Dissonance*. Evanston, IL: Row, Peterson.

Fields, Billy, and John L. Renne. 2021. *Adaptation Urbanism and Resilient Communities: Transforming Streets to Address Climate Change*. London: Routledge.

Fimrite, Peter. 2020. "New Reason to Conserve Redwoods—They're Best at Storing Polluting Carbon." *San Francisco Chronicle*, April 30. https://www.sfchronicle.com /environment/article/New-reason-to-conserve-California-s-redwoods-15238034 .php.

Fingerhut, Hannah. 2016. "Is Treatment of Minorities a Key Election Issue? Views Differ by Race, Party." Pew Research Center, July 13. https://www.pewresearch.org /short-reads/2016/07/13/partisan-racial-divides-exist-over-how-important -treatment-of-minorities-is-as-a-voting-issue/.

Finkel, Eli J., Christopher A. Bail, Mina Cikara, Peter H. Ditto, Shanto Iyengar, Samara Klar, Lilliana Mason, et al. 2020. "Political Sectarianism in America." *Science* 370:533–36. https://doi.org/10.1126/science.abe1715.

Fiorina, Morris P. 1999. "Whatever Happened to the Median Voter?" Paper presented at the MIT Conference on Parties and Congress, Cambridge, MA, October 2. http://web.stanford.edu/~mfiorina/Fiorina%20Web%20Files/MedianVoterPaper.pdf.

Fiorina, Morris P., and Samuel J. Abrams. 2008. "Political Polarization in the American Public." *Annual Review of Political Science* 11 (1): 563–88. https://doi.org/10.1146/annurev.polisci.11.053106.153836.

——. 2009. *Disconnect: The Breakdown of Representation in American Politics.* Illus. ed. Norman: University of Oklahoma Press.

Fischer, Michael, Mathew Werber, and Peter V. Schwartz. 2009. "Batteries: Higher Energy Density Than Gasoline?" *Energy Policy* 37 (7): 2639–41. https://doi.org/10.1016/j.enpol.2009.02.030.

Fischman, Robert L. 2005. "Cooperative Federalism and Natural Resources Law." *New York University Environmental Law Journal* 14 (1): 179–231.

Fisher, Elizabeth. 2007. *Risk Regulation and Administrative Constitutionalism.* Oxford: Hart.

Fisher, Elizabeth, and Sidney Shapiro. 2020. *Administrative Competence: Reimagining Administrative Law.* Cambridge: Cambridge University Press.

Fishkin, Joseph, and William E. Forbath. 2022. *The Anti-oligarchy Constitution: Reconstructing the Economic Foundations of American Democracy.* Cambridge, MA: Harvard University Press.

Fiske, Susan T., and Shelley E. Taylor. 2021. *Social Cognition: From Brains to Culture.* 4th ed. London: Sage.

Flavelle, Christopher. 2021. "Rising Seas Threaten an American Institution: The 30-Year Mortgage." *New York Times*, June 19, 2020, updated March 2. https://www.nytimes.com/2020/06/19/climate/climate-seas-30-year-mortgage.html.

Flavelle, Christopher, and Patricia Mazzei. 2021. "Miami Says It Can Adapt to Rising Seas. Not Everyone Is Convinced." *New York Times*, March 2. https://www.nytimes.com/2021/03/02/climate/miami-sea-level-rise.html.

Flavin, Patrick. 2015. "Campaign Finance Laws, Policy Outcomes, and Political Equality in the American States." *Political Research Quarterly* 68 (1): 77–88. https://doi.org/10.1177/1065912914554041.

Fleury, Jean-Baptiste, and Alain Marciano. 2018. "The Sound of Silence: A Review Essay of Nancy MacLean's *Democracy in Chains: The Deep History of the Radical Right's Stealth Plan for America.*" *Journal of Economic Literature* 56 (4): 1492–537.

Fong, Christian, and Sam Mardell. 2021. "Securitization in Action: How US States Are Shaping an Equitable Coal Transition." RMI, March 4. https://rmi.org/securitization-in-action-how-us-states-are-shaping-an-equitable-coal-transition/.

Forstall, Alfred E. 1900. "Government Control of the Price of Gas." In *Proceedings of the American Gas Light Association*, i–x. New York: Charles F. Bloom.

Forsyth, Ann, Emily Salomon, and Laura Smead. 2017. *Creating Healthy Neighborhoods: Evidence-Based Planning and Design Strategies.* London: Routledge.

Foxhall, Emily, and Alex Ford. 2023. "What You Need to Know About Texas' Complex—but Important—Electricity Market Reform Plan." *Texas Tribune*, March 1. https://www.texastribune.org/2023/03/01/texas-power-market-public-utility-commission-electricity-credits/.

Fox-Penner, Peter. 2010. *Smart Power: Climate Change, the Smart Grid, and the Future of Electric Utilities.* Anniversary ed. Washington, DC: Island Press.

Francis, Raymond L. 1950. "Mark Twain and H. L. Mencken." *Prairie Schooner* 24:31–40.

Franta, Benjamin. 2018. "Shell and Exxon's Secret 1980s Climate Change Warnings." *The Guardian*, September 19, 2018. https://www.theguardian.com/environment /climate-consensus-97-per-cent/2018/sep/19/shell-and-exxons-secret-1980s -climate-change-warnings.

Fredericks, Sarah E. 2021. Introduction to *Environmental Guilt and Shame: Signals of Individual and Collective Responsibility and the Need for Ritual Responses*, 1–24. Oxford: Oxford University Press.

Freeman, Jody. 2015. "A Critical Look at 'the Moral Case for Fossil Fuels.'" *Energy Law Journal* 36:327–53.

——. 2022. "Will the Supreme Court Frustrate Efforts to Slow Climate Change?" *New York Times*, February 26. https://www.nytimes.com/2022/02/26/opinion/climate -change-supreme-court.html.

Freeman, Jody, and David B. Spence. 2014. "Old Statutes, New Problems." *University of Pennsylvania Law Review* 163 (1): 1–93.

Freeman, Jody, and Matthew C. Stephenson. 2022. "The Anti-democratic Major Questions Doctrine." *Supreme Court Review* 2022:1–43. https://doi.org/10.1086/724919.

Freeman, John Leiper. 1965. *The Political Process: Executive Bureau–Legislative Committee Relations*. New York: Random House.

Frenkel, Sheera, and Daisuke Wakabayashi. 2018. "After Florida School Shooting, Russian 'Bot' Army Pounced." *New York Times*, February 20. https://www.nytimes .com/2018/02/19/technology/russian-bots-school-shooting.html.

Frey, William H. 2021. "Turnout in 2020 Election Spiked Among Both Democratic and Republican Voting Groups, New Census Data Shows." *Brookings*, May 5. https:// www.brookings.edu/articles/turnout-in-2020-spiked-among-both-democratic -and-republican-voting-groups-new-census-data-shows/.

Friedkin, Noah E., and Francesco Bullo. 2017. "How Truth Wins in Opinion Dynamics Along Issue Sequences." *Proceedings of the National Academy of Sciences* 114 (43): 11380–85. https://doi.org/10.1073/pnas.1710603114.

Friedman, Lisa. 2022. "Manchin Won a Pledge from Democrats to Finish a Contested Pipeline." *New York Times*, August 1. https://www.nytimes.com/2022/08/01/climate /manchin-climate-mountain-valley-pipeline.html.

Friedman, Vanessa. 2021. "Liz Cheney: The Model of a Modern Never-Trumper." *New York Times*, May 18, updated October 21. https://www.nytimes.com/2021/05/18/style /liz-cheney-trump-image.html.

Frimer, Jeremy A., Mark J. Brandt, Zachary Melton, and Matt Motyl. 2019. "Extremists on the Left and Right Use Angry, Negative Language." *Personality & Social Psychology Bulletin* 45 (8): 1216–31. https://doi.org/10.1177/0146167218809705.

Fuller, Jaime. 2016. "The Long Fight Between the Bundys and the Federal Government, from 1989 to Today." *Washington Post*, January 4. https://www.washi ngtonpost.com/news/the-fix/wp/2014/04/15/everything-you-need-to-know-about -the-long-fight-between-cliven-bundy-and-the-federal-government/.

Funigiello, Philip J. 1973. *Toward a National Power Policy: The New Deal and the Electric Utility Industry, 1933–1941*. Pittsburgh: University of Pittsburgh Press.

Furch, Jan, Vlastimil Konečný, and Zdeněk Krobot. 2022. "Modelling of Life Cycle Cost of Conventional and Alternative Vehicles." *Scientific Reports* 12 (1): art. 10661. https://doi.org/10.1038/s41598-022-14715-8.

Furlong, Scott R., and Cornelius M. Kerwin. 2005. "Interest Group Participation in Rule Making: A Decade of Change." *Journal of Public Administration Research and Theory* 15 (3): 353–70. https://doi.org/10.1093/jopart/mui022.

Galston, William A., and Elaine Kamarck. 2022. "Is Democracy Failing and Putting Our Economic System at Risk?" *Brookings*, January 4. https://www.brookings.edu/articles/is-democracy-failing-and-putting-our-economic-system-at-risk/.

Gandel, Stephen. 2021. "Zoom's Pandemic Profits Exceeded $670 Million. Its Federal Tax Payment? Zilch." CBS News, March 24. https://www.cbsnews.com/news/zoom-no-federal-taxes-2020/.

Gardiner, David. 2017. "The Growing Demand for Renewable Energy Among Major U.S. and Global Manufacturers." David Gardiner and Associates, September. https://www.dgardiner.com/wp-content/uploads/2017/09/Renewable-Energy-and-Climate-Commitments-in-the-Manufacturing-Sector_FINAL9.19.2017FINAL.pdf.

Gardner, Amy. 2022. "A Majority of GOP Nominees Deny or Question the 2020 Election Results." *Washington Post*, October 19. https://www.washingtonpost.com/nation/2022/10/06/elections-deniers-midterm-elections-2022/.

Gardner, Amy, Reis Thebault, and Robert Klemko. 2022. "Election Deniers Lose Races for Key State Offices in Every 2020 Battleground." *Washington Post*, November 14. https://www.washingtonpost.com/elections/2022/11/13/election-deniers-defeated-state-races/.

Garrett, R. Kelly, and Robert M. Bond. 2021. "Conservatives' Susceptibility to Political Misperceptions." *Science Advances* 7 (23). https://doi.org/10.1126/sciadv.abf1234.

Garzia, Diego, and Frederico Ferreira da Silva. 2022. "The Electoral Consequences of Affective Polarization? Negative Voting in the 2020 US Presidential Election." *American Politics Research* 50 (3): 303–11. https://doi.org/10.1177/1532673X221074633.

Gearino, Dan. 2023. "Cities Stand to Win Big with the Inflation Reduction Act. How Do They Turn This Opportunity Into Results?" *Inside Climate News*, June 1. https://insideclimatenews.org/news/01062023/inside-clean-energy-inflation-reduction-act-cities/.

Geiger, Abigail. 2014. "Political Polarization in the American Public." Pew Research Center, June 12. https://www.pewresearch.org/politics/2014/06/12/political-polarization-in-the-american-public/.

Gelinas, Donald J. 2003. *Final Report on Price Manipulation in Western Markets*. Federal Energy Regulatory Commission Docket no. PA02-02-000. Washington, DC: Federal Regulatory Commission, March.

Geller, Richard S. 2010. "The Legality of Form-Based Zoning Codes." *Journal of Land Use & Environmental Law* 26 (1): 35–91.

Gelles, David. 2022. "West Virginia Punishes Banks That It Says Don't Support Coal." *New York Times*, July 28. https://www.nytimes.com/2022/07/28/business/west-virginia-fossil-fuel-banks.html.

George, Violet. 2023. "Forest Carbon Offset Project in Canada Damaged by Raging Wildfires." *Carbon Herald* (blog), June 27. https://carbonherald.com/forest-carbon-offset-project-in-canada-damaged-by-raging-wildfires/.

Gerson, Noel L., and Sherri Goodman. 2007. *National Security and the Threat of Climate Change*. Alexandria, VA: CNA Corp.

Gerstenzang, James. 2000. "Gore Plays It Warm, Fuzzy on 'Oprah.'" *Los Angeles Times*, September 12. https://www.latimes.com/archives/la-xpm-2000-sep-12-mn-19723-story.html.

Gewin, Virginia. 2018. "The Slow-Motion Catastrophe Threatening America's 350-Year-Old Farms." *The Atlantic*, March 2. https://www.theatlantic.com/science/archive/2018/03/maryland-salt-farms/554663/.

Gilbert, Alex. 2020. "We Need Both Nuclear and Renewables to Protect the Climate." Breakthrough Institute, October 8. https://thebreakthrough.org/issues/energy/we -need-both-nuclear-and-renewables.

Gilens, Martin, and Benjamin I. Page. 2014. "Testing Theories of American Politics: Elites, Interest Groups, and Average Citizens." *Perspectives on Politics* 12 (3): 564– 81. https://doi.org/10.1017/S1537592714001595.

Gillingham, Kenneth, and James H. Stock. 2018. "The Cost of Reducing Greenhouse Gas Emissions." *Journal of Economic Perspectives* 32 (4): 53–72. https://doi.org/10 .1257/jep.32.4.53.

Gillis, Ash, Michael Vandenbergh, Kaitlin Raimi, Alex Maki, and Ken Wallston. 2021. "Convincing Conservatives: Private Sector Action Can Bolster Support for Climate Change Mitigation in the United States." *Energy Research & Social Science* 73: art. 101947. https://doi.org/10.1016/j.erss.2021.101947.

Gimon, Eric. 2022. "Let's Get Organized! Long-Term Market Design for a High Pen-etration Grid." Energy Innovation White Paper, September. https://energyin novation.org/wp-content/uploads/2022/09/Lets-Get-Organized-Long-Term-Market -Design-for-a-High-Penetration-Grid.pdf.

Gladwell, Malcolm. 2000. *The Tipping Point: How Little Things Can Make a Big Differ-ence.* Boston: Back Bay.

Global Environmental Change: Research Pathways for the Next Decade. 1999. Washing-ton, DC: National Academies Press.

Gluck, Abbe R., Mark Regan, and Erica Turret. 2020. "The Affordable Care Act's Liti-gation Decade." *Georgetown Law Journal* 108 (6): 1471–534.

Gold, Russell. 2014. *The Boom: How Fracking Ignited the American Energy Revolution and Changed the World.* New York: Simon & Schuster.

——. 2019. *Superpower: One Man's Quest to Transform American Energy.* New York: Simon & Schuster.

Goldberg, Bernard. 2001. *Bias: A CBS Insider Exposes How the Media Distort the News.* Washington, DC: Regnery.

Golden, Marissa Martino. 1998. "Interest Groups in the Rule-Making Process: Who Participates? Whose Voices Get Heard?" *Journal of Public Administration Research and Theory* 8 (2): 245–70. https://doi.org/10.1093/oxfordjournals.jpart.a024380.

Goldstein, Bonnie. 2006. "Inside Fox News." *Slate*, November 17. https://slate.com /news-and-politics/2006/11/fox-senior-vice-president-for-news-john-moody -reports-you-decide-2.html.

Gopnik, Adam. 2019. *A Thousand Small Sanities: The Moral Adventure of Liberalism.* New York: Basic.

Gordon, John Steele. 1988. *The Scarlet Woman of Wall Street: Jay Gould, Jim Fisk, Cor-nelius Vanderbilt, and the Erie Railway Wars.* New York: Grove Press.

Gordon, Sanford C., and Steven D. Rashin. 2021. "Stakeholder Participation in Pol-icy Making: Evidence from Medicare Fee Schedule Revisions." *Journal of Politics* 83 (1): 409–14. https://doi.org/10.1086/709435.

"Grid 2030": A National Vision for Electricity's Second 100 Years. 2015. N.p.: CreateSpace.

Griffin, James M., and Henry B. Steele. 1986. *Energy Economics and Policy.* 2nd ed. Orlando, FL: Academic Press College Division.

Griffin, Paul. 2017. *CDP Carbon Majors Report 2017.* Snowmass, CO: Climate Account-ability Institute. https://cdn.cdp.net/cdp-production/cms/reports/documents/000 /002/327/original/Carbon-Majors-Report-2017.pdf?1501833772.

Grimmer, Justin, Sean J. Westwood, and Solomon Messing. 2015. *The Impression of Influence: Legislator Communication, Representation, and Democratic Accountabil-ity.* Princeton, NJ: Princeton University Press.

Grose, Christian R., Neil Malhotra, and Robert Parks Van Houweling. 2015. "Explaining Explanations: How Legislators Explain Their Policy Positions and How Citizens React." *American Journal of Political Science* 59 (3): 724–43. https://doi.org/10.1111/ajps.12164.

Gross, Samuel R. 1998. "Update: American Public Opinion on the Death Penalty—It's Getting Personal." *Cornell Law Review* 83 (6): 1448–75.

Grullón Paz, Isabella. 2022. "Seattle and Rest of the Pacific Northwest Engulfed by 'Dangerous' Heat." *New York Times*, July 26. https://www.nytimes.com/2022/07/26/us/pacific-northwest-heat-warnings.html.

Guber, Deborah Lynn. 2013. "A Cooling Climate for Change? Party Polarization and the Politics of Global Warming." *American Behavioral Scientist* 57 (1): 93–115. https://doi.org/10.1177/0002764212463361.

Hall, Richard L., and Frank W. Wayman. 1990. "Buying Time: Moneyed Interests and the Mobilization of Bias in Congressional Committees." *American Political Science Review* 84 (3): 797–820. https://doi.org/10.2307/1962767.

Hall, Timothy L. 2021. "Religion and Civic Virtue: A Justification of Free Exercise." *Tulane Law Review* 67 (1): 87–134.

Halper, Evan. 2023. "Can Vacuums Slow Global Warming? Administration Bets $1.2 Billion on It." *Washington Post*, August 11. https://www.washingtonpost.com/business/2023/08/11/carbon-capture-vacuum-biden/.

Hamid, Shadi. 2018. "The Rise of Anti-liberalism." *Brookings*, February 21. https://www.brookings.edu/articles/the-rise-of-anti-liberalism/.

Hamilton, Alexander, James Madison, and John Jay. [1787–1788] n.d. *The Federalist Papers*. Full Text of *The Federalist Papers*, Library of Congress. https://guides.loc.gov/federalist-papers/full-text.

Hand, Learned. 1944. "The Spirit of Liberty." May 21. https://www.thefire.org/research-learn/spirit-liberty-speech-judge-learned-hand-1944.

Hanley, Steve. 2020. "Agrovoltaics Could Help Calm Fears About Renewables for Iowa Farmers." CleanTechnica, January 21. https://cleantechnica.com/2020/01/21/agrovoltaics-could-help-calm-fears-about-renewables-for-iowa-farmers/.

Hannah-Jones, Nikole. 2019. "Our Democracy's Founding Ideals Were False When They Were Written. Black Americans Have Fought to Make Them True." *New York Times Magazine*, August 14. https://www.nytimes.com/interactive/2019/08/14/magazine/black-history-american-democracy.html.

Hanson, Jon D., and Douglas A. Kysar. 1999. "Taking Behavioralism Seriously: Some Evidence of Market Manipulation." *Harvard Law Review* 112 (7): 1420–572. https://doi.org/10.2307/1342413.

Hardin, Garrett. 1968. "The Tragedy of the Commons." *Science* 162 (3859): 1243–48. https://doi.org/10.1126/science.162.3859.1243.

Hardin, Russell. 1982. *Collective Action*. Baltimore, MD: Johns Hopkins University Press.

Harold, Jason, Valentin Bertsch, Thomas Lawrence, and Magie Hall. 2021. "Drivers of People's Preferences for Spatial Proximity to Energy Infrastructure Technologies: A Cross-Country Analysis." International Association for Energy Economics 0(4). https://ideas.repec.org/a/aen/journl/ej42-4-harol.html.

Harrington, Michael. 1989. *Socialism: Past and Future*. New York: Arcade.

Harris, Leslie M. 2020. "I Helped Fact-Check the 1619 Project. The *Times* Ignored Me." *Politico*, March 6. https://www.politico.com/news/magazine/2020/03/06/1619-project-new-york-times-mistake-122248.

Harrison, Conor, and Shelley Welton. 2021. "The States That Opted Out: Politics, Power, and Exceptionalism in the Quest for Electricity Deregulation in the United States South." *Energy Research & Social Science* 79 (September): 1–11. https://doi.org/10.1016/j.erss.2021.102147.

Hartig, Hannah, Andrew Daniller, Scott Keeter, and Ted Van Green. 2023. "Republican Gains in 2022 Midterms Driven Mostly by Turnout Advantage." Pew Research Center, July 12. https://www.pewresearch.org/politics/2023/07/12/republican-gains-in-2022-midterms-driven-mostly-by-turnout-advantage/.

Hartmann, Thom. 2023. "The Right's 'Red Caesar' Plan: GOP's New Order Marches Onward—Only Voters Can Stop It." *Salon*, October 9.

Hasen, Richard L. 2023. "Trump Trial: Jan. 6 Charges Will Be the Most Important Case in U.S. History." *Slate*, August 1. https://slate.com/news-and-politics/2023/08/trump-trial-2024-historic-jack-smith-indictment.html.

Hauter, Wenonah. 2022. "Carbon Capture Won't Work, but It Will Funnel Billions to Corporations." Truthout, July 31. https://truthout.org/articles/carbon-capture-wont-work-but-it-will-funnel-billions-to-corporations/.

Hawkins, Lori. 2021. "As Some Texans See Electric Bills Skyrocket, Most Central Texans Should Be Spared Pricing Spikes." *Austin-American Statesman*, February 22. https://www.statesman.com/story/news/2021/02/21/some-texans-report-sky-high-bills-customers-austin-energy-bluebonnet-electric-cooperative-and-pedern/4532667001/.

Hayek, F. A. 1944. *The Road to Serfdom: Text and Documents—the Definitive Edition.* Edited by Bruce Caldwell. Chicago: University of Chicago Press.

——. 1948. *Individualism and Economic Order.* Chicago: University of Chicago Press.

Hayhoe, Katharine. 2021. *Saving Us: A Climate Scientist's Case for Hope and Healing in a Divided World.* New York: Atria/One Signal.

Heern, Jared. 2023. "Who's Controlling Our Energy Future? Industry and Environmental Representation on United States Public Utility Commissions." *Energy Research & Social Science* 101 (July): 1–11. https://doi.org/10.1016/j.erss.2023.103091.

Heglar, Mary Annaïse, and Amy Westervelt. 2021. " 'Nice' Isn't Going to Save the Planet." *The Nation*, November 10. https://www.thenation.com/article/environment/climate-cop26-civility/.

Heller, Michael A. 1998. "The Tragedy of the Anticommons: Property in the Transition from Marx to Markets." *Harvard Law Review* 111 (3): 621–88. https://doi.org/10.2307/1342203.

Hemmer, Nicole. 2021. "History Shows We Ignore Tucker Carlson at Our Peril." CNN, April 15. https://www.cnn.com/2021/04/15/opinions/tucker-carlson-replacement-theory-peter-brimelow-republican-party-hemmer/index.html.

——. 2022. *Partisans: The Conservative Revolutionaries Who Remade American Politics in the 1990s.* New York: Basic.

Hempling, Scott. 2014. " 'Regulatory Capture': Sources and Solutions." *Emory Corporate Governance and Accountability Review* 1 (1): 23–35.

Herndon, Astead W. 2020. "Conor Lamb, House Moderate, on Biden's Win, 'the Squad,' and the Future of the Democratic Party." *New York Times*, November 8. https://www.nytimes.com/2020/11/08/us/politics/conor-lamb-democrats-biden.html.

Herring, David. 2020. "Are There Positive Benefits from Global Warming?" Climate.gov, October 29. http://www.climate.gov/news-features/climate-qa/are-there-positive-benefits-global-warming.

Hertel-Fernandez, Alexander, Matto Mildenberger, and Leah C. Stokes. 2019. "Legislative Staff and Representation in Congress." *American Political Science Review* 113 (1): 1–18. https://doi.org/10.1017/S0003055418000606.

Hibbard, Paul J., Susan F. Tierney, Pavel G. Darling, and Sarah Cullinan. 2018. "An Expanding Carbon Cap-and-Trade Regime? A Decade of Experience with RGGI

Charts a Path Forward." *Electricity Journal* 31 (5): 1–8. https://doi.org/10.1016/j.tej
.2018.05.015.

Hickman, Kristin E. 2021. "Nondelegation as Constitutional Symbolism." *George Washington Law Review* 89 (5): 1079–142.

——. 2022. "The Roberts Court's Structural Incrementalism." *Harvard Law Review* 136 (1): F75–F96.

Hicks, J. R. 1975. "The Scope and Status of Welfare Economics." *Oxford Economic Papers* 27 (3): 307–26. https://doi.org/10.1093/oxfordjournals.oep.a041321.

Hill, Bruce. 2021. "Geologic Storage Is Permanent: An FAQ with Bruce Hill." Clean Air Task Force, March 9. https://www.catf.us/2021/03/geologic-storage-is-perm anent-faq/.

Hledik, Ryan, and Kate Peters. 2023. *Real Reliability: The Value of Virtual Power.* Boston: Brattle Group.

Hobbes, Thomas. [1651] 2005. *Leviathan.* Critical ed. London: Continuum.

Hobhouse, L. T. 1911. *Liberalism.* London: Williams and Norgate.

Hochschild, Arlie Russell. 2016. *Strangers in Their Own Land: Anger and Mourning on the American Right.* New York: New Press.

Hofstadter, Richard. 1955. *The Age of Reform: From Bryan to F.D.R.* New York: Vintage.

Hogan, Michael. 2023. "Tapping the Mother Lode: Employing Price-Responsive Demand to Reduce the Investment Challenge." Energy Systems Integration Group White Paper. https://www.raponline.org/knowledge-center/tapping-the -mother-lode-employing-price-responsive-demand-to-reduce-the-investment -challenge/.

Hogan, William W. 2005. "On an 'Energy Only' Electricity Market Design for Resource Adequacy." Harvard University Center for Business and Government, September.

Holleran, Max. 2022. *Yes to the City: Millennials and the Fight for Affordable Housing.* Princeton, NJ: Princeton University Press.

Holzman, Jael. 2022. "Biden Admin Eyes Funding Canadian Mining." *E&E News,* August 23. https://www.eenews.net/articles/biden-admin-eyes-funding-canadian -mining/.

Hopkins, Daniel J. 2018. *The Increasingly United States: How and Why American Political Behavior Nationalized.* Chicago: University of Chicago Press.

Hopman, Erika Street, and Bridgett Ennis. 2022. "A Conversation with a Woman Who Promotes Renewable Energy in Rural Communities." Yale Climate Connections, June. http://yaleclimateconnections.org/2022/06/a-conversation-with-a-woman -who-promotes-renewable-energy-in-rural-communities/.

Horsley, Scott. 2019. "This Economic Theory Could Be Used to Pay for the Green New Deal." NPR, July 17. https://www.npr.org/2019/07/17/742255158/this-economic-theory -could-be-used-to-pay-for-the-green-new-deal.

Horton, Helena. 2023. "Young Climate Activist Tells Greenpeace to Drop 'Old-Fashioned' Anti-nuclear Stance." *The Guardian,* August 29. https://www.the guardian.com/environment/2023/aug/29/young-climate-activist-tells-greenpeace -to-drop-old-fashioned-anti-nuclear-stance.

Houghton, J. T., L. G. Meira Filho, B. A. Callander, N. Harris, A. Kattenberg, and K. Maskell, eds. 1996. *Climate Change 1995: The Science of Climate Change.* Second Assessment Report of the Intergovernmental Panel on Climate Change. Cambridge: Cambridge University Press.

Houghton, J. T., Y. Ying, D. J. Griggs, M. Noguer, P. J. van der Linden, X. Dai, K. Maskell, and C. A. Johnson, eds. 2001. *Climate Change 2001: The Scientific Basis.* Third Assessment Report of the Intergovernmental Panel on Climate Change. Cambridge: Cambridge University Press.

House, Billy. 2019. "Progressive Group That Backed AOC Takes Aim at Incumbents Across U.S." *Bloomberg*, August 22. https://www.bloomberg.com/news/articles/2019 -08-22/liberals-seek-to-repeat-ocasio-cortez-feat-by-ousting-incumbents.

Hovenkamp, Herbert. 1994. *Federal Antitrust Policy: The Law of Competition and Its Practice*. St. Paul, MN: West Information.

Howarth, Robert. 2013. Comment in "Should Nuclear Power Receive Environmental Subsidies?" OurEnergyPolicy, posted September 21. https://www.ourenergypolicy .org/should-nuclear-power-receive-environmental-subsidies/#comment-1449.

Huxley, Aldous. 1934. Introduction to Samuel Butler, *Erewhon: Or, Over the Range* (1872). Norwalk, CT: Easton Press.

Idel, Robert. 2022. "Levelized Full System Costs of Electricity." *Energy* 259 (November): art. 124905. https://doi.org/10.1016/j.energy.2022.124905.

Intergovernmental Panel on Climate Change (IPCC). 1992. *FAR Climate Change: Scientific Assessment of Climate Change*. Geneva: IPCC. https://www.ipcc.ch/report/ar1 /wg1/.

——. 2014. *Climate Change 2014: Synthesis Report*. Contribution of Working Groups I, II, and III to the Fifth Assessment Report of the Intergovernmental Panel on Climate Change (IPCC). Geneva: IPCC. https://epic.awi.de/id/eprint/37530/1/IPCC _AR5_SYR_Final.pdf.

——. 2019. *Global Warming of 1.5°C*. Cambridge: Cambridge University Press. https:// www.ipcc.ch/site/assets/uploads/sites/2/2019/06/SR15_Full_Report_Low_Res .pdf.

——. 2023. *AR6 Synthesis Report: Climate Change 2023*. Contribution of Working Groups I, II, and III to the Sixth Assessment Report of the Intergovernmental Panel on Climate Change (IPCC). Geneva: IPCC. https://www.ipcc.ch/report/sixth -assessment-report-cycle/.

Israel, Tania. 2020. *Beyond Your Bubble: How to Connect Across the Political Divide, Skills and Strategies for Conversations That Work*. Washington, DC: APA LifeTools.

Iyengar, Shanto, and Douglas S. Massey. 2019. "Scientific Communication in a Posttruth Society." *Proceedings of the National Academy of Sciences* 116 (16): 7656–61. https://doi.org/10.1073/pnas.1805868115.

Jacobs, Sharon, and Dave Owen. 2023. "Community Energy Exit." *Duke Law Journal* 73 (2): 251–326.

Jacobs, Struan. 1997. "Michael Polanyi and Spontaneous Order, 1941–1951." *Tradition and Discovery* 24 (2): 14–28. https://philpapers.org/rec/JACMPA and http:// polanyisociety.org/TAD%20WEB%20ARCHIVE/TAD24-2/TAD24-2-pg14-28-pdf .pdf.

Jacobson, Mark Z., Robert W. Howarth, Mark A. Delucchi, Stan R. Scobie, Jannette M. Barth, Michael J. Dvorak, Megan Klevze, et al. 2013. "Examining the Feasibility of Converting New York State's All-Purpose Energy Infrastructure to One Using Wind, Water, and Sunlight." *Energy Policy* 57:585–601. https://doi.org/10.1016/j .enpol.2013.02.036.

Jacquet, Jennifer. 2015. *Is Shame Necessary? New Uses for an Old Tool*. New York: Pantheon.

James, Steve. 2014. "Deep Freeze Puts $5 Billion Chill on Economy." CNBC, January 8. https://www.cnbc.com/2014/01/08/deep-freeze-puts-5-billion-chill-on-economy .html.

Jamieson, Kathleen Hall, and Joseph N. Cappella. 2008. *Echo Chamber: Rush Limbaugh and the Conservative Media Establishment*. Oxford: Oxford University Press.

Janis, Irving L. 1972. *Victims of Groupthink: A Psychological Study of Foreign-Policy Decisions and Fiascoes*. Boston: Houghton Mifflin.

Jayashankar, Aparna, Prithvi Kalkunte, Anil Kumar, and Pia Orrenius. 2023. "Hotter Summer Days Heat Up Texans but Chill the State Economy." Federal Reserve Bank of Dallas, October 18. https://www.dallasfed.org/research/swe/2023/swe2309.

Jefferson, Thomas. [1818] n.d. "Thomas Jefferson's Explanation of the Three Volumes Bound in Marbeld Paper (the So-Called 'ANAS'), 4 February 1818." Founders Online. https://founders.archives.gov/documents/Jefferson/03-12-02-0343-0002.

Jenkins, Jesse D. 2022. "The Inflation Reduction Act and the Path to a Net-Zero America." Center for Policy Research on Energy and the Environment, Princeton University, September 12. https://cpree.princeton.edu/events/2022/inflation-reduction-act-and-path-net-zero-america.

——. 2023. "How the Climate Fight Was Almost Lost." *Heatmap News*, August 18. https://heatmap.news/politics/inflation-reduction-act-jesse-jenkins.

Jenkins, Jesse D., Erin N. Mayfield, Jamil Farbes, Greg Schivley, Neha Patankar, and Ryan Jones. 2023. "Climate Progress and the 117th Congress: The Impacts of the Inflation Reduction Act and Infrastructure Investment and Jobs Act." July 14. https://doi.org/10.5281/ZENODO.8087805.

Jensen, Jacob, Suresh Naidu, Ethan Kaplan, Laurence Wilse-Samson, David Gergen, Michael Zuckerman, and Arthur Spirling. 2012. "Political Polarization and the Dynamics of Political Language: Evidence from 130 Years of Partisan Speech." *Brookings Papers on Economic Activity* 2012 (2): 1–81. https://doi.org/10.1353/eca.2012.0017.

The Jewish Peril: Protocols of the Learned Elders of Zion. 1920. London: Eyre & Spottiswoode.

Johnsen, D. Bruce. 1991. "Property Rights to Cartel Rents: The Socony-Vacuum Story." *Journal of Law & Economics* 34 (1): 177–203. https://doi.org/10.1086/467223.

Johnson, Robert. 2023. "The Energy Transition: Opportunities and Challenges for Indigenous Communities in the US and Canada." Paper presented at the Center on Global Energy Policy, Columbia University, February 8. https://www.energypolicy.columbia.edu/events/the-energy-transition-opportunities-and-challenges-for-indigenous-communities-in-the-us-and-canada/.

Jolls, Christine, Cass R. Sunstein, and Richard Thaler. 1998. "A Behavioral Approach to Law and Economics." *Stanford Law Review* 50 (5): 1471–550. https://doi.org/10.2307/1229304.

Jones, Bryan D., and Frank R. Baumgartner. 2005. "A Model of Choice for Public Policy." *Journal of Public Administration Research and Theory* 15 (3): 325–51. https://doi.org/10.1093/jopart/mui018.

Jones, Jeff. 2020. "In Election 2020, How Did the Media, Electoral Process Fare? Republicans, Democrats Disagree." Knight Foundation, December. https://knightfoundation.org/articles/in-election-2020-how-did-the-media-electoral-process-fare-republicans-democrats-disagree/.

Jones, Thomas A. 2011. "Wind Turbine Syndrome and Vibroacoustic Disease." *Wind Wise MA* (blog), October 14. https://windwisema.org/about/noise/wind-turbine-syndrome-and-vibroacoustic-disease/.

Joskow, Paul L. 1988. "Asset Specificity and the Structure of Vertical Relationships: Empirical Evidence." *Journal of Law, Economics, and Organization* 4 (1): 95–117. https://doi.org/10.1093/oxfordjournals.jleo.a036950.

——. 2008. *Capacity Payments in Imperfect Electricity Markets: Need and Design*. Cambridge, MA: MIT Center for Energy and Environmental Policy Research.

Joskow, Paul L., Douglas R. Bohi, and Frank M. Gollop. 1989. "Regulatory Failure, Regulatory Reform, and Structural Change in the Electrical Power Industry." *Brookings Papers on Economic Activity* 1989:125–208. https://doi.org/10.2307/2534721.

Jurkowitz, Mark, and Jeffrey Gottfried. 2022. "Twitter Is the Go-to Social Media Site for U.S. Journalists, but Not for the Public." Pew Research Center, June 27. https://www.pewresearch.org/short-reads/2022/06/27/twitter-is-the-go-to-social-media-site-for-u-s-journalists-but-not-for-the-public/.

Kahan, Dan M., Donald Braman, John Monahan, Lisa Callahan, and Ellen Peters. 2010. "Cultural Cognition and Public Policy: The Case of Outpatient Commitment Laws." *Law and Human Behavior* 34 (2): 118–40. https://doi.org/10.1007/s10979-008-9174-4.

Kahan, Dan M., Donald Braman, Paul Slovic, John Gastil, and Geoffrey L. Cohen. 2007. "The Second National Risk and Culture Study: Making Sense of—and Making Progress in—the American Culture War of Fact." George Washington University Legal Studies Research Paper no. 370, Yale Law School Public Law Working Paper no. 154, Harvard Law School Program on Risk Regulation Research Paper no. 08-26.

Kahan, Dan M., Hank Jenkins-Smith, and Donald Braman. 2011. "Cultural Cognition of Scientific Consensus." *Journal of Risk Research* 14 (2): 147–74. https://doi.org/10.1080/13669877.2010.511246.

Kahneman, Daniel. 2011. *Thinking, Fast and Slow.* New York: Farrar, Straus and Giroux.

Kahneman, Daniel, and Amos Tversky. 1979. "Prospect Theory: An Analysis of Decision Under Risk." *Econometrica* 47 (2): 263–91. https://doi.org/10.2307/1914185.

——. 1984. "Choices, Values, and Frames." *American Psychologist* 39 (4): 341–50. https://doi.org/10.1037/0003-066X.39.4.341.

Kalla, Joshua L., and David E. Broockman. 2018. "The Minimal Persuasive Effects of Campaign Contact in General Elections: Evidence from 49 Field Experiments." *American Political Science Review* 112 (1): 148–66. https://doi.org/10.1017/S0003055417000363.

——. 2020. "Reducing Exclusionary Attitudes Through Interpersonal Conversation: Evidence from Three Field Experiments." *American Political Science Review* 114 (2): 410–25. https://doi.org/10.1017/S0003055419000923.

Kalmoe, Nathan P., and Lilliana Mason. 2022. *Radical American Partisanship: Mapping Violent Hostility, Its Causes, and the Consequences for Democracy.* Chicago: University of Chicago Press.

Kalt, Joseph P., and Mark A. Zupan. 1990. "The Apparent Ideological Behavior of Legislators: Testing for Principal-Agent Slack in Political Institutions." *Journal of Law & Economics* 33 (1): 103–31. https://doi.org/10.1086/467201.

Karni, Annie. 2019. "No One Attacked Trump More in 2016 Than Republicans. It Didn't Work." *New York Times*, August 13. https://www.nytimes.com/2019/08/13/us/politics/trump-attacks-republicans-democrats.html.

Karpf, David. 2016. *Analytic Activism: Digital Listening and the New Political Strategy.* New York: Oxford University Press.

Kashwan, Prakash. 2020. "American Environmentalism's Racist Roots Have Shaped Global Thinking About Conservation." *The Conversation*, September 2. http://theconversation.com/american-environmentalisms-racist-roots-have-shaped-global-thinking-about-conservation-143783.

Katz, A. J. 2023. "These Are the Top-Rated Cable News Shows of 2022." *Adweek*, January 3. https://www.adweek.com/tvnewser/these-are-the-top-rated-cable-news-shows-of-2022/521247/.

Kaufman, Noah, John Larsen, Ben King, and Peter Marsters. 2020. "Output-Based Rebates: An Alternative to Border Carbon Adjustments for Preserving US Competitiveness." Center on Global Energy Policy, Columbia University. https://www.energypolicy.columbia.edu/publications/output-based-rebates-an-alternative-to-border-carbon-adjustments-for-preserving-us-competitiveness/.

Kelton, Stephanie. 2020. *The Deficit Myth: Modern Monetary Theory and the Birth of the People's Economy.* New York: PublicAffairs.

Kennedy, Brian, Cary Funk, and Alec Tyson. 2023. "What Americans Think About an Energy Transition from Fossil Fuels to Renewables." Pew Research Center, June 28. https://www.pewresearch.org/science/2023/06/28/what-americans-think-about-an-energy-transition-from-fossil-fuels-to-renewables/.

Kennedy, Brian, Alec Tyson, and Cary Funk. 2022. "Americans Divided Over Direction of Biden's Climate Change Policies." Pew Research Center, July 14. https://www.pewresearch.org/science/2022/07/14/americans-divided-over-direction-of-bidens-climate-change-policies/.

Kennedy, Ryan. 2022. "California Cuts Rooftop Solar Net Metering: An Industry Reacts." *PV Magazine USA*, December 20. https://pv-magazine-usa.com/2022/12/20/california-cuts-rooftop-solar-net-metering-an-industry-reacts/.

Kenny, Christopher T., Cory McCartan, Tyler Simko, Shiro Kuriwaki, and Kosuke Imai. 2023. "Widespread Partisan Gerrymandering Mostly Cancels Nationally, but Reduces Electoral Competition." *Proceedings of the National Academy of Sciences* 120 (25): art. e2217322120. https://doi.org/10.1073/pnas.2217322120.

Kersh, Rogan. 2007. "The Well-Informed Lobbyist: Information and Interest Group Lobbying." In *Interest Group Politics*, 7th ed., edited by Allan J. Cigler and Burdett A. Loomis, 389–411. Washington, DC: CQ Press.

Kessler, Jeremy K., and David E. Pozen. 2018. "The Search for an Egalitarian First Amendment." *Columbia Law Review* 118 (7): 1953–2010.

Kessler, Richard. 2023. "US Clean Grid Progress Hits Hurdle as Speed of High-Voltage Power Line Build-out Sags." *Recharge*, January 19. https://www.rechargenews.com/wind/us-clean-grid-progress-hits-hurdle-as-speed-of-high-voltage-power-line-build-out-sags/2-1-1390978.

Khan, Yusuf. 2023. "Copper Shortage Threatens Green Transition." *Wall Street Journal*, April 18. https://www.wsj.com/articles/copper-shortage-threatens-green-transition-620df1e5.

Kiesling, L. Lynne. 2009. *Deregulation, Innovation, and Market Liberalization: Electricity Regulation in a Continually Evolving Environment.* London: Routledge.

Kim, Doyob, and Alyssa Fischer. 2021. "Distributed Energy Resources for Net Zero: An Asset or a Hassle to the Electricity Grid? Analysis." International Energy Agency, September. https://www.iea.org/commentaries/distributed-energy-resources-for-net-zero-an-asset-or-a-hassle-to-the-electricity-grid.

Kinder, Molly, and Laura Stateler. 2020. "Amazon and Walmart Have Raked in Billions in Additional Profits During the Pandemic, and Shared Almost None of It with Their Workers." *Brookings* (blog), December 22. https://www.brookings.edu/articles/amazon-and-walmart-have-raked-in-billions-in-additional-profits-during-the-pandemic-and-shared-almost-none-of-it-with-their-workers/.

King, Carey W. 2020. *The Economic Superorganism: Beyond the Competing Narratives on Energy, Growth, and Policy.* Cham, Switzerland: Springer International.

King, Gary, Benjamin Schneer, and Ariel White. 2017. "How the News Media Activate Public Expression and Influence National Agendas." *Science* 358 (6364): 776–80. https://doi.org/10.1126/science.aao1100.

Kingdon, John W. 2003. *Agendas, Alternatives, and Public Policies*. 2nd ed. London: Longman.

Klass, Alexandra B., Joshua Macey, Shelley Welton, and Hannah Wiseman. 2022. "Grid Reliability Through Clean Energy." *Stanford Law Review* 74 (5): 969–1071.

Klass, Alexandra B., and Danielle Meinhardt. 2015. "Transporting Oil and Gas: U.S. Infrastructure Challenges." *Iowa Law Review* 100 (3): 947–1054.

Klass, Alexandra B., and Jim Rossi. 2017. "Reconstituting the Federalism Battle in Energy Transportation." *Harvard Environmental Law Review* 41 (2): 423–92.

Klein, Maury. 2008. *The Power Makers: Steam, Electricity, and the Men Who Invented Modern America*. New York: Bloomsbury Press.

Kleinfeld, Rachel. 2021. "The Rise of Political Violence in the United States." *Journal of Democracy* 32 (4): 160–76.

Klumpp, Tilman, Hugo M. Mialon, and Michael A. Williams. 2016. "The Business of American Democracy: *Citizens United*, Independent Spending, and Elections." *Journal of Law & Economics* 59 (1): 1–43. https://doi.org/10.1086/685691.

Knutson, Jacob. 2020. "11 Republican Congressional Nominees Support the QAnon Conspiracy Theory." *Axios*, July 12. https://www.axios.com/2020/07/12/qanon -nominees-congress-gop.

Koerth, Maggie. 2018. "How Money Affects Elections." *FiveThirtyEight* (blog), September 10. https://fivethirtyeight.com/features/money-and-elections-a-complicated -love-story/.

Kolko, Gabriel. 1962. *Wealth and Power in America: An Analysis of Social Class and Income Distribution*. New York: Praeger.

——. 1965. *Railroads and Regulation, 1877–1916*. Princeton, NJ: Princeton University Press.

Kosnik, Lea-Rachel. 2010. "River Basin Water Management in the U.S.: A Regulatory Anticommons." *Environmental & Energy Law & Policy Journal* 5 (2): 365–94.

Kovvali, Aneil, and Joshua C. Macey. 2023. "The Corporate Governance of Public Utilities." *Yale Journal on Regulation* 40 (2): 569–619.

Kramer, Anna. 2018. "The Unaffordable City: Housing and Transit in North American Cities." *Cities* 83:1–10. https://doi.org/10.1016/j.cities.2018.05.013.

Kramer, Bruce M., and Owen L. Anderson. 2005. "The Rule of Capture—an Oil and Gas Perspective." *Environmental Law* 35 (4): 899–954.

Krastev, Ivan, and Stephen Holmes. 2020. *The Light That Failed: Why the West Is Losing the Fight for Democracy*. New York: Pegasus.

Krebs, Tom. 2023. "Modern Climate Policy: Moving Beyond the Market-Liberal Paradigm." Newforum, January 10. https://newforum.org/en/studie/modern-climate -policy-moving-beyond-the-market-liberal-paradigm/.

Krehbiel, Keith. 1992. *Information and Legislative Organization*. Paperback ed. Ann Arbor: University of Michigan Press.

——. 1998. *Pivotal Politics: A Theory of U.S. Lawmaking*. Chicago: University of Chicago Press.

Krishnan, Mekala, Hamid Samandari, Jonathan Woetzel, Sven Smit, Daniel Pacthod, Dickon Pinner, Tomas Nauclér, et al. 2022. "Sectors Are Unevenly Exposed in the Net-Zero Transition." *McKinsey Insights*, January.

Krugman, Paul. 2009. "Health Care Realities." *New York Times*, July 30. https://www .nytimes.com/2009/07/31/opinion/31krugman.html.

——. 2023. "Why We Should Politicize the Weather." *New York Times*, July 17. https:// www.nytimes.com/2023/07/17/opinion/weather-climate-politics-republican.html.

Kubin, Emily, Curtis Puryear, Chelsea Schein, and Kurt Gray. 2021. "Personal Experiences Bridge Moral and Political Divides Better Than Facts." *Proceedings of the*

National Academy of Sciences, 118 (6): art. e2008389118. https://doi.org/10.1073/pnas
.2008389118.

Kuckro, Rod. 2015. "Northeast Blizzard Evokes Polar Vortex—and Region's Gas Pipeline Shortages." *E&E News*, January 27. https://subscriber.politicopro.com/article
/eenews/2015/01/27/northeast-blizzard-evokes-polar-vortex-and-regions-gas
-pipeline-shortages-100289.

Kuipers, Dean. 2012. "Unabomber Billboard Continues to Hurt Heartland Institute."
Los Angeles Times, May 9. https://www.latimes.com/science/la-xpm-2012-may-09-la
-me-gs-unabomber-billboard-continues-to-hurt-heartland-institute-20120509
-story.html.

Kuran, Timur. 1995. *Private Truths, Public Lies: The Social Consequences of Preference
Falsification*. Cambridge, MA: Harvard University Press.

Kustoff, Alexander, Maikol Cerda, Akhil Rajan, Frances Rosenbluth, and Ian Shapiro. 2021. "The Rise of Safe Seats and Party in Discipline in the US Congress."
Unpublished paper. On file with the author.

Kysar, Douglas A., and James Salzman. 2003. "Environmental Tribalism." *Minnesota
Law Review* 87 (4): 1099–137.

Lacey, Stephen. 2014. "This Is What the Utility Death Spiral Looks Like." *GTM* (Greentech Media), March 4. https://www.greentechmedia.com/articles/read/this-is
-what-the-utility-death-spiral-looks-like.

LaFrance, Adrienne. 2019. "Fox Got It Wrong With '3 Mexican Countries,' but Also
Got It Right." *The Atlantic*, March 31. https://www.theatlantic.com/ideas/archive
/2019/03/foxs-3-mexican-countries-chyron-message/586195/.

Lakhani, Nina. 2022. "Schumer and Manchin's 'Dirty Side Deal' to Fast-Track Pipelines Faces Backlash." *The Guardian*, September 22. https://www.theguardian.com
/us-news/2022/sep/22/schumer-manchin-side-deal-pipelines-backlash.

Lanham, J. Drew. 2021. "What Do We Do About John James Audubon?" *Audubon*,
Spring. https://www.audubon.org/magazine/spring-2021/what-do-we-do-about
-john-james-audubon.

Larsen, Patrick. 2022. "State Official Tells Regulators RGGI Repeal Process Is Imminent." *VPM*, August 31. https://www.vpm.org/news/2022-08-31/state-official-tells
-regulators-rggi-repeal-process-is-imminent.

Lawson, Ashley J. 2021. *The Clean Electricity Performance Program (CEPP): In Brief*.
Congressional Research Service (CRS) report. Washington, DC: CRS.

Lawson, M. Asher, and Hemant Kakkar. 2022. "Of Pandemics, Politics, and Personality: The Role of Conscientiousness and Political Ideology in the Sharing of Fake
News." *Journal of Experimental Psychology* 151 (5): 1154–77. https://doi.org/10.1037
/xge0001120.

Leahy, Michael Patrick. 2009. *Rules for Conservative Radicals: Lessons from Saul Alinsky, the Tea Party Movement, and the Apostle Paul in the Age of Collaborative Technologies*. Edited by Gina Loudon, Legacy Group. N.p.: C-Rad Press.

Lee, A. L. 2023. "U.S. Energy Department Announces $1.2 Billion to Build Two Car-
bon Dioxide Removal Sites in Texas, Louisiana." UPI, August 11. https://www.upi
.com/Top_News/US/2023/08/11/energy-department-announces-12-billion-to
-build-direct-air-capture-facilities/3491691748180/.

Lee, Frances E. 2015. "How Party Polarization Affects Governance." *Annual Review of
Political Science* 18 (1): 261–82. https://doi.org/10.1146/annurev-polisci-072012-113747.

Lee, Hoesung, Katherine Calvin, Dipak Dasgupta, Oliver Geden, Bronwyn Hayward,
Nicholas P. Simpson, Edmond Totin, et al. 2023. *Synthesis Report of the IPCC Sixth
Assessment Report (AR6)*. Geneva: Intergovernmental Panel on Climate Change.
https://report.ipcc.ch/ar6syr/pdf/IPCC_AR6_SYR_SPM.pdf.

Lee, Hoesung, Katherine Calvin, Dipak Dasgupta, Gerhard Krinner, Aditi Mukherji, Peter Thorne, Christopher Risos, et al. 2023. "IPCC, 2023: Summary for Policymakers." In *Climate Change 2023: Synthesis Report*. Contribution of Working Groups I, II, and III to the Sixth Assessment Report of the Intergovernmental Panel on Climate Change (IPCC). Geneva: IPCC. https://www.ipcc.ch/report/ar6/syr/.

Lenzi, Dominic. 2022. "How Should We Respond to Climate Change? Virtue Ethics and Aggregation Problems." *Journal of Social Philosophy* 54 (3): 421–36. https://doi.org/10.1111/josp.12488.

Leonhardt, David. 2023. "Trump's Indictment Is Unavoidably Political." *New York Times*, June 10. https://www.nytimes.com/2023/06/10/briefing/trump-indictment -political.html.

Leonhardt, David, and Ashley Wu. 2021. "Fighting the Dixie Fire." *New York Times*, October 11. https://www.nytimes.com/2021/10/11/briefing/dixie-fire-battle-climate -change.html.

Lepore, Jill. 2007. "Party Time." *The New Yorker*, September 10. https://www.newyorker .com/magazine/2007/09/17/party-time.

Lerer, Lisa, and Astead W. Herndon. 2021. "Menace Enters the Republican Mainstream." *New York Times*, November 12. https://www.nytimes.com/2021/11/12/us /politics/republican-violent-rhetoric.html.

Levendusky, Matthew S. 2018. "Americans, Not Partisans: Can Priming American National Identity Reduce Affective Polarization?" *Journal of Politics* 80 (1): 59–70. https://doi.org/10.1086/693987.

Levi, Michael. 2012. "Would Cap and Trade Have Increased U.S. Emissions?" *Council on Foreign Relations* (blog), October 24. https://www.cfr.org/blog/would-cap-and -trade-have-increased-us-emissions.

Levin, Aaron M., and Joshua C. Macey. 2018. "Dodd-Frank Is a Pigouvian Regulation." *Yale Law Journal* 127 (5): 1336–415.

Levin, Todd, John Bistline, Ramteen Sioshansi, Wesley J. Cole, Jonghwan Kwon, Scott P. Burger, George W. Crabtree, et al. 2023. "Energy Storage Solutions to Decarbonize Electricity Through Enhanced Capacity Expansion Modelling." *Nature Energy*, September, 1199–208. https://doi.org/10.1038/s41560-023-01340-6.

LeVine, Marianne. 2014. "Minorities Aren't Well Represented in Environmental Groups, Study Says." *Los Angeles Times*, July 28. https://www.latimes.com/nation /la-na-environmental-groups-diversity-20140728-story.html.

Levitsky, Steven, and Daniel Ziblatt. 2019. *How Democracies Die*. New York: Broadway.

Levy, David L., and Ans Kolk. 2002. "Strategic Responses to Global Climate Change: Conflicting Pressures on Multinationals in the Oil Industry." *Business and Politics* 4 (3): 275–300.

Levy, Ro'ee. 2021. "Social Media, News Consumption, and Polarization: Evidence from a Field Experiment." *American Economic Review* 111 (3): 831–70. https://doi.org /10.1257/aer.20191777.

Lewis, Michael. 2010. *The Big Short: Inside the Doomsday Machine*. New York: Norton.

——. 2017. *The Undoing Project: A Friendship That Changed Our Minds*. New York: Norton.

——. 2018. *Has Anyone Seen the President?* Audiobook. New York: Simon & Schuster Audio.

Libgober, Brian D. 2020. "Strategic Proposals, Endogenous Comments, and Bias in Rulemaking." *Journal of Politics* 82 (2): 642–56. https://doi.org/10.1086/706891.

Lindblom, Charles E. 1959. "The Science of 'Muddling Through.'" *Public Administration Review* 19 (2): 79–88. https://doi.org/10.2307/973677.

Lipsitz, Raina. 2022. *The Rise of a New Left: How Young Radicals Are Shaping the Future of American Politics*. London: Verso.

Livermore, Michael A. 2014. "Cost–Benefit Analysis and Agency Independence." *University of Chicago Law Review* 81 (2): 609–88.

Logan, Erin B., and Anumita Kaur. 2022. "Republicans Who Voted Against Biden's Infrastructure Bill Are Touting Its Projects Anyway." *Los Angeles Times*, January 24. https://www.latimes.com/politics/story/2022-01-24/these-republicans-voted-against-bidens-infrastructure-bill-theyre-running-on-it-anyway.

Lomborg, Bjørn. 2020. *False Alarm: How Climate Panic Costs Us Trillions, Hurts the Poor, and Fails to Fix the Planet*. New York: Basic.

Lopez, German. 2023. "An Enemy in Mexico." *New York Times*, July 31. https://www.nytimes.com/2023/07/31/briefing/mexico.html.

Lopez, Nadia. 2023. "Analysis: California's Early EV Adopters Are Affluent, White, Asian, Educated, and Urban." *Times of San Diego*, March 26. https://timesofsandiego.com/business/2023/03/26/analysis-californias-early-ev-adopters-are-affluent-white-asian-educated-and-urban/.

Lord, Charles G., Lee Ross, and Mark R. Lepper. 1979. "Biased Assimilation and Attitude Polarization: The Effects of Prior Theories on Subsequently Considered Evidence." *Journal of Personality and Social Psychology* 37 (11): 2098–109. https://doi.org/10.1037/0022-3514.37.11.2098.

Lovelock, James E., and Lynn Margulis. 1974. "Atmospheric Homeostasis by and for the Biosphere: The Gaia Hypothesis." *Tellus* 26 (1–2): 2–10. https://doi.org/10.1111/j.2153-3490.1974.tb01946.x.

Lowe, Chris. 2001. "The Trouble with Tribe." *Learning for Justice*, Spring. https://www.learningforjustice.org/magazine/spring-2001/the-trouble-with-tribe.

Lustgarten, Abrahm. 2020. "The Great Climate Migration Has Begun." *New York Times Magazine*, July 23. https://www.nytimes.com/interactive/2020/07/23/magazine/climate-migration.html.

Luttig, J. Michael. 2023. "Ex–Federal Judge and Prominent Conservative: 'There Is No Republican Party.'" Interview by Shawna Mizelle. CNN, August 9. https://www.cnn.com/2023/08/09/politics/michael-luttig-conservative-judge-republicans-cnntv/index.html.

Macey, Joshua C. 2020. "Zombie Energy Laws." *Vanderbilt Law Review* 73 (4): 1077–126.

Macey, Joshua C., and Jackson Salovaara. 2020. "Rate Regulation Redux." *University of Pennsylvania Law Review* 168 (5): 1181–267.

Macey, Joshua C., Shelley Welton, and Hannah Jacobs Wiseman. 2023. "Grid Reliability in the Electric Era." *Yale Journal on Regulation* 41:164–247.

MacKay, Alexander, and Ignacia Mercadal. 2021. "Deregulation, Market Power, and Prices: Evidence from the Electricity Sector." Posted February 26. https://doi.org/10.2139/ssrn.3793305.

MacLean, Nancy. 2017. *Democracy in Chains: The Deep History of the Radical Right's Stealth Plan for America*. New York: Viking Press.

MacNeil, Robert. 2012. "Alternative Climate Policy Pathways in the US." *Climate Policy* 13 (2): 259–76. https://doi.org/10.1080/14693062.2012.714964.

Magat, Wesley, Alan J. Krupnick, and Winston Harrington. 2013. *Rules in the Making: A Statistical Analysis of Regulatory Agency Behavior*. London: Routledge.

Malik, Naureen S. 2017. "Cold Snap Makes New England the World's Priciest Gas Market." *Boston Globe*, December 27. https://www.bostonglobe.com/metro/2017/12/27/cold-snap-makes-new-england-world-priciest-gas-market/ILRzKrRTCtW4uNYRZeEIvK/story.html.

Malthus, Joseph Robert. 1789. *An Essay on the Principle of Population*. London: J. Johnson.

Marcacci, Silvio. 2023. "2023 Energy Predictions: IRA Spurs Clean Energy Boom, Electric Trucks Accelerate, Battery Demand Surges, EPA Cuts Power Sector Pollution." *Forbes*, January 9. https://www.forbes.com/sites/energyinnovation/2023/01/09/2023-energy-predictions-ira-spurs-clean-energy-tribal-renewables-surge-electric-trucks-accelerate-battery-demand-grows-epa-cuts-power-sector-pollution/.

Marchese, David. 2019. "Why Stacey Abrams Is Still Saying She Won." *New York Times Magazine*, April 28. https://www.nytimes.com/interactive/2019/04/28/magazine/stacey-abrams-election-georgia.html.

Marcus, Josh. 2023. "I Took a Deep Dive Into Rumble—and the Issues Go Far Further Than Russell Brand." *The Independent*, October 13. https://www.independent.co.uk/voices/rumble-russell-brand-trump-biden-b2423379.html.

Marks, Joseph, Eloise Copland, Eleanor Loh, Cass R. Sunstein, and Tali Sharot. 2019. "Epistemic Spillovers: Learning Others' Political Views Reduces the Ability to Assess and Use Their Expertise in Nonpolitical Domains." *Cognition* 188:74–84. https://doi.org/10.1016/j.cognition.2018.10.003.

Martel, Cameron, Gordon Pennycook, and David G. Rand. 2020. "Reliance on Emotion Promotes Belief in Fake News." *Cognitive Research: Principles and Implications* 5 (1): art. 47. https://doi.org/10.1186/s41235-020-00252-3 or https://www.researchgate.net/publication/345991064_Reliance_on_emotion_promotes_belief_in_fake_news.

Martin, Albro. 1974. "The Troubled Subject of Railroad Regulation in the Gilded Age—a Reappraisal." *Journal of American History* 61 (2): 339–71. https://doi.org/10.2307/1903953.

Martin, Jonathan, and Alexander Burns. 2021. "Republicans Splinter Over Whether to Make a Full Break from Trump." *New York Times*, January 8. https://www.nytimes.com/2021/01/07/us/politics/trump-republicans.html.

Martin, Ralf, Mirabelle Muûls, and Ulrich J. Wagner. 2016. "The Impact of the European Union Emissions Trading Scheme on Regulated Firms: What Is the Evidence After Ten Years?" *Review of Environmental Economics and Policy* 10 (1): 129–48. https://doi.org/10.1093/reep/rev016.

Martorana, Megan. 2007. "Jargon Alert: Pareto Efficiency." *Econ Focus*, Federal Reserve Bank of Richmond, 11 (1): 8.

Marx, Karl. 1887. *Capital: A Critique of Political Economy*. Translated by Samuel Moore and Edward Aveling. Moscow: Progress.

——. 1994. *The Eighteenth Brumaire of Louis Bonaparte*. Translated by D. D. L. (1897). New York: International.

Marx, Karl, and Frederick Engels. 2014. *The Communist Manifesto*. Translated by Samuel Moore. New York: International.

Mason, Lilliana. 2016. "A Cross-Cutting Calm: How Social Sorting Drives Affective Polarization." *Public Opinion Quarterly* 80 (S1): 351–77. https://doi.org/10.1093/poq/nfw001.

Massarella, Kate, Susannah M. Sallu, Jonathan E. Ensor, and Rob Marchant. 2018. "REDD+, Hype, Hope and Disappointment: The Dynamics of Expectations in Conservation and Development Pilot Projects." *World Development* 109:375–85. https://doi.org/10.1016/j.worlddev.2018.05.006.

Massey, William L., and Nora Mead Brownell. 2003. "Fact-Finding Investigation Into Possible Manipulation of Electric and Natural Gas Prices, Docket No. PA02-2-005." Federal Energy Regulatory Commission.

Mastrangelo, Dominick. 2022. "Fox Tops 2022 Cable Ratings." *The Hill* (blog), December 15. https://thehill.com/homenews/3776681-fox-news-tops-2022-cable-ratings/#:~:text=Fox%20News%20notched%20its%20seventh,to%20Nielsen%20Media%20Research%20figures.

Mastroianni, Adam. 2023. "Your Brain Has Tricked You Into Thinking Everything Is Worse." *New York Times*, June 20. https://www.nytimes.com/2023/06/20/opinion/psychology-brain-biased-memory.html.

Mattison, Nathaniel. 2022. "Beyond Gas Bans: Alternative Pathways to Reduce Building Emissions in Light of State Preemption Laws." Guarini Center, New York University School of Law. https://guarinicenter.org/document/beyond-gas-bans/.

Mayer, Jane. 2016. *Dark Money: The Hidden History of the Billionaires Behind the Rise of the Radical Right*. New York: Knopf Doubleday.

Mayhew, David R. 1974. "Congressional Elections: The Case of the Vanishing Marginals." *Polity* 6 (3): 295–317. https://doi.org/10.2307/3233931.

——. 2004. *Congress: The Electoral Connection*. New Haven, CT: Yale University Press.

Mays, Jacob, Michael Craig, L. Lynne Kiesling, Joshua Macey, Blake Shaffer, and Han Shu. 2021. "Private Risk and Social Resilience in Liberalized Electricity Markets." *Joule* 6 (2): 369–80. https://doi.org/10.2139/ssrn.3936984.

Mazzei, Patricia. 2023. "DeSantis's Latest Target: A Small College of 'Free Thinkers.'" *New York Times*, February 14. https://www.nytimes.com/2023/02/14/us/ron-desantis-new-college-florida.html.

McCarter, Joan. 2010. "Ben Nelson to Filibuster Climate Bill." *Daily Kos*, July 16. https://www.dailykos.com/stories/2010/7/16/884853/-.

McCartney, Laton. 2009. *The Teapot Dome Scandal: How Big Oil Bought the Harding White House and Tried to Steal the Country*. New York: Random House Trade Paperbacks.

McCright, Aaron M., and Riley E. Dunlap. 2011. "The Politicization of Climate Change and Polarization in the American Public's Views of Global Warming, 2001–2010." *Sociological Quarterly* 52 (2): 155–94. https://doi.org/10.1111/j.1533-8525.2011.01198.x.

McDevitt, Casey. 2022. "Heat Pumps vs. Furnaces." *Energy Sage* (blog), October 24. https://news.energysage.com/heat-pumps-vs-furnaces/.

McDonald, Stephen L. 1971. *Petroleum Conservation in the United States: An Economic Analysis*. Baltimore, MD: Johns Hopkins University Press.

McDonnell Nieto del Rio, Guilia, Nicholas Bogel-Burroughs, and Ivan Penn. 2021. "His Lights Stayed on During Texas' Storm. Now He Owes $16,752." *New York Times*, February 20. https://www.nytimes.com/2021/02/20/us/texas-storm-electric-bills.html.

McGarity, Thomas O. 2013. *Freedom to Harm: The Lasting Legacy of the Laissez Faire Revival*. New Haven, CT: Yale University Press.

——. 2014. "The Disruptive Politics of Climate Disruption." *Nova Law Review* 38 (3): 393–472.

McGarity, Thomas O., and Wendy Wagner. 2023. "U.S. Agency Experts in Shackles: The Quest for Information." *Journal of Environmental Law* 35 (1): 65–86. https://doi.org/10.1093/jel/eqad005.

McGraw, Seamus. 2015. *Betting the Farm on a Drought: Stories from the Front Lines of Climate Change*. Austin: University of Texas Press.

McKibben, Bill. 2015. "Power to the People: Why the Rise of Green Energy Makes Utility Companies Nervous." *The New Yorker*, June 22. https://www.newyorker.com/magazine/2015/06/29/power-to-the-people.

McLaughlin, Dan. 2022. "Democrats Need to Call Off Targeting Supreme Court Justices After Armed Assassin Arrested at Kavanaugh's House." *National Review* (blog), June 8. https://www.nationalreview.com/corner/democrats-need-to-call-off -targeting-supreme-court-justices-after-armed-assassin-arrested-at-kavanaughs -house/.

McLean, Bethany, and Peter Elkind. 2003. *The Smartest Guys in the Room: The Amazing Rise and Scandalous Fall of Enron*. New York: Portfolio/Penguin.

Meckling, Jonas. 2011. *Carbon Coalitions: Business, Climate Politics, and the Rise of Emissions Trading*. Cambridge, MA: MIT Press.

Mellers, Barbara, Philip Tetlock, and Hal R. Arkes. 2019. "Forecasting Tournaments, Epistemic Humility, and Attitude Depolarization." *Cognition* 188:19–26. https://doi .org/10.1016/j.cognition.2018.10.021.

Memmott, Trevor, Sanya Carley, Michelle Graff, and David M. Konisky. 2021. "Sociodemographic Disparities in Energy Insecurity Among Low-Income Households Before and During the COVID-19 Pandemic." *Nature Energy* 6 (2): 186–93. https:// doi.org/10.1038/s41560-020-00763-9.

Mena, Bryan. 2021. "Gov. Greg Abbott and Other Republicans Blamed Green Energy for Texas' Power Woes. But the State Runs on Fossil Fuels." *Texas Tribune*, February 18. https://www.texastribune.org/2021/02/17/abbott-republicans-green-energy/.

Mensching, Leah McBride. 2017. "Wind Energy Isn't a Breeze." *Slate*, August 24. https://slate.com/technology/2017/08/why-farmers-in-iowa-hope-wind-energy -will-blow-over.html.

Merrell, Alexandrea. 2010. *Rules for Republican Radicals . . . and How Conservatives Can Create a Republican Revolution to Stop It*. N.p.: Hey Blondie.

Metzger, Bryan. 2021. "Manchin Says He's 'Never Been a Liberal in Any Way, Shape, or Form' as He Calls for $2 Trillion in Cuts to Reconciliation Bill." *Business Insider*, September 30. https://www.businessinsider.com/joe-manchin-never-been-liberal -2-trillion-cuts-reconciliation-bill-2021-9.

Meyer, Robinson. 2018. "The GOP Just Lost Its Most Important Climate Moderates." *The Atlantic*, November 8. https://www.theatlantic.com/science/archive/2018/11 /how-many-house-republicans-believe-climate-change/575233/.

——. 2023. "Why America Is Betting on Carbon Removal." *Heatmap News*, August 16.

Meyerson, Harold. 2023. "The Divisions in DSA." *The American Prospect*, October 17. https://prospect.org/blogs-and-newsletters/tap/2023-10-17-divisions-in-dsa-israel -gaza/.

Michelson, Joan. 2023. "Wave of 'Anti-ESG' Investing Legislation, New Study Found." *Forbes*, August 29. https://www.forbes.com/sites/joanmichelson2/2023/08/29/wave -of-anti-esg-investing-legislation-new-study-found/.

Mildenberger, Matto. 2019. "The Tragedy of 'the Tragedy of the Commons.'" *Scientific American*, April 23. https://blogs.scientificamerican.com/voices/the-tragedy -of-the-tragedy-of-the-commons/.

Milgram, Stanley. 1963. "Behavioral Study of Obedience." *Journal of Abnormal and Social Psychology* 67 (4): 371–78.

Milheim, Russ. 2023. "James Cameron Voices Support for Thanos' Depopulation Plan." *TheDirect.Com*, February 20. https://thedirect.com/article/james-cameron -thanos-depopulation-plan.

Mill, John Stuart. 1838. *Essays on Bentham and Coleridge*. London: Baldwin, Cradock, and Joy.

Miller, Kimberly. 2020. "Climate Change: Sea Level Rise Causes Record King Tide Water Highs." *Palm Beach Post*, October 20. https://www.palmbeachpost.com /story/weather/2020/10/20/climate-change-sea-level-rise-causes-record-king-tide -water-highs/5992756002/.

Miller, Tim. 2022. *Why We Did It: A Travelogue from the Republican Road to Hell.* New York: Harper.

Mills, C. Wright. 1956. *The Power Elite.* New York: Oxford University Press.

Milman, Oliver, and Dominic Rushe. 2017. "New EPA Head Scott Pruitt's Emails Reveal Close Ties with Fossil Fuel Interests." *The Guardian*, February 22. https://www.theguardian.com/environment/2017/feb/22/scott-pruitt-emails -oklahoma-fossil-fuels-koch-brothers.

Min, Yohan, Maarten Brinkerink, Jesse Jenkins, and Erin Mayfield. 2023. "Effects of Renewable Energy Provisions of the Inflation Reduction Act on Technology Costs, Materials Demand, and Labor." June 8. https://zenodo.org/records/8020818.

Monast, Jonas J. 2022. "Precautionary Ratemaking." *UCLA Law Review* 69 (2): 520–70.

Moore, Adrian, and Michael Lynch. 2001. "Power Tripped." *Reason* (blog), June 1. https://reason.com/2001/06/01/power-tripped-2/.

Moore, Thomas Gale. 1996. "Global Warming: Costs and Benefits." *World Climate Report Essays* 1 (23). https://web.stanford.edu/~moore/costs-benefits.html.

Morita, Kanako, and Ken'ichi Matsumoto. 2023. "Challenges and Lessons Learned for REDD+ Finance and Its Governance." *Carbon Balance and Management* 18 (1): art. 8. https://doi.org/10.1186/s13021-023-00228-y.

Moss, David A., and Daniel Carpenter. 2014. "Conclusion: A Focus on Evidence and Prevention." In *Preventing Regulatory Capture: Special Interest Influence and How to Limit It*, edited by Daniel Carpenter and David A. Moss, 451–66. New York: Cambridge University Press.

Mullen, Brian, Jennifer L. Atkins, Debbie S. Champion, Cecelia Edwards, Dana Hardy, John E. Story, and Mary Vanderklok. 1985. "The False Consensus Effect: A Meta-analysis of 115 Hypothesis Tests." *Journal of Experimental Social Psychology* 21 (3): 262–83. https://doi.org/10.1016/0022-1031(85)90020-4.

Muller, Nicholas Z., Robert Mendelsohn, and William Nordhaus. 2011. "Environmental Accounting for Pollution in the United States Economy." *American Economic Review* 101 (5): 1649–75. https://doi.org/10.1257/aer.101.5.1649.

Murphy, Bruce Allen. 1982. *The Brandeis/Frankfurter Connection: The Secret Political Activities of Two Supreme Court Justices.* New York: Oxford University Press.

Mutz, Diana C. 2006. *Hearing the Other Side: Deliberative Versus Participatory Democracy.* Cambridge: Cambridge University Press.

Nelson, Robert H. 2012. "Rethinking Church and State: The Case of Environmental Religion." *Pace Environmental Law Review* 29 (1): 121–217. https://doi.org/10.58948 /0738-6206.1684.

Neufeld, John L. 2016. *Selling Power: Economics, Policy, and Electric Utilities Before 1940.* Chicago: University of Chicago Press.

Newport, Frank. 2021. "Deconstructing Americans' Views of Socialism, Capitalism." Gallup, December 17. https://news.gallup.com/opinion/polling-matters/358178 /deconstructing-americans-views-socialism-capitalism.aspx.

Nichols, Michelle. 2023. "UN Chief to Fossil Fuel Firms: Stop Trying to 'Knee-Cap' Climate Progress." Reuters, June 15. https://www.reuters.com/business/enviro nment/un-chief-fossil-fuel-firms-stop-trying-knee-cap-climate-progress-2023 -06-15/.

Nickerson, Raymond S. 1998. "Confirmation Bias: A Ubiquitous Phenomenon in Many Guises." *Review of General Psychology* 2 (2): 175–220. https://doi.org/10.1037/1089 -2680.2.2.175.

Nierenberg, Nicolas, Walter R. Tschinkel, and Victoria J. Tschinkel. 2010. "Early Climate Change Consensus at the National Academy: The Origins and Making of

Changing Climate." *Historical Studies in the Natural Sciences* 40 (3): 318–49. https://doi.org/10.1525/hsns.2010.40.3.318.

Nikolov, Dimitar, Alessandro Flammini, and Filippo Menczer. 2021. "Right and Left, Partisanship Predicts (Asymmetric) Vulnerability to Misinformation." *Harvard Kennedy School Misinformation Review* 1 (7). https://doi.org/10.37016/mr-2020-55.

Nilsen, Ella. 2022. "Wind and Solar Power Are 'Bailing Out' Texas Amid Record Heat and Energy Demand." CNN, June 14. https://www.cnn.com/2022/06/14/us/texas-energy-record-solar-wind-climate/index.html.

Niskanen, William A. 1971. *Bureaucracy and Representative Government*. Chicago: Aldine, Atherton.

NOAA National Centers for Environmental Information. 2023. *September 2021 National Climate Report*. Washington, DC: NOAA National Centers for Environmental Information. https://www.ncei.noaa.gov/access/monitoring/monthly-report/national/202109.

Nordhaus, Ted. 2020. "Must Growth Doom the Planet?" *New Atlantis*, Winter. https://www.thenewatlantis.com/publications/must-growth-doom-the-planet.

——. 2021. "Ted Nordhaus on How Green Activists Mislead and Hold Back Progress." *The Economist*, November 19. https://www.economist.com/by-invitation/2021/11/19/ted-nordhaus-on-how-green-activists-mislead-and-hold-back-progress.

North American Electricity Reliability Corporation (NERC). 2022. *2022 Long-Term Reliability Assessment 13*. Washington, DC: NERC. https://www.nerc.com/pa/RAPA/ra/Reliability%20Assessments%20DL/NERC_LTRA_2022.pdf.

Novachek, Frank. 2019. "Building a Carbon-Free Future." Hydrogen@Scale: Chemical Energy Storage Panel, Annual Fuel Cell Seminar and Exposition, November 5. https://www.energy.gov/sites/prod/files/2019/12/f69/fcto-fcs-h2-scale-2019-workshop-16-novachek.pdf.

Obama, Barack. 2020. "Remarks by Former President Barack Obama in Support of Senator Joe Biden at the 2020 Democratic National Convention." August 19. https://www.pbs.org/newshour/politics/read-obamas-full-speech-at-the-democratic-national-convention.

Obama, Michelle. 2016. "Remarks by the First Lady at the Democratic National Convention." July 25. https://obamawhitehouse.archives.gov/the-press-office/2016/07/25/remarks-first-lady-democratic-national-convention.

O'Dowd, Peter. 2023. "Are We Witnessing the End of a Digital Media Era? Author Ben Smith Thinks So." *Here & Now*, WBUR, May 8. https://www.wbur.org/hereandnow/2023/05/08/digital-media-end-buzzfeed.

Okun, Eli. 2023. "Playbook PM: Did the Supreme Court Just Flip the House?" *Politico*, June 8. https://www.politico.com/newsletters/playbook-pm/2023/06/08/did-the-supreme-court-just-flip-the-house-00101047.

Ollman, Bertell. 2017. "Toward a Marxist Interpretation of the US Constitution." *Jacobin*, July 4. https://jacobin.com/2017/07/founding-fathers-constitutional-convention.

Olson, Arne, Nick Schlag, Greg Gangelhoff, and Anthony Fratto. 2023. "Every Load an Island: Requiring Hourly Matching of Clean Electricity Purchases Would Raise Emissions." *Utility Dive*, August 29. https://www.utilitydive.com/news/hourly-matching-clean-electricity-renewable-energy-purchases-e3/692099/.

Olson, Mancur. 1965. *The Logic of Collective Action: Public Goods and the Theory of Groups*. Cambridge, MA: Harvard University Press.

Olya, Gabrielle. 2021. "Will Zoom and These 5 Other Companies Continue Their Incredible Runs in 2021?" *Yahoo Finance*, January 14. https://finance.yahoo.com/news/zoom-5-other-companies-continue-130003766.html.

O'Neill, Brian C. 2023. "Envisioning a Future with Climate Change." *Nature Climate Change* 13 (9): 874–76. https://doi.org/10.1038/s41558-023-01784-4.

Oreskes, Naomi. 2004. "The Scientific Consensus on Climate Change." *Science* 306 (5702): 1686. https://www.science.org/doi/10.1126/science.1103618.

Oreskes, Naomi, and Erik M. Conway. 2010. *Merchants of Doubt: How a Handful of Scientists Obscured the Truth on Issues from Tobacco Smoke to Climate Change*. New York: Bloomsbury Press.

Ortiz, Erik. 2021. " 'The Numbers Don't Lie': The Green Movement Remains Overwhelmingly White, Report Finds." NBC News, January 13. https://www.nbcnews.com/news/us-news/numbers-don-t-lie-green-movement-remains-overwhelmingly-white-report-n1253972.

Orwell, George. 1945. "Notes on Nationalism." *Polemic*. https://www.orwellfoundation.com/the-orwell-foundation/orwell/essays-and-other-works/notes-on-nationalism/.

——. 1968. "Review of *A Coat of Many Colours: Occasional Essays* by Herbert Read" (1945). In *In Front of Your Nose, 1945–1950*, vol. 4 of *The Collected Essays, Journalism, and Letters of George Orwell*, edited by Sonia Orwell and Ian Angus, 48–51. London: Secker & Warburg.

Osaka, Shannon. 2022. "These 'Nuclear Bros' Say They Know How to Solve Climate Change." *Washington Post*, September 30. https://www.washingtonpost.com/climate-environment/2022/09/30/nuclear-bros-power-activists/.

Osofsky, Hari M., and Hannah J. Wiseman. 2014. "Hybrid Energy Governance." *University of Illinois Law Review* 2014 (1): 1–66.

Owens, Renee. 2016. "The Unpleasant Secrets of Clean Solar Energy." *Desert Report*, December. https://www.desertreport.org/wp-content/uploads/2016/12/DR-Winter2016.pdf.

Ozone Depletion, the Greenhouse Effect, and Climate Change. 1986. Washington, DC: U.S. Government Printing Office.

Pachauri, Rajendra K., and Andy Reisinger. 2007. *Climate Change 2007: Synthesis Report*. Contribution of Working Groups I, II, and III to the Fourth Assessment Report of the Intergovernmental Panel on Climate Change (IPCC). Geneva: IPCC. https://research.usq.edu.au/item/q6wyo/climate-change-2007-synthesis-report-contribution-of-working-groups-i-ii-and-iii-to-the-fourth-assessment-report-of-the-intergovernmental-panel-on-climate-change.

Paddock, LeRoy C., and Max Greenblum. 2016. "Community Benefit Agreements for Wind Farm Siting in Context." In *Sharing the Costs and Benefits of Energy and Resource Activity: Legal Change and Impact on Communities*, edited by Lila Barrera-Hernández, Barry Barton, Lee Godden, Alastair Lucas, and Anita Rønne, 155–72. Oxford: Oxford University Press.

Pahwa, Nitish. 2023. "Farewell Transmission." *Slate*, April 27. https://slate.com/business/2023/04/texas-power-grid-senate-plan-gas-fossil-fuels-renewables.html.

Pariser, Eli. 2011. *The Filter Bubble: How the New Personalized Web Is Changing What We Read and How We Think*. New York: Penguin.

Payne, Heather. 2017. "Game Over: Regulatory Capture, Negotiation, and Utility Rate Cases in an Age of Disruption" *University of San Francisco Law Review* 52:75–114.

Pearson, Kathryn. 2015. *Party Discipline in the U.S. House of Representatives*. Ann Arbor: University of Michigan Press.

Peck, Reece. 2019. *Fox Populism: Branding Conservatism as Working Class*. Cambridge: Cambridge: University Press.

Peltzman, Sam. 1976. "Toward a More General Theory of Regulation." *Journal of Law & Economics* 19 (2): 211–40. https://doi.org/10.1086/466865.

Pengelly, Martin. 2023a. "Kari Lake's Vow to Defend Trump with Guns Threatens Democracy, Democrat Says." *The Guardian*, June 12. https://www.theguardian.com /us-news/2023/jun/12/kari-lake-trump-nra-threat-threatens-democracy-arizona -democrat-ruben-gallego.

Pengelly, Martin. 2023b. "Sarah Palin Says US Civil War 'Is Going to Happen' Over Trump Prosecutions." *The Guardian*, August 25. https://www.theguardian.com/us -news/2023/aug/25/sarah-palin-us-civil-war-donald-trump-prosecutions.

Penn, Ivan. 2021. "PG&E Aims to Curb Wildfire Risk by Burying Many Power Lines." *New York Times*, July 21. https://www.nytimes.com/2021/07/21/business/energy -environment/pge-underground-powerlines-wildfires.html.

Penn, Ivan, and Peter Eavis. 2023. "Hawaiian Electric Was Warned of Its System's Fragility Before Wildfire." *New York Times*, August 19. https://www.nytimes.com /2023/08/19/business/energy-environment/hawaiian-electric-maui-wildfire -climate-change.html.

Pennycook, Gordon, Tyrone D. Cannon, and David G. Rand. 2018. "Prior Exposure Increases Perceived Accuracy of Fake News." *Journal of Experimental Psychology* 147 (12): 1865–80. https://doi.org/10.1037/xge0000465.

Pennycook, Gordon, and David G. Rand. 2019. "Lazy, Not Biased: Susceptibility to Partisan Fake News Is Better Explained by Lack of Reasoning Than by Motivated Reasoning." *Cognition* 188:39–50. https://doi.org/10.1016/j.cognition.2018.06.011.

Penrod, Emma. 2023. "US Grid Interconnection Backlog Jumps 40%, with Wait Times Expected to Grow as IRA Spurs More Renewables." *Utility Dive*, April 11. https:// www.utilitydive.com/news/grid-interconnection-queue-berkeley-lab-lbnl-watt -coalition-wind-solar-renewables/647287/.

Perkins, David N., Michael Farady, and Barbara Bushey. 1991. "Everyday Reasoning and the Roots of Intelligence." In *Informal Reasoning and Education*, edited by James F. Voss, David N. Perkins, and Judith W. Segal, 83–106. Hillsdale, NJ: Lawrence Erlbaum Associates.

Perkins, David N., Richard Allen, and James Hafner. 1983. "Difficulties in Everyday Reasoning." In *Thinking, the Expanding Frontier*, edited by William Maxwell, 177–90. Philadelphia: Franklin Institute Press.

Perl, Libby. 2018. *LIHEAP: Program and Funding*. RL31865. Washington, DC: Congressional Research Service.

Peskoe, Ari. 2021. "Is the Utility Transmission Syndicate Forever?" *Energy Law Journal* 42 (1): 1–66.

Philippon, Thomas. 2019. "The Economics and Politics of Market Concentration." *The Reporter* (National Bureau of Economic Research), no. 4 (December). https://www .nber.org/reporter/2019number4/economics-and-politics-market-concentration.

Pierce, Richard J., Jr. 1983. "Reconsidering the Roles of Regulation and Competition in the Natural Gas Industry." *Harvard Law Review* 97 (2): 345–85. https://doi.org/10 .2307/1340851.

——. 1986. "A Proposal to Deregulate the Market for Bulk Power." *Virginia Law Review* 72 (7): 1183–235. https://doi.org/10.2307/1073090.

——. 1987. "State Regulation of Natural Gas in a Federally Deregulated Market: The Tragedy of the Commons Revisited." *Cornell Law Review* 73 (1): 15–53.

——. 1988. "Reconstituting the Natural Gas Industry from Wellhead to Burnertip." *Energy Law Journal* 9 (1): 1–57.

Pierce, William L. 1978. *The Turner Diaries*. Mill Point, WV: National Vanguard.

Pigou, A. C. 1929. *The Economics of Welfare*. London: Macmillan.

Pilkington, Ed. 2020. "Ronan Farrow: Master #MeToo Reporter Hit by Surprise *New York Times* Takedown." *The Guardian*, May 18. https://www.theguardian

.com/media/2020/may/18/ronan-farrow-new-york-times-too-good-critique-ben-smith.

Piper, Jessica. 2023. "Anti-vaccine Nonprofits Saw Revenues Spike During the Covid-19 Pandemic." *Politico*, September 24. https://datawrapper.dwcdn.net/BaDRx/1/.

Pitz, Gordon F., Leslie Downing, and Helen Reinhold. 1967. "Sequential Effects in the Revision of the Subjective Probabilities." *Canadian Journal of Psychology* 21:381–93. https://doi.org/10.1037/h0082998.

Plaven, George. 2023. "Oregon Governor Calls for Pause on Offshore Wind Turbines." *Capital Press*, June 12. https://www.capitalpress.com/ag_sectors/water/oregon-governor-members-of-congress-call-for-pause-on-offshore-wind-turbines/article_006dc7ca-0943-11ee-aebb-03dace78973d.html.

Pollin, Robert. 2022. "Nationalize the U.S. Fossil Fuel Industry to Save the Planet." American Prospect, April 8. https://prospect.org/api/content/07f725d0-b6b6-11ec-9d60-12274efc5439/.

Poole, Keith T., and Howard Rosenthal. 2007. *Ideology & Congress*. 2nd ed. New Brunswick, NJ: Transaction.

Pope, James Gray. 1990. "Republican Moments: The Role of Direct Popular Power in the American Constitutional Order." *University of Pennsylvania Law Review* 139 (2): 287–368. https://doi.org/10.2307/3312284.

Popova, Maria. 2015. "Hope, Cynicism, and the Stories We Tell Ourselves." *Marginalian* (blog), February 9. https://www.themarginalian.org/2015/02/09/hope-cynicism/.

Popper, Karl. 1945. *The Open Society and Its Enemies*. Abingdon-on-Thames, U.K.: Routledge.

——. 1998. *The World of Parmenides: Essays on the Presocratic Enlightenment*. Edited by Arne Friemuth Petersen and Jorgen Mejer. London: Routledge.

Porch, Scott. 2015. "The Book That Changed Campaigns Forever." *Politico*, June. https://www.politico.com/magazine/story/2015/04/22/teddy-white-political-journalism-117090.

Porsius, Jarry T., Liesbeth Claassen, Tjabe Smid, Fred Woudenberg, and Danielle R. M. Timmermans. 2014. "Health Responses to a New High-Voltage Power Line Route: Design of a Quasi-experimental Prospective Field Study in the Netherlands." *BMC Public Health* 14 (1): art. 237. https://doi.org/10.1186/1471-2458-14-237.

Porter, Jeffrey R. 2022. "Our Justice System Can't Work If the End Justifies Any Means." *Lexology* (blog), May 4. https://www.lexology.com/library/detail.aspx?g=423124ed-9787-434b-93fe-e5fcd5929043.

Posner, Richard A. 1977. *Economic Analysis of Law*. 2d ed. Boston: Little, Brown.

Possible Health Effects of Exposure to Residential Electric and Magnetic Fields. 1997. Washington, DC: National Academies Press.

Postman, Neil. 2006. *Amusing Ourselves to Death: Public Discourse in the Age of Show Business*. 2nd ed. New York: Penguin.

Potters, Jan, and Frans van Winden. 1992. "Lobbying and Asymmetric Information." *Public Choice* 74 (3): 269–92. https://doi.org/10.1007/BF00149180.

Powell, Miles A. 2015. "Pestered with Inhabitants: Aldo Leopold, William Vogt, and More Trouble with Wilderness." *Pacific Historical Review* 84 (2): 195–226. https://doi.org/10.1525/phr.2015.84.2.195.

Prentice, Robert. 2008. "Enron: A Brief Behavioral Autopsy." *American Business Law Journal* 40 (2): 417–44. https://doi.org/10.1111/j.1744-1714.2002.tb00851.x.

Prentice, Robert A., and Mark E. Roszkowski. 1992. "Tort Reform and the Liability Revolution: Defending Strict Liability in Tort for Defective Products." *Gonzaga Law Review* 27 (2): 251–302.

Purcell, Edward A. 1967. "Ideas and Interests: Businessmen and the Interstate Commerce Act." *Journal of American History* 54 (3): 561–78. https://doi.org/10.2307/2937407.

Pyper, Julia. 2017. "The Latest Trends in Corporate Renewable Energy Procurement." *GTM* (Greentech Media), June 30. https://www.greentechmedia.com/articles/read/the-latest-trends-in-corporate-renewable-energy-procurement.

Pyszczynski, Tom, and Jeff Greenberg. 1987. "Toward an Integration of Cognitive and Motivational Perspectives on Social Inference: A Biased Hypothesis-Testing Model." *Advances in Experimental Social Psychology* 20:297–340. https://doi.org/10.1016/S0065-2601(08)60417-7.

Quinn, Melissa. 2023. *"Dominion Voting v. Fox News* Lawsuit: Who's Who in the High-Stakes Defamation Trial?" CBS News, April 17. https://www.cbsnews.com/news/fox-news-dominion-whos-who/.

Rabe, Barry G. 2023. "Methane Comes Front and Center in Climate Change Policy." *Brookings*, January 6. https://www.brookings.edu/articles/methane-comes-front-and-center-in-climate-change-policy/.

Rachlinski, Jeffrey J. 1996. "Gains, Losses, and the Psychology of Litigation." *Southern California Law Review* 70 (1): 113–85.

——. 1998. "A Positive Psychological Theory of Judging in Hindsight." *University of Chicago Law Review* 65 (2): 571–625. https://doi.org/10.2307/1600229.

——. 2000. "The Psychology of Global Climate Change." *University of Illinois Law Review* 2000 (1): 299–320.

Rakove, Jack N. 1996. *Original Meanings: Politics and Ideas in the Making of the Constitution*. New York: Knopf.

——. 2017. "Jack Rakove Reviews *Democracy in Chains*." *Critical Inquiry* (blog), November 1. https://criticalinquiry.uchicago.edu/jack_rakove_reviews_democracy_in_chains/.

Ramirez, Rachel. 2022. "Power Outages Are on the Rise, Led by Texas, Michigan, and California. Here's What's to Blame." CNN, September 14. https://www.cnn.com/2022/09/14/us/power-outages-rising-extreme-weather-climate/index.html.

Randall, Eric. 2012. "The Koch Brothers Pledged $60 Million to Defeat Obama." *The Atlantic*, February 3. https://www.theatlantic.com/politics/archive/2012/02/koch-brothers-pledged-60-million-defeat-obama/332244/.

Rasmussen, Dennis C. 2017. *The Infidel and the Professor: David Hume, Adam Smith, and the Friendship That Shaped Modern Thought*. Princeton, NJ: Princeton University Press.

Ray, Douglas. 2021. "Lazard's Levelized Cost of Energy Analysis—Version 15.0." Lazard. https://www.lazard.com/media/sptlfats/lazards-levelized-cost-of-energy-version-150-vf.pdf.

Reid, Carlton. 2019. "Drive Shame Needs to Join Flight Shame, If We Are to Save the Planet." *Forbes*, December 11. https://www.forbes.com/sites/carltonreid/2019/12/11/drive-shame-needs-to-join-flight-shame-if-we-are-to-save-the-planet/.

Rhodes, Joshua D. 2022. *The Impact of Renewables in ERCOT*. Austin, TX: Ideasmiths, October.

——. 2023. *The Economic Impact of Renewable Energy and Energy Storage in Rural Texas*. Austin, TX: Ideasmiths, January. https://www.ideasmiths.net/wp-content/uploads/2023/01/Economic-Impact-of-Renewable-Energy_JAN2023.pdf.

Richardson, Nathan. 2015. "Trading Unmoored: The Uncertain Legal Foundation for Emissions Trading Under S. 111 of the Clean Air Act." *Penn State Law Review* 120 (1): 181–249.

——. 2023. "Antideference: COVID, Climate, and the Rise of the Major Questions Canon." *Virginia Law Review Online* 108: 174–206. https://virginialawreview.org/wp-content/uploads/2022/04/Richardson_Book.pdf.

Ricks, Thomas E. 2020. *First Principles: What America's Founders Learned from the Greeks and Romans and How That Shaped Our Country.* New York: Harper.

Ricks, Morgan, Ganesh Sitaraman, Shelley Welton, and Lev Manand. 2022. *Networks, Platforms, and Utilities: Law and Policy.* N.p.: Self-published.

Ricks, Wilson, Qingyu Xu, and Jesse D. Jenkins. 2023. "Minimizing Emissions from Grid-Based Hydrogen Production in the United States." *Environmental Research Letters* 18 (1): art. 014025. https://doi.org/10.1088/1748-9326/acacb5.

Riker, William H. 1982. *Liberalism Against Populism: A Confrontation Between the Theory of Democracy and the Theory of Social Choice.* San Francisco: W. H. Freeman.

Ripley, Amanda, Rehka Tenjarla, and Angela Y. He. 2019. "The Geography of Partisan Prejudice." *The Atlantic*, March 4, 2019. https://www.everand.com/article/401049201/The-Geography-Of-Partisan-Prejudice.

Ripley, Randall B. 1975. *Congress: Process and Policy.* New York: Norton.

Rix, Kevin, Nora J. Demchur, David F. Zane, and Lawrence H. Brown. 2021. "Injury Rates per Mile of Travel for Electric Scooters Versus Motor Vehicles." *American Journal of Emergency Medicine* 40 (February): 166–68. https://doi.org/10.1016/j.ajem.2020.10.048.

Roberts, David. 2013. "Goodbye for Now." *Grist* (blog), August 19. https://grist.org/article/goodbye-for-now/.

——. 2019. "3 Key Solutions to California's Wildfire Safety Blackout Mess." *Vox*, October 22. https://www.vox.com/energy-and-environment/2019/10/22/20916820/california-wildfire-climate-change-blackout-insurance-pge.

Robertson, Cassandra Burke. 2001. "Bringing the Camel Into the Tent: State and Federal Power Over Electricity Transmission." *Cleveland State Law Review* 49 (1): 71–103.

Rohac, Dalibor, Liz Kennedy, and Vikram Singh. 2018. "Drivers of Authoritarian Populism in the United States: A Primer." Center for American Progress, May 10. https://www.americanprogress.org/article/drivers-authoritarian-populism-united-states/.

Rohr, John A. 1986. *To Run a Constitution: The Legitimacy of the Administrative State.* Lawrence: University of Kansas Press.

Rome, Adam. 2003. " 'Give Earth a Chance': The Environmental Movement and the Sixties." *Journal of American History* 90 (2): 525–54. https://doi.org/10.2307/3659443.

Romero, Simon, and Clifford Krauss. 2011. "Ecuador Judge Orders Chevron to Pay $9 Billion." *New York Times*, February 15. https://www.nytimes.com/2011/02/15/world/americas/15ecuador.html.

Romoser, James. 2023. "The Supreme Court Gift List: Paintings, Guns, and a Sculpture of a Hand." *Yahoo News*, May 24. https://news.yahoo.com/bronze-sculptures-cowboy-boots-guns-192918023.html.

Roose, Kevin. 2021. "What Is QAnon, the Viral Pro-Trump Conspiracy Theory?" *New York Times*, September 3. https://www.nytimes.com/article/what-is-qanon.html.

Rosenberg, Matthew. 2021. "A QAnon Supporter Is Headed to Congress." *New York Times*, November 4. https://www.nytimes.com/2020/11/03/us/politics/qanon-candidates-marjorie-taylor-greene.html.

Rosenwald, Brian. 2019. *Talk Radio's America: How an Industry Took Over a Political Party That Took Over the United States.* Cambridge, MA: Harvard University Press.

Ross, Lauren, Ariel Drehobl, and Brian Stickles. 2018. "The High Cost of Energy in Rural America: Household Energy Burdens and Opportunities for Energy

Efficiency." American Council for an Energy-Efficient Economy, July 18. https://www.aceee.org/research-report/u1806.

Ross, Lee, David Greene, and Pamela House. 1977. "The 'False Consensus Effect': An Egocentric Bias in Social Perception and Attribution Processes." *Journal of Experimental Social Psychology* 13 (3): 279–301. https://doi.org/10.1016/0022-1031(77)900 49-X.

Ross, Michael L. 2012. *The Oil Curse: How Petroleum Wealth Shapes the Development of Nations*. Princeton, NJ: Princeton University Press.

Roston, Eric. 2016. "The Caucus to Save the World." *Bloomberg*, February 11. https://www.bloomberg.com/news/articles/2016-02-11/can-only-congress-prevent-climate-change.

Roth, Sammy. 2023. "The Revolving Door at Public Utilities Commissions? It's Alive and Well." *Los Angeles Times*, June 8. https://www.latimes.com/environment/newsletter/2023-06-08/the-revolving-door-at-public-utilities-commissions-its-alive-and-well-boiling-point.

Rothbard, Murray N. [1982] 2003. *The Ethics of Liberty*. Paperback ed. New York: New York University Press.

Rothkopf, Joanna. 2014. "There Are Two Environmentalist Movements: One for Rich Whites, the Other for Poor Minorities." *Salon*, August 11. https://www.salon.com/2014/08/11/there_are_two_environmentalist_movements_one_for_rich_whites_the_other_for_poor_minorities/.

Rule, Troy A. 2015. "Solar Energy, Utilities, and Fairness." *San Diego Journal of Climate & Energy Law* 6:115–48.

Russell, Bertrand. 1959. "Message to Future Generations." https://www.youtube.com/watch?v=ihaB8AFOhZo&feature=youtu.be&ab_channel=PhilosophieKanal.

——. 2009. "An Outline of Intellectual Rubbish (1943)." In *Russell: Unpopular Essays*, 82–123. London: Routledge.

Rutenberg, Jim. 2016. "Trump Is Testing the Norms of Objectivity in Journalism." *New York Times*, August 8. https://www.nytimes.com/2016/08/08/business/balance-fairness-and-a-proudly-provocative-presidential-candidate.html.

Safire, William. 1986. "Essay: About Roy Cohn." *New York Times*, August 4.

Samantray, Abhishek, and Paolo Pin. 2019. "Credibility of Climate Change Denial in Social Media." *Palgrave Communications* 5:1–8.

Samenow, Jason. 2012. "Heartland Institute Launches Campaign Linking Terrorism, Murder, and Global Warming Belief." *Washington Post*, May 4. https://www.washingtonpost.com/blogs/capital-weather-gang/post/heartland-institute-launches-campaign-linking-terrorism-murder-and-global-warming-belief/2012/05/04/gIQAJJ3Q1T_blog.html.

Sandel, Michael J. 1997. "It's Immoral to Buy the Right to Pollute." *New York Times*, December 15. https://www.nytimes.com/1997/12/15/opinion/it-s-immoral-to-buy-the-right-to-pollute.html.

——. 2020. *The Tyranny of Merit: What's Become of the Common Good?* New York: Farrar, Straus and Giroux.

Sanders, Katie. 2022. "Are Republicans and Democrats Driven by Hatred of One Another? Less Than You Think." Annenberg School of Communication, University of Pennsylvania, May. https://www.asc.upenn.edu/news-events/news/are-republicans-and-democrats-driven-hatred-one-another-less-you-think.

Sandler, Todd. 1992. *Collective Action: Theory and Applications*. Ann Arbor: University of Michigan Press.

Saric, Ivana. 2022. "The Times Trump Has Advocated for Violence." *Axios*, May 2. https://www.axios.com/2022/05/02/trump-call-violence-presidency.

Sautter, John A., James Landis, and Michael H. Dworkin. 2009. "The Energy Trilemma in the Green Mountain State: An Analysis of Vermont's Energy Challenges and Policy Options." *Vermont Journal of Environmental Law* 10 (3): 477–506. https://doi.org/10.2307/vermjenvilaw.10.3.477.

Sax, Joseph L. 1970. "The Public Trust Doctrine in Natural Resource Law: Effective Judicial Intervention." *Michigan Law Review* 68 (3): 471–566. https://doi.org/10.2307/1287556.

Schäfer, Mike S., and James Painter. 2021. "Climate Journalism in a Changing Media Ecosystem: Assessing the Production of Climate Change–Related News Around the World." *Wiley Interdisciplinary Reviews: Climate Change* 12 (1). https://doi.org/10.1002/wcc.675.

Schapiro, Robert A. 2005. "Toward a Theory of Interactive Federalism." *Iowa Law Review* 91 (1): 243–317.

Schattschneider, E. E. 1960. *The Semisovereign People: A Realist's View of Democracy in America*. Hinsdale, IL: Dryden Press.

Scheufele, Dietram A., and Nicole M. Krause. 2019. "Science Audiences, Misinformation, and Fake News." *Proceedings of the National Academy of Sciences* 116 (16): 7662–69. https://doi.org/10.1073/pnas.1805871115.

Scheyder, Ernest. 2023. "U.S. Bans Mining in Parts of Minnesota, Dealing Latest Blow to Antofagasta's Copper Project." Reuters, January 26. https://www.reuters.com/legal/litigation/us-blocks-mining-parts-minnesota-dealing-latest-blow-antofagastas-copper-project-2023-01-26/.

Schiffman, John. 2021. "How AT&T Helped Build Far Right One America News." Reuters, October 6. https://www.reuters.com/investigates/special-report/usa-oneamerica-att/.

Schilbach, Leonhard, Simon B. Eickhoff, Thomas Schultze, Andreas Mojzisch, and Kai Vogeley. 2013. "To You I Am Listening: Perceived Competence of Advisors Influences Judgment and Decision-Making Via Recruitment of the Amygdala." *Social Neuroscience* 8 (3): 189–202. https://doi.org/10.1080/17470919.2013.775967.

Schlozman, Kay, Sidney Verba, and Henry E. Brady. 2012. *The Unheavenly Chorus: Unequal Political Voice and the Broken Promise of American Democracy*. Princeton, NJ: Princeton University Press.

Schmidt, Jesper Hvass, and Mads Klokker. 2014. "Health Effects Related to Wind Turbine Noise Exposure: A Systematic Review." *PLOS One* 9 (12): art. e114183. https://doi.org/10.1371/journal.pone.0114183.

Schmidt, Michael S., Alan Feuer, Maggie Haberman, and Adam Goldman. 2023. "Trump Supporters' Violent Rhetoric in His Defense Disturbs Experts." *New York Times*, June 11. https://www.nytimes.com/2023/06/10/us/politics/trump-supporter-violent-rhetoric.html.

Schmidt, Susan, and James V. Grimaldi. 2005. "The Fast Rise and Steep Fall of Jack Abramoff." *Washington Post*, December 29. https://www.washingtonpost.com/archive/politics/2005/12/29/the-fast-rise-and-steep-fall-of-jack-abramoff/56987391-1b47-414d-866e-531bc2b0a603/.

Schoenbrod, David. 1995. *Power Without Responsibility: How Congress Abuses the People Through Delegation*. New Haven, CT: Yale University Press.

Schroeder, Christopher H. 1993. "Cool Analysis Versus Moral Outrage in the Development of Federal Environmental Criminal Law." *William and Mary Law Review* 35 (1): 251–69.

Schulte, David M., Karin M. Dridge, and Mark H. Hudgins. 2015. "Climate Change and the Evolution and Fate of the Tangier Islands of Chesapeake Bay, USA." *Scientific Reports* 5 (1). https://doi.org/10.1038/srep17890.

Schumpeter, Joseph A. [1942] 1987. *Capitalism, Socialism, and Democracy.* 6th ed. London: Unwin Paperbacks.

Schwartz, John. 2017. " 'A Conservative Climate Solution': Republican Group Calls for Carbon Tax." *New York Times*, February 8. https://www.nytimes.com/2017/02/07/science/a-conservative-climate-solution-republican-group-calls-for-carbon-tax.html.

Scott, Eugene. 2022. "What Happened to the 10 Republicans Who Voted to Impeach Trump?" *Washington Post*, November 26. https://www.washingtonpost.com/politics/2022/11/23/gop-trump-impeachment-house/.

Segers, Grace. 2020. "Incoming House Member Says 'Masks Are Oppressive' as U.S. Breaks Record for Daily COVID-19 Cases." CBS News, November 13. https://www.cbsnews.com/news/marjorie-taylor-greene-incoming-house-member-says-masks-are-oppressive-covid-19-surge/.

Selezneva, Elizabeth. 2021. "Priming Caution Does Not Decrease Receptivity to Fake News." *Revue YOUR Review* (York Online Undergraduate Research) 8 (August): 98–112.

Semple, Robert B., Jr. 2022. "This Environmental Law Made Half of America's Fresh Waters Swimmable and Fishable." *New York Times*, October 26. https://www.nytimes.com/2022/10/26/opinion/environment/clean-water-act-sackett-epa.html.

Sen, Amartya. 2017. *Collective Choice and Social Welfare.* Exp. ed. Cambridge, MA: Harvard University Press.

Serwer, Adam. 2019. "The Fight Over the 1619 Project Is Not About the Facts." *The Atlantic*, December 23. https://www.theatlantic.com/ideas/archive/2019/12/historians-clash-1619-project/604093/.

Shah, Simmone. 2023. "Electric Grids Across U.S. Need Updating Amid Climate Change." *Time*, August 18. https://time.com/6306121/maui-fire-hawaiian-electric-grids/.

Shanor, Amanda, Mary-Hunter McDonnell, and Timothy Werner. 2021. "Corporate Political Power: The Politics of Reputation & Traceability." *Emory Law Journal* 71 (2): 153–216.

Shapiro, Ben. 2019. "Calling for 'Reason and Civility' Doesn't Make You Hitler." *Daily Wire*, September 3. https://www.dailywire.com/news/shapiro-calling-reason-and-civility-doesnt-make-daily-wire.

Shapiro, Sidney A., and Joseph P. Tomain. 2003. *Regulatory Law and Policy: Cases and Materials.* New York: LexisNexis.

Shellenberger, Michael. 2019. "Why Renewables Can't Save the Planet." https://www.congress.gov/116/meeting/house/109694/documents/HHRG-116-II06-20190625-SD005.pdf.

Shepard, Steven. 2023. "Our New Poll Shows Just How Much GOP Voters Have Diverged from Everyone Else on Vaccines." *Politico*, September 23. https://www.politico.com/news/2023/09/23/gop-voters-vaccines-poll-00117125.

Sherman, Gabriel. 2018. *The Loudest Voice in the Room: How the Brilliant, Bombastic Roger Ailes Built Fox News—and Divided a Country.* New York: Ballantine.

Shughart, William F., and Fred S. McChesney. 2010. "Public Choice Theory and Antitrust Policy." *Public Choice* 142 (3–4): 385–406.

Silver, Nate. 2020. "The Senate's Rural Skew Makes It Very Hard for Democrats to Win the Supreme Court." *FiveThirtyEight* (blog), September 20. https://fivethirtyeight.com/features/the-senates-rural-skew-makes-it-very-hard-for-democrats-to-win-the-supreme-court/.

Simon, Herbert A. 1946. "The Proverbs of Administration." *Public Administration Review* 6 (1): 53–67.

——. 1984. "Human Nature in Politics: The Dialogue of Psychology with Political Science." *American Political Science Review* 79 (2): 293–304. https://doi.org/10.2307/1956650.

Sinopoli, Richard C. 1987. "Liberalism, Republicanism, & the Constitution." *Polity* 19 (3): 331–52. https://doi.org/10.2307/3234793.

Sirota, David. 2021. "WEEKEND READER: Corporate Media Reveals Its True Colors." *The Lever*, October 3. https://www.levernews.com/weekend-reader-mainstream-media-reveals-its-true-colors-exclusive-for-subscribers/.

Skaife, Hollis A., and Timothy Werner. 2020. "Changes in Firms' Political Investment Opportunities, Managerial Accountability, and Reputational Risk." *Journal of Business Ethics* 163 (2): 239–63. https://doi.org/10.1007/s10551-019-04224-6.

Skocpol, Theda, and Alexander Hertel-Fernandez. 2016. "The Koch Network and Republican Party Extremism." *Perspectives on Politics* 14 (3): 681–99. https://doi.org/10.1017/S1537592716001122.

Slade, Stephanie. 2022. "Both Left and Right Are Converging on Authoritarianism." *Reason*, October. https://reason.com/2022/09/13/the-authoritarian-convergence/.

Slattery, Michael C., Becky L. Johnson, Jeffrey A. Swofford, and Martin J. Pasqualetti. 2012. "The Predominance of Economic Development in the Support for Large-Scale Wind Farms in the U.S. Great Plains." *Renewable and Sustainable Energy Reviews* 16 (6): 3690–701. https://doi.org/10.1016/j.rser.2012.03.016.

Slocum, Tyson. 2007. "The Failure of Electricity Deregulation: History, Status, and Needed Reforms." Public Citizen's Energy Program. https://www.ftc.gov/sites/default/files/documents/public_events/Energy%20Markets%20in%20the%2021st%20Century:%20Competition%20Policy%20in%20Perspective/slocum_dereg.pdf.

Sloman, Steven A., and Nathaniel Rabb. 2019. "Thought as a Determinant of Political Opinion." *Cognition* 188:1–7. https://doi.org/10.1016/j.cognition.2019.02.014.

Smeltzer, David. 2021. "Review of the ERCOT Scarcity Pricing Mechanism." Public Utility Commission of Texas.

Smith, Adam. [1776] 1850. *An Inquiry Into the Nature and Causes of the Wealth of Nations.* 5th ed. London: A. Strahan & T. Cadell.

——. [1759] n.d. *The Theory of Moral Sentiments.* London: Andrew Millar. Library of Congress. https://www.loc.gov/item/18015943/.

Smith, Ben. 2023. *Traffic: Genius, Rivalry, and Delusion in the Billion-Dollar Race to Go Viral.* New York: Penguin.

Smith, Mark A. 2000. *American Business and Political Power: Public Opinion, Elections, and Democracy.* Chicago: University of Chicago Press.

Smith, Michael. 2023. "DeSantis Proposes Tax Exemption for Gas Stoves, Ridicules Talk of Ban." *Bloomberg*, February 2. https://www.bloomberg.com/news/articles/2023-02-02/gas-stoves-in-florida-would-be-tax-exempt-with-desantis-proposal.

Snyder, Timothy. 2017. *On Tyranny.* New York: Penguin Random House.

——. 2021. "The American Abyss." *New York Times Magazine*, January 9. https://www.nytimes.com/2021/01/09/magazine/trump-coup.html.

Solomon, Michelle, Eric Gimon, Mike O'Boyle, Umed Paliwal, and Amol Phadke. 2023. *Coal Cost Crossover 3.0: Local Renewables Plus Storage Create New Economic and Reliability Opportunities.* San Francisco: Energy Innovation. https://energyinnovation.org/wp-content/uploads/2023/01/Coal-Cost-Crossover-3.0.pdf.

Solomon, Susan, Dahe Qin, Martin Manning, Melinda Marquis, and Kristen Averyt, eds. 2007. *Climate Change 2007: The Physical Science Basis: Contribution of Working Group I to the Fourth Assessment Report of the Intergovernmental Panel on Climate Change.* Cambridge: Cambridge University Press.

Sonner, Scott. 2023. "9th Circuit Denies Bid by Environmentalists and Tribes to Block Nevada Lithium Mine." *AP News*, July 17. https://apnews.com/article/nevada-thacker-pass-lithium-mine-4ad772a6940eb8edd507b50a179202f2.

Soroka, Stuart N., and Christopher Wlezien. 2010. *Degrees of Democracy: Politics, Public Opinion, and Policy.* Cambridge: Cambridge University Press.

Sorrel, Charlie. 2017. "Dutch Cyclists Have Had It with Motorized Scooters Invading Bike Lanes." Fast Company, June 28. https://www.fastcompany.com/3068522/dutch-cyclists-have-had-it-with-motorized-scooters-invading-bike-lanes.

Spence, David B. 1995. "Paradox Lost: Logic, Morality, and the Foundations of Environmental Law in the 21st Century." *Columbia Journal of Environmental Law* 20 (1): 145–82.

——. 1999a. "Imposing Individual Liability as a Legislative Policy Choice: Holmesian 'Intuitions' and Superfund Reform." *Northwestern University Law Review* 93 (2): 389–452.

——. 1999b. "Managing Delegation ex Ante: Using Law to Steer Administrative Agencies." *Journal of Legal Studies* 28 (2): 413–59. https://doi.org/10.1086/468057.

——. 2001. "The Shadow of the Rational Polluter: Rethinking the Role of Rational Actor Models in Environmental Law." *California Law Review* 89 (4): 917–98. https://doi.org/10.2307/3481289.

——. 2002. "A Public Choice Progressivism, Continued." *Cornell Law Review* 87 (2): 397–448.

——. 2008. "Can Law Manage Competitive Energy Markets?" *Cornell Law Review* 93 (4): 765–817.

——. 2013. "Federalism, Regulatory Lags, and the Political Economy of Energy Production." *University of Pennsylvania Law Review* 161 (2): 431–508.

——. 2014. "The Political Economy of Local Vetoes." *Texas Law Review* 93 (2): 351–413.

——. 2017. "Naïve Energy Markets." *Notre Dame Law Review* 92 (3): 973–1030.

——. 2019. "Regulation and the New Politics of (Energy) Market Entry." *Notre Dame Law Review* 95 (1): 327–96.

——. 2022. "Naïve Administrative Law: Complexity, Delegation, and Climate Policy." *Yale Journal on Regulation* 39 (2): 963–1010.

Spence, David B., and Frank B. Cross. 2000. "A Public Choice Case for the Administrative State." *Georgetown Law Journal* 89 (1): 97–127.

Squitieri, Chad. 2021. "Who Determines Majorness?" *Harvard Journal of Law & Public Policy* 44:463–522. https://journals.law.harvard.edu/jlpp/wp-content/uploads/sites/90/2021/04/Squitieri-Who-Determines-Majorness.pdf.

Steele, David. 2022. "Afraid to Speak Up or Out." *Inside Higher Ed* (blog), June 1. https://www.insidehighered.com/news/2022/06/02/survey-college-students-still-dont-feel-free-speak-campus.

Stein, Amy L. 2016. "Distributed Reliability." *University of Colorado Law Review* 87 (3): 887–962.

Steuart, James. 1767. *An Inquiry Into the Principles of Political Oeconomy: Being an Essay on the Science of Domestic Policy in Free Nations.* London: A. Millan & T. Cadell.

Stevens, Stuart. 2020. *It Was All a Lie: How the Republican Party Became Donald Trump.* New York: Knopf.

Stieglitz, Stefan, and Linh Dang-Xuan. 2013. "Emotions and Information Diffusion in Social Media—Sentiment of Microblogs and Sharing Behavior." *Journal of Management Information Systems* 29 (4): 217–48. https://doi.org/10.2753/MIS0742-1222290408.

Stigler, George J. 1971. "The Theory of Economic Regulation." *Bell Journal of Economics and Management Science* 2 (1): 3–21. https://doi.org/10.2307/3003160.

Stigler, George J., and Claire Friedland. 1962. "What Can Regulators Regulate? The Case of Electricity." *Journal of Law & Economics* 5:1–16.

Stokes, Leah. 2020. *Short Circuiting Policy: Interest Groups and the Battle Over Clean Energy and Climate Policy in the American States.* Oxford: Oxford University Press.

———. 2023. "Before We Invest Billions in This Clean Fuel, Let's Make Sure It's Actually Clean." *New York Times*, April 14. https://www.nytimes.com/2023/04/14/opinion/hydrogen-fuel-tax-credit-climate-change.html.

Stolberg, Sheryl Gay. 2019. " 'The Squad' Rankles, but Pelosi and Ocasio-Cortez Make Peace for Now." *New York Times*, July 26. https://www.nytimes.com/2019/07/26/us/politics/aoc-squad-pelosi.html.

Stolte, Justin. 2006. "The Energy Policy Act of 2005: The Path to Energy Autonomy?" *Journal of Legislation* 33 (1): 119–43.

Stone, Christopher D. 1972. "Should Trees Have Standing?—Toward Legal Rights for Natural Objects." *Southern California Law Review* 45:450–501.

Storrow, Benjamin. 2023a. "4 Lawsuits Threaten Vineyard Wind." *E&E News*, March 29. https://www.eenews.net/articles/4-lawsuits-threaten-vineyard-wind/.

———. 2023b. "Solar Power Bails Out Texas Grid During Major Heat Wave." *Scientific American*, June 26. https://www.scientificamerican.com/article/solar-power-bails-out-texas-grid-during-major-heat-wave/.

Stossel, John. 2003. *Give Me a Break: How I Exposed Hucksters, Cheats, and Scam Artists and Became the Scourge of the Liberal Media.* New York: Harper Perennial.

Strong, Frank. 2021. "How 2,400 Journalists Use Social Media for Reporting [and Why PR Should Get Serious About Social] [*sic*]." *Sword and the Script* (blog), March 30. https://www.swordandthescript.com/2021/03/journalists-social-media/.

Sunstein, Cass R. 1992. "What's Standing After *Lujan*? Of Citizen Suits, 'Injuries,' and Article III." *Michigan Law Review* 91 (2): 163–236. https://doi.org/10.2307/1289685.

———. 2000. "Deliberative Trouble? Why Groups Go to Extremes." *Yale Law Journal* 110 (1): 71–119. https://doi.org/10.2307/797587.

Sutcliffe, John B. 2008. "Public Participation in Local Politics: The Impact of Community Activism on the Windsor–Detroit Border Decision Making Process." *Canadian Journal of Urban Research* 17 (2): 57–83.

Svitek, Patrick. 2022. "Texas Puts Final Estimate of Winter Storm Death Toll at 246." *Texas Tribune*, January 2. https://www.texastribune.org/2022/01/02/texas-winter-storm-final-death-toll-246/.

Sweeney, Richard, Robert Stavins, Robert Stowe, and Gabriel Chan. 2012. "The US Sulphur Dioxide Cap and Trade Programme and Lessons for Climate Policy." Center for Economic and Policy Research, August 12. https://cepr.org/voxeu/columns/us-sulphur-dioxide-cap-and-trade-programme-and-lessons-climate-policy.

Sweet, William V., John P. Krasting, Benjamin D. Hamlington, Eric Larour, Robert E. Kopp, and Doug Marcy. 2022. *2022 Sea Level Rise: Technical Report.* Washington, DC: NOAA. https://oceanservice.noaa.gov/hazards/sealevelrise/sealevelrise-tech-report.html.

Tamborrino, Kelsey, and Josh Siegel. 2023. "Big Winners from Biden's Climate Law: Republicans Who Voted Against It." *Politico*, January 23. https://www.politico.com/news/2023/01/23/red-states-are-winning-big-from-dems-climate-law-00078420.

Tandanpolie, Tatyana. 2023. "Fox News' Greg Gutfeld Suggests 'Civil War' Because 'Elections Don't Work.'" *Salon*, October 6. https://www.salon.com/2023/10/06/fox-news-greg-gutfeld-suggests-civil-war-because-elections-dont-work/.

Tarbell, Ida. [1904] 1966. *The History of the Standard Oil Company: Briefer Version*. Edited by David M. Chalmers. New York: Harper & Row.

Tavernise, Sabrina, and Nate Cohn. 2019. "The America That Isn't Polarized." *New York Times*, September 24. https://www.nytimes.com/2019/09/24/upshot/many-americans-not-polarized.html.

Taylor, Astra. 2020. "A New Group of Leftist Primary Challengers Campaign Through Protests and the Coronavirus." *The New Yorker*, June 17. https://www.newyorker.com/news/the-political-scene/a-new-group-of-leftist-primary-challengers-campaign-through-protests-and-the-coronavirus.

Tebor, Celina. 2021. "Here Are Some Things to Know About the Extreme Drought in the Western U.S." *Los Angeles Times*, June 19. https://www.latimes.com/world-nation/story/2021-06-19/western-united-states-drought.

Teirstein, Zoya. 2021. "Poll: The Partisan Gap on Climate Change Is Widening." *Grist*, April 13. https://grist.org/politics/poll-the-partisan-gap-on-climate-change-is-widening/.

——. 2023. "Minnesota's New Climate Bill Is Ambitious: 100% Clean Energy by 2040." Canary Media, February 6. https://www.canarymedia.com/articles/politics/minnesotas-new-climate-bill-is-ambitious-100-clean-energy-by-2040.

Tenbrunsel, Ann E., and David M. Messick. 2004. "Ethical Fading: The Role of Self-Deception in Unethical Behavior." *Social Justice Research* 17 (2): 223–36. https://doi.org/10.1023/B:SORE.0000027411.35832.53.

Tesich, Steve. 1992. "A Government of Lies." *The Nation*, January 6.

Teske, Paul Eric. 2004. *Regulation in the States*. Washington, DC: Brookings Institution Press.

Thaler, Richard, and Cass R. Sunstein. 2009. *Nudge: Improving Decisions About Health, Wealth, and Happiness*. New York: Penguin.

Theriault, Sean M. 2008. *Party Polarization in Congress*. Cambridge: Cambridge University Press.

——. 2015. *Party Warriors: The Ugly Side of Party Polarization in Congress*. Cambridge: Cambridge University Press.

Thiel, Peter. 2009. "The Education of a Libertarian." *Cato Unbound: A Journal of Debate*, April 13. https://www.cato-unbound.org/2009/04/13/peter-thiel/education-libertarian/

Thompson, Hunter S. 1994. *Better Than Sex: Confessions of a Political Junkie*. New York: Ballantine.

Thrush, Glenn. 2020. "'We're Not a Democracy,' Says Mike Lee, a Republican Senator. That's a Good Thing, He Adds." *New York Times*, October 8. https://www.nytimes.com/2020/10/08/us/elections/mike-lee-democracy.html.

Tietenberg, Thomas H. 1992. *Environmental and Natural Resource Economics*. 3rd ed. HarperCollins.

Timm, Jane C., Amanda Terkel, and Dareh Gregorian. 2023. "'I Hate Him Passionately': Tucker Carlson Was Fed Up with Trump After the 2020 Election." *NBC News* (blog), March 7. https://www.nbcnews.com/politics/donald-trump/private-fox-news-text-messages-emails-released-dominion-suit-rcna72693.

Tokita, Christopher K., Andrew M. Guess, and Corina E. Tarnita. 2021. "Polarized Information Ecosystems Can Reorganize Social Networks Via Information Cascades." In "Dynamics of Political Polarization," special issue, *Proceedings of the*

National Academy of Sciences 118 (50): art. e2102147118. https://doi.org/10.1073/pnas .2102147118.

Tol, Richard S. J. 2005. "The Marginal Damage Costs of Carbon Dioxide Emissions: An Assessment of the Uncertainties." *Energy Policy* 33 (16): 2064–74. https://doi.org /10.1016/j.enpol.2004.04.002.

Townsend, Mark, and Paul Harris. 2004. "Now the Pentagon Tells Bush: Climate Change Will Destroy Us." *The Observer*, February 22.

Trabish, Herman K. 2018. "California Utilities Prep Nation's Biggest Time-of-Use Rate Rollout." *Utility Dive*, December 6. https://www.utilitydive.com/news/california -utilities-prep-nations-biggest-time-of-use-rate-roll-out/543402/.

——. 2023. "Hawai'i Leads the Way on Advanced Rate Design with Default Time-of-Use Rates, Fixed Charge Innovations." *Utility Dive*, May 9. https://www.utilitydive .com/news/hawaii-advanced-rate-design-default-time-of-use-fixed-charge -innovations/648994/.

Truman, David B. 1951. *The Governmental Process: Political Interests and Public Opinion*. New York: Knopf.

Tufekci, Zeynep. 2018. "YouTube, the Great Radicalizer." *New York Times*, March 10. https://www.nytimes.com/2018/03/10/opinion/sunday/youtube-politics-radical .html.

Tully-McManus, Katherine. 2020. "QAnon goes to Washington: Two Supporters Win Seats in Congress." *Roll Call*, November 5. https://rollcall.com/2020/11/05/qanon -goes-to-washington-two-supporters-win-seats-in-congress/.

Tyler, Tom R. 1990. *Why People Obey the Law*. New Haven, CT: Yale University Press.

Tyson, Alec, Cary Funk, and Brian Kennedy. 2022. "Americans Largely Favor U.S. Taking Steps to Become Carbon Neutral by 2050." Pew Research Center, March 1. https://www.pewresearch.org/science/2022/03/01/americans-largely-favor-u-s -taking-steps-to-become-carbon-neutral-by-2050/.

Upadhyayula, Venkata K. K., Venkataramana Gadhamshetty, Dimitris Athanassiadis, Mats Tysklind, Fanran Meng, Qing Pan, Jonathan M. Cullen, et al. 2022. "Wind Turbine Blades Using Recycled Carbon Fibers: An Environmental Assessment." *Environmental Science & Technology* 56 (2): 1267–77. https://doi.org/10.1021 /acs.est.1c05462.

Urofsky, Melvin I. 2009. *Louis D. Brandeis: A Life*. New York: Pantheon.

Vadari, Mani. 2018. *Smart Grid Redefined: Transformation of the Electric Utility*. Boston: Artech House.

Van Boven, Leaf, Phillip J. Ehret, and David K. Sherman. 2018. "Psychological Barriers to Bipartisan Public Support for Climate Policy." *Perspectives on Psychological Science* 13 (4): 492–507. https://doi.org/10.1177/1745691617748966.

Vance, J. D. 2016. *Hillbilly Elegy: A Memoir of a Family and Culture in Crisis*. London: William Collins.

Vandenbergh, Michael P. 2005. "Order Without Social Norms: How Personal Norm Activation Can Protect the Environment." *Northwestern University Law Review* 99 (3): 1101–66.

Vanderford, Richard. 2022. "Florida's DeSantis Takes Aim at 'Woke Capital.'" *Wall Street Journal*, July 28. https://www.wsj.com/articles/floridas-desantis-takes-aim -at-woke-capital-11659043495.

Van Horn, Jodie, and Mary Anne Hitt. 2019. "In the Face of Climate Change, Cities and States Continue to Lead on Clean Energy." *Sierra Club* (blog), April 5. https:// www.sierraclub.org/articles/2019/04/face-climate-change-cities-and-states -continue-lead-clean-energy.

Vargas, Melany, Kara McNutt, and Chris Seiple. 2023. "Green Hydrogen: What the Inflation Reduction Act Means for Production Economics and Carbon Intensity." Wood Mackenzie, March 14. https://www.woodmac.com/news/opinion/green-hydrogen-IRA-production-economics/.

Varian, Hal R. 1990. *Intermediate Microeconomics: A Modern Approach.* 2nd ed. New York: Norton.

Verchick, Rob. 2023. *The Octopus in the Parking Garage: A Call for Climate Resilience.* New York: Columbia University Press.

Vermeule, Adrian. 2024. "Why I Lost Interest in the Liberalism Debate." *The New Digest,* February 3.

Voelkel, Jan, Michael Stagnaro, James Chu, Sophia Pink, Joseph Mernyk, Chrystal Redekopp, Matthew Cashman, et al. 2022. "Megastudy Identifying Successful Interventions to Strengthen Americans' Democratic Attitudes." Northwestern Institute for Policy Research Working Paper Series. https://www.ipr.northwestern.edu/documents/working-papers/2022/wp-22-38.pdf.

Volcovici, Valerie. 2023. "Why Native American Tribes Struggle to Tap Billions in Clean Energy Incentives." Reuters, September 8. https://www.reuters.com/sustainability/climate-energy/why-us-tribes-struggle-tap-billions-clean-energy-incentives-2023-09-08/.

Von Kaenel, Camille. 2022. "California's Latest Power Grid Problems Are Just the Beginning." *Politico,* September 23. https://www.politico.com/news/2022/09/23/californias-lofty-climate-goals-clash-with-reality-00058466.

Vosoughi, Soroush, Deb Roy, and Sinan Aral. 2018. "The Spread of True and False News Online." *Science* 359 (6380): 1146–51. https://doi.org/10.1126/science.aap9559.

Wagner, Wendy. 2004. "Commons Ignorance: The Failure of Environmental Law to Produce Needed Information on Health and the Environment." *Duke Law Journal* 53:1619–745.

——. 2010. "Administrative Law, Filter Failure, and Information Capture." *Duke Law Journal* 59 (7): 1321–432.

Wagner, Wendy, Katherine Barnes, and Lisa Peters. 2011. "Rulemaking in the Shade: An Empirical Study of EPA's Air Toxic Emission Standards." *Administrative Law Review* 63 (1): 99–158.

Wald, Matthew L. 2009. "Giving the Power Grid Some Backbone." *Scientific American,* March 1. https://doi.org/10.1038/scientificamericanearth0309-52.

Waldholz, Rachel. 2017. "Alaskan Village, Citing Climate Change, Seeks Disaster Relief in Order to Relocate." NPR, January 10. https://www.npr.org/2017/01/10/509176361/alaskan-village-citing-climate-change-seeks-disaster-relief-in-order-to-relocate.

Walker, Christopher J. 2022. "A Congressional Review Act for the Major Questions Doctrine." *Harvard Journal of Law & Public Policy* 45 (3): 773–93.

Walker, Jack L. 1991. *Mobilizing Interest Groups in America: Patrons, Professions, and Social Movements.* Ann Arbor: University of Michigan Press.

Wallace-Wells, David. 2022a. "Beyond Catastrophe: A New Climate Reality Is Coming Into View." *New York Times Magazine,* October 26. https://www.nytimes.com/interactive/2022/10/26/magazine/climate-change-warming-world.html.

——. 2022b. "Gov. Jay Inslee Is Taking a Well-Earned Climate Victory Lap." *New York Times,* August 31. https://www.nytimes.com/2022/08/31/opinion/environment/jay-inslee-ira-climate-change.html.

Walter, Amy. 2023. "The Underappreciated Third-Party Threats to Biden." *Cook Political Report,* October 13. https://www.cookpolitical.com/analysis/national/national-politics/underappreciated-third-party-threats-biden.

Walters, Daniel E. 2019. "Capturing the Regulatory Agenda: An Empirical Study of Agency Responsiveness to Rulemaking Petitions." *Harvard Environmental Law Review* 43 (1): 175–223.

Walters, Daniel E., and Andrew N. Kleit. 2023. "Grid Governance in the Energy Tri-lemma Era: Remedying the Democracy Deficit." *Alabama Law Review* 74 (4): 1033–88. https://doi.org/10.2139/ssrn.4051765.

Ward, Bud. 2013. "*Grist*'s David Roberts: A Hot Light on Warming Planet Goes Stone-Cold." *Yale Climate Connections* (blog), September 4. http://yaleclimateconnections .org/2013/09/grists-david-roberts-a-hot-light-on-warming-planet-goes-stone -cold/.

Ward, Ian. 2023. "The Federalist Society Isn't Quite Sure About Democracy Anymore." *Politico*, March 17. https://www.politico.com/news/magazine/2023/03/17/federalist -society-democracy-opinion-00087270.

Warren, Michael, and Jamie Gangel. 2021. "McConnell Privately Says He Wants Trump Gone as Republicans Quietly Lobby Him to Convict." CNN, January 22. https://www.cnn.com/2021/01/22/politics/mcconnell-trump-impeachment -conviction-republicans/index.html.

Wash, Lacey. 2023. "Power Cost Adjustment Impacts New Puget Sound Energy Rates." Washington Utilities and Transportation Commission, January 12. https://www .utc.wa.gov/news/2023/power-cost-adjustment-impacts-new-puget-sound-energy -rates.

Wasik, John F. 2006. *The Merchant of Power: Sam Insull, Thomas Edison, and the Cre-ation of the Modern Metropolis*. New York: St. Martin's Press.

Wasserman, David. 2023. "In the End, Redistricting Didn't Hurt (and May Have Even Helped) House Democrats." *Cook Political Report*, September 25. https://www .cookpolitical.com/analysis/house/redistricting/end-redistricting-didnt-hurt -and-may-have-even-helped-house-democrats.

Watkins, Matthew. 2022. "Texas Breaks Power Demand Record During June Heat Wave." *Texas Tribune*, June 12. https://www.texastribune.org/2022/06/12/texas-heat -wave-grid/.

Weaver, David H., and G. Cleveland Wilhoit. 1986. *The American Journalist: A Portrait of U.S. News People and Their Work*. Bloomington: Indiana University Press.

Wei, Yifan, Jinyuan Song, Timothy Werner, and Nan Jia. 2022. "Strategic Conse-quences of Democratic Backsliding: The Trump Effect on Firm Regulatory Risk." *Academy of Management Proceedings* 2022 (1): art. 11945. https://doi.org/10 .5465/AMBPP.2022.11945abstract.

Weigel, David. 2014. "Rolling Coal: Conservatives Who Show Their Annoyance with Liberals, Obama, and the EPA by Blowing Black Smoke from Their Trucks." *Slate*, July 3. https://slate.com/news-and-politics/2014/07/rolling-coal-conservatives-who -show-their-annoyance-with-liberals-obama-and-the-epa-by-blowing-black -smoke-from-their-trucks.html.

Weingast, Barry R., and William J. Marshall. 1988. "The Industrial Organization of Congress; or, Why Legislatures, Like Firms, Are Not Organized as Markets." *Jour-nal of Political Economy* 96 (1): 132–63. https://doi.org/10.1086/261528.

Weiss, Daniel J. 2010. "Anatomy of a Senate Climate Bill Death." Center for Ameri-can Progress, October 12. https://www.americanprogress.org/article/anatomy-of -a-senate-climate-bill-death/.

Weissman, Steven, and Romany Webb. 2014. "Addressing Climate Change Without Legislation: Volume 2: FERC." https://escholarship.org/uc/item/5rm2d5xw.

Welsh, Nick. 2023. "The Electrifying Leah Stokes." *Santa Barbara Independent*, April 19. https://www.independent.com/2023/04/19/the-electrifying-leah-stokes/.

Welton, Shelley. 2017. "Clean Electrification." *University of Colorado Law Review* 88 (3): 571–652.

——. 2021. "Rethinking Grid Governance for the Climate Change Era." *California Law Review* 109 (January): 209–75.

——. 2023. "The Public–Private Blur in Clean Energy Siting." Working paper presented at Berkeley-Penn Energy Law Scholars Workshop, University of California at Berkeley School of Law, May, and Energizing Private Law Workshop, Kings College London, June.

Welton, Shelley, and Joel Eisen. 2019. "Clean Energy Justice: Charting an Emerging Agenda." *Harvard Environmental Law Review* 43 (2): 307–71.

Wenner, Lettie M. 1982. *The Environmental Decade in Court*. Bloomington: Indiana University Press.

Westwick, Peter. 2019. "California Is Uniquely Fire-Prone Thanks to Its Long Romance with High-Voltage Power Lines." *Los Angeles Times*, January 28. https://www.latimes.com/opinion/op-ed/la-oe-westwick-fires-california-history-electricity-20190128-story.html.

Westwood, Sean J., Justin Grimmer, Matthew Tyler, and Clayton Nall. 2022. "Current Research Overstates American Support for Political Violence." *Proceedings of the National Academy of Sciences* 119 (12): art. e2116870119. https://doi.org/10.1073/pnas.2116870119.

White, Adam J. 2020. "A Republic, If We Can Keep It." *The Atlantic*, February 4. https://www.theatlantic.com/ideas/archive/2020/02/a-republic-if-we-can-keep-it/605887/.

White, Theodore H. 1961. *The Making of the President 1960*. New York: Atheneum House.

——. 1969. *The Making of the President 1968*. New York: Atheneum House.

Wilkinson, Claire. 2021. "Property Insurers Tighten Coverage as Climate Change Continues." *Business Insurance*, August 17. https://www.businessinsurance.com/article/20210817/NEWS06/912343906/Property-insurers-tighten-coverage-as-climate-change-continues.

Williams, Emily L., Sydney A. Bartone, Emma K. Swanson, and Leah C. Stokes. 2022. "The American Electric Utility Industry's Role in Promoting Climate Denial, Doubt, and Delay." *Environmental Research Letters* 17 (9): art. 094026. https://doi.org/10.1088/1748-9326/ac8ab3.

Williamson, Oliver E. 1976. "Franchise Bidding for Natural Monopolies—in General and with Respect to CATV." *Bell Journal of Economics* 7 (1): 73–104. https://doi.org/10.2307/3003191.

Wilson, Anne E., Victoria A. Parker, and Matthew Feinberg. 2020. "Polarization in the Contemporary Political and Media Landscape." *Current Opinion in Behavioral Sciences* 34:223–28. https://doi.org/10.1016/j.cobeha.2020.07.005.

Wing, Nick. 2017. "Joe Manchin Shoots Cap-and-Trade Bill with Rifle in New Ad." *HuffPost*, December 6. https://www.huffpost.com/entry/joe-manchin-ad-dead-aim_n_758457.

Wiser, Ryan, Karen Jenni, Joachim Seel, Erin Baker, Maureen Hand, Eric Lantz, and Aaron Smith. 2016. "Forecasting Wind Energy Costs and Cost Drivers." International Energy Agency Wind. https://pdfs.semanticscholar.org/a719/42aaa18a002b03512219e3c7c902913cab6d.pdf.

Witko, Christopher. 2011. "Campaign Contributions, Access, and Government Contracting." *Journal of Public Administration Research and Theory* 21 (4): 761–78. https://doi.org/10.1093/jopart/muroo5.

Wlezien, Christopher. 2004. "Patterns of Representation: Dynamics of Public Preferences and Policy." *Journal of Politics* 66 (1): 1–24. https://doi.org/10.1046/j.1468-2508.2004.00139.x.

Wolfe, Rebecca, Ann E. Tenbrunsel, John M. Darley, and Kristina A. Diekmann. 2004. "Collective Punishment: When Is Our Group Responsible for Our Actions?" Paper presented at the IACM Conference, October 26. https://papers.ssrn.com/sol3/papers.cfm?abstract_id=609305.

Wolman, Jordan. 2022. "Republicans Plan Surge of Attacks on 'Woke' Investing After the Midterms." *Politico*, November 1. https://www.politico.com/news/2022/11/01/republicans-sustainable-investing-midterms-00064326.

Wood, Gordon S. 1987. "Ideology and the Origins of Liberal America." *William and Mary Quarterly* 44 (3): 628–40. https://doi.org/10.2307/1939783.

World Bank. 2022. *State and Trends of Carbon Pricing 2022*. Washington, DC: World Bank.

World Health Organization. 2007. *Extremely Low Frequency Fields*. Geneva: World Health Organization.

Wright, Georgia, Liat Olenick, and Amy Westervelt. 2021. "The Dirty Dozen: Meet America's Top Climate Villains." *The Guardian*, October 27. https://www.theguardian.com/commentisfree/2021/oct/27/climate-crisis-villains-americas-dirty-dozen.

Wright, Tom, and Bradley Hope. 2018. *Billion Dollar Whale: The Man Who Fooled Wall Street, Hollywood, and the World*. New York: Hachette.

Yackee, Jason Webb, and Susan Webb Yackee. 2006. "A Bias Towards Business? Assessing Interest Group Influence on the U.S. Bureaucracy." *Journal of Politics* 68 (1): 128–39. https://doi.org/10.1111/j.1468-2508.2006.00375.x.

Yackee, Susan Webb. 2022. "Regulatory Capture's Self-Serving Application." *Public Administration Review* 82 (5): 866–75. https://doi.org/10.1111/puar.13390.

Yadin, Sharon. 2019. "Regulatory Shaming." *Environmental Law* 49 (2): 407–51.

Yergin, Daniel. [1990] 2008. *The Prize: The Epic Quest for Oil, Money, and Power*. With a new epilogue. New York: Simon & Schuster.

Yin, Jianjun. 2023. "Rapid Decadal Acceleration of Sea Level Rise Along the U.S. East and Gulf Coasts During 2010–22 and Its Impact on Hurricane-Induced Storm Surge." *Journal of Climate* 36 (13): 4511–29. https://doi.org/10.1175/JCLI-D-22-0670.1.

Yost, Keith. 2010. "The Story BCG Offered Me $16,000 Not to Tell." *The Tech*, April 9. https://thetech.com/2010/04/09/dubai-v130-n18.

Yourish, Karen, Larry Buchanan, and Denise Lu. 2021. "The 147 Republicans Who Voted to Overturn Election Results." *New York Times*, January 7. https://www.nytimes.com/interactive/2021/01/07/us/elections/electoral-college-biden-objectors.html.

Zeitlin, Matthew. 2023a. "Beware a Battery Backlash." *Heatmap News*, August 2. https://heatmap.news/politics/lithium-ion-battery-fires-storage.

——. 2023b. "Everyone's Mad at Offshore Wind Developers." *Heatmap News*, November 1. https://heatmap.news/economy/everyones-mad-at-offshore-wind-developers.

Zekeria, Tesnim, and Judd Legum. 2021. "The Georgia Legislators Pushing Voter Suppression Bills Are Backed by Millions in Corporate Cash." January. https://popular.info/p/georgia.

Zimmer, Ben. 2017. "The Roots of the 'What About?' Ploy." *Wall Street Journal*, June 9. https://www.wsj.com/articles/the-roots-of-the-what-about-ploy-1497019827.

Zingales, Luigi. 2015. "Presidential Address: Does Finance Benefit Society?" *Journal of Finance* 70 (4): 1327–63. https://doi.org/10.1111/jofi.12295.

———. 2017. "Towards a Political Theory of the Firm." *Journal of Economic Perspectives* 31 (3): 113–30. https://doi.org/10.1257/jep.31.3.113.

Zito, Salena. 2016. "Taking Trump Seriously, Not Literally." *The Atlantic*, September 23. https://www.theatlantic.com/politics/archive/2016/09/trump-makes-his-case-in-pittsburgh/501335/.

Zuckerman, Gregory. 2013. *The Frackers: The Outrageous Inside Story of the New Billionaire Wildcatters*. New York: Portfolio/Penguin.

Zuckerman, Jake. 2021. "Ohio Utility Regulator Lobbied for Legislation to Save FirstEnergy Millions, Texts Show." *Ohio Capital Journal*, November 9. https://ohiocapitaljournal.com/2021/11/09/ohio-utility-regulator-lobbied-for-legislation-to-save-firstenergy-millions-texts-show/.

Zuckert, Catherine. 2018. "The Prince of the People: Machiavelli Was No 'Machiavellian.'" Aeon, November 19. https://aeon.co/essays/the-prince-of-the-people-machiavelli-was-no-machiavellian.

INDEX